Complete Book of Crochet-Stitch Designs

500 Classic & Original Patterns

Linda P. Schapper

 Sterling Publishing Co., Inc.   New York

D1214144

ACKNOWLEDGMENTS

I would like to thank Anna Kunz-Schapper of Wetzikon, Switzerland, who welcomed me into her family and passed on her techniques and love of crochet.
I would also like to thank Mr. Jagdish Chavda, of the University of Central Florida in Orlando who took the time to make the photographs.

Edited by Barbara Busch

Library of Congress Cataloging in Publication Data

Schäpper, Linda.
  Complete book of crochet-stitch designs.

  Includes index.
  1. Crocheting—Patterns. I. Title
  TT820.S28 1985   746-43′4041   85-9905
  ISBN 0-8069-5722-0
  ISBN 0-8069-6222-4 (pbk.)

7   9   10   8   6

Copyright © 1985 by Sterling Publishing Co., Inc.
Two Park Avenue, New York, N.Y. 10016
Distributed in Australia by Capricorn Book Co., Pty. Ltd.
Unit 5C1 Lincoln St., Lane Cove, N.S.W. 2066
Distributed in the United Kingdom by Blandford Press
Link House, West Street, Poole, Dorset BH15 1LL, England
Distributed in Canada by Oak Tree Press Ltd.
℅ Canadian Manda Group, P.O. Box 920, Station U
Toronto, Ontario, Canada M8Z 5P9
Manufactured in the United States of America
All rights reserved

Contents

Introduction

Although crochet is thought to have originated as early as the Stone Age when there were no needles available to join clothing and a rough crude hook was formed, very little about early crochet survived in the way of a written record. It is possible that we have adopted the French word for hook, *crochet*, as the name of the craft, because the French did more than any other group to record crochet patterns.

Since very little in the way of written instructions were available for crochet, patterns were passed down through families, and new patterns were copied by examining the design with a magnifying glass. In the last century, written instructions became more popular as reading levels of women improved. Instructions, however, often can be long and tedious, and although perfectly clear to the writer, were frequently difficult for the crocheter.

Introduced in more extensive form in this book is the international crochet symbol system. It is easy to read after you have worked out the four or five basic stitches, and it makes crocheting easier. By using the system, it is easier to see the whole pattern in proportion, and it is a nice experience to be able to pick up a crochet book in Russian and understand the crochet symbols. The symbols themselves look a great deal like the actual crochet stitches and, as you will see, are not difficult to follow. These start on page 13.

On the following pages are instructions in the basic stitches referred to in the designs. On page 15, starts a Pictorial Index. This provides (greatly reduced) an overall view of each crochet design, along with the page numbers on which they can be found.

Crochet itself is based on a few simple stitches used in endless variation. It begins with a chain and the way the stitches are formed determines the pattern. You only need a hook, your hand and the thread. It is easy to carry with you and do anywhere. Unlike knitting and weaving, it is difficult to make a mistake which cannot be corrected immediately.

Crochet is versatile. It can make generous lace patterns, mimic knitting, patchwork or weaving and it can form any number of textile patterns. I found the challenge of making 500 different patterns with the same white thread exhilarating and never-ending. The original 500 could easily lead to another 1000.

Abbreviations

ch(s)	chain(s)
dc	double crochet
hdc	half-double crochet
rep	repeat(ing)
sc	single crochet
sk	skip
sl st	slip stitch(es)
trc	triple crochet
*	used to mark the beginning of a set of instructions that are to be repeated

Notes for those using the written instructions

1. Stitch is always counted from the last stitch used.
2. I always use at least 1 extra chain. Some people like the extra chain in the beginning of the first row. If you prefer your crochet tighter, leave off the extra chain.
3. The abbreviations used are the American ones. British readers should keep this in mind, since a few British abbreviations are different.
4. The diagrams are easier, once you have learned them. When in doubt, check the diagrams.

Stitches

Chain
Make a slipknot.

1

Pass the hook through the loop, under the thread and catch the thread with the hook.

2

Wrap the yarn around the hook and draw up a loop through both the chain and the loop on the hook.

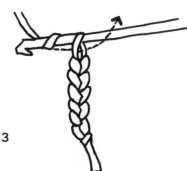

3

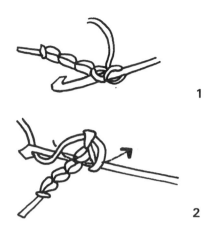

1

2

Slip Stitch

Make a chain the length desired. Place thread over the hook and insert it into the 2nd chain from the hook.

Place the thread over the hook and pull it back through the first loop. Repeat this procedure of catching the thread on the hook and pulling it through the hole until you make the desired number of chains.

Single Crochet

This is a short tight stitch.

Make the chain as long as you want it. Insert the hook into the 2nd chain on the hook. Wrap the thread around the hook coming towards you.

Pull the thread through the 2 loops on the hook.

Continue by inserting the hook into the next chain.

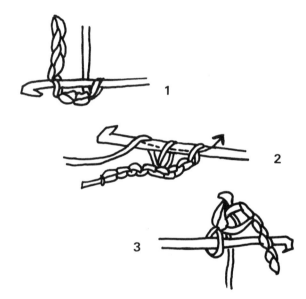

1

2

3

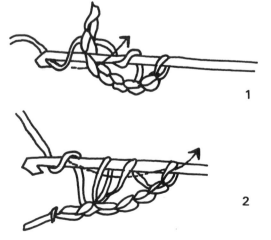

1

2

Half-Double Crochet

This stitch gives a lot of body and structure and resembles knitting. Make the chain the desired length. Wrap the thread around the hook and insert the hook into the 5th chain from the hook, and pull it through the chain.

There should be 3 loops on the hook now. Wrap the thread over the hook. Pull the thread through the 3 loops on the hook.

Double Crochet

This is perhaps the most popular and frequently used crochet stitch. Make the chain the desired length. Wrap the thread over the hook, and insert the hook into the chain.

Wrap the thread over again and pull the thread through. Wrap the thread around the hook again and pull the thread through 2 loops, leaving 2 loops on the hook. Wrap the thread around the hook and pull the thread through the 2 loops on the hook.

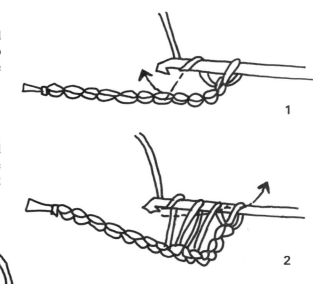

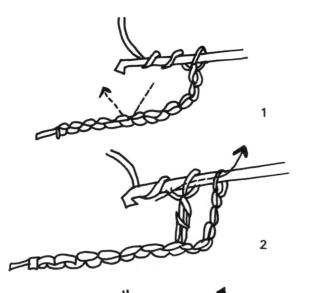

Triple Crochet

Work a chain to the desired length, wrap the thread around the hook twice and insert the hook into the desired chain.

Place the thread around the hook and pull it through 1 loop, leaving 4 loops on the needle. Wrap the thread around the hook and pull it through 2 loops on the hook, leaving 3 loops on the hook. Wrap the thread around the hook and pull it through 2 loops on the hook. Place the thread around the hook and pull it through the last 2 loops.

Puff Stitch

Chain to the length needed. Insert the hook into the desired chain, yarn over, insert hook again, yarn over, as many times as desired, only pulling the yarn through all the loops at once at the end. A pull stitch can be made with 2 to 6 loops.

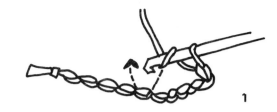

1

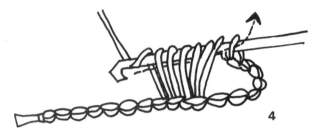

2

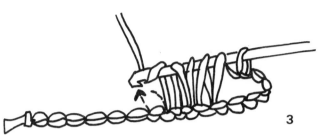

3

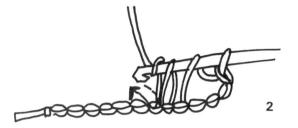

4

Cluster Stitch

Chain the row to the desired length. Wrap the thread around the hook towards you. Insert hook, wrap thread around and pull through 2 loops, leaving 2 on the hook. Wrap thread around the hook, insert it into the same chain, draw it through 2 loops, leaving 3 on the hook, until you have the number of stitches on the hook that you need. Then, wrap thread around the hook towards you and pull it through all the loops, leaving 1 on the hook. Can be worked with 2 to 6 loops.

1

2

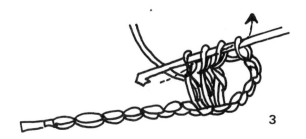

3

Popcorn Stitch

Chain to the length needed. Make 3 or more double crochet, as desired, in the same chain, turn and chain 1. Make 1 single crochet around the chain after the last double crochet, chain 1 and turn. Can be worked with 2 to 6 loops.

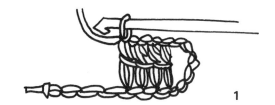

1

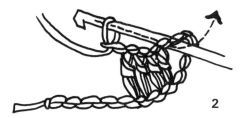

2

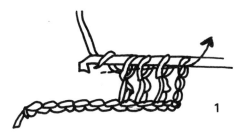

1

Inverted V-Stitch

Work chain to needed length. Begin double crochet in desired chain, yarn over and pull yarn through 2 loops, yarn over. Begin 2nd double crochet, pull yarn through 2 loops and continue until necessary number of double crochet are made, then yarn over and pull through all the loops on the hook.

2

Picot

After single or double crochet, chain 3 and insert the last chain back into the 1st chain.

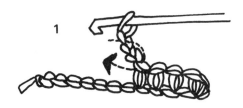

1

2

Triple X-Stitch

Wrap thread around the needle towards you twice. Begin 1 triple crochet, pull yarn through 2 loops, leaving 3 on the hook. Begin 2nd triple crochet in the 2nd chain, and pull the yarn through 2 loops, 3 times. Chain 1 and work 1 double crochet in the joint of the base of the 2 triple crochet.

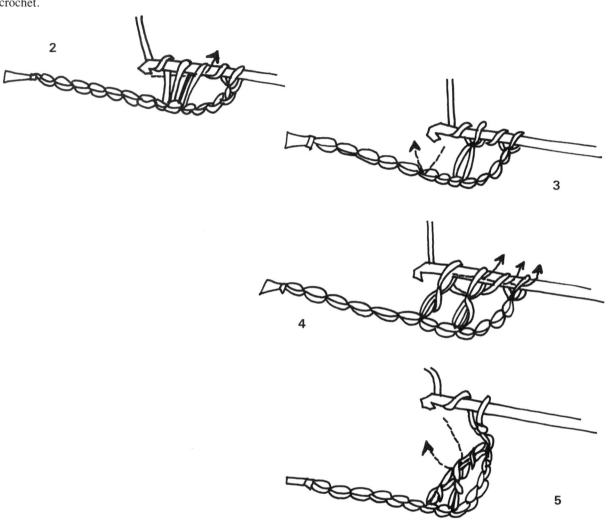

Small X-Stitch

Work 1 double crochet in the 2nd or 3rd double crochet, chain 1 or 2, depending on the pattern. Work 1 double crochet backwards 1 or 2 stitches.

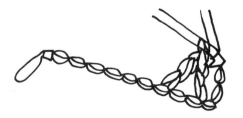

Y-Stitch

Wrap yarn around needle twice, as if doing a triple crochet. Pull yarn through 3 times.

Wrap yarn around hook once. Insert in the middle of the triple crochet, and make a double crochet in the middle of that stitch.

Begin next stitch.

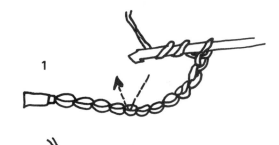

1

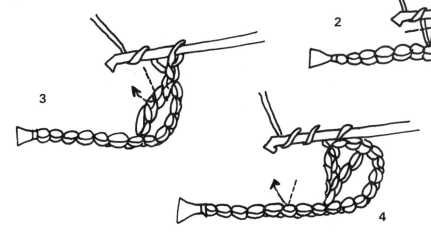

2

3

4

From the front.

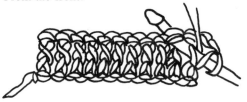

Relief Double Crochet

Same as the double crochet except that instead of the hook being inserted in the hole, the crochet is formed by circling the post of the crochet stitch below, either from the front and out again or from the back and out again.

From the back.

V-Stitch or Shells

Shells are most often formed by inserting more than 1 double crochet in the same chain. They are made from 2 double crochet for a V-stitch to 3 or more double crochet to as many as 14 or 15 double crochet, depending on the fullness desired. They also can be interspaced with chains.

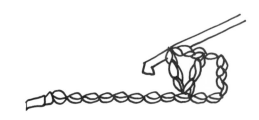

International Crochet Symbols

chain stitch	⌀	∞∞∞∞∞
slip stitch	<	< < < < <
single crochet	+	+ + + + +
half-double crochet	T	T T T T T
double crochet	Ŧ	ŦŦŦŦŦ
triple crochet	Ŧ	ŦŦŦŦŦ
relief double crochet from the front	ʓ	ʓʓʓʓʓ
relief double crochet from the back	Ʒ	ƷƷƷƷƷ
picot	✿	✿ ✿ ✿ ✿ ✿
popcorn (3-looped)	🌽	🌽🌽🌽🌽🌽
popcorn (4-looped)	🌽	🌽🌽🌽🌽🌽
popcorn (5-looped)	🌽	🌽🌽🌽🌽🌽

puff stitch (2-looped)

puff stitch (3-looped)

puff stitch (4-looped)

puff stitch (5-looped)

cluster (2-looped)

cluster (3-looped)

cluster (4-looped)

cluster (5-looped)

small X-stitch

triple X-stitch

V-stitch

shell (3-looped)

shell (4-looped)

shell (5-looped)

inverted V-stitch (3-looped)

inverted V-stitch (4-looped)

inverted V-stitch (5-looped)

4-looped shell with chains

6-looped shell with chains

dropped stitch, dropped double crochet

wraparound stitch

Y-stitch

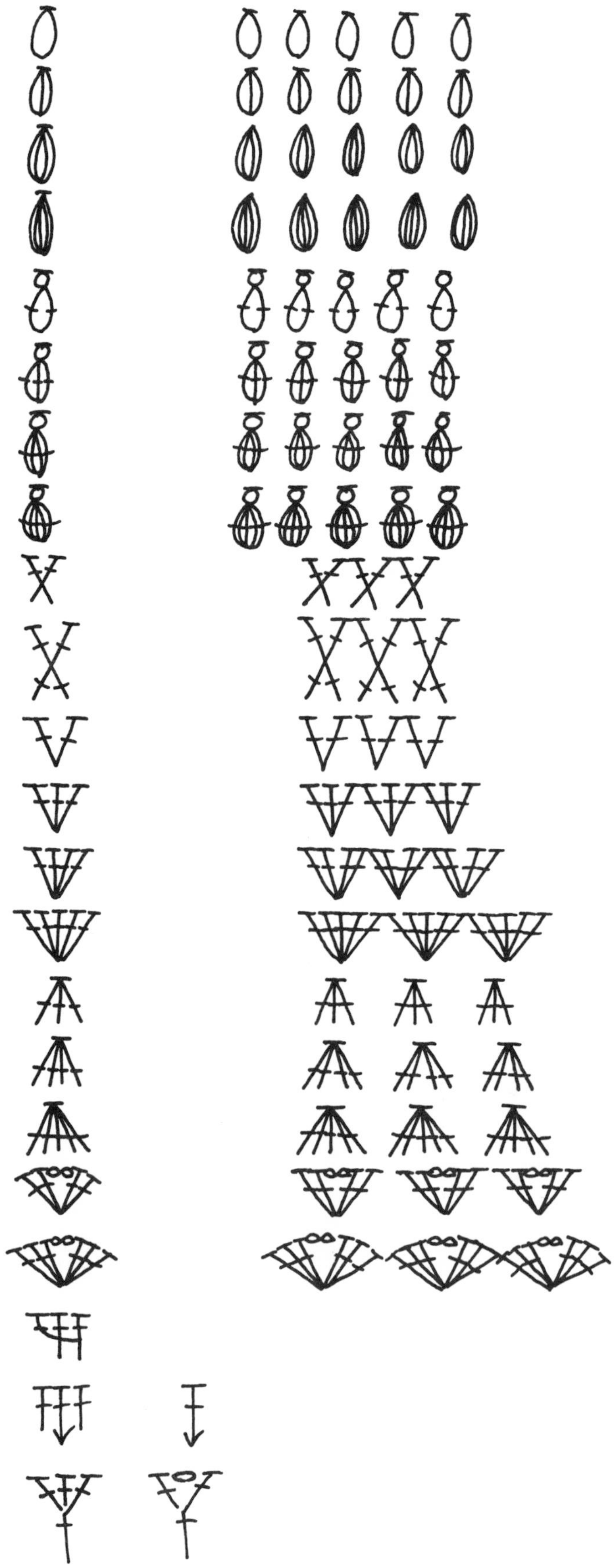

Pictorial Index

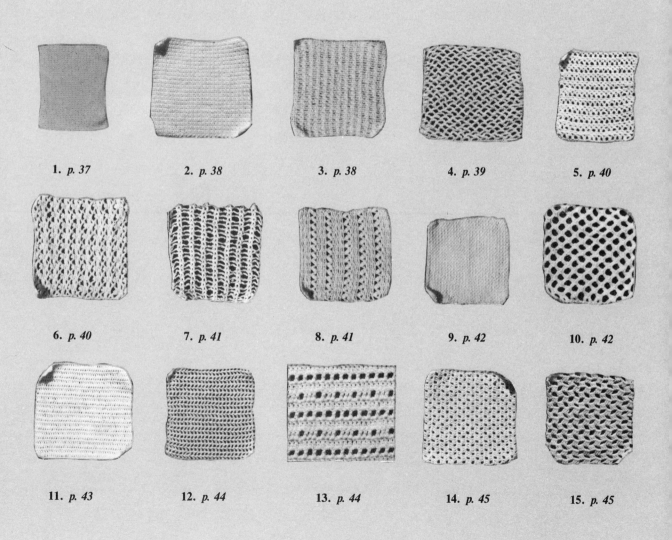

1. *p. 37*   2. *p. 38*   3. *p. 38*   4. *p. 39*   5. *p. 40*

6. *p. 40*   7. *p. 41*   8. *p. 41*   9. *p. 42*   10. *p. 42*

11. *p. 43*   12. *p. 44*   13. *p. 44*   14. *p. 45*   15. *p. 45*

16   **Complete Book of Crochet**

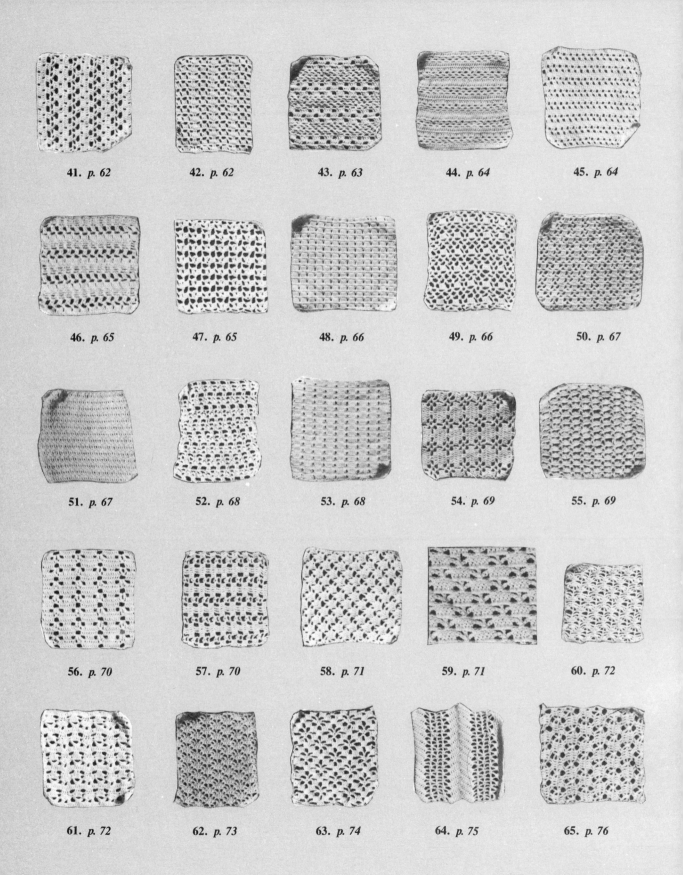

41. *p. 62*   42. *p. 62*   43. *p. 63*   44. *p. 64*   45. *p. 64*

46. *p. 65*   47. *p. 65*   48. *p. 66*   49. *p. 66*   50. *p. 67*

51. *p. 67*   52. *p. 68*   53. *p. 68*   54. *p. 69*   55. *p. 69*

56. *p. 70*   57. *p. 70*   58. *p. 71*   59. *p. 71*   60. *p. 72*

61. *p. 72*   62. *p. 73*   63. *p. 74*   64. *p. 75*   65. *p. 76*

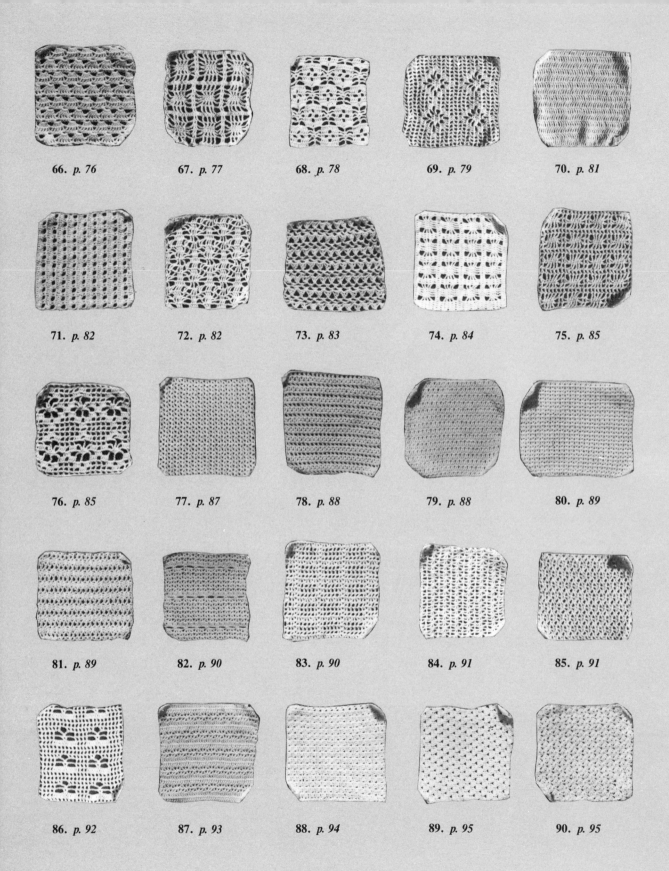

66. *p. 76* 67. *p. 77* 68. *p. 78* 69. *p. 79* 70. *p. 81*

71. *p. 82* 72. *p. 82* 73. *p. 83* 74. *p. 84* 75. *p. 85*

76. *p. 85* 77. *p. 87* 78. *p. 88* 79. *p. 88* 80. *p. 89*

81. *p. 89* 82. *p. 90* 83. *p. 90* 84. *p. 91* 85. *p. 91*

86. *p. 92* 87. *p. 93* 88. *p. 94* 89. *p. 95* 90. *p. 95*

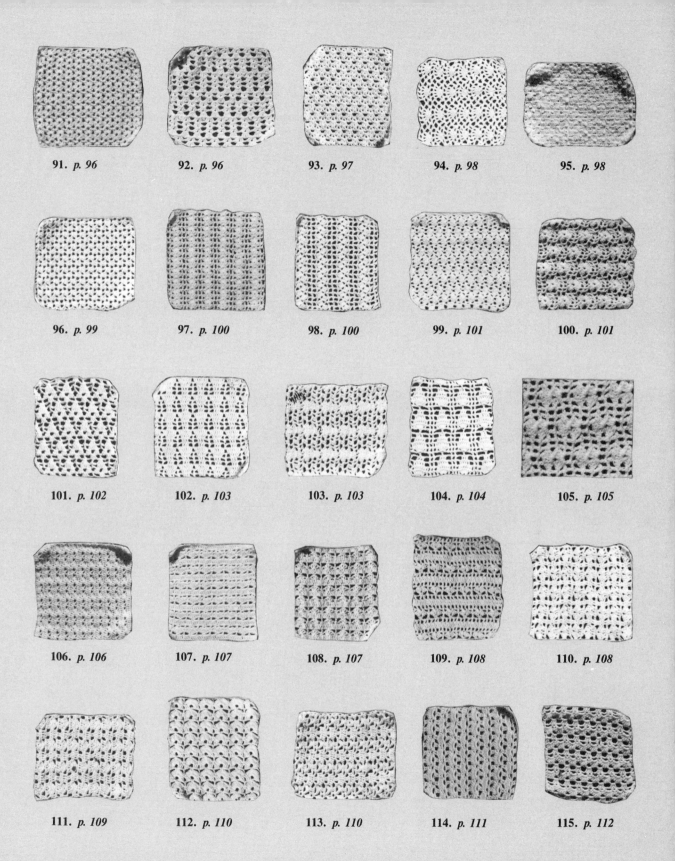

91. *p. 96*　　92. *p. 96*　　93. *p. 97*　　94. *p. 98*　　95. *p. 98*

96. *p. 99*　　97. *p. 100*　　98. *p. 100*　　99. *p. 101*　　100. *p. 101*

101. *p. 102*　　102. *p. 103*　　103. *p. 103*　　104. *p. 104*　　105. *p. 105*

106. *p. 106*　　107. *p. 107*　　108. *p. 107*　　109. *p. 108*　　110. *p. 108*

111. *p. 109*　　112. *p. 110*　　113. *p. 110*　　114. *p. 111*　　115. *p. 112*

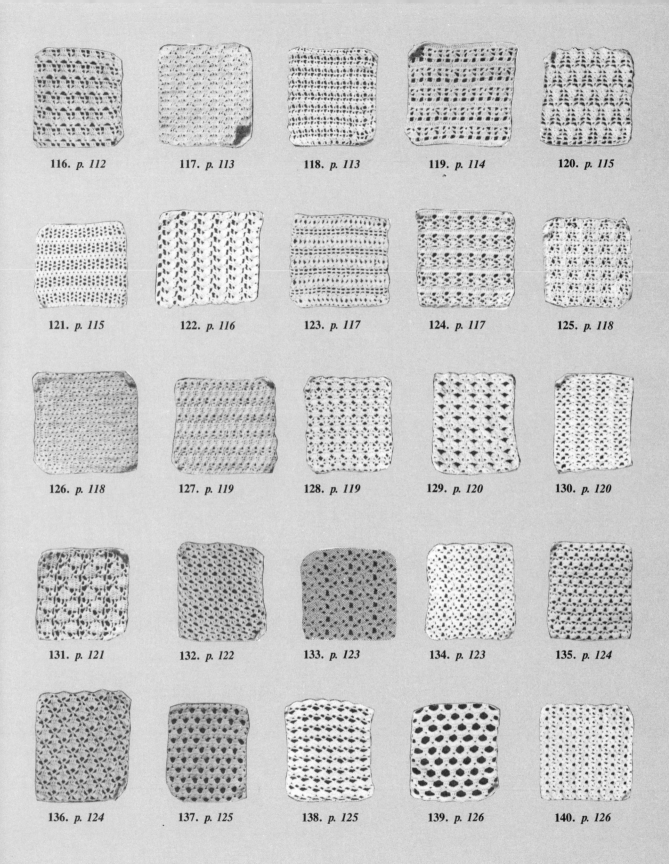

116. *p. 112* 117. *p. 113* 118. *p. 113* 119. *p. 114* 120. *p. 115*

121. *p. 115* 122. *p. 116* 123. *p. 117* 124. *p. 117* 125. *p. 118*

126. *p. 118* 127. *p. 119* 128. *p. 119* 129. *p. 120* 130. *p. 120*

131. *p. 121* 132. *p. 122* 133. *p. 123* 134. *p. 123* 135. *p. 124*

136. *p. 124* 137. *p. 125* 138. *p. 125* 139. *p. 126* 140. *p. 126*

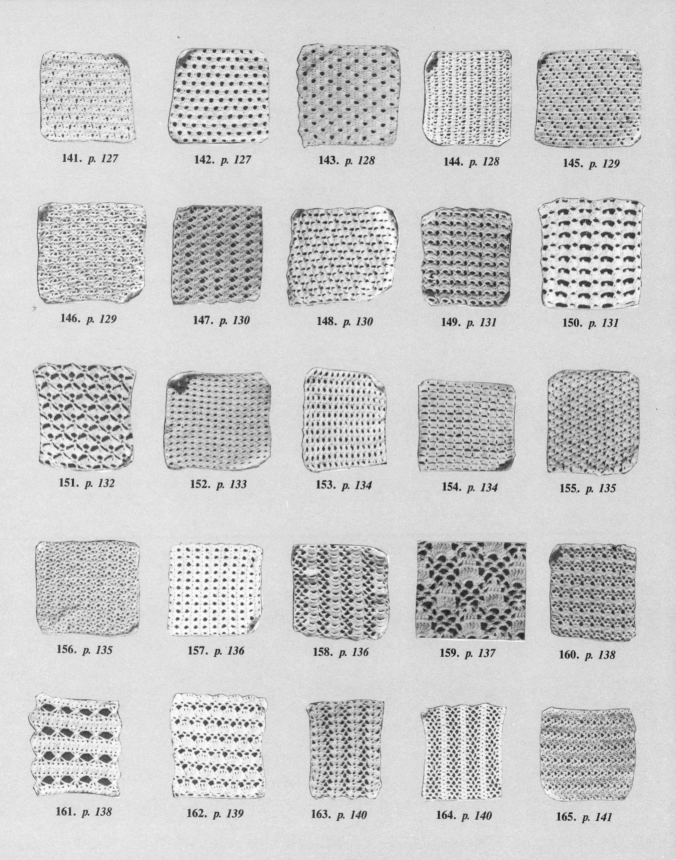

141. *p. 127*

142. *p. 127*

143. *p. 128*

144. *p. 128*

145. *p. 129*

146. *p. 129*

147. *p. 130*

148. *p. 130*

149. *p. 131*

150. *p. 131*

151. *p. 132*

152. *p. 133*

153. *p. 134*

154. *p. 134*

155. *p. 135*

156. *p. 135*

157. *p. 136*

158. *p. 136*

159. *p. 137*

160. *p. 138*

161. *p. 138*

162. *p. 139*

163. *p. 140*

164. *p. 140*

165. *p. 141*

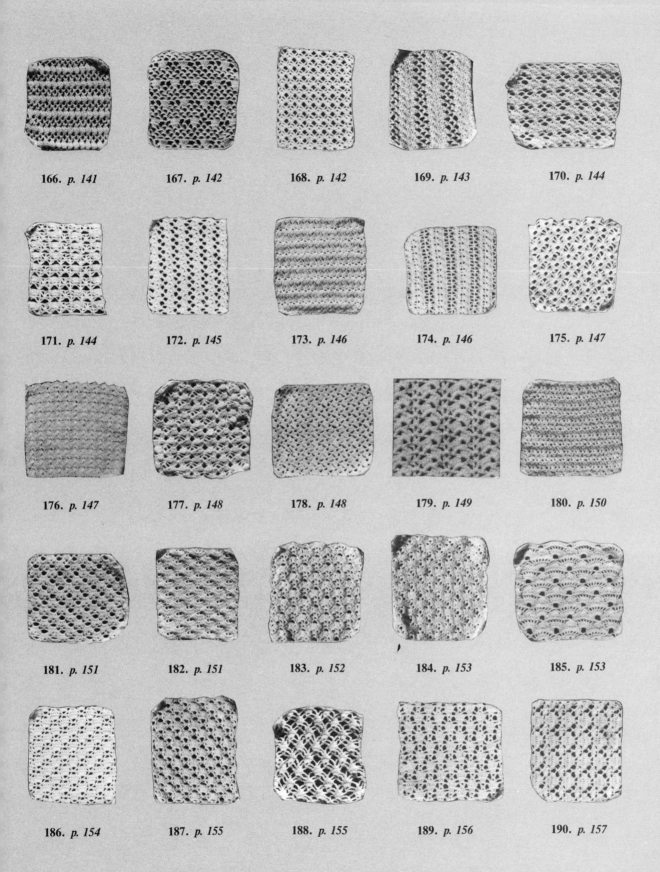

166. *p. 141*   167. *p. 142*   168. *p. 142*   169. *p. 143*   170. *p. 144*

171. *p. 144*   172. *p. 145*   173. *p. 146*   174. *p. 146*   175. *p. 147*

176. *p. 147*   177. *p. 148*   178. *p. 148*   179. *p. 149*   180. *p. 150*

181. *p. 151*   182. *p. 151*   183. *p. 152*   184. *p. 153*   185. *p. 153*

186. *p. 154*   187. *p. 155*   188. *p. 155*   189. *p. 156*   190. *p. 157*

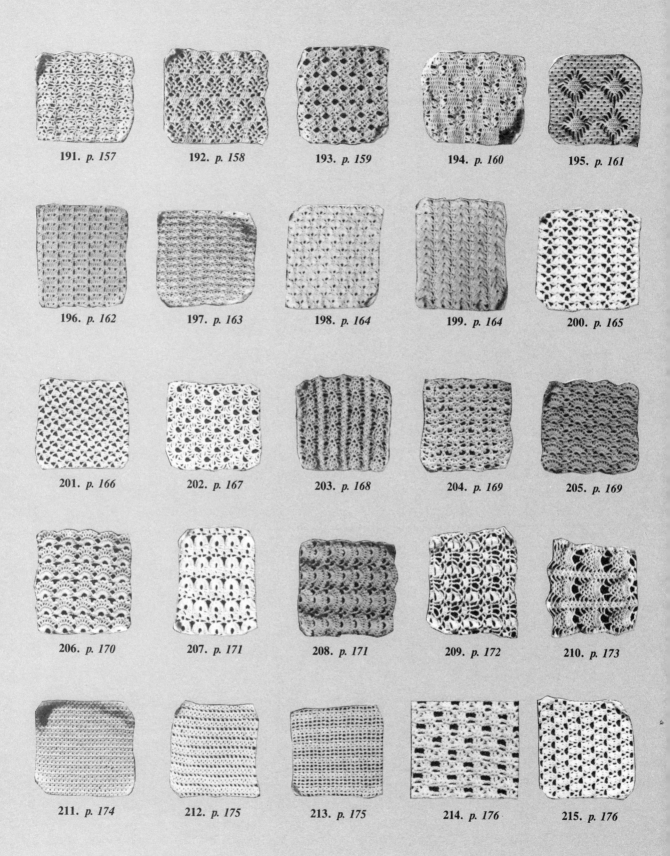

191. *p. 157*   192. *p. 158*   193. *p. 159*   194. *p. 160*   195. *p. 161*

196. *p. 162*   197. *p. 163*   198. *p. 164*   199. *p. 164*   200. *p. 165*

201. *p. 166*   202. *p. 167*   203. *p. 168*   204. *p. 169*   205. *p. 169*

206. *p. 170*   207. *p. 171*   208. *p. 171*   209. *p. 172*   210. *p. 173*

211. *p. 174*   212. *p. 175*   213. *p. 175*   214. *p. 176*   215. *p. 176*

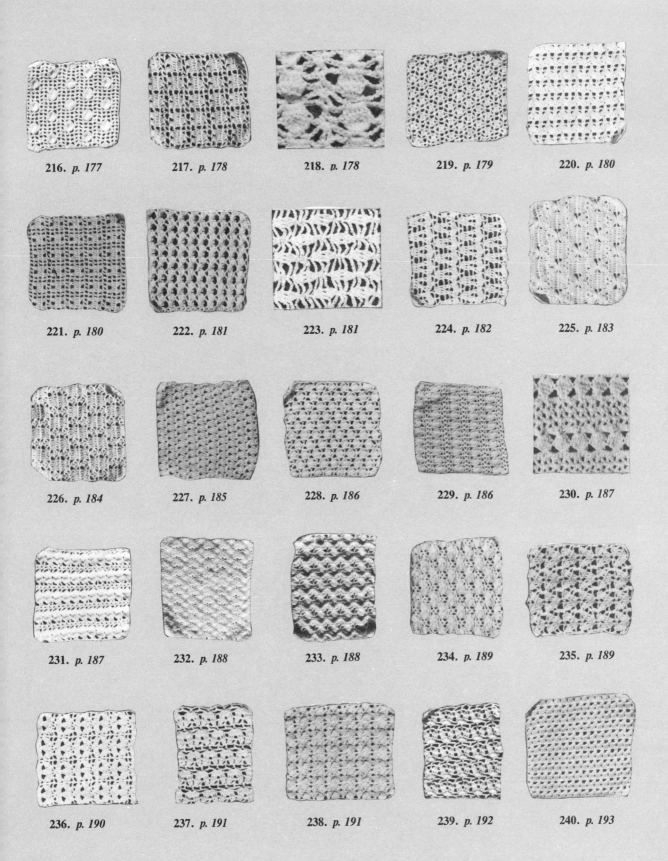

216. *p. 177*   217. *p. 178*   218. *p. 178*   219. *p. 179*   220. *p. 180*

221. *p. 180*   222. *p. 181*   223. *p. 181*   224. *p. 182*   225. *p. 183*

226. *p. 184*   227. *p. 185*   228. *p. 186*   229. *p. 186*   230. *p. 187*

231. *p. 187*   232. *p. 188*   233. *p. 188*   234. *p. 189*   235. *p. 189*

236. *p. 190*   237. *p. 191*   238. *p. 191*   239. *p. 192*   240. *p. 193*

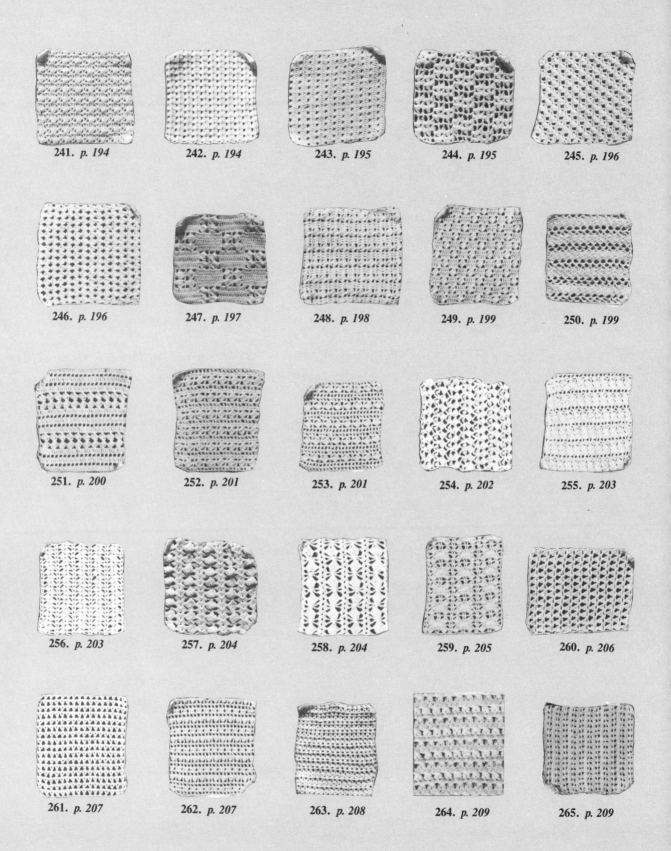

241. *p. 194*   242. *p. 194*   243. *p. 195*   244. *p. 195*   245. *p. 196*

246. *p. 196*   247. *p. 197*   248. *p. 198*   249. *p. 199*   250. *p. 199*

251. *p. 200*   252. *p. 201*   253. *p. 201*   254. *p. 202*   255. *p. 203*

256. *p. 203*   257. *p. 204*   258. *p. 204*   259. *p. 205*   260. *p. 206*

261. *p. 207*   262. *p. 207*   263. *p. 208*   264. *p. 209*   265. *p. 209*

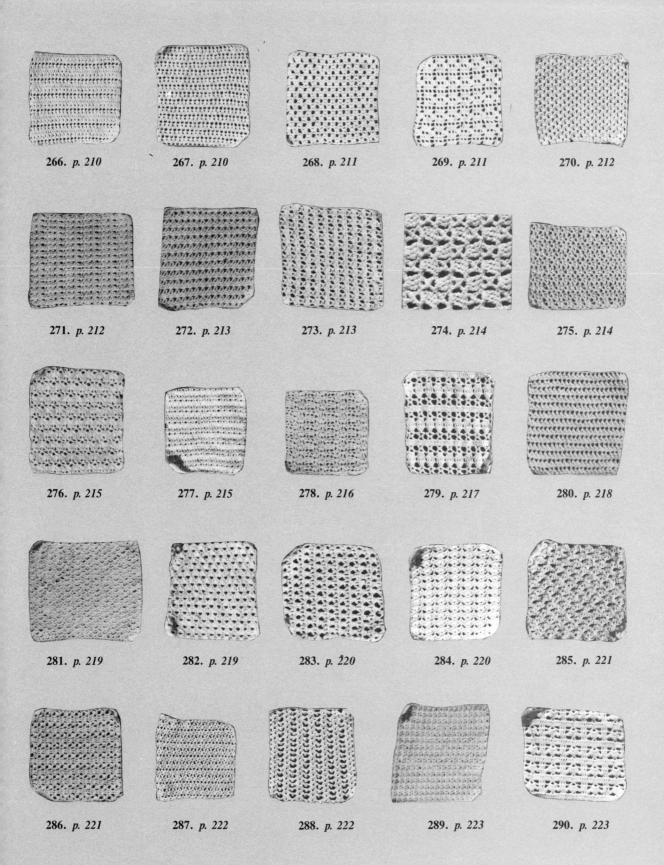

266. *p. 210* 267. *p. 210* 268. *p. 211* 269. *p. 211* 270. *p. 212*

271. *p. 212* 272. *p. 213* 273. *p. 213* 274. *p. 214* 275. *p. 214*

276. *p. 215* 277. *p. 215* 278. *p. 216* 279. *p. 217* 280. *p. 218*

281. *p. 219* 282. *p. 219* 283. *p. 220* 284. *p. 220* 285. *p. 221*

286. *p. 221* 287. *p. 222* 288. *p. 222* 289. *p. 223* 290. *p. 223*

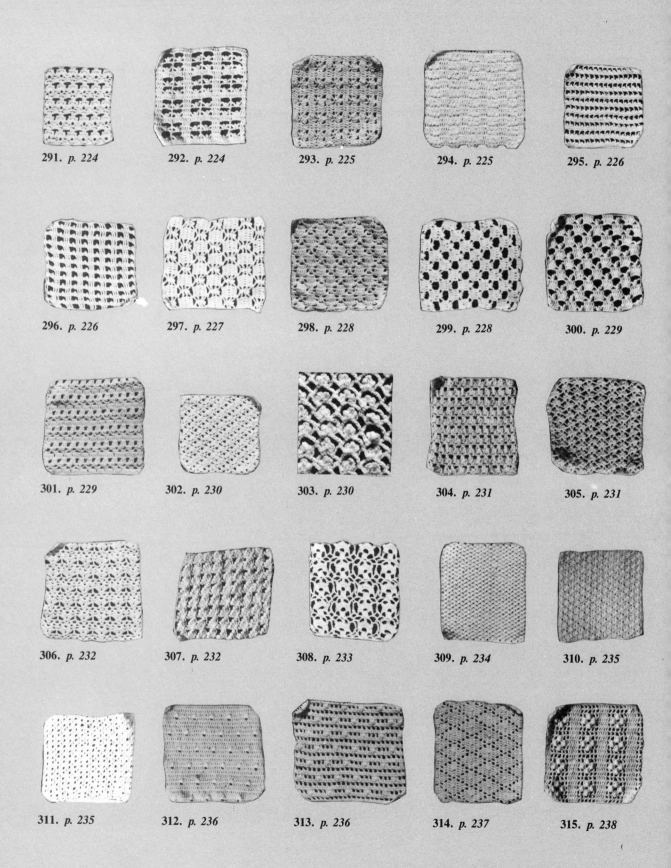

291. *p. 224*   292. *p. 224*   293. *p. 225*   294. *p. 225*   295. *p. 226*

296. *p. 226*   297. *p. 227*   298. *p. 228*   299. *p. 228*   300. *p. 229*

301. *p. 229*   302. *p. 230*   303. *p. 230*   304. *p. 231*   305. *p. 231*

306. *p. 232*   307. *p. 232*   308. *p. 233*   309. *p. 234*   310. *p. 235*

311. *p. 235*   312. *p. 236*   313. *p. 236*   314. *p. 237*   315. *p. 238*

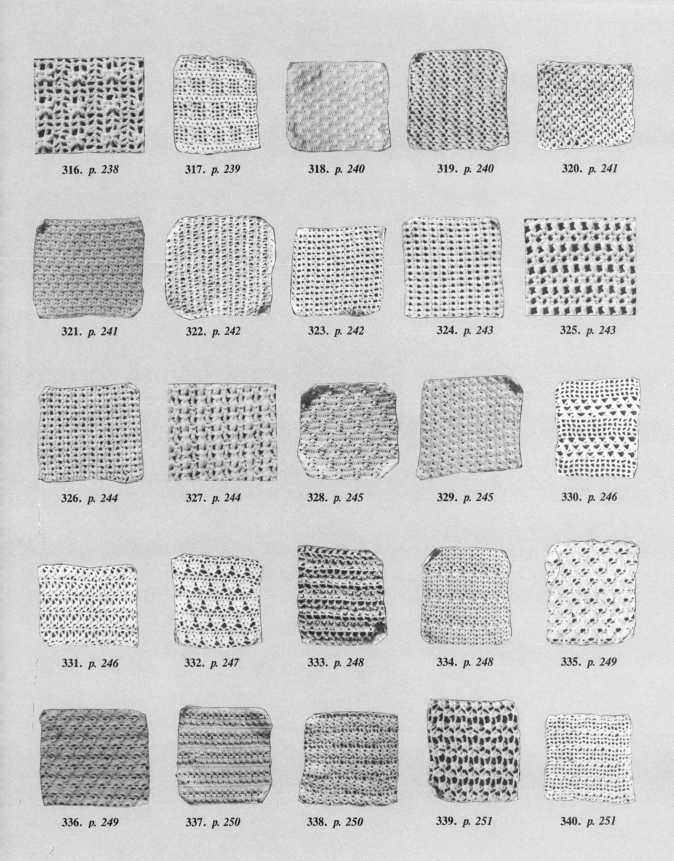

316. *p. 238*   317. *p. 239*   318. *p. 240*   319. *p. 240*   320. *p. 241*

321. *p. 241*   322. *p. 242*   323. *p. 242*   324. *p. 243*   325. *p. 243*

326. *p. 244*   327. *p. 244*   328. *p. 245*   329. *p. 245*   330. *p. 246*

331. *p. 246*   332. *p. 247*   333. *p. 248*   334. *p. 248*   335. *p. 249*

336. *p. 249*   337. *p. 250*   338. *p. 250*   339. *p. 251*   340. *p. 251*

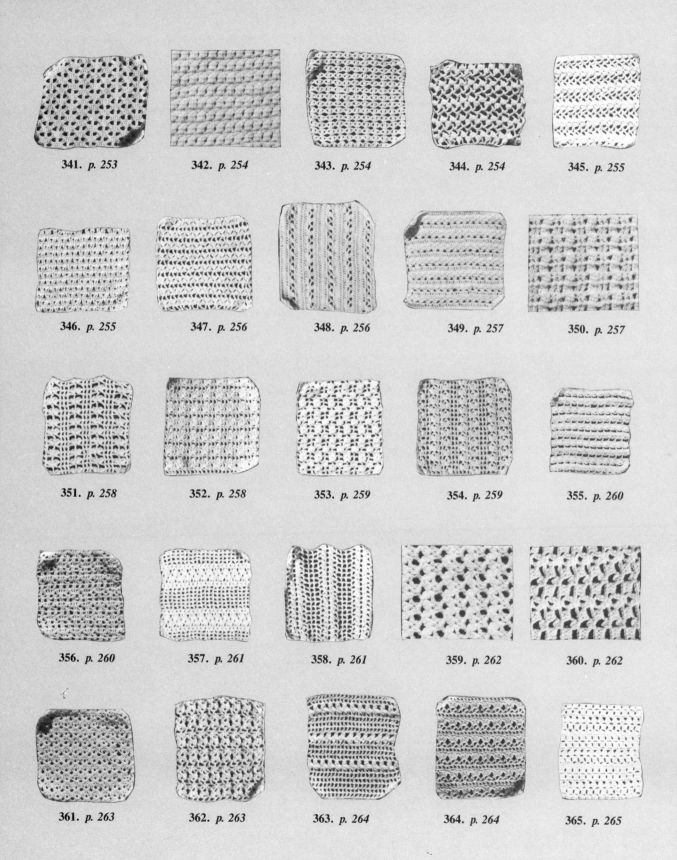

341. *p. 253*   342. *p. 254*   343. *p. 254*   344. *p. 254*   345. *p. 255*

346. *p. 255*   347. *p. 256*   348. *p. 256*   349. *p. 257*   350. *p. 257*

351. *p. 258*   352. *p. 258*   353. *p. 259*   354. *p. 259*   355. *p. 260*

356. *p. 260*   357. *p. 261*   358. *p. 261*   359. *p. 262*   360. *p. 262*

361. *p. 263*   362. *p. 263*   363. *p. 264*   364. *p. 264*   365. *p. 265*

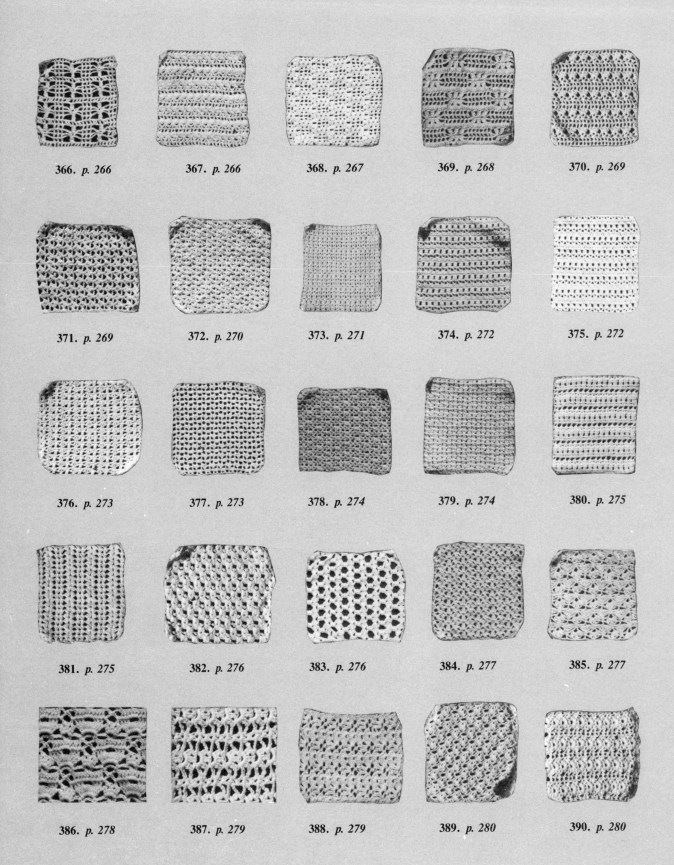

366. *p. 266*   367. *p. 266*   368. *p. 267*   369. *p. 268*   370. *p. 269*

371. *p. 269*   372. *p. 270*   373. *p. 271*   374. *p. 272*   375. *p. 272*

376. *p. 273*   377. *p. 273*   378. *p. 274*   379. *p. 274*   380. *p. 275*

381. *p. 275*   382. *p. 276*   383. *p. 276*   384. *p. 277*   385. *p. 277*

386. *p. 278*   387. *p. 279*   388. *p. 279*   389. *p. 280*   390. *p. 280*

391. *p. 281*   392. *p. 282*   393. *p. 282*   394. *p. 283*   395. *p. 284*

396. *p. 285*   397. *p. 286*   398. *p. 287*   399. *p. 287*   400. *p. 288*

401. *p. 289*   402. *p. 290*   403. *p. 291*   404. *p. 291*   405. *p. 292*

406. *p. 292*   407. *p. 293*   408. *p. 293*   409. *p. 294*   410. *p. 294*

411. *p. 295*   412. *p. 296*   413. *p. 297*   414. *p. 298*   415. *p. 298*

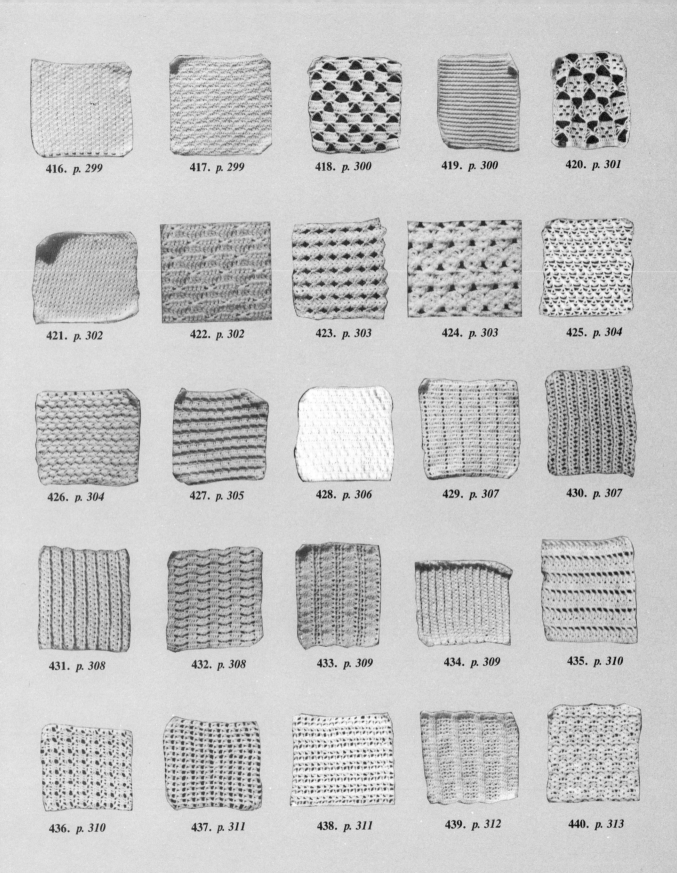

416. *p. 299*   417. *p. 299*   418. *p. 300*   419. *p. 300*   420. *p. 301*

421. *p. 302*   422. *p. 302*   423. *p. 303*   424. *p. 303*   425. *p. 304*

426. *p. 304*   427. *p. 305*   428. *p. 306*   429. *p. 307*   430. *p. 307*

431. *p. 308*   432. *p. 308*   433. *p. 309*   434. *p. 309*   435. *p. 310*

436. *p. 310*   437. *p. 311*   438. *p. 311*   439. *p. 312*   440. *p. 313*

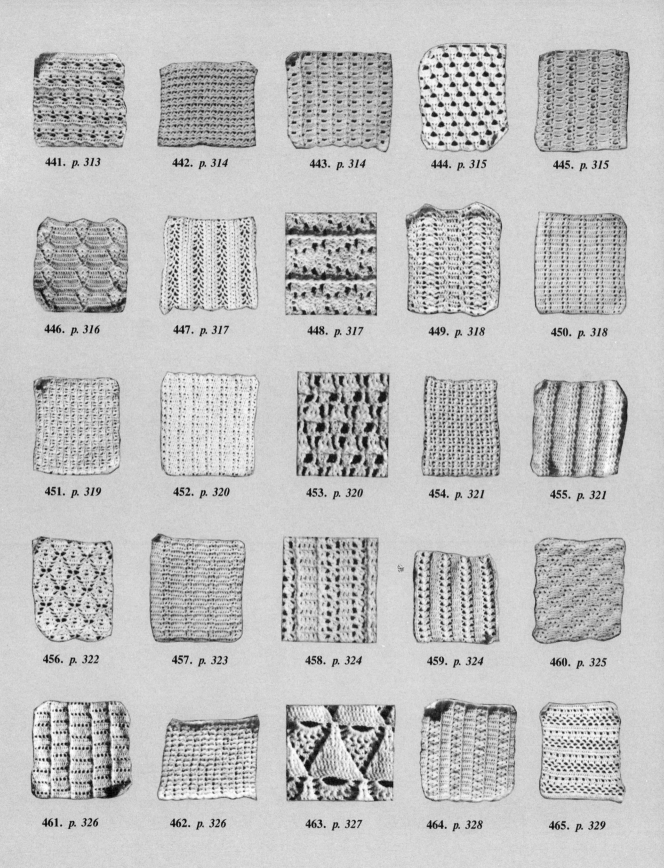

441. *p. 313* 442. *p. 314* 443. *p. 314* 444. *p. 315* 445. *p. 315*

446. *p. 316* 447. *p. 317* 448. *p. 317* 449. *p. 318* 450. *p. 318*

451. *p. 319* 452. *p. 320* 453. *p. 320* 454. *p. 321* 455. *p. 321*

456. *p. 322* 457. *p. 323* 458. *p. 324* 459. *p. 324* 460. *p. 325*

461. *p. 326* 462. *p. 326* 463. *p. 327* 464. *p. 328* 465. *p. 329*

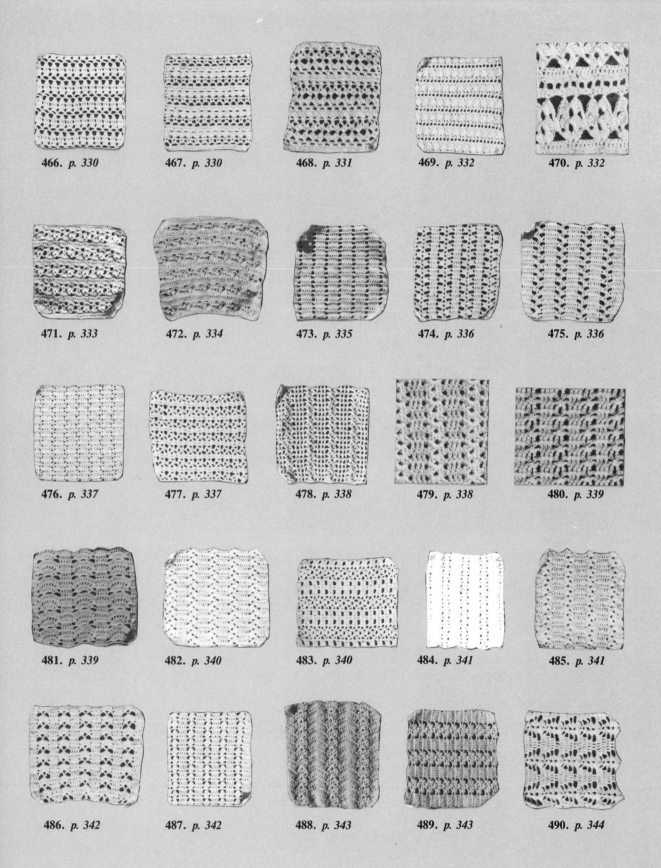

466. *p. 330*   467. *p. 330*   468. *p. 331*   469. *p. 332*   470. *p. 332*

471. *p. 333*   472. *p. 334*   473. *p. 335*   474. *p. 336*   475. *p. 336*

476. *p. 337*   477. *p. 337*   478. *p. 338*   479. *p. 338*   480. *p. 339*

481. *p. 339*   482. *p. 340*   483. *p. 340*   484. *p. 341*   485. *p. 341*

486. *p. 342*   487. *p. 342*   488. *p. 343*   489. *p. 343*   490. *p. 344*

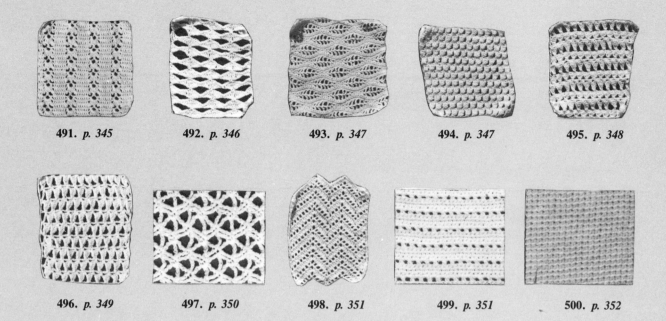

491. *p. 345*   492. *p. 346*   493. *p. 347*   494. *p. 347*   495. *p. 348*

496. *p. 349*   497. *p. 350*   498. *p. 351*   499. *p. 351*   500. *p. 352*

◆ *1* ◆
Single Crochet

1. Chain any multiple, plus 1.

Row 1: Sc in 2nd ch, continue until end of row, turn, ch 1.
Row 2: Sc across row, ch 1, turn.

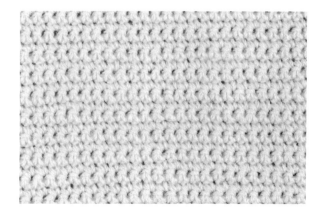

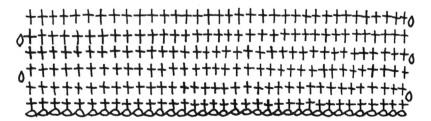

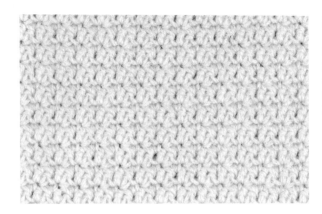

2. Chain multiples of 2 plus 2.

Row 1: 2 sc in the 4th ch, * 2 sc in the 2nd ch, rep from *, ending row with last set, ch 2 and turn.
Row 2: 2 sc in the 2nd stitch, * 2 sc in the 2nd stitch, rep from *, ending row with regular set, ch 2 and turn.
Pattern formed by rep rows 1–2.

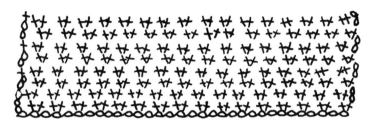

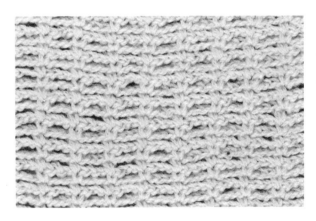

3. Chain multiples of 4 plus 1.

Row 1: 1 sc in the 1st and the 2nd ch, * ch 3, 1 sc in the 4th ch, rep from *, ending row with an extra sc, ch 1 and turn.
Row 2: Same as row 1 except that the sc are worked in the sc.
Pattern formed by rep rows 1–2.

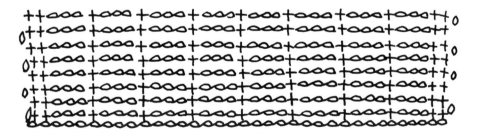

· 2 ·
Chains and Single Crochet

4. Chain multiples of 4 plus 2.

Row 1: 1 sc in the 2nd ch, * ch 5, 1 sc in the 4th ch, rep from *, ending row with last sc, ch 5 and turn.
Row 2: * 1 sc around 5-ch, ch 5, rep from *, ending row with last sc, ch 2, dc in sc, ch 1 and turn.
Pattern formed by rep rows 1–2.

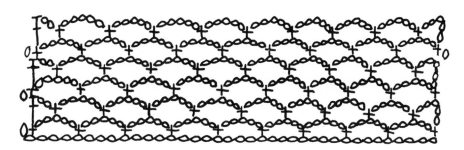

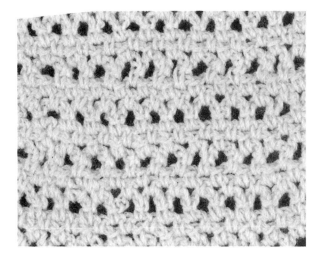

5. Chain multiples of 3 plus 1.

Row 1: 1 sc in 2nd ch, * ch 5, 1 sc in the 3rd ch, rep from *, ending row with 1 sc, ch 4 and turn.
Row 2: 1 sc around the middle of the 5-ch, * ch 2, 1 sc around the middle of the 5-ch, rep from *, ending row with 1 ch and 1 dc, ch 1 and turn.
Row 3: 1 sc in dc, 1 sc in the 1-ch, * ch 2, 1 sc around the 2-ch, rep from *, ending row with 1 sc in the turning ch, ch 5 and turn.
Row 4: * 1 sc around 2-ch, ch 5, rep from *, ending row with 2 chs and 1 dc, ch 1 and turn.
Row 5: 1 sc in dc, * ch 2, 1 sc around middle of the 5-ch, rep from *, ending row with 1 sc, ch 1 and turn.
Row 6: 1 sc in 1st sc, ch 1, * 1 sc around 2-ch, ch 2, rep from *, ending row with a sc, ch 1 and turn.
Pattern formed by rep rows 1–6.

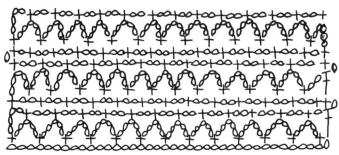

6. Chain multiples of 5 plus 1.

Row 1: 1 sc in the 2nd ch, * ch 5, 1 sc in the 4th ch, ch 3, 1 sc in the next ch, rep from *, ending row with 1 sc in the last ch, ch 5 and turn.
Row 2: * 1 sc around the 5-ch, ch 5, 1 sc around the middle of the 5-ch, ch 5, rep from *, ending row with 2 chs and 1 dc in the sc, ch 1 and turn.
Row 3: 1 sc in the 1st dc, * ch 3, 2 sc around the middle of the 5-ch, rep from *, ending row with sc in turning ch, ch 1 and turn.
Row 4: 1 sc in every ch and every sc all across the row, ending with the last sc in the last sc, ch 1 and turn.
Row 5: Same as row 1.
Pattern formed by rep rows 1–4.

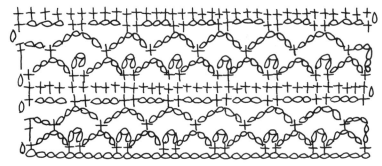

7. Chain multiples of 6 plus 6.

Row 1: 1 sc in the 6th ch, * ch 5, 1 sc in the 6th ch, ch 5, 1 sc in the same ch used for the 1st sc, rep from *, ending row with 5 chs and 1 dc in the last ch, ch 3 and turn.
Row 2: 1 dc in the 1st dc, * ch 5, 1 sc around the middle of the next 5-ch, ch 5, 1 sc in the 5-ch just used, rep from *, ending row with 1 dc in the sc, ch 3 and turn.
Pattern formed by rep rows 1–2.

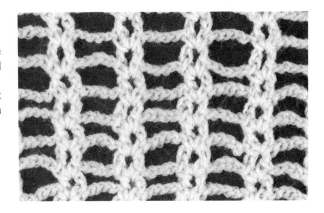

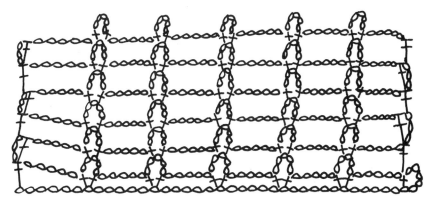

8. Chain multiples of 4 plus 1.

Row 1: 1 sc in the 2nd ch and the next ch, * ch 3, 1 sc in the 4th ch, rep from *, ending row with a sc, ch 1 and turn.
Rows 2–5: Same as row 1, ch 2 and turn.
Row 6: * 1 sl st in the 1st ch, ch 3, 1 dc in the next sc, ch 1, work 3 sc around the dc, rep from *, ending row with 1 sl st in the last sc, ch 4 and turn.
Row 7: * 1 sc in the top of the 3-ch, ch 3, rep from *, ending row with 3 chs and a dc in the turning ch, ch 1 and turn.
Pattern formed by rep rows 1–7.

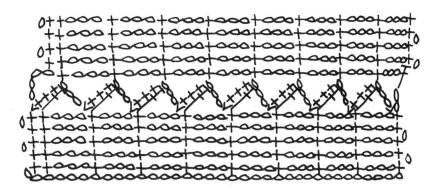

9. Chain multiples of any even number plus 1.

Row 1: 1 sc in the 2nd ch from the hook and all across the row, ch 1 and turn.
Row 2: * 1 sc in the sc, ch 1, 1 sc in the 2nd sc, ch 1, rep from *, ending row with last sc, ch 1 and turn.
Row 3: 1 sc in the 1st sc, * 1 sc around the ch, ch 1, 1 sc around the ch, ch 1, rep from *, ending row with sc in the last sc, ch 1 and turn.
Row 4: Sc in the sc, ch 1, sc in the ch, * ch 1, 1 sc in the ch, rep from *, ending row with last sc, ch 1 and turn.
Pattern formed by rep rows 2–3.

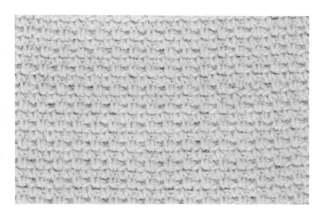

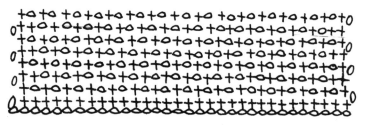

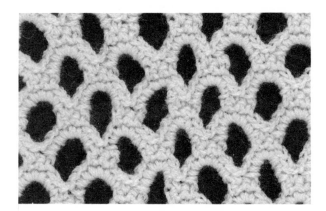

10. Chain multiples of 6 plus 1.

Row 1: 1 sc in the 2nd ch, * ch 6, 1 sc in the 6th ch, rep from *, ending row after last set, ch 1 and turn.
Row 2: 1 sc in the 1st sc, * 7 sc around the 6-ch, 1 sc in the sc, rep from *, ending row after last set, ch 7 and turn.
Row 3: 1 sc in the 4th sc and in the 2 sc following, * ch 6, 1 sc in the 6th sc, and in the following 2 sc, rep from *, ending row with 3 chs and 1 trc in the last sc.
Row 4: 1 sc in the trc, 1 sc in each of the next 3 chs, 1 sc in the middle of the 3 sc, * 7 sc around the 7-ch, 1 sc in the middle of the 3 sc, rep from *, ending row with 4 sc in the turning ch, ch 1 and turn.
Pattern formed by rep rows 1–4.

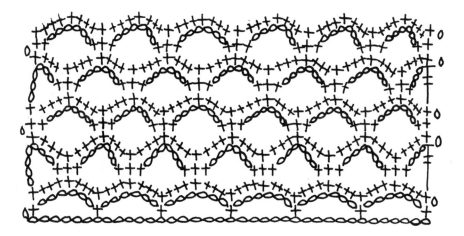

• 3 •
Double Crochet and Chain

11. Chain any multiple plus 3.

Row 1: Dc in the 5th ch and in each ch all across the row, ch 3 and turn.
Row 2: 1 dc in the 5th dc and all the way across the row, ch 3 and turn.
Pattern formed by rep rows 1–2.

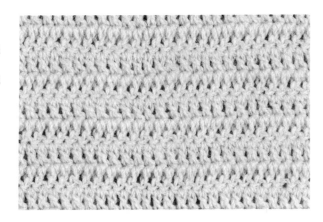

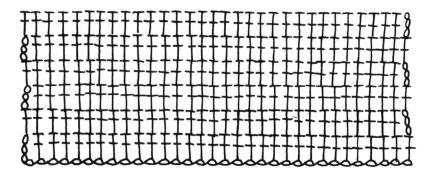

12. Chain multiples of 2 plus 6.

Row 1: 1 dc in the 6th ch, * ch 1, 1 dc in the 2nd ch, rep from *,
ending row with last dc, ch 4 and turn.
Pattern formed by rep row 1.

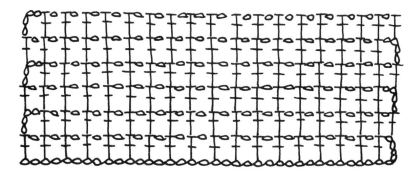

13. Chain multiples of 4 plus 3.

Row 1: 1 dc in the 5th ch and in each ch all across the row, ch 4 and
turn.
Row 2: 1 dc in the 3rd dc, * ch 1, 1 dc in the 2nd dc, rep from *,
ending row with 1 ch and 1 dc in the turning ch, ch 3 and turn.
Row 3: 1 dc in each ch and in each dc all across the row, ch 3 and
turn.
Row 4: 1 dc in the 2nd and next dc, * ch 1, 1 dc in the 2nd dc and
the 2 after that, rep from *, ending row with 1 dc in the turning
ch, ch 3 and turn.
Row 5: 1 dc in each ch and dc all across the row, ch 3 and turn.
Pattern formed by rep rows 1–4.

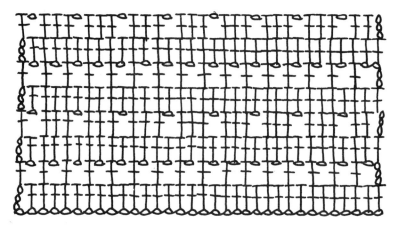

14. Chain multiples of 4 plus 4.

Row 1: 1 dc in the 5th ch and the ch after, * ch 1, 1 dc in the 2nd ch and the 2 following chs, rep from *, ending row with 3 dc, ch 4 and turn.
Row 2: 1 dc in the 3rd dc, * 1 dc in the ch, 1 dc in the 1st dc, ch 1, 1 dc in the 2nd dc, rep from *, ending row with 1 ch and 1 dc in the turning ch, ch 3 and turn.
Pattern formed by rep rows 1–2.

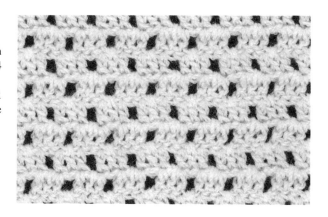

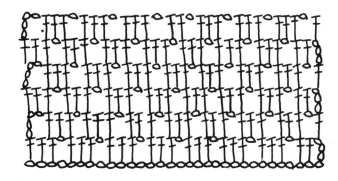

15. Chain multiples of 6 plus 2.

Row 1: 1 dc in the 5th ch from the hook, 1 dc in the next ch, * ch 3, 1 dc in the 4th ch and the 2 chs afterwards, rep from *, ending row with 3 chs and 1 dc in the last ch, ch 3 and turn.
Row 2: 3 dc around the 1st 3-ch, * ch 3, 3 dc around the next 3-ch, rep from *, ending row with 3 chs and 1 dc in the turning ch, ch 3 and turn.
Pattern formed by rep rows 1–2.

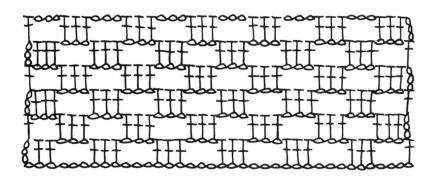

Double Crochet and Chain 45

16. Chain multiples of 6 plus 4.

Row 1: 1 dc in the 5th ch and all the way across the row, ch 3 and turn.

Row 2: 1 dc in the 2nd dc, * ch 3, 1 dc in the 4th dc and in each of the next 2 dc, rep from *, ending row with 1 dc in the last dc and 1 dc in the turning ch, ch 4 and turn.

Row 3: * 1 dc around each of the 3 chs, ch 3, rep from *, ending row with 1 ch and 1 dc in the turning ch, ch 3 and turn.

Row 4: 1 dc in the 1st 1-ch, * ch 3, and 1 dc around each of the next 3 chs, rep from *, ending row with 2 dc in the turning ch, ch 3 and turn.

Row 5: 1 dc in each ch and dc, ch 3 and turn.

Row 6: 1 dc in each dc, ch 3 and turn.

Row 7: Same as row 1.

Pattern formed by rep rows 1–6.

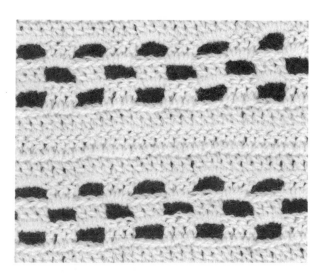

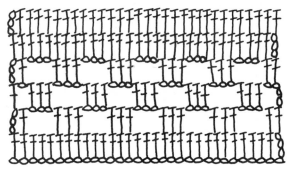

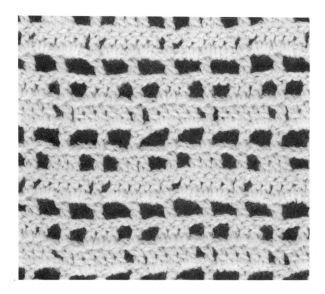

17. Chain multiples of 8 plus 4.

Row 1: 1 dc in 5th ch, 1 dc in next ch, * ch 1, 1 dc in 2nd ch, 1 ch, 1 dc in 2nd ch, dc in each of the next 4 chs, rep from *, ending row with 3 dc, ch 3 and turn.

Row 2: 1 dc in 2nd dc, * ch 2, 1 dc in dc, ch 2, 1 dc in 2nd dc and in next 2 dc, rep from *, ending row with 1 dc in last dc and 1 in the turning ch, ch 6 and turn.

Row 3: 1 dc in 3rd dc, * ch 3, 1 dc in 2nd dc, rep from *, ending row with 1 dc in the turning ch, ch 4 and turn.

Row 4: * 1 dc in 2nd ch, 1 in next ch, 1 in the dc and 1 in each of the 2 chs following the dc, ch 1, 1 dc in the next dc, ch 1, rep from *, row ending in 1 ch and 1 dc in turning ch, ch 5 and turn.

Row 5: * 1 dc in 2nd dc, in the next 2 dc, ch 2, 1 dc in 2nd dc, ch 2, rep from *, ending row with 2 chs and 1 dc, ch 6 and turn.

Row 6: * 1 dc in the middle of the 3 dc, ch 3, 1 dc in 2nd dc, ch 3, rep from *, row ending with 1 dc in turning ch.

Pattern formed by rep rows 1–6.

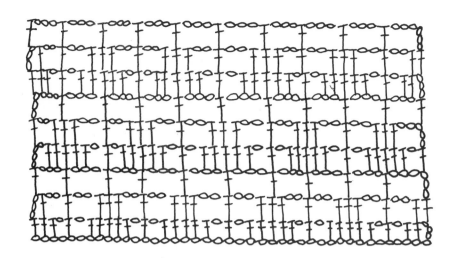

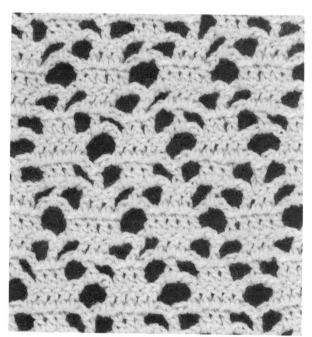

18. Chain multiples of 10 plus 7.

Row 1: 1 dc in the 11th ch, * 1 dc in the next 2 chs, ch 3, 1 dc in the 4th ch, ch 3, 1 dc in the 4th ch, rep from *, ending with 3 chs and 1 dc, ch 5 and turn.

Row 2: * 1 dc in the 3rd ch, 1 dc in each of the next 3 dc, 1 dc in the next ch, ch 5, rep from *, ending row with 2 chs and 1 dc in the turning ch, ch 6 and turn.

Row 3: Sk 1 dc,* 1 dc in the 2nd dc and in the next 2 dc, ch 3, 1 dc in the middle of the 5-ch, ch 3, rep from *, ending row with 3 chs, and 1 dc in the turning ch, ch 3 and turn.

Row 4: 1 dc in the 2nd ch, * ch 3, 1 dc in the 2nd dc, ch 3, 1 dc in 3rd ch, 1 dc in the dc, 1 dc in the 1st ch following the dc, rep from *, ending row with 2 dc in the turning ch, ch 3 and turn.

Row 5: 1 dc in the 2nd dc, 1 dc in the ch following the dc, * ch 5, 1 dc in the last ch before the dc and in the 3 dc, and in the 1st ch following the 3 dc, rep from *, ending row with 1 dc in the last ch before the dc in the dc and in the turning ch, ch 3 and turn.

Row 6: 1 dc in the 2nd dc, * ch 3, 1 dc around the 5-ch, ch 3, 1 dc in the 2nd dc and also the next 2 dc, rep from *, ending row in 2 dc, ch 6 and turn.

Pattern formed by rep rows 1–6.

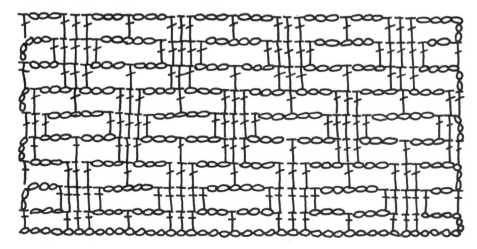

19. Chain multiples of 8 plus 5.

Row 1: 1 dc in the 7th ch, * ch 1, 1 dc in the 2nd ch, rep from *, all across row, ch 4 and turn.
Row 2: 1 dc in the 2nd dc, ch 1, * 1 dc in the dc, the ch, the dc, the ch and the dc, ch 1, 1 dc in the next dc, ch 1, rep from *, ending row with 1 dc in the turning ch, ch 4 and turn.
Row 3: Same as row 2.
Row 4: Same as row 1.
Pattern formed by rep rows 1–4.

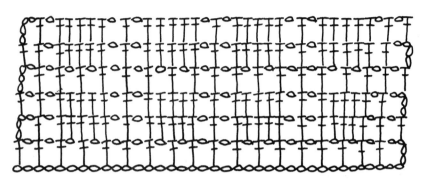

20. Chain multiples of 18 plus 6.

Row 1: 1 dc in the 8th ch, * ch 2, 1 dc in the 3rd ch, ch 2, 1 dc in the 3rd ch and 1 dc in each of the following 9 chs, ch 2, 1 dc in the 3rd ch, rep from *, ending row with the 10 dc, ch 3 and turn.
Row 2: 1 dc in the 2nd dc and the 2 dc after that, * ch 2, 1 dc in the 3rd dc and the 3 dc after that, ch 2, 1 dc in the dc, 1 dc in each of the 2-chs, 1 dc in the dc, ch 2, 1 dc in the next dc and the 3 dc after that, rep from *, ending row with 1 dc in the turning ch, ch 5 and turn.
Row 3: Sk 1 dc, * dc in the dc, ch 2, 1 dc in the 3rd dc, ch 2, 1 dc in the next dc and the 3 dc after that, 1 dc in each of the 2 chs, 1 dc in each of the next 4 dc, ch 2, rep from *, ending row with 1 dc in the turning ch, ch 5 and turn.
Row 4: 1 dc in the 4th dc, * ch 2, 1 dc in the 3rd dc, ch 2, 1 dc in the 3rd dc, 1 dc in each of the next 2 chs, the dc, the 2 chs, the dc, the 2 chs and the next dc, ch 2, 1 dc in the 3rd dc, rep from *, ending row with 3 dc in the turning ch, ch 3 and turn.
Row 5: 1 dc in the 2nd dc, and the next 2 dc, * ch 2, 1 dc in the 3rd dc and the 3 dc following, ch 2, 1 dc in the dc, 1 dc in each of the 2 chs, dc in the dc, ch 2, dc in the dc, and 1 in each of the 3 dc, rep from *, ending row with 1 dc in the turning ch, ch 5 and turn.
Row 6: Sk the 1st dc, * dc in the next dc, ch 2, 1 dc in the 3rd dc, ch 2, 1 dc in each of the next 4 dc, the 2-ch, and the 4 dc, ch 2, rep from *, ending row with 1 dc in the turning ch.
Pattern formed by rep rows 1–6.

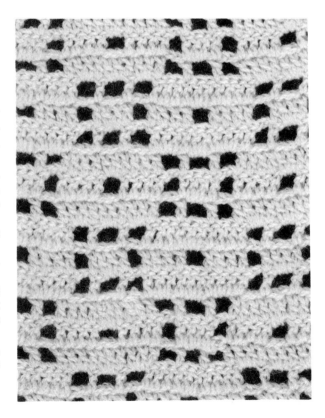

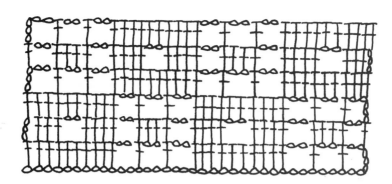

21. Chain multiples of 24 plus 6.

Row 1: 1 dc in the 9th ch *, ch 2, 1 dc in the 3rd ch, ch 2, 1 dc in the 3rd ch, 1 dc in the 6 chs following, ch 2 and dc in the 3rd ch, 4 times, repeat from *, ending row with 1 dc in each of the last 4 chs, ch 5 and turn.

Row 2: Sk 1 dc.* dc in the 3rd dc and the 2 chs after that, dc in the dc, ch 2, dc in the dc 4 times, 1 dc in each of the 2 chs, dc in the dc, ch 2, dc in the 3rd dc, ch 2, rep from *, ending row with 1 dc in the turning ch, ch 5 and turn.

Row 3: Sk 1st dc, * dc in dc, dc in each of next 2 chs, dc in dc, ch 2, 1 dc in 3rd dc, ch 2, dc in dc 2 times, ch 2, dc in 3rd dc, dc in each of next 2 chs, dc in dc, ch 2, dc in dc, ch 2, rep from * ending row with 1 dc in the turning ch, ch 5 and turn.

Row 4: Sk 1st dc * 1 dc in the dc, ch 2, dc in the dc, ch 2, dc in the 3rd dc, dc in each of the 2-chs, the dc and the next 2 chs and dc, ch 2, dc in the 3rd dc, ch 2, dc in the dc, ch 2, dc in the dc, ch 2, rep from *, ending row with 3 dc in the turning ch, ch 3 and turn.

Row 5: 1 dc in the 2nd dc and the 2 dc after that, * ch 2 and dc in dc 6 times, 1 dc in each of the next 6 dc, rep from *, ending row with 1 dc in the turning ch, ch 5 and turn.

Row 6: Same as row 3.

Row 7: Same as row 2.

Row 8: Same as row 1.

Pattern formed by rep rows 1–8.

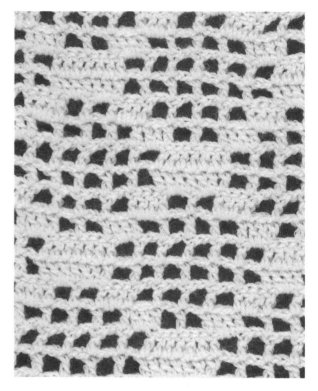

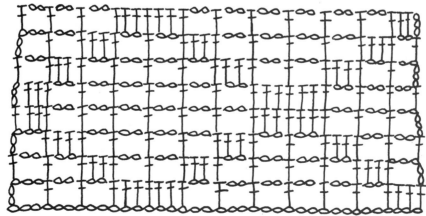

22. Chain multiples of 24 plus 4.

Row 1: 1 dc in the 7th ch, ch 1, 1 dc in the 2nd ch 6 times, 1 dc in the next 2 chs, ch 1, 1 dc in the 2nd ch 7 times, ch 4 and turn.

Row 2: 1 dc in the 2nd dc, ch 1, 1 dc in the dc 5 times, 1 dc in the ch, 1 dc in each of the next 3 dc, in the next 1-ch and in the dc, ch 1 and 1 dc in the next dc 5 times, ch 1 and 1 dc in the turning ch, ch 4 and turn.

Row 3: Sk 1st dc, dc in the next dc, ch 1 and dc in the dc 4 times, 1 dc in the 1-ch, 1 dc in each of the 3 dc, ch 1, 1 dc in the 2nd dc, 1 dc in each of the next 2 dc, dc in the 1-ch, dc in the dc, ch 1 and dc in the dc 4 times, ch 1 and dc in the turning chain, ch 4 and turn.

Row 4: 1 dc in the 2nd dc, ch 1, dc in the dc 3 times, dc in the 1-ch, 1 dc in each of the 3 dc, ch 1, dc in the 2nd dc, ch 1, dc in the dc, ch 1, dc in the 2nd dc, dc in the next 2 dc, dc in the 1-ch and the dc after that, ch 1 and dc in the dc 3 times, ch 1 and dc in the turning ch, ch 4 and turn.

Row 5: Sk 1st dc, dc in the next dc, ch 1, dc in the dc, ch 1, dc in the dc, 1 dc in the 1-ch, 1 dc in each of the 3 dc, ch 1, 1 dc in the 2nd dc, ch 1 and dc in the dc 3 times, ch 1, dc in the 2nd dc, dc in the next 2 dc, dc in the 1-ch, dc in the dc, ch 1, dc in the dc, ch 1, dc in the dc, ch 1, dc in the turning ch, ch 4 and turn.

Row 6: Sk 1 dc, dc in dc, ch 1, 2 times, ch 1, dc in 2nd dc, and in each of next 2 dc, dc in 1-ch, dc in dc, ch 1, dc in dc 3 times, dc in 1-ch, dc in each of next 3 dc, ch 1, dc in 2nd dc, ch 1, dc in dc 2 times, ch 1, dc in turning ch, ch 4 and turn.

Row 7: Sk 1st dc, dc in the dc, ch 1 and dc in the dc 3 times, ch 1, 1 dc in the 2nd dc, 1 dc in each of the next 2 dc, dc in the 1-ch, dc in the dc, ch 1, dc in the next dc, dc in the 1-ch, 1 dc in each of the 3 dc, ch 1, dc in the 2nd dc, ch 1, dc in the dc 3 times, ch 1, dc in the turning ch, ch 4 and turn.

Row 8: Sk 1 dc, dc in the dc, ch 1 and dc in the dc 4 times, ch 1 and dc in the 2nd dc, 1 dc in each of the next 2 dc, dc in the 1-ch, 1 dc in each of the next 3 dc, ch 1 and dc in the 2nd dc, ch 1 and dc in the dc 4 times, ch 1, dc in the turning ch, ch 4 and turn.

Row 9: Sk 1 dc, dc in the dc, ch 1 and dc in the dc 5 times, ch 1, dc in the 2nd dc, dc in each of the next 2 dc, ch 1, dc in the 2nd dc, ch 1, dc in the dc 5 times, ch 1, dc in the turning ch.

Pattern formed by rep rows 1–9.

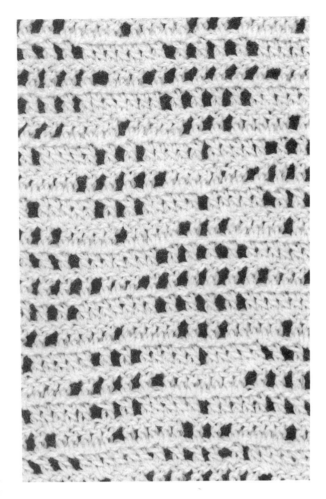

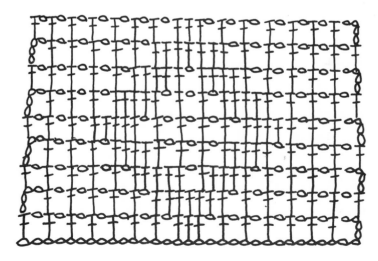

23. Chain multiples of 9 plus 4.

Row 1: 1 dc in the 5th ch and the 1 after that, * ch 2, 1 dc in the 3rd ch and in the 6 chs following, repeat from *, ending row with 5 dc, ch 3 and turn.

Row 2: 1 dc in the 2nd dc, * and in the next 3 dc, 2 dc around the 2-ch, ch 2, 1 dc in 3rd dc and next dc, rep from *, ending row with 2 chs and 1 dc in the turning ch, ch 3 and turn.

Row 3: * 2 dc around the 2-ch, 1 dc in each of the next 5 dc, ch 2, rep from *, ending row with 1 ch and 1 dc in the turning ch, ch 3 and turn.

Row 4: 1 dc in the 1-ch, * ch 2, 1 dc in the 3rd dc and in the next 4 dc, 2 dc in the 2-ch, rep from *, ending row with 5 dc in the dc and 1 in the turning ch, ch 3 and turn.

Row 5: 1 dc in the 2nd dc and in the next 2 dc, * ch 2, 2 dc in the 2-ch, 5 dc in the next 5 dc, rep from *, ending row with 2 dc in the 2-ch, 1 in the dc and 1 in the turning ch, ch 3 and turn.

Row 6: Sk 1 dc, 1 dc in each of the next 3 dc, * 2 dc around the 2-ch, ch 2, 1 dc in the 3rd dc and in the next 4 dc, repeat from *, ending row with 1 dc in the last dc and 1 in the turning ch, ch 4 and turn.

Row 7: * 2 dc in the 2-ch, 1 dc in each of the next 5 dc, ch 2, rep from *, ending row with 2 dc in the 2-ch, 5 dc in the dc and 1 in the turning ch, ch 5 and turn.

Row 8: 1 dc in the 4th dc, * dc in the next 4 dc, 2 dc around the 2-ch, ch 2, 1 dc in the 3rd dc, rep from *, ending row with 2 dc in the turning ch, ch 3 and turn.

Row 9: 1 dc in the 2nd dc, and the next 3 dc, * ch 2, 2 dc around the 2-ch, 1 dc each in the next 5 dc, rep from *, ending row with 3 dc in the turning ch, ch 3 and turn.

Pattern formed by rep rows 1–9.

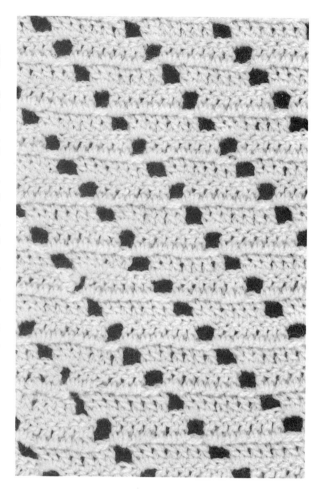

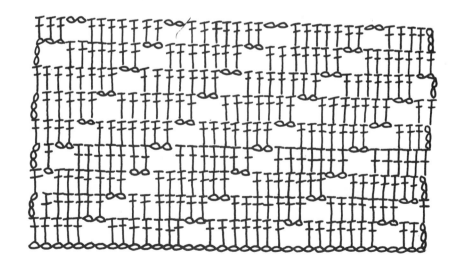

24. Chain multiples of 16 plus 5.

Row 1: 1 dc in the 7th ch, * ch 1, 1 dc in the 2nd ch, ch 1, 1 dc in the 2nd ch, ch 1, 1 dc in each of the next 3 chs, ch 1, dc in the 2nd ch, ch 1, 1 dc in the 2nd ch, ch 1, dc in the 2nd ch, ch 1, dc in the 2nd ch, rep from *, ending row with dc, ch 4 and turn.

Rows 2–4: Same as row 1, ch 4 and turn.

Row 5: Sk 1 dc, 1 dc in the dc, * ch 1, dc in the dc, ch 1, dc in the dc, dc in the 1-ch, dc in the dc and in the next 2 dc, 1 dc in the 1-ch, 1 dc in the dc, ch 1, dc in the dc, ch 1, dc in the dc, ch 1, dc in the dc, rep from *, ending row with dc in the turning ch, ch 3 and turn.

Row 6: 1 dc in the 1-ch, 1 dc in the dc, ch 1, * dc in the dc, ch 1, dc in the dc, ch 1, dc in the dc, dc in the 1-ch, 1 dc in each of the next 7 dc, 1 dc in the 1-ch, 1 dc in the dc, ch 1, rep from *, ending row with dc in the turning ch, ch 4 and turn.

Row 7: Sk 1st dc, * 1 dc in the dc, dc in the 1-ch, dc in each of the next 11 dc, 1 dc in the 1-ch, dc in the dc, ch 1 and rep from *, ending row with dc in the turning ch, ch 3 and turn.

Row 8: Same as row 6.

Row 9: Same as row 5.

Pattern formed by rep rows 1–9.

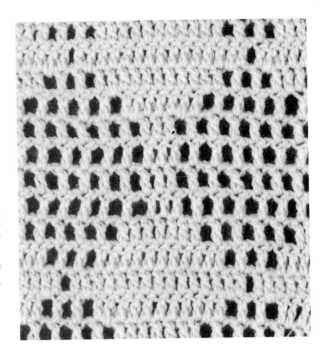

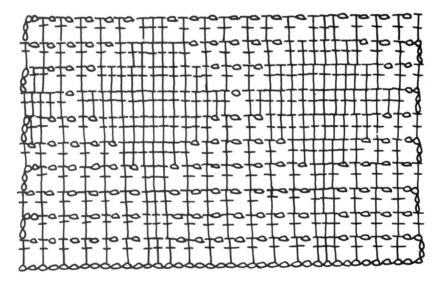

25. Chain multiples of 14 plus 4.

Row 1: 1 dc in the 5th ch and in the 6 chs following, * ch 1, dc in the 2nd ch, ch 1, dc in the 2nd ch, ch 1, dc in the 2nd ch, ch1, dc in the 2nd ch, 1 dc in each of the next 6 chs, rep from *, ending row with dc, ch 3 and turn.

Rows 2–3: Same as row 1, ch 4 and turn.

Row 4: 1 dc in the 3rd dc, ch 1 and dc in the 2nd dc 3 times, * form 6 dc, 1 in the dc, 1 in the ch, dc, ch, dc, ch, ch 1, dc in the 2nd dc 3 times and ch 1, rep from *, ending row with 1 dc in the turning ch, ch 4 and turn.

Rows 5–6: Rep row 4.

Pattern formed by rep rows 1–6.

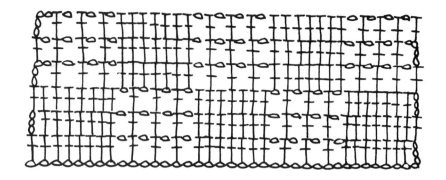

• *4* •
Single Crochet, Double Crochet, Chain

26. Chain multiples of 10 plus 6.

Row 1: 1 sc in the 3rd ch and the next 3 chs, * work 1 dc in each of the next 5 chs, work 1 sc in each of the next 5 chs, repeat from *, ending with last set, ch 3 and turn.
Row 2: Make 1 dc in each of the sc, * make 1 sc in each of the dc and work 1 dc in each of the sc, repeat from *, ending row with 1 dc in the sc, ch 1 and turn.
Pattern formed by rep rows 1–2.

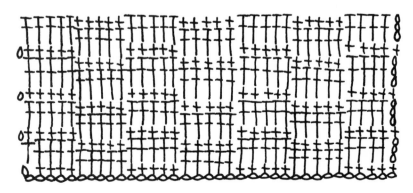

27. Chain multiples of 2 plus 2.

Row 1: 1 sc in the 4th ch, * 1 dc in the next ch, 1 sc in the next ch, rep from *, ending row with 1 dc in the last stitch, ch 2 and turn.
Row 2: * 1 dc in the sc of the previous row, 1 sc in the dc of the row before, rep from *, ending row with 1 dc in the turning ch, ch 2 and turn.
Pattern formed by rep rows 1–2.

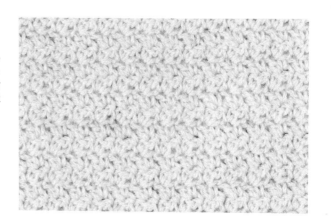

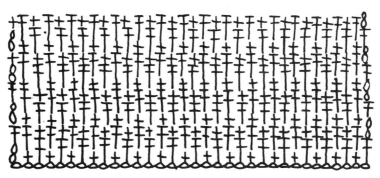

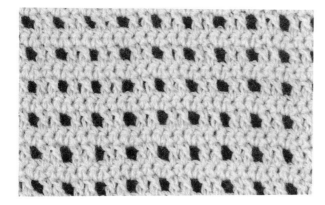

28. Chain multiples of 3 plus 4.

Row 1: 1 sc in the 2nd ch and in each ch all across the row, ch 4 and turn.
Row 2: 1 dc in the 3rd sc and the sc following that, * ch 1, dc in the 2nd sc and the sc after that, rep from *, ending row with 1 dc, ch 1 and turn.
Row 3: Same as row 1 except that the sc are formed in each ch and each dc.
Pattern formed by rep rows 1–2.

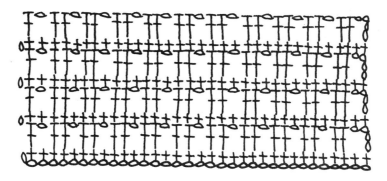

Single Crochet, Double Crochet, Chain 55

29. Chain multiples of 4 plus 1.

Row 1: 1 sc in the 2nd ch and the ch after that, * ch 2, 1 sc in the 3rd ch and the ch after that, rep from *, ending row with 2 sc, ch 3 and turn.
Row 2: 1 dc in the 2nd sc, * ch 2, 1 dc in each of the next 2 sc, rep from *, ending row with 2 dc, ch 1 and turn.
Row 3: Same as row 1 except that the sc are worked in the dc.
Pattern formed by rep rows 1–2.

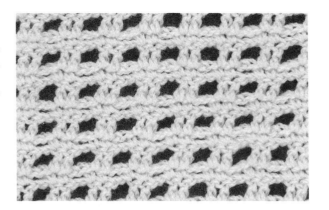

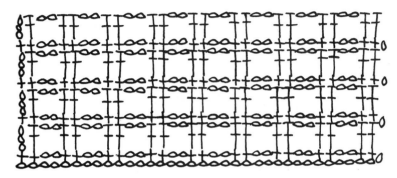

30. Chain multiples of 6 plus 5.

Row 1: 1 dc in the 5th ch, 1 dc in the next ch, * ch 3, 1 dc in the 4th ch and also in the next 2 chs, rep from *, ending row with 3 dc, ch 1 and turn.
Row 2: 1 sc in the 1st 3 dc, * ch 3, 1 sc in each of the 3 dc, rep from *, ending row with 2 sc in the last 2 dc and 1 in the turning ch, ch 1 and turn.
Row 3: 1 sc in the 1st 3 sc, * ch 3, 1 sc in each of the 3 sc, rep from *, ending row with 3 sc, ch 3 and turn.
Pattern formed by rep rows 1–3.

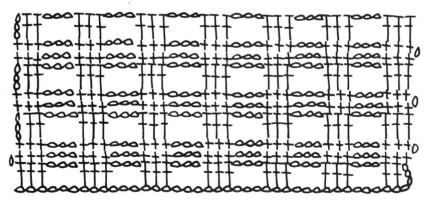

31. Chain multiples of any even number plus 3.

Row 1: 1 dc in the 5th ch and in each ch all the way across the row, ch 1 and turn.
Row 2: 1 sc in the 1st dc, * ch 2, 1 sc between the 2nd and 3rd dc, rep from *, ending row with 1 sc in the turning ch, ch 3 and turn.
Row 3: 2 dc around the 2-ch, * 2 dc around the 2-ch, rep from *, ending row with last set and 1 dc in the last sc, ch 1 and turn.
Pattern formed by rep rows 1–3.

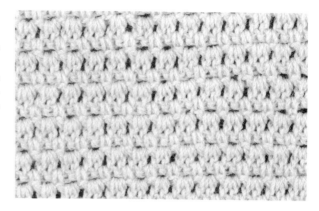

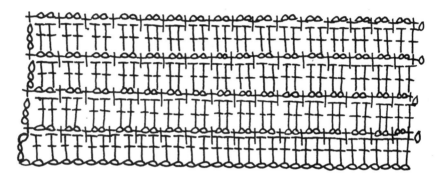

32. Chain multiples of 4 plus 4.

Row 1: 1 dc in the 5th ch and in each ch all across the row, ch 1 and turn.
Row 2: 1 sc in the 1st and the next dc, * ch 2, 1 sc in the 3rd dc and the dc after that, rep from *, ending row with 2 sc and 1 additional sc in the turning ch, ch 3 and turn.
Row 3: 1 dc in each sc and in each ch all across the row, ch 1 and turn.
Pattern formed by rep rows 1–2.

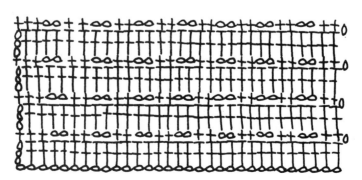

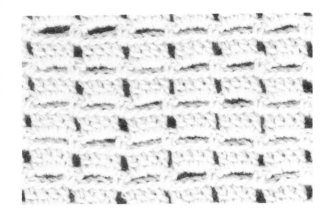

33. Chain multiples of 5 plus 4.

Row 1: 1 dc in the 5th ch and 1 dc in each of the next 3 chs, * ch 1, 1 dc in the 2nd ch and dc in each of the following 3 chs, repeat from *, ending row after last set with 1 additional dc, ch 1 and turn.
Row 2: 1 sc between the 1st and the 2nd dc, * ch 4, 1 sc in the 1-ch, rep from *, ending row with 1 sc in the turning ch, ch 3 and turn.
Pattern formed by rep rows 1–2.

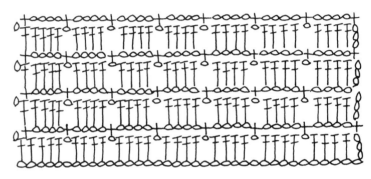

34. Chain multiples of 4 plus 1.

Row 1: 1 dc in the 11th ch, * ch 3, 1 dc in the 4th ch, rep from *, ending row with 1 dc in the last ch, ch 5 and turn.
Row 2: * 1 sc around the 3-ch, ch 2, 1 dc in the dc, ch 2, rep from *, ending row with 2 chs and 1 dc, ch 6 and turn.
Pattern formed by rep rows 1–2.

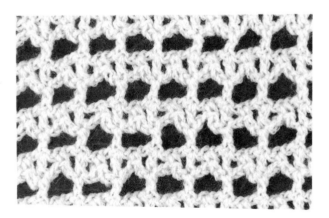

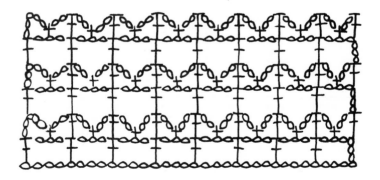

35. Chain multiples of 6 plus 6.

Row 1: 1 sc in 10th ch, * ch 3, 1 dc in 3rd ch, ch 3, 1 sc in 3rd ch, rep from *, ending row with 1 dc, ch 3 and turn.
Row 2: 1 dc in ch just following dc, * ch 3, 1 dc just before dc, 1 dc in the dc, 1 dc just after the dc, rep from *, ending row with 2 dc in turning ch, ch 6 and turn.
Row 3: Same as row 1, only sc should be placed in the middle of the 3-ch, and the dc should be placed in the middle dc.
Pattern formed by rep rows 1–3.

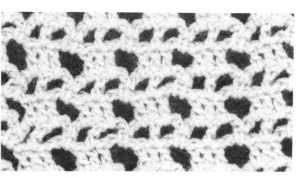

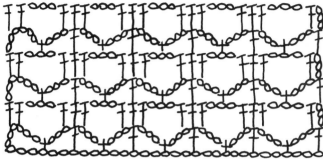

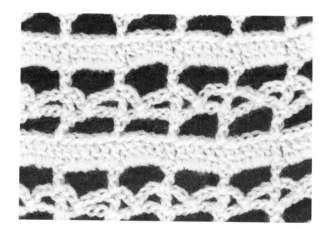

36. Chain multiples of 6 plus 4.

Row 1: 1 dc in 5th ch and continue dc in each ch all across the row, ch 8 and turn.
Row 2: 1 dc in 7th dc, * ch 5, 1 dc in 6th dc, rep from *, ending row with 1 dc, ch 6 and turn.
Row 3: 1 sc around the middle of the 5-ch, * ch 3, 1 dc in dc, ch 3, 1 sc around the middle of the 5-ch, rep from *, ending in 1 dc in the turning ch, ch 8 and turn.
Row 4: Sk 1 dc, * 1 dc in dc, ch 5, rep from *, ending in 1 dc, ch 3 and turn.
Row 5: 1 dc in each of the 5-chs, * 1 dc in the dc, 1 dc in the next 5-ch, rep from *, ch 8 and turn.
Pattern formed by rep rows 1–4.

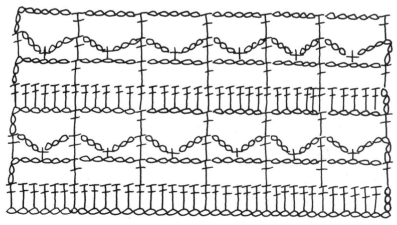

37. Chain multiples of 7 plus 7.

Row 1: 1 sc in 10th ch, * ch 3, 1 dc in 3rd ch, 1 dc in next ch, ch 3, 1 sc in 3rd ch, rep from *, ending row with 1 dc in last ch, ch 1 and turn.

Row 2: 1 sc in 1st dc, * 1 sc in 1st ch, ch 3, 1 sc in last ch before the 2 dc, 1 sc in each of the next 2 dc, 1 sc in the 1st ch, rep from *, ending row with 2 sc in the turning ch, ch 6 and turn.

Pattern formed by rep rows 1–2.

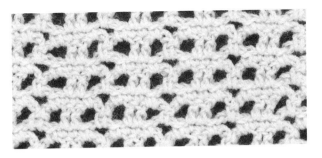

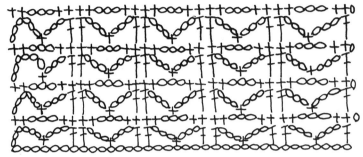

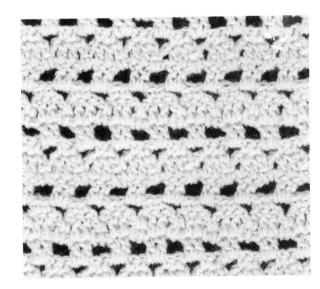

38. Chain multiples of 4 plus 5.

Row 1: 1 dc in 5th ch, * ch 2, 1 dc in 3rd ch, 1 dc in next ch, rep from *, ending row with 2 dc, ch 3 and turn.

Row 2: 1 dc in 2nd dc, * ch 2, 1 sc around 2-ch, ch 2, 1 dc in next dc, 1 dc in next dc, rep from *, ending row with 1 dc, and 1 dc in turning ch, ch 1 and turn.

Row 3: 1 sc in 1st dc, 1 sc in next dc, * ch 2, 1 sc in next dc, 1 sc in next dc, rep from *, ending row with 1 sc in last dc, and 1 sc in the turning ch, ch 4 and turn.

Row 4: 2 dc around 2-ch, * ch 2, 2 dc around 2-ch, rep from *, ending row with 1 dc in last sc, ch 1 and turn.

Row 5: 1 sc in 1st dc, * ch 2, 1 dc in each of the next 2 dc, ch 2, 1 sc around 2-ch, rep from *, ending row with 2 dc in last 2 dc, ch 2 and 1 sc in turning ch, ch 4 and turn.

Row 6: 1 sc in 1st dc, * 1 sc in next dc, ch 2, 1 sc in top of dc, rep from *, ending row with 1 ch and 1 dc in last sc, ch 3 and turn.

Pattern formed by rep rows 1–6.

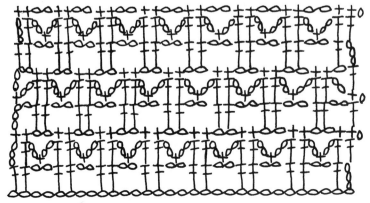

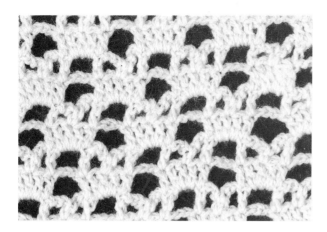

39. Chain multiples of 8 plus 4.

Row 1: 1 dc in the 5th ch, and 1 dc in each of the next 3 chs, * ch 3, 1 sc in the 2nd ch, ch 3, 1 dc in the 2nd ch, 1 dc in each of the next 4 chs, rep from *, ending row after the ch set with 1 dc, ch 6 and turn.
Row 2: Sk 1 dc, * 1 dc in the next dc, ch 3, 1 sc in the 2nd dc, ch 3, 1 dc in the 2nd dc, ch 3, rep from *, ending row after the ch·set with 1 dc in the turning ch, ch 6 and turn.
Row 3: 1 dc in the 2nd dc of the ch set, * 1 dc in each of the next 3 chs and the dc, ch 3 and 1 dc in the next dc, rep from *, ending row with 5 dc, ch 6 and turn.
Row 4: Rep row 1.
Patterns formed by rep rows 1–3.

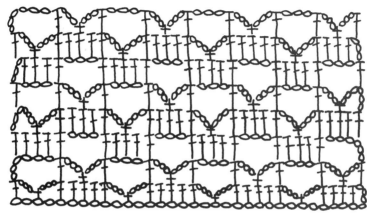

40. Chain multiples of 9 plus 6.

Row 1: 1 dc in 9th ch, * 1 dc in each of the next 5 chs, ch 5, 1 dc in 4th ch, rep from *, ending row with 2 chs and 1 dc in the last ch, ch 1 and turn.
Row 2: 1 sc in the 1st dc, * ch 3, 1 dc in the 1st dc, ch 1, 1 dc in the 5th dc, ch 3, 1 sc in the middle of the 5-ch, rep from *, ending row with 1 sc in the turning ch, ch 5 and turn.
Row 3: Same as row 1, except that the 1st 2 dc should be made in the last ch before the dc, the middle 2 in the 1-ch between the 2 dc, and the last 2 dc should be made in the 1st ch after the dc.
Pattern formed by rep rows 1–2.

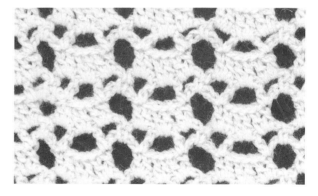

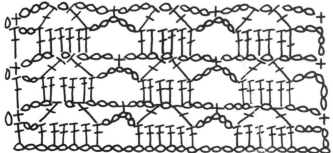

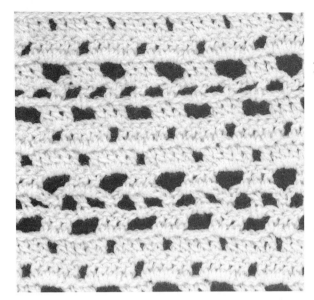

41. Chain multiples of 6 plus 4.

Row 1: 1 dc in the 5th ch and in the ch following, * ch 1, 1 dc in the 2nd ch, and in 4 chs following, repeat from *, ending row with 3 dc, ch 3 and turn.

Row 2: 1 dc in the 2nd dc and the next dc, * 1 dc in the ch and also in the 2 dc which follow, ch 1, 1 dc in the 2nd dc and the 1 following, rep from *, ending row with last set and 1 extra dc in the turning ch, ch 3 and turn.

Row 3: 1 dc in the 2nd dc, * ch 3, 1 dc in the last dc before the ch, 1 dc in the ch and 1 dc in the 1st dc after the ch, rep from *, ending row with 1 dc in the last dc and 1 in the turning ch, ch 1 and turn.

Row 4: 1 sc in the 1st dc, * ch 3, 1 dc around the 3-ch, ch 3, 1 sc in the middle of the 3 dc, rep from *, ending row with last sc in the turning ch, ch 5 and turn.

Row 5: * 1 dc in the 3rd ch, 1 dc in the dc, 1 dc in the 1st ch after the dc, ch 3, rep from *, ending row with last set, 1 ch and 1 trc in the turning ch, ch 3 and turn.

Pattern formed by rep rows 1–5.

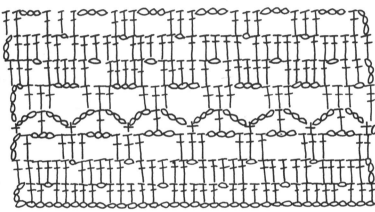

42. Chain multiples of 11 plus 7.

Row 1: 1 sc in the 10th ch, * ch 5, 1 sc in the 4th ch, ch 3, 1 dc in the 3rd ch and in the next ch, ch 3, 1 sc in the 3rd ch, rep from *, ending row with 3 chs and 1 dc, ch 3 and turn.

Row 2: 2 dc in the 1st dc and the 1st ch, * ch 1, 3 dc around the 5-ch, ch 1, 1 dc in the ch, and 2 dc in the 1st dc, 2 dc in the 2nd dc, 1 dc in the 1st ch, rep from *, ending row with 3 dc in the turning ch, ch 6 and turn.

Row 3: Same as row 1, except that the sc is worked in the ch.

Pattern formed by rep rows 1–2.

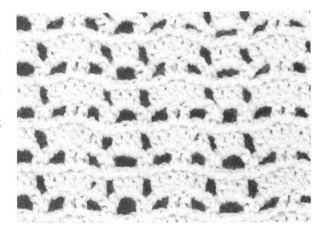

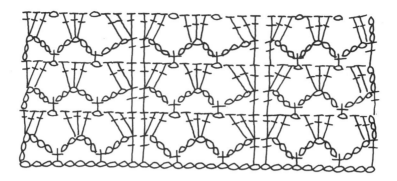

43. Chain multiples of 6 plus 5.

Row 1: 1 dc in the 5th ch and the 2 chs after that, * ch 2, 1 dc in the 3rd ch and the 3 chs following, rep from *, ending row with last set, ch 5 and turn.

Row 2: * 1 dc in the last of the 4 dc, 1 dc in each of the next 2 chs, 1 dc in the 1st of the dc of the next 4-set, ch 2, rep from *, ending row with 2 chs and 1 dc in the turning ch, ch 3 and turn.

Row 3: * 1 dc in each of the 1-ch, 1 dc in the 1st dc of the next set, ch 2, 1 dc in the last of the 4 dc of the next set, rep from *, ending row with last set and 3 dc in the turning ch, ch 1 and turn.

Row 4: * 1 sc in the 1st dc of the set, ch 3, 1 sc in the last dc of the set, ch 3, rep from *, ending row with 1 sc in the turning ch, ch 4 and turn.

Row 5: * 1 sc around the 3-ch, ch 3, rep from *, ending row with sc around the last 3-ch, ch 1 and 1 dc in the last sc, ch 1 and turn.

Row 6: 1 sc in the 1st dc, * ch 3, 1 sc in the 3-ch, rep from *, ending row with sc in the turning ch, ch 4 and turn.

Row 7: * 1 sc in the 3-ch, ch 3 and rep from *, ending row with 1 sc in the last 3-ch, ch 1 and 1 dc in the last sc, ch 1 and turn.

Row 8: 1 sc in the 1st dc, * ch 3, 1 sc around the 3-ch, rep from *, ending row with 1 sc in the turning ch, ch 3 and turn.

Row 9: * work 2 dc around the 3-ch, 1 dc in the sc, ch 2, 1 dc in the next sc, rep from *, ending row with 1 dc in the last sc.
Pattern formed by rep rows 1–9.

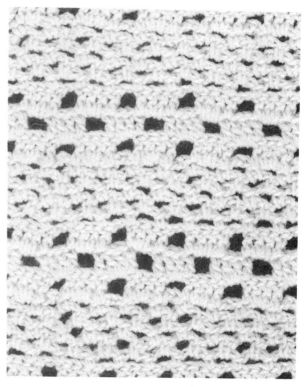

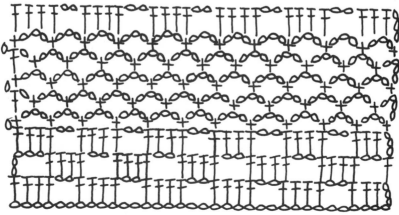

44. Chain multiples of 3 plus 3.

Row 1: 1 dc in the 5th ch and in all the chs all the way across the row, ch 1 and turn.
Row 2: 1 sc in the 1st dc, ch 3, * 1 sc in the 3rd dc, ch 3 and rep from *, ending row with 1 sc in the turning ch, ch 3 and turn.
Row 3: * 1 sc around the 3-ch, ch 3, 1 sc around the next 3-ch, rep from *, ending row with last sc around the 3-ch, ch 1 and 1 hdc in the sc, ch 1.
Row 4: 1 sc in the 1st hdc, * ch 3, 1 sc around the middle of the 3-ch, rep from *, ending row with 1 sc in the turning ch, ch 3 and turn.
Row 5: * work 2 dc around the 3-ch, 1 dc in the sc, rep from *, ending the row with last dc in the last sc, ch 3 and turn.
Pattern formed by rep rows 1–5.

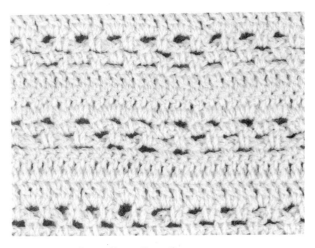

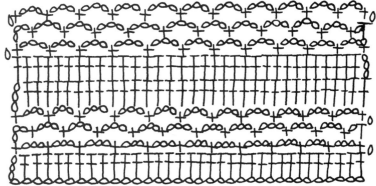

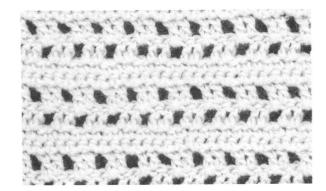

45. Chain multiples of 2 plus 3.

Row 1: 1 sc in the 2nd ch and in each ch all across the row, ch 1 and turn.
Row 2: 1 sc in the 1st sc and all the way across the row, ch 3 and turn.
Row 3: 1 dc in the 1st sc and 1 dc in the next sc, * ch 2, 1 dc in the 3rd sc and the sc after that, rep from *, ending row with 1 dc in each of the last 2 sc, ch 4 and turn.
Row 4: * 2 dc around the 2-ch, ch 2, rep from *, ending row with 1 dc in the turning ch, ch 1 and turn.
Pattern formed by rep rows 1–4.

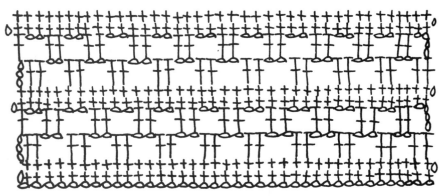

46. Chain multiples of 8 plus 1.

Row 1: 1 sc in the 2nd ch, * ch 3, 1 sc in the 4th ch, rep from *, ending row with last sc, ch 1 and turn.
Rows 2–3: Same as row 1, ch 3 and turn.
Row 4: * sc in the sc, ch 4, rep from *, ending row with the sc, ch 4 and turn.
Row 5: * work 2 dc around the 4-ch, ch 3, rep from *, ending row with 2 dc in the last 4-ch, ch 1 and 1 dc in the sc, ch 1 and turn.
Row 6: 1 sc in the 1st dc, * ch 4, 1 sc in the middle of the 3 chs, rep from *, ending row with 1 sc in the turning ch, ch 3 and turn.
Row 7: * work 4 dc around the 4-ch, rep from *, ending row after last set with 1 extra dc in the sc, ch 1 and turn.
Row 8: Same as row 1 except that the sc is worked in the middle of the 2 sets, ch 1 and turn.
Pattern formed by rep rows 1–8.

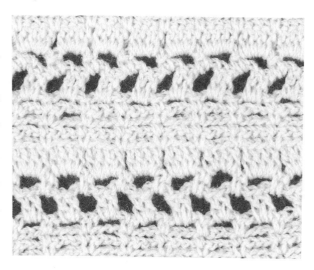

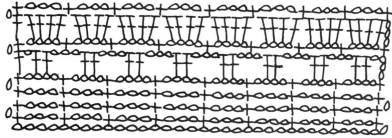

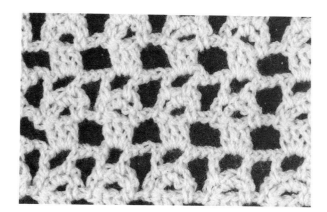

47. Chain multiples of 6 plus 6.

Row 1: 1 dc in 7th ch, 1 dc in next ch, 1 dc in next ch, * ch 5, turn to reverse side, attach chs to ch where it meets the dc, so that it forms a loop, reverse again, ch 3, 1 sc in the middle of the ch below, ch 3, attach to the last dc, ch 3, 1 dc in 4th ch, 1 dc in next ch, 1 dc in next ch, rep from *, ending with 1 ch and 1 dc, 1 ch 6 and turn.
Row 2: * 1 dc just before sc, ch 3, 1 dc just after the sc, forming a small arch, ch 2, rep from *, ending row with 1 ch and 1 trc in turning ch, ch 4 and turn.
Row 3: Same as row 1, except that 3 dc are worked in 3-ch.
Pattern formed by rep rows 1–3.

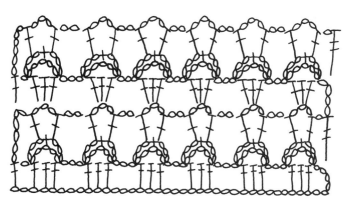

Single Crochet, Double Crochet, Chain 65

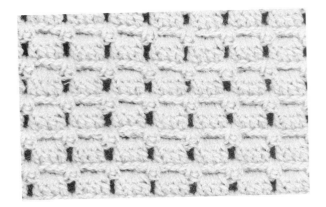

48. Chain multiples of 4 plus 1.

Row 1: 1 sc in the 2nd ch, 1 sc in the next ch, * ch 2, 1 sc in the 3rd ch and in the ch after that, rep from *, ending row with 2 sc, ch 3 and turn.
Row 2: * 4 dc around the middle of the 2-ch, rep from *, ending row with last set, and then 1 dc in the last sc and turn.
Row 3: Same as row 1 except that the 2 sc are worked in the space between the 2 sets of 4.
Pattern formed by rep rows 1–2.

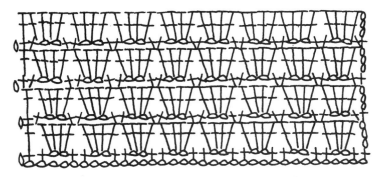

49. Chain multiples of 8 plus 1.

Row 1: 1 sc in the 2nd ch, * ch 5, 1 sc in the 4th ch, rep from *, ending row after the last set, ch 5 and turn.
Row 2: * 1 sc around the 1st 5-ch, ch 5, rep from *, ending row with 1 sc around the last 5-ch, ch 2 and 1 dc in the last sc, ch 3 and turn.
Row 3: 1 dc in the 1st dc, * ch 2, 4 dc around the 5-ch, ch 2, work 1 dc around the next 5-ch, rep from *, ending row with 2 chs and 1 dc in the turning ch, ch 5 and turn.
Row 4: * 1 sc in the 2-ch, ch 5, 1 sc in the next 2-ch, rep from *, ending row with last sc, ch 2 and 1 dc in the turning ch, ch 1 and turn.
Pattern formed by rep rows 1–4.

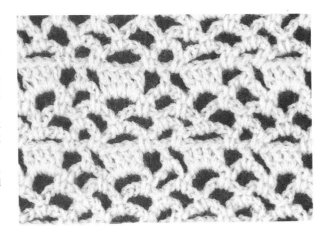

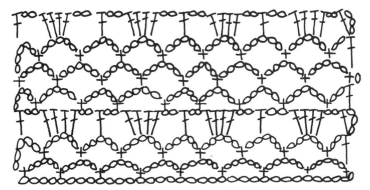

50. Chain multiples of 6 plus 4.

Row 1: 1 sc in the 6th ch, * ch 3, 1 sc in the 3rd ch, rep from *, ending row with sc, 1 ch and 1 hdc in the 2nd ch, ch 3 and turn.
Row 2: 1 dc in the 1-ch, * ch 3, 1 sc around the 3-ch, ch 3, 3 dc around the next 3-ch, rep from *, ending row with sc, 3 chs and 2 dc in the turning ch, ch 3 and turn.
Row 3: 1 sc in the 1st ch, * ch 3, 1 sc in the last ch before the dc, ch 3, 1 sc in the 1st ch after the 3 dc, rep from *, ending row with 1 ch and 1 hdc in the turning ch, ch 3 and turn.
Row 4: Same as row 2, ch 3 and turn.
Row 5: Same as row 3, ch 3 and turn.
Row 6: Same as rows 2 and 4, ch 3 and turn.
Row 7: Same as rows 1, 3 and 5, ch 1 and turn.
Row 8: 1 sc in the hdc, * ch 3, work 3 dc in the next 3-ch, ch 3, 1 sc in the next 3-ch, rep from *, ending row with 3 chs and 1 sc in the turning ch (this row is alternated with the 1st 3).
Pattern formed by rep rows 1–8.

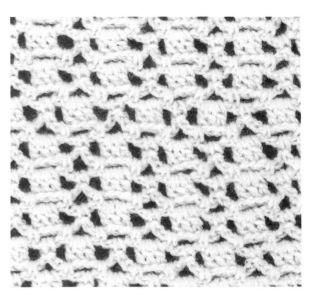

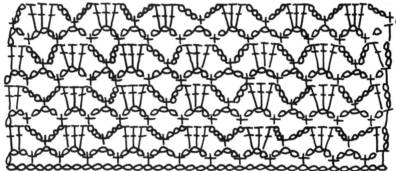

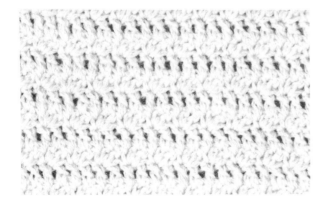

51. Chain multiples of 2 plus 1.

Row 1: 1 sc in the 2nd ch, * ch 1, 1 dc in same ch as the sc, 1 sc in 2nd ch, rep from *, ending row with 1 sc in last ch, ch 3 and turn.
Row 2: * 1 dc in the ch, and 1 dc in the sc, rep from *, row ending with last set, ch 1 and turn.
Pattern formed by rep rows 1–2.

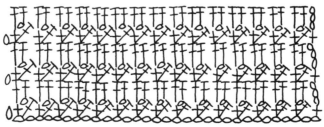

Single Crochet, Double Crochet, Chain 67

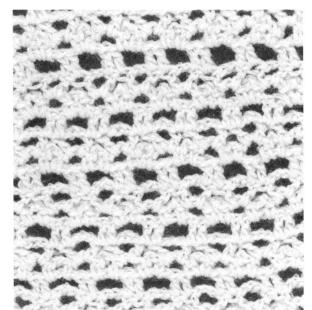

52. Chain multiples of 5 plus 7.

Row 1: 1 dc in 11th ch, 1 dc in next ch, * ch 3, 1 dc in 4th ch, 1 dc in next ch, rep from *, ending row with 3 chs and 1 dc, ch 1 and turn.

Row 2: 1 sc in 1st dc, 1 sc in 1st ch, ch 3, * 1 sc in 3rd ch, ch 3, 1 sc in 1st ch after 2 dc, ch 3 and rep from *, ending row with 2 sc in turning ch, ch 4 and turn.

Row 3: 1 dc in 1st sc, * 1 dc in 1st ch after sk 1st 3-ch group, ch 3, 1 dc back in the same 3-ch group, rep from *, ending row with 1 dc in end sc, 1 ch and 1 dc in same sc, ch 4 and turn.

Row 4: 1 dc in 2nd dc, 1 dc in next dc, * ch 3, 1 dc in next dc and in the dc after that, rep from *, ending row with 1 ch and 1 dc in the turning ch, ch 1 and turn.

Row 5: 1 sc in 1st dc, 1 sc in ch, * ch 3, sk 2 dc, sc in 1st ch afterwards, ch 3, 1 sc at the end of the same 3-ch, rep from *, ending row with 2 sc in the turning ch, ch 2 and turn.

Row 6: * 1 dc in 1st ch, ch 3, 1 dc back in same 3-ch, rep from *, ending row with 3 chs and 2 dc finished together in last 2 sc, ch 6 and turn.

Pattern formed by rep rows 1–6.

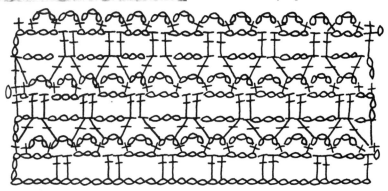

53. Chain multiples of 5 plus 7.

Row 1: 1 sc in the 7th ch, * ch 2, 1 sc in the 3rd ch, ch 4, 1 sc in the 2nd ch, rep from *, ending row with 2 ch and 1 dc in the next ch, ch 1 and turn.

Row 2: 1 sc in the dc, * work 4 dc around the 2-ch, 1 sc around the middle of the 4-ch, rep from *, ending row with last 4 dc and 1 sc in the turning ch, ch 5 and turn.

Pattern formed by rep rows 1–2.

54. Chain multiples of 12 plus 4.

Row 1: 1 dc in the 5th ch and also in the next 3 chs, * ch 3, 1 dc in the 3rd ch, and in the next 9 chs, rep from *, ending row with 5 dc, ch 3 and turn.

Row 2: 1 dc in the 2nd dc, 1 dc in the next dc, * ch 3, 1 sc around the middle of the 3-ch, ch 3, 1 dc in the 3rd dc and in the next 5 dc, rep from *, ending row with 3 dc, the last 1 in the turning ch, ch 6 and turn.

Row 3: * 1 sc in the middle of the 3-ch, ch 3, 1 sc in the middle of the next 3-ch, ch 3, 1 dc in the 3rd dc and the next dc, ch 3 and rep from *, ending row with 1 dc in the turning ch, ch 3 and turn.

Row 4: 2 dc in the 3-ch, * ch 3, 1 sc in the middle of the 2nd 3-ch, ch 3, 2 dc in the next 3-ch, 1 dc in each of the next 2 dc, 2 dc around the 3-ch, rep from *, ending row with 3 dc in the turning ch, ch 3 and turn.

Pattern formed by rep rows 1–4.

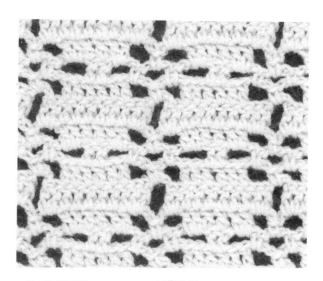

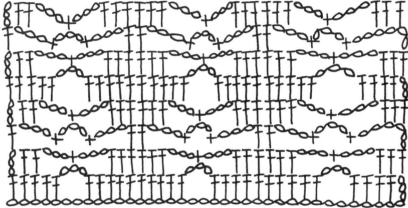

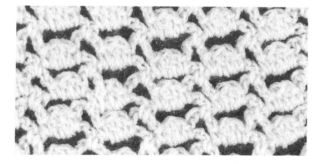

55. Chain multiples of 5 plus 1.

Row 1: 1 sc in the 2nd ch, * ch 5, 1 sc in the 5th ch, rep from *, ending row with 1 sc, ch 3 and turn.

Row 2: 1 dc in the 1st sc, ch 2, * 1 sc in the 2nd ch, 2 dc in the next ch, 1 sc in the next ch, ch 5, rep from *, ending row after last set with 2 chs and 1 dc in the sc, ch 1 and turn.

Row 3: 1 sc in the dc, * ch 5, 1 sc in the middle of the 5-ch, rep from *, ending row with a sc in the last dc, ch 3 and turn.

Pattern formed by rep rows 1–3.

56. Chain multiples of 11 plus 4.

Row 1: 1 dc in the 5th ch and in the next 2 chs, * ch 3, 1 dc in the 4th ch and also in the 7 chs, rep from *, ending row with 4 dc, ch 3 and turn.

Row 2: 1 dc in the 2nd dc, * ch 4, 1 sc in the 1st ch, ch 7, 1 sc in the 3rd ch, ch 4, 1 dc in the 3rd dc and in the next 3 dc, rep from *, ending row with 2 dc, 1 in turning ch, ch 3 and turn.

Row 3: 1 dc in the 2nd dc, * 1 dc in each of the 1st 2-chs, ch 1, 1 sc in the 7-ch, ch 1, 1 dc in each of the last 2 chs of the 4-ch, 1 dc in each of the next 4 dc, rep from *, ending row with 1 extra dc in the turning ch, ch 3 and turn.

Pattern formed by rep rows 1–3.

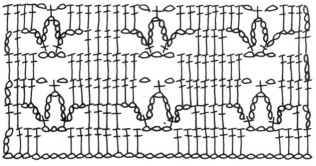

57. Chain multiples of 9 plus 4.

Row 1: 1 dc in 5th ch, 1 dc in each of the next 2 chs, * ch 8, 1 dc back in 1st ch, 1 dc in 3rd ch and in each of next 6 chs, rep from *, ending row with 4 dc, ch 4 and turn.

Row 2: 1 trc in 2nd dc, * ch 2, 1 sc in middle of 8-ch, ch 3, 1 sc in same 8-ch, ch 2, 1 trc in 3rd dc, same in the next dc and the next dc, rep from *, ending row with 2 trc in last dc and turning ch, ch 3 and turn.

Pattern formed by rep rows 1–2.

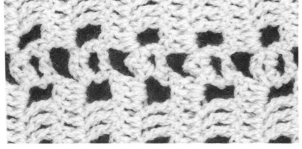

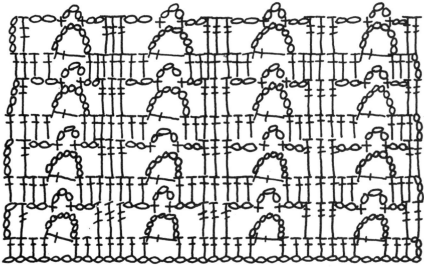

58. Chain multiples of 8 plus 4.

Row 1: 1 dc in the 5th ch, * ch 3, 1 sc in the 2nd ch and in the next ch, ch 3, 1 dc in the 2nd ch and 1 dc in each of the next 3 chs, rep from *, ending row with 1 sc in the last ch, ch 4 and turn.
Row 2: * 1 sc in each of the 4 dc, ch 4, rep from *, ending row with 2 sc, 1 in the last dc and 1 in the turning ch, ch 1 and turn.
Row 3: 1 sc in the 1st sc, * ch 3, 1 dc in each of the 4-ch, ch 3, 1 sc in the 2nd sc and in the next, rep from *, ending row with 2 dc in the turning ch, ch 1 and turn.
Row 4: 1 sc in each of the 1st 2 dc, * ch 4, 1 sc in each of the next 4 dc, rep from *, ending row with 1 ch and 1 dc in the turning ch, ch 3 and turn.
Pattern formed by rep rows 1–4.

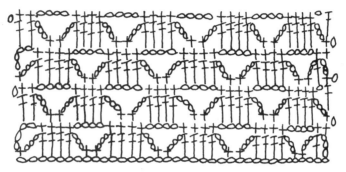

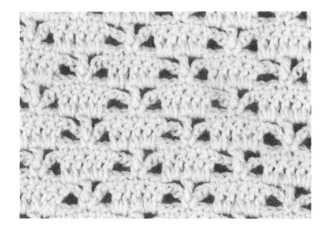

59. Chain multiples of 10 plus 1.

Row 1: 1 sc in 2nd ch, * ch 3, 1 dc in 3rd ch, 1 dc in each of next 4 chs, ch 3, 1 sc in 3rd ch, rep from *, row ending with 3 chs and 1 sc in the last ch, ch 5 and turn.
Row 2: * 1 sc in each of the 5 dc, ch 2, 1 dc in sc, ch 2, rep from *, ending row with 2 chs and 1 dc in turning ch, ch 3 and turn.
Row 3: 2 dc in 2-ch, * ch 3, 1 sc in the 3rd and middle sc, ch 3, 2 dc around the 2-ch, 1 dc in the dc, 2 dc around the 2-ch, rep from *, ending row with 3 dc, ch 1 and turn.
Row 4: 1 sc in each of the 1st 3 dc, * ch 2, 1 dc in the sc, ch 2, 1 sc in each of the next 5 dc, rep from *, ending row with 3 sc in the 2 dc and the turning ch, ch 1 and turn.
Pattern formed by rep rows 1–4.

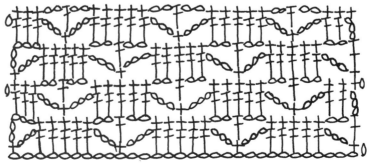

Single Crochet, Double Crochet, Chain   71

60. Chain multiples of 10 plus 7.

Row 1: 1 sc in 10th ch, * sc in each of next 4 chs, totalling 5, ch 3, 1 dc in 3rd ch, ch 3, 1 sc in 3rd ch, rep from *, ending row with 3 chs and 1 dc in 3rd ch, ch 1 and turn.

Row 2: 1 sc in 1st dc, 1 sc in 1st ch, * ch 3, 1 sc in 2nd sc, 1 sc in next 2 sc, ch 3, 1 sc in last ch before the dc, 1 sc in the dc, 1 sc in ch after dc, rep from *, ending row with 2 sc in the turning ch, ch 1 and turn.

Row 3: 1 sc in 1st sc, * ch 5, 1 sc in 2nd sc, ch 5, 1 sc in 2nd sc, rep from *, ending row with 1 sc, ch 1 and turn.

Row 4: 1 sc in 1st sc, ch 4, * 1 dc in next sc, ch 4, 1 sc in next sc, ch 4, rep from *, ending row with 1 sc, ch 1 and turn.

Row 5: 1 sc in 1st sc, 1 sc in each of next 2-ch, * ch 3, 1 dc in 1st dc, ch 3, 1 sc in 3rd ch, 1 sc in next ch, 1 sc in sc, 1 sc in each of next 2 chs, rep from *, row ending with 3 sc, ch 1 and turn.

Row 6: 1 sc in 1st sc and 1 in the 2nd, * ch 3, 1 sc in 3rd ch, 1 sc in the top of the dc, 1 sc in the next ch, ch 3, 1 sc in the 2nd and next 2 sc, rep from *, ending row with 2 sc, ch 1 and turn.

Row 7: 1 sc in 1st sc, * ch 5, 1 sc in 2nd sc, ch 5, 1 sc in 2nd sc, rep from *, row ending with 1 sc, ch 7 and turn.

Row 8: * 1 sc in 1st sc, ch 4, 1 dc in next sc, ch 4, rep from *, ending row with 1 dc, ch 6 and turn.

Pattern formed by rep rows 1–8.

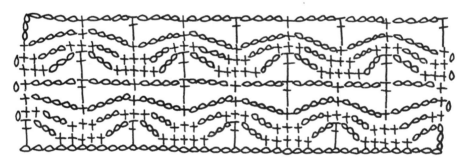

61. Chain multiples of 11 plus 7.

Row 1: 1 dc in the 7th ch, * 1 dc in the 4th ch and in the next 2 chs, ch 5 and turn, attach the 5-ch between the 1st of the 3 dc and the dc before the set of 3, turn again and work 7 sc around the 5-ch, secure 7th ch in the last ch, 1 dc in the 4th ch, ch 3, 1 dc in the same ch just used, 1 dc in next ch, ch 3, dc in ch just used, rep from *, ending row after the last set with 1 dc, 3 ch and 1 dc, ch 3 and turn.

Row 2: 2 dc around the 3-ch, * ch 2, 1 sc in the 4th sc, ch 2, 2 dc around the 3-ch, 1 dc in the dc and 1 in the next dc, 2 dc in the 3-ch, rep from *, ending row with 3 dc in the turning ch, ch 6 and turn.

Row 3: Same as row 1, except that the 3 dc are worked in the ch, the sc and the ch and the 4 dc, interspaced with chs, are worked in the middle 2 dc.

Pattern formed by rep rows 1–2.

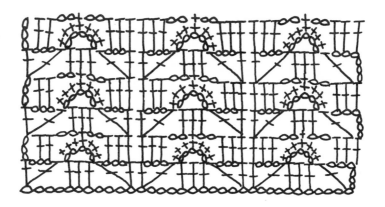

62. Chain multiples of 11 plus 9.

Row 1: 1 sc in the 3rd ch and the 2 chs after that, * ch 3, 1 dc in the 4th ch, ch 3, 1 sc in the 4th ch and the 4 chs following, rep from *, ending row with 3 chs and 1 dc in the 4th and last ch, ch 1 and turn.

Row 2: 1 sc in the dc and the 1st ch, * ch 3, 1 sc in the 2nd sc and the 2 sc after that, ch 3, 1 sc in the last of the 3-ch, 1 sc in the dc, and 1 sc in the 1st of the next 3-ch, rep from *, ending row with 2 sc in the sc and 1 in the turning ch, ch 2 and turn.

Row 3: 1 dc in the 2nd sc, * ch 3, 1 sc in the last of the 3-ch, 1 sc in each of the next 3 sc, 1 sc in the 1st of the next 3-ch, ch 3, 1 dc in the 2nd sc, rep from *, ending row with 3 sc, ch 1 and turn.

Row 4: 1 sc in each of the 1st 2 sc, * ch 3, 1 sc in the last of the 3-ch, 1 sc in the dc, 1 sc in the 1st of the 3-ch, ch 3, 1 sc in the 2nd sc and the 2 sc after that, rep from *, ending row with 3 sc, the last of which is in the turning ch, ch 1 and turn.

Row 5: 1 sc in each of the 1st 3 sc and 1 in the 1st of the 3-ch, * ch 3, 1 dc in the 2nd sc, ch 3, 1 sc in the last of the 3-ch and in each of the next 3 sc, 1 sc in the 1st part of the next 3-ch, rep from *, ending row with 1 dc in the last sc, ch 1 and turn.

Pattern formed by rep rows 1–4.

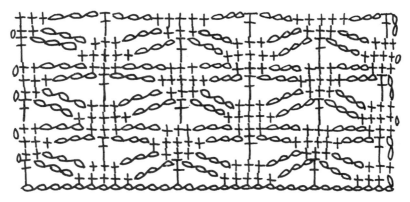

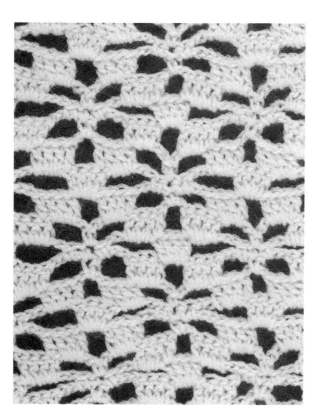

63. Chain multiples of 17 plus 4.

Row 1: 1 dc in the 5th ch, * ch 5, 1 sc in the 6th ch and in the 2 chs following, ch 5, 1 dc in the 6th ch and in the 3 chs following, rep from *, ending row with 2 dc in the last 2 chs, ch 3 and turn.

Row 2: 1 dc in the 2nd dc and 3 dc in the ch following, * ch 4, 1 sc in the 2nd sc, ch 4, 3 dc in the last ch, 1 dc in the 1st dc, ch 3, 1 dc in the 3rd dc and 3 dc in the 1st ch, rep from *, ending row with 3 dc in the ch and 1 dc in the dc and 1 dc in the turning ch, ch 1 and turn.

Row 3: 1 sc in the 1st dc, * ch 4, 1 dc in the 4th dc of the set, 3 dc in the 1st ch, ch 2, 3 dc in the last ch before the 4 dc, 1 dc in the 1st dc, ch 4, 1 sc in the 3-ch, rep from *, ending row with 4 chs and 1 sc in the turning ch, ch 8 and turn.

Row 4: * 4 dc in the 2-ch, ch 5, 1 sc in the last of the 4-ch, 1 sc in the sc, 1 sc in the 1st of the next set of 4-ch, ch 5, rep from *, ending row with 1 dc in the sc, ch 1 and turn.

Row 5: 1 sc in the dc, * ch 4, 3 dc in the last part of the 5-ch, 1 dc in the 1st dc, ch 3, 1 dc in the 3rd dc, and 3 dc in the 1st part of the next 5-ch, ch 4, 1 sc in the 2nd sc, rep from *, ending row with 4 chs and 1 sc in the turning ch, ch 5 and turn.

Row 6: * 3 dc in the last part of the 4-ch, 1 dc in the 1st dc, ch 4, 1 sc around the 3-ch, ch 4, 1 dc in the last of the next set of dc, 3 dc in the 1st part of the 4-ch, ch 2 and rep from *, ending row with 4 dc and 1 trc in the turning ch, ch 3 and turn.

Pattern formed by rep rows 1–6.

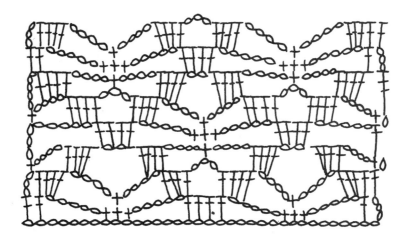

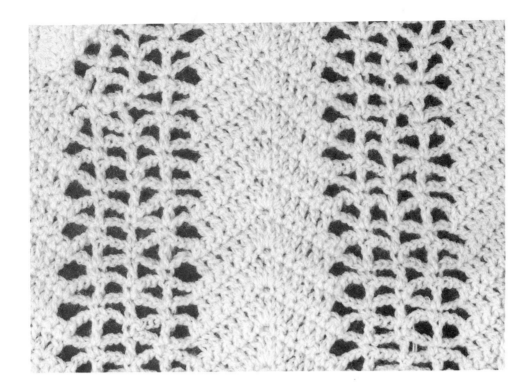

64. Chain multiples of 26 plus 3.

Row 1: 2 dc in the 4th ch, 1 dc in each of the next 5 chs, * ch 3, 1 sc in the 5th ch, ch 3, 1 dc in the 3rd ch, ch 3, 1 sc in the 3rd ch, ch 3, 1 dc in the 5th ch and in the next 4 chs, 2 dc in the next ch, ch 1, 2 dc in the same ch, 1 dc in the next 5-ch, rep from *, ending row with 3 chs, 1 sc, 3 ch and 1 dc, ch 1 and turn.

Row 2: * 1 sc in the dc, ch 3, 1 dc in next sc, ch 3, 1 sc in each of next 7 dc, ch 1, sc in each of next 7 dc, ch 3, 1 dc in the sc, ch 3, rep from *, ending row with extra sc in the turning ch.

Row 3: Same as row 1, 2 dc worked in the 1st sc and in the 2 before and after the ch section will be unused.

Pattern formed by rep rows 1–2.

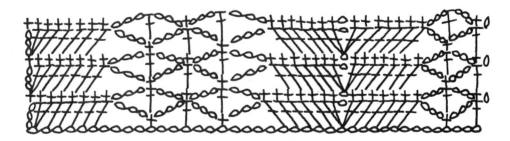

65. Chain multiples of 9 plus 4.

Row 1: 1 dc in the 5th ch and in the 2 chs after that, * ch 5, 1 dc in the 6th ch and in the following 3 chs, rep from *, ending row with 4 dc, ch 3 and turn.
Row 2: 1 dc in the 2nd dc and in the next 2 dc, * ch 3, 1 sc around the middle of the 5-ch underneath and the 5-ch underneath that, ch 3, 1 dc in the next dc and the 3 after that, rep from *, ending row with 4 dc, the last 1 in the turning ch, ch 7 and turn.
Row 3: 1 dc in the 3rd dc and 1 in the next dc, * 1 dc in each of the next 2 dc, ch 5, 1 dc in each of the next 2 dc, rep from *, ending row with 4 chs and 1 dc in the turning ch, ch 7 and turn.
Row 4: 1 dc in the 2nd dc and the 3 following that, * ch 5, 1 dc in each of the next 4 dc, rep from *, ending row with 4 chs and 1 dc in the turning ch, ch 6 and turn.
Row 5: 1 sc around the middle of the 4-ch, and the 2 chs below, * ch 3, 1 dc in each of the next 4 dc, ch 3, 1 sc around the middle of the 5-ch from the rows below, rep from *, ending row with last set and 1 dc in the turning ch, ch 3 and turn.
Row 6: 1 dc in the 1st 3-ch, * 1 dc in each of the next 2 dc, ch 5, 1 dc in each of the next 2 dc, rep from *, ending row with 2 dc in the turning ch, ch 3 and turn.
Pattern formed by rep rows 1–6.

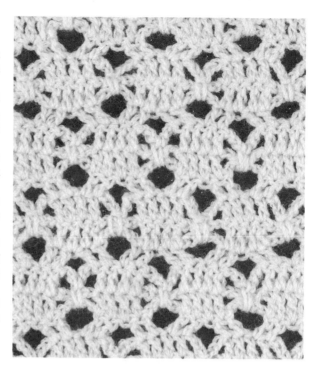

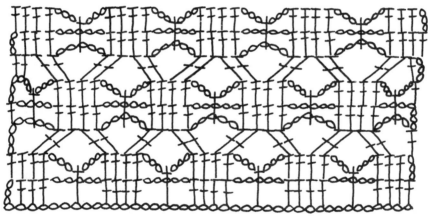

66. Chain multiples of 7 plus 1.

Row 1: 1 sc in the 2nd ch and the 2 following, * ch 3, 1 sc in the 4th ch and the 3 chs after that, rep from *, ending row with 3 sc in the last 3 chs, ch 4 and turn.
Row 2: * work 5 dc around the 3-ch, ch 3, rep from *, ending row with last set, 1 ch and 1 dc in the last sc, ch 3 and turn.
Row 3: * 1 dc and 1 ch in the 1st 4 dc of the set, 1 dc in the 5th dc, rep from *, ending row after last set with 1 dc in the turning ch, ch 1 and turn.
Row 4: 1 sc in the 1st dc, ch 1, * 1 sc in each of the 1-ch, ch 3, rep from *, ending row with 1 ch and 1 sc in the turning ch, ch 3 and turn.
Row 5: 2 dc in the 1-ch, * ch 3, work 5 dc around the 3-ch, rep from *, ending row with 3 dc in the last sc, ch 4 and turn.
Row 6: 1 dc in the 2nd dc, ch 1, 1 dc in the next dc, * 1 dc in the dc

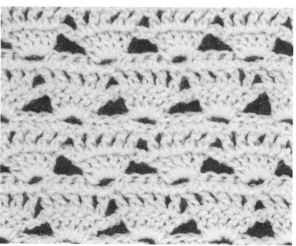

and 1 ch, rep 4 times, 1 dc in the last of the set of 5, rep from *, ending row with 1 dc, 1 ch, 1 dc in the last dc, 1 ch, 1 dc in the turning ch.

Row 7: 1 sc in the 1st dc, 1 sc in each of the next 1-ch, * ch 3, 1 sc in each of the 1-ch, rep from *, ending row with 1 extra sc in the turning ch, ch 4 and turn.

Pattern formed by rep rows 2–7.

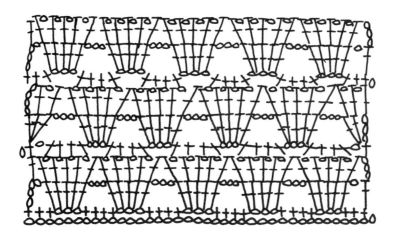

67. Chain multiples of 15 plus 3.

Row 1: 1 hdc in the 5th ch and in each ch all across the row, ch 3 and turn.

Row 2: 1 dc in the 2nd hdc, * ch 3, 1 trc in the 4th hdc, ch 1, 1 trc in the 2nd hdc, ch 1, 1 trc in the 2nd hdc, ch 1, 1 trc in the 2nd hdc, ch 3, 1 dc in the 4th hdc and the hdc after that, rep from *, ending row with 2 dc, the last in the turning ch, ch 3 and turn.

Row 3: 1 dc in the 2nd dc, * ch 5, 1 dc in each of the 4 trc, ch 5, 1 dc in each of the 2 dc, rep from *, ending row with 1 dc in the last dc and 1 in the turning ch, ch 3 and turn.

Row 4: 1 dc in the 2nd dc, * ch 5, 1 sc in each of the 4 dc, ch 5, 1 dc in each of the 2 dc, rep from *, ending row with 1 dc in the last dc and 1 in the turning ch, ch 3 and turn.

Row 5: 1 dc in the 2nd dc, * ch 5, 1 sc in each of the 4 sc, ch 5, 1 dc in each of the 2 dc, rep from *, ending row with 1 dc in the last dc and 1 in the turning ch, ch 3 and turn.

Row 6: 1 dc in the 2nd dc, * ch 3, 1 dc in the 1st sc, ch 1, dc in the next sc, ch 1, dc in the next sc, ch 1, 1 dc in the next sc, ch 3, 1 dc in each of the next 2 dc, rep from *, ending row with 1 dc in the last dc and 1 in the turning ch, ch 3 and turn.

Row 7: 1 dc in the 2nd dc, * ch 3, 1 trc in the dc, ch 1, trc in the next dc, ch 1, trc in the next dc, ch 1, 1 trc in the next dc, ch 3, 1 dc

in each of the next 2 dc, rep from *, ending row with 1 dc in the last dc and 1 in the turning ch, ch 3 and turn.

Row 8: Same as row 1 except that 1 hdc is made in each ch and in each stitch all across the row.

Pattern formed by rep rows 1–8.

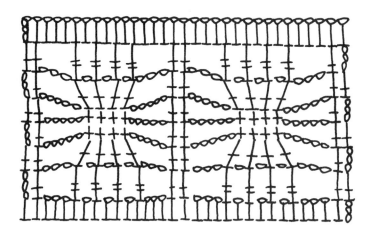

68. Chain multiples of 20 plus 4.

Row 1: 1 dc in the 5th ch and the 8 chs following, * ch 4, 1 dc in the 5th ch, ch 4, 1 dc in the 5th ch and the 9 chs following, rep from *, ending row with 4 chs and 1 dc in the 5th and last ch, ch 1 and turn.

Row 2: 1 sc in the dc, ch 4, * 1 dc in each of the 1st 4 dc, ch 2, dc in the 3rd dc and the 3 dc after that, ch 4, 1 sc in the dc, ch 4, rep from *, ending row with 3 dc and 1 in the turning ch, ch 3 and turn.

Row 3: 1 dc in the 2nd dc, ch 2, 1 dc in each of the 2-chs, ch 2, 1 dc in the 3rd dc and the dc after that, * ch 4, 1 sc in the last of the 4-chs, ch 1, 1 sc in the 1st of the 4-chs, ch 4, 1 dc in each of the 1st 2 dc, ch 2, 1 dc in each of the 2-chs, ch 2, 1 dc in the 3rd dc and the dc after that, rep from *, ending row with sc in the sc, ch 1 and turn.

Row 4: Sc in the sc, ch 4, * 1 dc in each of the 2 dc, 1 dc in each of the 2-chs, ch 2, 1 dc in each of the 2-chs, 1 dc in each of the 2 dc, ch 4, 1 sc in the 1-ch, ch 4 and rep from *, ending row with 1 dc in the turning ch, ch 3 and turn.

Row 5: 1 dc in the 2nd dc and the next 2 dc, 1 in each of the 2-chs, 1 in each of the 4 dc, * ch 4, 1 dc in the sc, ch 4, 1 dc in each of the 4 dc, 1 in each of the 2-chs and 1 in each of the 4 dc, rep from *, ending row with 1 dc in the sc, ch 3 and turn.

Row 6: 5 dc in the 4-ch, * ch 4, 1 dc in the 5th dc, ch 4, work 5 dc in the 4-ch, work 5 dc in the next 4-ch, rep from *, ending row with 1 dc in the turning ch, ch 7 and turn.

Row 7: Sk 1st dc 1 sc in the dc, ch 4, * 1 dc in each of the next 4 dc, ch 2, 1 dc in the 3rd dc and the 3 dc after that, ch 4, 1 sc in the dc, ch 4 and rep from *, ending row with 1 dc in the turning ch, ch 3, and turn.

Row 8: 1 dc in the 2nd dc and the 4 dc after that, * ch 4, 1 sc in the

end of the 4-ch, ch 1, 1 sc in the 1st of the 4-ch, ch 4, 1 dc in the dc and the 1 after that, ch 2, 1 dc in each of the 2-chs, ch 2, 1 dc in the 3rd dc and the 1 after that, rep from *, ending row with 1 dc in the turning ch, ch 7 and turn.

Row 9: 1 sc in the 1-ch, ch 4, * 1 dc in each of the 2 dc, 1 dc in each of the 2-chs, ch 2, 1 dc in each of the 2-chs, 1 dc in each of the 2 dc, ch 4, 1 sc in the 1-ch, ch 4, rep from *, ending row with 1 ch and 1 dc in the turning ch, ch 3 and turn.

Row 10: 1 dc in the 1-ch and 1 dc in each of the 4 dc, * ch 4, 1 dc in the sc, ch 4, 1 dc in each of the 4 dc, 1 dc in each of the 2-chs, 1 dc in each of the 4 dc, rep from *, ending row with 1 dc in the turning ch.

Pattern formed by rep rows 1–10.

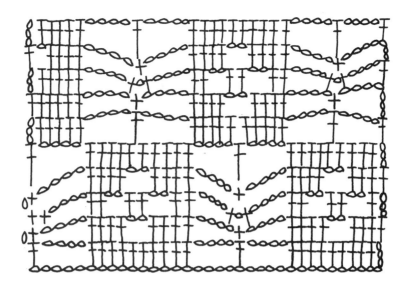

69. Chain multiples of 24 plus 5.

Row 1: 1 dc in the 7th ch, * ch 1 and dc in the 2nd ch, rep from *, ending row with dc in the last ch, ch 4 and turn.

Row 2: Sk 1 dc, dc in the next dc, ch 1 and dc in the dc 6 times, 1 dc in the 1-ch, dc in the next dc, ch 1 and dc in the dc 6 times, ch 1 and dc in the turning ch, ch 4 and turn.

Row 3: Sk 1st dc, dc in the dc, ch 1 and dc in the dc 5 times, 1 dc in 1-ch, dc in next dc, ch 3, dc in the 2nd dc, dc in the 1-ch, dc in the dc, ch 1 and dc in the dc 5 times, ch 1 and dc in the turning ch.

Row 4: Sk the 1st dc, dc in the dc, ch 1 and dc in the dc 4 times, dc in the 1-ch and in the next dc, ch 3, sc in the 3-ch, ch 3, dc in the 3rd dc, dc in the 1-ch and the next dc, ch 1 and dc in the dc 4 times, ch 1 and dc in the turning ch, ch 4 and turn.

Row 5: Sk 1st dc, dc in the next dc, ch 1, dc in the dc 3 times, dc in the 1-ch, dc in the dc, ch 4, sc in the last of the 3-ch, sc in sc, sc in 1st sc, ch 4, dc in the 3rd dc, dc in the 1-ch, dc in the dc, ch 1, dc in the dc 3 times, ch 1 and dc in the turning ch, ch 4 and turn.

Row 6: Sk 1st dc, dc in the dc, ch 1 and dc in the dc 2 times, dc in the 1-ch, dc in the dc, ch 4, sc in the last of the 4-ch, sc in each of the 3 sc, sc in the 1st of the 4-ch, ch 4, dc in the 3rd dc, dc in the 1-ch, dc in the dc, ch 1 and dc in the dc 2 times, ch 1 and dc in the turning ch, ch 4 and turn.

Row 7: Sk 1st dc, dc in the dc, ch 1 and dc in the dc 2 times, ch 1, dc in the 2nd dc, 1 dc in each of the 1st 2 chs, ch 4, sc in the 2nd sc and each of the next 2 sc, ch 4, 1 dc in each of the last 2 chs, dc in the dc, ch 1 and dc in the 2nd dc, ch 1 and dc in the dc 2 times, ch 1 and dc in the turning ch, ch 4 and turn.

Row 8: Sk 1st dc, dc in the dc, ch 1 and dc in the dc 3 times, ch 1, dc in the 2nd dc, 1 dc in each of the next 2 chs, ch 3, sc in the 2nd sc, ch 3, 1 dc in each of the last 2 chs, dc in the dc, ch 1, dc in the 2nd dc, ch 1, dc in the dc 3 times, ch 1, dc in the turning ch, ch 4 and turn.

Row 9: Sk 1 dc, dc in the dc, ch 1 and dc in the dc 4 times, ch 1 and dc in the 2nd dc, 1 dc in each of the 1st 2 chs, ch 1, 1 dc in each of the last 2 chs, dc in the dc, ch 1, dc in the 2nd dc, ch 1 and dc in the dc 4 times, ch 1 and dc in the turning ch, ch 4 and turn.

Row 10: Sk 1st dc, dc in the 2nd dc, ch 1 and dc in the dc 5 times, ch 1 and dc in the 2nd dc, dc in the 1-ch, dc in the dc, ch 1, dc in the 2nd dc, ch 1 and dc in the dc 5 times, ch 1 and dc in the turning ch, ch 4 and turn.

Single Crochet, Double Crochet, Chain   79

Row 11: Sk 1st dc, dc in the dc, ch 1 and dc in the dc 6 times, ch 1 and dc in the 2nd dc, ch 1 and dc in the dc 6 times, ch 1 and dc in the turning ch, ch 4 and turn.

Row 12: Sk 1st dc, dc in the dc, dc in the 1-ch, dc in the dc, ch 1 and dc in the dc 11 times, dc in the 1-ch, dc in the dc, ch 1 and dc in the turning ch, ch 3 and turn.

Row 13: Sk 1st dc, dc in the 1-ch, dc in the dc, ch 3, dc in the 2nd dc, dc in the 1-ch, dc in the dc, ch 1 and dc in the dc 9 times, dc in the 1-ch, dc in the dc, ch 3, dc in the 2nd dc and 2 dc in the turning ch.

Pattern formed by rep rows 1–11 and then alternating order in rows 12–22.

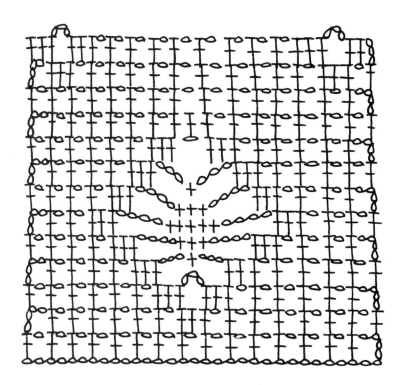

· 5 ·
Triple, Double and Single Crochet and Chain

70. Chain any number.

Row 1: Trc in the 6th ch and in each ch all across the row, ch 4 and turn.
Pattern formed by rep row 1.

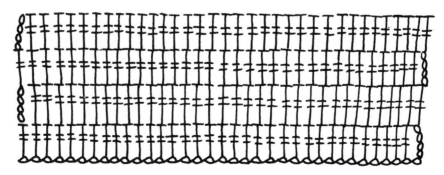

71. Chain multiples of 4 plus 5.

Row 1: 1 dc in the 6th ch, 1 dc in the next ch, * 1 trc in the next ch and the ch after, 1 dc in each of the next 2 chs, rep from *, ending row after the 2 dc with 1 trc, ch 5 and turn.
Row 2: * 1 dc in each of the 2 trc, ch 2, rep from *, ending row with 2 chs and 1 dc in the turning ch, ch 4 and turn.
Row 3: Same as row 1, except that the trc are worked in the dc, and the dc are worked in the chs.
Pattern formed by rep rows 1–2.

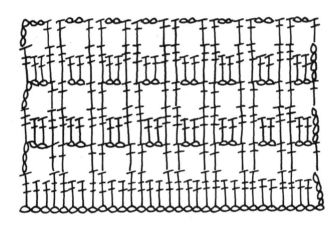

72. Chain multiples of 16 plus 4.

Row 1: 1 dc in the 5th ch and the ch after that, * ch 4, 1 trc in the 5th ch and in the 2 chs following, ch 4, 1 dc in the 5th ch and the 4 chs after that, rep from *, ending row with 1 dc in each of the last 3 chs, ch 3 and turn.
Row 2: 1 dc in the 2nd dc, * ch 3, 1 trc in the 1st trc, ch 2, 1 trc in the trc just used, 1 trc in each of the next 2 trc, ch 2, 1 trc in the trc just used, ch 3, 1 dc in the 2nd dc and in each of the next 2 dc, rep from *, ending row with 1 dc in the last dc and 1 in the turning ch, ch 3 and turn.
Row 3: 1 dc in the 2nd dc, * 1 trc in the 1st trc, ch 2, trc in the next trc, ch 2, trc in the trc just used, trc in each of the next 2 trc, ch 2, trc in the trc just used, ch 2, trc in the next trc, 1 dc in each of the 3 dc, rep from *, ending row with 1 dc in the last dc and 1 in the turning ch, ch 4 and turn.
Row 4: * 1 trc in the 1st trc, ch 2, trc in the next trc, ch 2, trc in the trc just used, ch 2, 1 trc in each of the next 3 trc, ch 2, trc in the next trc, ch 2, trc in the trc just used, ch 2, trc in the next trc, 1 trc in the 2nd dc, rep from *, ending row with 1 trc in the turning ch, ch 4 and turn.
Row 5: Trc in the 3rd trc, * ch 4, 1 dc in the last ch before the 3 trc, 1 dc in each of the 3 trc, 1 dc in the 1st ch after the 3 trc, ch 4, 1 trc in the 2nd trc, trc in the 2nd trc, trc in the 2nd trc, rep from *, ending row with 1 trc in the turning ch, ch 4 and turn.

Row 6: 1 trc in the 2nd trc, ch 2, 1 trc in the same trc just used, * ch 3, 1 dc in the 2nd dc and the 2 dc after that, ch 3, 1 trc in the next trc, ch 2, 1 trc in the same trc just used and in the next 2 trc, ch 2, trc in the same trc just used, rep from *, ending row with 1 trc in the turning ch, ch 4 and turn.

Row 7: Trc in the 2nd trc, ch 2, trc in the same trc, ch 2, trc in the next trc, * 1 dc in each of the 3 dc, trc in the trc, ch 2, trc in the next trc, ch 2, trc in the trc just used, trc in the next trc and trc after that, ch 2, trc in the trc just used, ch 2, trc in the next trc, rep from *, ending row with 1 trc in the turning ch, ch 4 and turn.

Row 8: 1 trc in the 2nd trc, * ch 2, trc in the next trc, ch 2, trc in the trc just used, ch 2, trc in the next trc, trc in the 2nd dc, trc in the next trc, ch 2, trc in the next trc, ch 2, trc in the trc just used, ch 2, trc in each of the next 3 trc, rep from *, ending row with 1 trc in the turning ch, ch 3 and turn.

Row 9: 1 dc in the 2nd trc, 1 dc in the 2-ch, * ch 4, trc in the 2nd trc 3 times, ch 4, 1 dc in the 2-ch before the 3 trc, 1 dc in each of the 3 trc, 1 dc in the 2-ch just after the 3 trc, rep from *, ending row with 1 dc in the turning ch.

Pattern formed by rep rows 1–9.

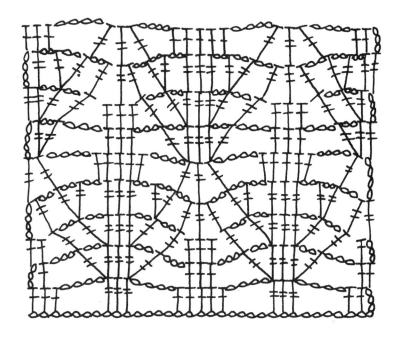

73. Chain multiples of 4 plus 1.

Row 1: 1 sc in the 2nd ch, * ch 5, 1 sc in the 4th ch, rep from *, ending row with 1 sc in the last ch, ch 5 and turn.

Row 2: * begin 1 trc in the sc, together with 1 dc in the middle of the 5-ch and 1 trc in the next sc, finish all 3 together, ch 5, rep from *, ending row with last set, 1 ch and 1 trc in the turning ch, ch 1 and turn.

Row 3: 1 sc in the trc, * ch 5, 1 sc in the middle of the 5-ch, rep from *, ending row with 1 sc in the turning ch, ch 6 and turn.

Row 4: * 1 sc around the 5-ch, ch 5, rep from *, ending row with 1 sc around the last 5-ch, ch 2, 1 trc in the turning ch, ch 2 and turn.

Row 5: 1 trc in the sc, * ch 5, begin 1 trc in the 1st sc just used, 1 dc around the middle of the 5-ch, and 1 trc in the next sc, finish all 3 together, rep from *, ending row with 1 trc in the last sc and 1 dc in the turning ch, finished together, ch 8 and turn.

Row 6: 1 sc around the 5-ch, ch 5, rep from *, ending row with sc in the middle of the last 5-ch, ch 2 and 1 trc in the turning ch, ch 1 and turn.

Pattern formed by rep rows 1–6.

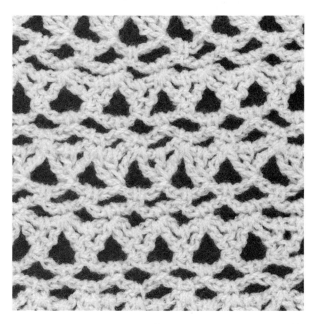

Triple, Double and Single Crochet and Chain   83

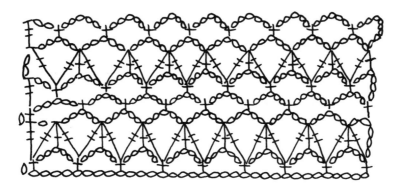

74. Chain multiples of 11 plus 4.

Row 1: 1 dc in 5th ch and in every ch all across the row, ch 3 and turn.

Row 2: 1 dc in 2nd dc, 1 dc in next dc, * ch 3, 1 trc in the 3rd dc and in the next 3 dc, ch 3, 1 dc in the 3rd dc and in the next 2 dc, rep from *, ending row with 3 dc in last 2 dc and in the turning ch, ch 3 and turn.

Row 3: 1 dc in 2nd dc and in the 3rd, * ch 3, 1 sc in each of the 4 trc, ch 3, 3 dc in the 3 dc, rep from *, ending row with 3 dc, ch 3 and turn.

Row 4: 1 dc in 2nd dc and in the next, * ch 3, 1 sc in each of the 4 sc, ch 3, 1 dc in each of the 3 dc, rep from *, ending row with 3 dc, ch 3 and turn.

Row 5: 1 dc in 2nd dc, 1 dc in the next dc, * ch 3, 1 sc in each of the next 4 sc, ch 3, 1 dc in each of the next 3 dc, rep from *, ending row with 3 dc, ch 3 and turn.

Row 6: 1 dc in 2nd dc and the next, * ch 3, 1 trc in each of the next 4 sc, ch 3, 1 dc in each of the next 3 dc, rep from *, ending row with 3 dc, ch 3 and turn.

Row 7: Rep row 1, dc all across the row, 1 in each ch and in each stitch.

Pattern formed by rep rows 1–6.

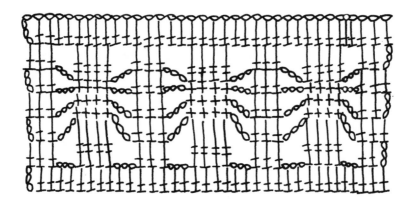

75. Chain multiples of 12 plus 5.

Row 1: 1 dc in the 7th ch, * ch 1, 1 dc in the 2nd ch, rep from *, ending row with the last set, ch 4 and turn.
Row 2: 1 dc in the 2nd dc, * ch 3, work 1 trc in each of the next 4 dc, ch 3, 1 dc in the next dc, ch 1, 1 dc in the next dc, rep from *, ending row with 1 dc in the turning ch, ch 4 and turn.
Row 3: 1 dc in the 2nd dc, * ch 3, 1 sc in each of the 4 trc, ch 3, 1 dc in the dc, ch 1, 1 dc in the dc, rep from *, ending row with 1 dc in the turning ch, ch 4 and turn.
Row 4: 1 dc in the 2nd dc, * ch 1, 1 trc in the next sc, ch 1, 1 trc in the next sc, ch 1, 1 trc in the next sc, ch 1, 1 trc in the next sc, ch 1, 1 dc in the next dc, ch 1, 1 dc in the next dc, rep from *, ending row with 1 dc in the turning ch, ch 4 and turn.
Pattern formed by rep rows 1–4.

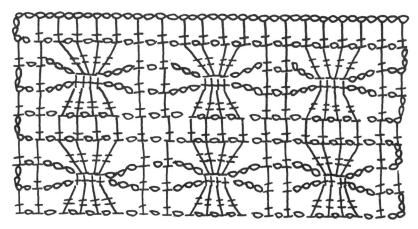

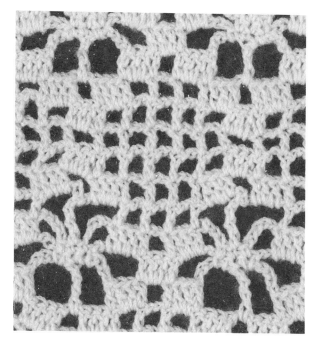

76. Chain multiples of 18 plus 4.

Row 1: 1 dc in the 5th ch, * ch 2, 1 dc in the 3rd ch, rep from * ending row with dc and 1 dc in the ch following, ch 3 and turn
Row 2: 1 dc in the 2nd dc, * ch 2, 1 dc in the dc, ch 2, 1 dc in the dc, 1 dc in each of the next 2 chs, 1 dc in the dc, ch 2, dc in the dc, ch 2, 1 dc in the dc, ch 2, 1 dc in the dc, rep from *, ending row with 1 extra dc following the last dc, ch 3 and turn.
Row 3: 1 dc in the 2nd dc, ch 2, * 1 dc in the dc, 1 dc in each of the next 2 chs, 1 dc in the dc, ch 2, 1 dc in the 3rd dc, 1 dc in each of the 2 chs, 1 dc in the dc, ch 2, 1 dc in the dc, ch 2, 1 dc in the dc, · ch 2, rep from *, ending row with 1 extra dc after the last dc, ch 3 and turn.
Row 4: Sk 1 dc, * dc in the next dc, 1 dc in each of the 2-chs, 1 dc in the next dc, ch 5, 1 trc in the middle of the 2-ch, ch 5, 1 dc in the 4th dc, 1 dc in each of the 2-chs, 1 dc in the dc, ch 2, rep from *, ending row with 1 extra dc, ch 3 and turn.
Row 5: 1 dc in the 2nd dc, * ch 5, 1 sc in the last of the 5-ch, 1 sc in the trc, 1 sc in the 1st of the 5-ch, ch 5, 1 dc in the 4th dc, 1 dc in each of the next 2 chs, 1 dc in the next dc, rep from *, ending row with 1 extra dc, ch 3 and turn.

Row 6: Sk 1 dc, * dc in the next dc, 1 dc around each of the 3 chs, ch 5, 1 sc in each of the 3 sc, ch 5, 1 dc around each of 3 chs, 1 dc in the next dc, ch 2, and rep from *, ending row with 1 extra dc, ch 3 and turn.

Row 7: 1 dc in the 2nd dc, ch 2, * 1 dc in the 3rd dc, ch 5, 1 trc in the 2nd sc, ch 5, 1 dc in the dc, ch 2, 1 dc in the 3rd dc, ch 2, 1 dc in the next dc, ch 2, rep from *, ending row with 1 extra dc in the turning ch, ch 3 and turn.

Row 8: 1 dc in the 2nd dc, * ch 2, 1 dc in the next dc, 3 dc in the next 4-ch, dc in next dc, ch 2, 3 dc in next 4-ch, dc in the next dc, ch 2, dc in next dc, ch 2, dc in next dc, rep from *, ending row with 1 extra dc in the turning ch, ch 3 and turn.

Row 9: 1 dc in the 2nd dc, ch 2, * 1 dc in the next dc, ch 2, 1 dc in the 3rd dc, 1 dc in each of the 2 chs, 1 dc in the next dc, ch 2, 1 dc in the 3rd dc, ch 2, dc in the dc, ch 2, dc in the dc, ch 2, rep from *, ending row with 1 extra dc in the turning ch, ch 3 and turn.
Pattern formed by rep rows 1–9.

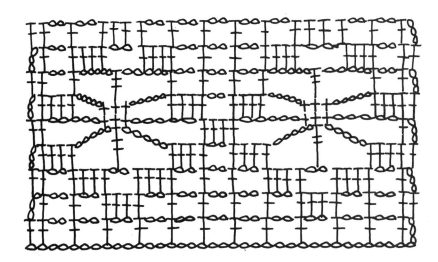

· 6 ·
V-Stitch

77. Chain multiples of any even number plus 3.

Row 1: 2 dc in the 5th ch, * work 2 dc in the 2nd ch, rep from *,
ending row with 1 dc in the turning ch, ch 3 and turn.
Row 2: * work 2 dc in the middle of the 2 dc worked together in
the row below, rep from *, ending with 1 dc in the turning ch, ch
3 and turn.
Pattern formed by rep rows 1–2.

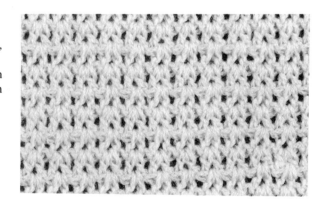

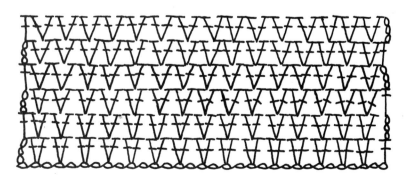

78. Chain multiples of any even number plus 6.

Row 1: 1 dc in the 6th ch, * ch 1, 1 dc in the 2nd ch, rep from *,
ending row with last set, ch 3 and turn.
Row 2: Work 2 dc in the 2nd dc, * work 2 dc in each dc, rep from
*, ending row with last set and 1 dc in the turning ch.
Pattern formed by rep rows 1–2.

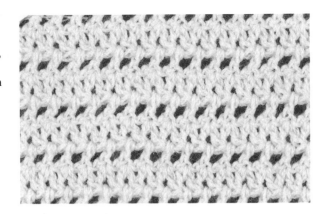

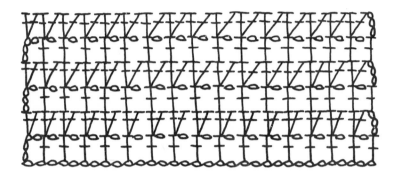

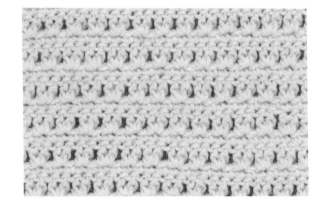

79. Chain multiples of 2 plus 1.

Row 1: 1 sc in each 2nd ch and all across the row, ch 3 and turn.
Row 2: 1 dc in the 1st sc, * 1 dc in the 2nd sc, 1 dc in the same sc
just used, rep from *, ending row with last set and the dc in the
last sc, ch 1 and turn.
Pattern formed by rep rows 1–2.

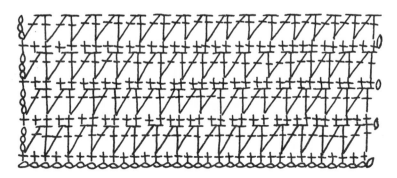

80. Chain multiples of 2 plus 4.

Row 1: 1 dc in the 5th ch, ch 1, 1 dc in the next ch, * 1 dc in the 2nd ch, ch 1, 1 dc in the next ch, rep from *, ending row after last set of dc in the 2nd ch, ch 3 and turn.
Row 2: * 1 dc in the 1-ch between the 2 dc, ch 1, 1 dc in the same 1-ch, rep from *, ending row with 1 dc in the turning ch, ch 3 and turn.
Pattern formed by rep rows 1–2.

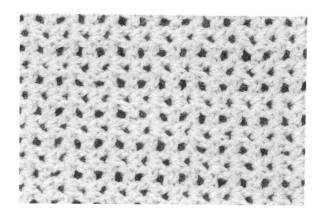

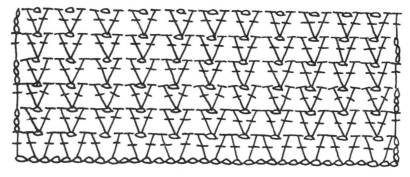

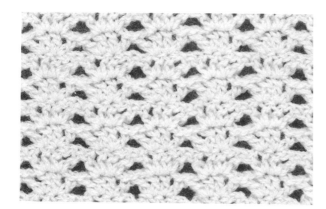

81. Chain multiples of 6 plus 5.

Row 1: 1 dc in the 5th ch, * 1 dc in the 5th ch, ch 1, 1 dc in the same ch, 1 dc in the next ch, ch 1, 1 dc in the same ch, rep from *, ending row with 1 dc, 1 ch and 1 dc in the last ch, ch 4 and turn.
Row 2: Same as row 1, except that the dc are worked in the tops of the middle dc of the set.
Pattern formed by rep row 1.

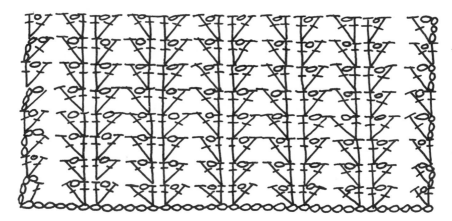

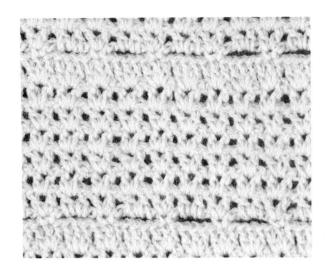

82. Chain multiples of 6 plus 4.

Row 1: 1 dc in the 4th ch, * 1 dc in the 3rd ch, ch 1, 1 dc in the same ch, rep from *, ending row with 2 dc in the 3rd and last ch, ch 3 and turn.
Row 2: Same as row 1, ch 3 and turn.
Row 3: 1 dc in the 1st dc, * 3 dc in the 1-ch, rep from *, ending row with 2 dc in the turning chain, ch 1 and turn.
Row 4: 1 sc in the 1st dc, * ch 5, 1 sc in the middle dc of the 2nd set of 3 dc, rep from *, ending row with 1 sc in the turning ch, ch 3 and turn.
Row 5: 1 dc in the sc, * 1 dc in the 5-ch, ch 1, 1 dc around the same 1-ch, 1 dc in the sc, ch 1, 1 dc in the same sc, rep from *, ending row with 2 dc in the turning ch, ch 3 and turn.
Rows 6–8: Same as row 5, ch 3 and turn.
Pattern formed by rep rows 1–8.

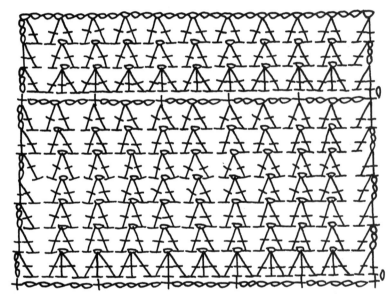

83. Chain multiples of 12 plus 4.

Row 1: 1 dc in 6th ch, * ch 1, 1 dc in same ch, 1 dc in 2nd ch, 1 dc in 2nd ch, ch 1, rep from *, ending row with 1 dc in end ch, ch 4 and turn.
Row 2: * 1 dc in 1st 1-ch, ch 1, 1 dc in next dc, 1 dc in next ch, ch 1, 1 dc in ch just used, 1 dc in next dc, ch 1, 1 dc in next ch, ch 1, 1 dc in next dc, ch 1, rep from *, ending row with 1 dc in the turning ch, ch 4 and turn.
Rows 3–4: Same as row 2.
Row 5: Sk 1 dc, * 1 dc in 1st dc, ch 1, 1 dc in dc just used, 1 dc in next dc, 1 dc in next 1-ch, ch 1, and 1 dc in ch just used, 1 dc in next dc, dc in next dc, ch 1, dc in dc just used, dc in dc, rep from *, row ending with 1 dc, ch 4 and turn.
Pattern formed by rep rows 1–5.

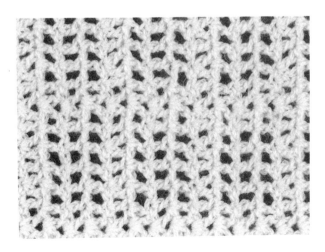

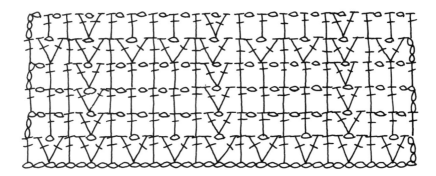

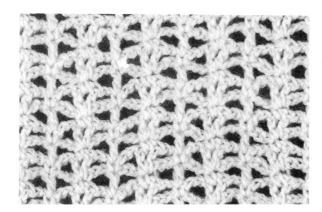

84. Chain multiples of 6 plus 1.

Row 1: 1 sc in the 2nd ch, * ch 3, 1 dc in the 3rd ch, ch 3, 1 sc in the 3rd ch, rep from *, ending row with 3 chs and 1 dc in the 3rd ch, ch 1 and turn.

Row 2: 1 sc in the 1st dc, * ch 2, 1 dc in the sc, ch 1, 1 dc in the same ch, ch 2, 1 sc in the dc, rep from *, ending row with 2 dc in the sc, ch 1 and turn.

Row 3: Same as row 1 except that the sc is worked in the 1-ch, and the dc is worked in the sc.

Pattern formed by rep rows 1–2.

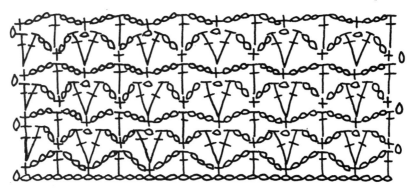

85. Chain multiples of 6 plus 6.

Row 1: 1 sc in the 9th ch, * ch 2, 1 dc in the 3rd ch, ch 2, 1 sc in the 3rd ch, rep from *, ending row with 2 chs and 1 dc in the last ch, ch 1 and turn.

Row 2: * 1 sc in the 1st dc, 1 dc in the sc, ch 3, 1 dc in the same sc, rep from *, ending row with 1 sc, ch 5 and turn.

Row 3: Same as row 1, except the sc is made around the 3-ch, dc in the sc.

Pattern formed by rep rows 1–2.

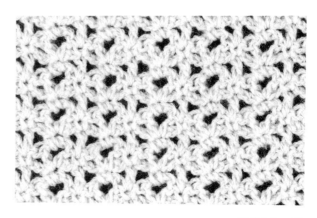

V-Stitch 91

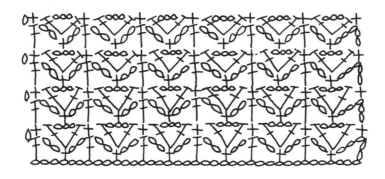

86. Chain multiples of 8 plus 5.

Row 1: 1 dc in the 7th ch, * ch 1, 1 dc in the 2nd ch, rep from *, ending row with last dc, ch 4 and turn.

Row 2: 1 dc in the 2nd dc, * ch 1, 1 dc in the next dc, 1 dc in each ch and in each dc 6 times, ch 1, 1 dc in the next dc, ch 1, 1 dc in the next dc, ch 1, 1 dc in the next dc, rep from *, ending row with 1 ch and 1 dc, ch 4 and turn.

Row 3: Sk 1st dc, * 1 dc in the next dc, ch 1, 1 dc in the next dc, ch 4, 1 dc in the 6th dc, ch 1, 1 dc in the same dc, ch 4, 1 dc in the 6th dc, ch 1, 1 dc in the next dc, ch 1, 1 dc in the next dc, ch 1, rep from *, ending row with 1 dc in the turning ch, ch 4 and turn.

Row 4: Sk 1st dc, 1 dc in the next dc, ch 1, dc in the dc, * ch 6, 1 sc in the 1-ch, ch 6, 1 dc in the dc and ch 1, 5 times, rep from *, ending row with 1 dc in the turning ch, ch 4 and turn.

Row 5: Sk 1st dc, * dc in the dc, ch 1, dc in the dc, ch 1, dc in the 6-ch, ch 1, dc in the 6-ch, ch 3, dc in the next 6-ch, ch 1, dc in the 6-ch, ch 1, dc in the dc 3 times, ch 1, and rep from *, ending row with dc in the turning ch, ch 4 and turn.

Row 6: Same as row 1, dc and ch in each dc, plus 1 dc in the 3-ch. Pattern formed by rep rows 1–5.

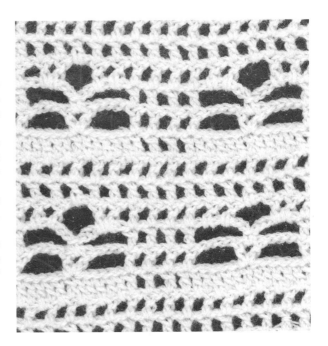

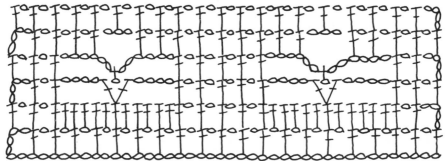

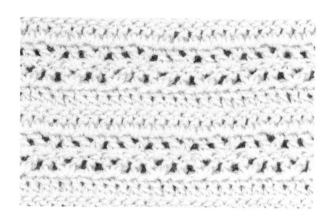

87. Chain multiples of 4 plus 4.

Row 1: 1 dc in the 5th ch and in each ch all across the row, ch 3 and turn.
Row 2: Same as row 1, ch 3 and turn.
Row 3: 1 dc in the 3rd dc, * ch 1, 1 dc in the dc just used, 1 dc in the 2nd dc, 1 dc in the 2nd dc, rep from *, ending row with last set and 1 dc in the turning ch, ch 3 and turn.
Row 4: 1 dc in the 1st dc, * 1 dc in the 1-ch between the 2 sides of the V-stitch, 1 dc in the dc, ch 1, 1 dc in the same dc, rep from *, ending row with last dc and 2 dc in the turning ch, ch 3 and turn.
Pattern formed by rep rows 1–4.

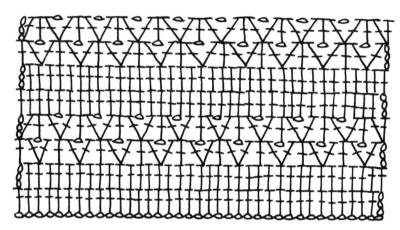

• 7 •
Simple Shell

88. Chain multiples of 3 plus 1.

Row 1: 1 sc in the 2nd ch, * ch 2, 1 sc in the 3rd ch, rep from *,
ending row with 1 sc in the last ch, ch 3 and turn.
Row 2: 1 dc in the 1st sc, * 3 dc in the next sc, rep from *, ending
row with 2 dc in the last sc.
Pattern formed by rep rows 1–2.

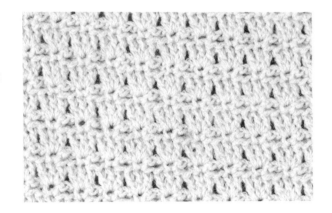

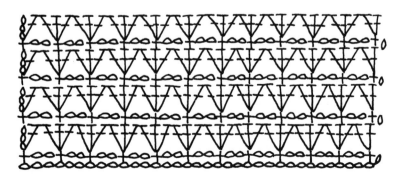

89. Chain multiples of 4 plus 4.

Row 1: 4 dc in the 6th ch, * 4 dc in the 4th ch, rep from *, ending row with 3 dc in the last ch, ch 1 and turn.
Row 2: 1 sc in the 1st dc and in every dc all across the row, with 1 extra in the turning ch, ch 3 and turn.
Row 3: 2 dc in the 2nd sc, * 4 dc in the 4th sc, rep from *, ending row with 1 dc after the last set, ch 1 and turn.
Row 4: 1 sc in each dc all across the row.
Pattern formed by rep rows 1–4.

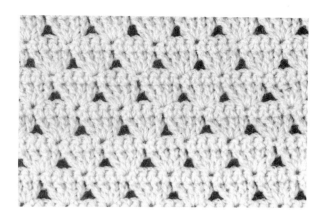

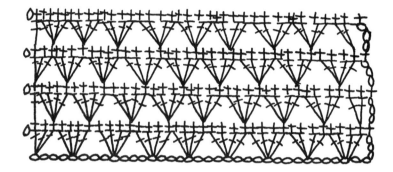

90. Chain multiples of 6 plus 4.

Row 1: 2 dc in the 7th ch, * ch 1, 2 dc in the same ch, 1 dc in the 3rd ch, 2 dc in the 3rd ch, rep from *, ending row with 1 dc after the last set, ch 1 and turn.
Row 2: 1 sc in the 1st dc and in every dc and ch all across the row, ending with 1 sc in the turning ch, ch 3 and turn.
Row 3: 2 dc in the 1st sc, * 1 dc in the 3rd sc, 2 dc in the 3rd sc, ch 1, 2 dc in the same sc, rep from *, ending row with 3 dc in the last sc, ch 1 and turn.
Row 4: 1 sc in the 1st dc and in each ch and dc all across the row, ch 3 and turn.
Pattern formed by rep rows 1–4.

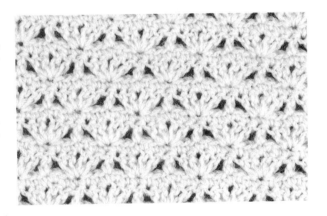

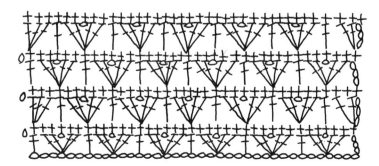

Simple Shell 95

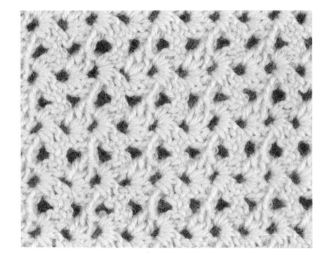

91. Chain multiples of 6 plus 4.

Row 1: 2 dc in the 6th ch, * ch 3, 2 dc in the same ch, 2 dc in the 4th ch, rep from *, ending row with 1 dc after the last set, ch 3 and turn.
Pattern formed by rep row 1.

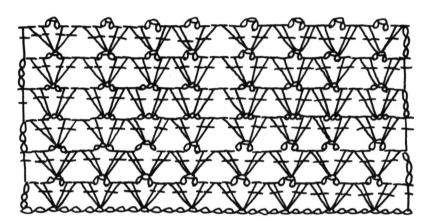

92. Chain multiples of 5 plus 4.

Row 1: 2 dc in the 4th ch, * ch 2, 2 dc in the 5th ch, ch 1, 2 dc in the same ch, rep from *, ending row with 3 dc in the last ch, ch 3 and turn.
Row 2: Same as row 1, ch 3 and turn.
Row 3: * 2 dc in the 2-ch, ch 1, 2 dc in the same 2-ch, ch 2, rep from *, ending row with 1 dc after the last set, ch 3 and turn.
Row 4: Same as row 3, ch 3 and turn.
Row 5: * 2 dc in the 1-ch, 1 picot, 2 dc in the same ch, ch 2, rep from *, ending row with 1 dc after the last set, ch 3 and turn.
Row 6: 2 dc in the 1st dc, * ch 2, 2 dc in the next 2-ch, ch 1, 2 dc in the same 2-ch, rep from *, ending row with 3 dc in the turning ch, ch 3 and turn.
Rows 7–9: Same as row 6.
Pattern formed by rep rows 1–9.

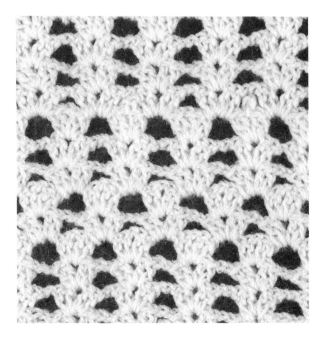

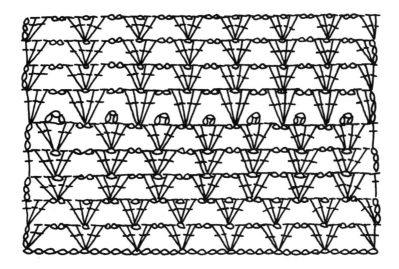

93. Chain multiples of 12 plus 6.

Row 1: 1 sc in the 8th ch, * ch 2, 5 dc in the 4th ch, ch 2, 1 sc in the 4th ch, ch 5, 1 sc in the 4th ch, rep from *, ending row with 3 dc in the last ch, ch 4 and turn.
Row 2: 1 dc in the 2nd dc, ch 1 and 1 dc in the next dc, * ch 2, 1 sc around the middle of the 5-ch, ch 2, 1 dc in the next dc and ch 1, 4 times, 1 dc in the next dc, rep from *, ending row with 2 chs and 1 sc in the turning ch, ch 3 and turn.
Row 3: * 1 dc in the dc, ch 2, 4 times, 1 dc in the last dc of the set, rep from *, ending row with 1 dc in the turning ch, ch 3 and turn.
Row 4: Same as row 1, except that the 5 dc are worked in the middle of the 5 dc of the set, 1 sc is worked in the last 2 chs of the set and the 1st 2.
Pattern formed by rep rows 1–4.

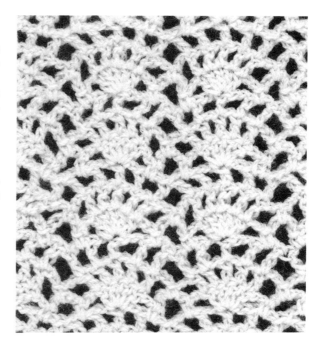

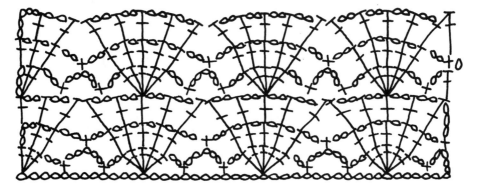

94. Chain multiples of 3 plus 4.

Row 1: 1 dc in 6th ch, * ch 1, 1 dc in the same ch, 1 dc in the 3rd ch, rep from *, ending row with 1 dc 2 chs after the last set, ch 3 and turn.
Row 2: 2 dc in 1st ch, ch 1, 2 dc in the same ch, * ch 1, 2 dc in the 2nd 1-ch, ch 1, 2 dc in the same 1-ch, rep from *, row ending with 1 extra dc finished in the turning ch, ch 3 and turn.
Row 3: Same as row 1, except that sets are worked in each 1-ch.
Pattern formed by rep rows 1–2.

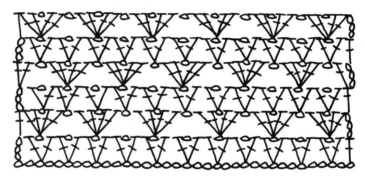

95. Chain multiples of 4 plus 4.

Row 1: 2 dc in the 6th ch, * ch 5, attach the end ch back into the 1st ch, 2 dc in the same ch, 2 dc in the 4th ch, rep from *, ending row with 1 dc in the 3rd ch after the last set, ch 3 and turn.
Row 2: 2 dc in the 1st dc, * 2 dc between the 2 sets, ch 5, attach the end ch back into the 1st ch, 2 dc in the same space just used, rep from *, ending row after the last set with 3 dc in the turning ch, ch 3 and turn.
Pattern formed by rep rows 1–2.

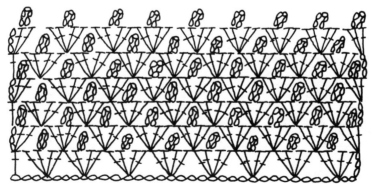

· 8 ·
Shells—Filet

96. Chain multiples of 6 plus 4.

Row 1: 1 dc in 4th ch, * ch 1, 1 dc in 3rd ch, ch 1, 3 dc in 3rd ch, rep from *, ending row with 2 dc in last ch, ch 4 and turn.
Row 2: * 3 dc in the single standing dc, ch 1, 1 dc in the middle of the 3 dc, ch 1, rep from *, ending row with 1 dc in the turning ch, ch 3 and turn.
Row 3: Same as row 1, dc placed alternatively.
Pattern formed by rep rows 1–2.

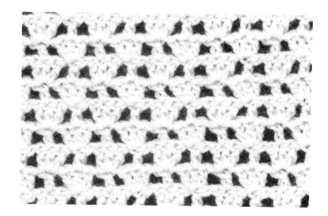

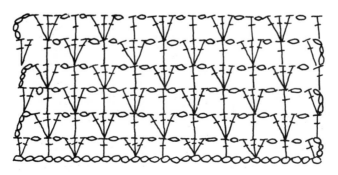

97. Chain multiples of 8.

Row 1: 1 dc in the 7th ch, * 5 dc in the 3rd ch, 1 dc in the 3rd ch, ch 1, 1 dc in the 2nd ch, rep from *, ending row with 1 ch and 1 dc, ch 4 and turn.
Row 2: Same as row 1, except that the 5 dc are worked in the 3rd (middle) of the dc, and the dc are worked in the dc.
Pattern formed by rep row 1.

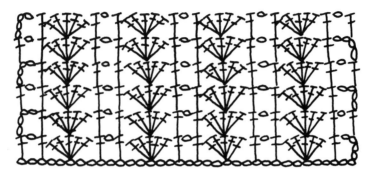

98. Chain multiples of 13 plus 4.

Row 1: 1 dc in 7th ch, * ch 2, 3 dc in same ch, 1 dc in 4th ch, ch 2, 1 dc in 3rd ch, ch 2, 1 dc in 3rd ch, 1 dc in 3rd ch, rep from *, ending row with 1 dc in last ch, ch 3 and turn.
Row 2: * 1 dc in 2-ch, ch 2, 3 dc in the same 2-ch, 1 dc in 2nd dc, ch 2, dc in next dc, ch 2, 1 dc in next dc, rep from *, ending row with 1 dc in the turning ch, ch 3 and turn.
Pattern formed by rep rows 1–2.

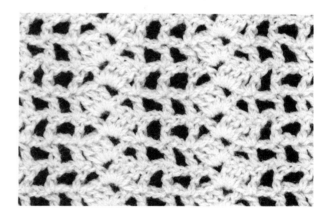

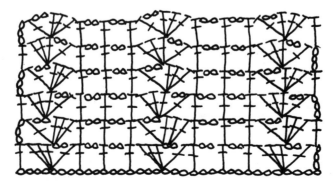

99. Chain multiples of 10 plus 5.

Row 1: 1 dc in the 7th ch, * 5 dc in the 3rd ch, 1 dc in the 3rd ch, ch 1, 1 dc in the 2nd ch, ch 1, 1 dc in the 2nd ch, rep from *, ending row with 1 dc, 1 ch and 1 dc, ch 3 and turn.
Row 2: 2 dc in the 1st dc, * 1 dc in the 2nd dc, ch 1, 1 dc in the 2nd dc, ch 1, 1 dc in the 2nd dc, sk 1 dc, 5 dc in the next dc, rep from *, ending row with 3 dc in the turning ch, ch 4 and turn.
Pattern formed by rep rows 1–2.

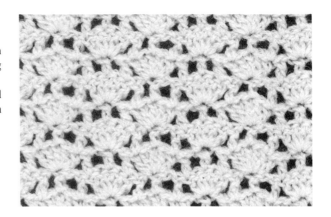

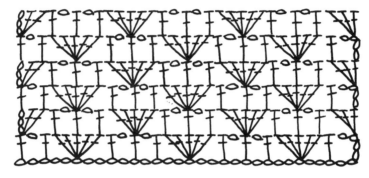

100. Chain multiples of 18 plus 5.

Row 1: 4 dc in the 10th ch, * ch 1, 4 dc in the ch just used, ch 1, 1 dc in the 5th ch, ch 1 and dc in the 2nd ch 4 times, ch 1, 4 dc in the 5th ch, rep from *, ending row with last dc, ch 4 and turn.
Row 2: Same as row 1, ch 4 and turn.
Row 3: Sk 1st dc, * dc in the next dc, ch 1, dc in the 2nd dc, ch 1, 1 dc in the 1-ch, ch 1, 1 dc in the 2nd dc, ch 1, 1 dc in the 2nd dc, ch 1, 4 dc in the 3rd dc, ch 1, 4 dc in the same dc, ch 1, rep from *, ending row with 1 dc in the turning ch, ch 4 and turn.
Row 4: Same as row 3, ch 5 and turn.
Pattern formed by rep rows 1–4.

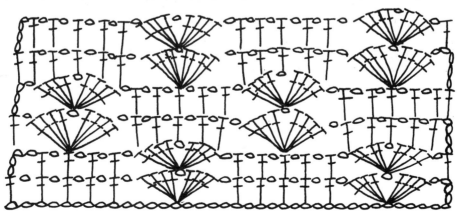

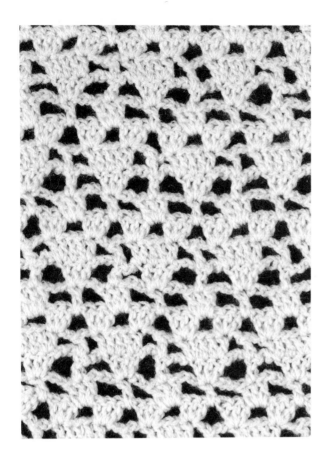

101. Chain multiples of 10 plus 7.

Row 1: 1 dc in the 12th ch, 2 other dc in the same ch, * ch 3, 1 dc in the 5th ch, ch 3, work 3 dc in the 5th ch, rep from *, ending row with 1 dc in the last ch, ch 3 and turn.
Row 2: 1 dc in the 1st dc, * ch 3, 1 dc in the 2nd dc, ch 3, work 3 dc in the single standing dc, rep from *, ending row with 2 dc in the turning ch, ch 3 and turn.
Row 3: 2 dc in the 2nd dc, * ch 2, 1 dc in the dc, ch 2, 2 dc in the 1st dc, 1 dc in the next dc, and 2 dc in the next dc, rep from *, ending row with 2 dc in the last dc and 1 dc in the turning ch, ch 3 and turn.
Row 4: 3 dc in the 3rd dc, * ch 1, 3 dc in the 2nd dc, ch 1, 3 dc in the 4th dc, rep from *, ending row with 3 dc in the 2nd to the last dc and 1 dc in the turning ch, ch 3 and turn.
Row 5: 1 dc in the 1st dc, * ch 3, 1 dc in the 1-ch, ch 3, work 3 dc in the next 1-ch, rep from *, ending row with 2 dc in turning ch, ch 6 and turn.
Row 6: * 3 dc in the single standing dc, ch 3, 1 dc in the middle of the 3 dc, ch 3, rep from *, ending row with 3 chs and 1 dc in the turning ch, ch 5 and turn.
Row 7: * 2 dc in the 1st of the 3 dc worked together, 1 dc in the next dc, 2 dc in the last of the 3 dc, ch 2, 1 dc in the dc, ch 2, rep from *, ending row with 2 chs and 1 dc, ch 3 and turn.
Row 8: * 3 dc in the 1st of the 5 dc worked in a group, ch 1, 3 dc in the 4th dc, ch 1, rep from *, ending row with 1 dc in the turning ch after the last set, ch 6 and turn.
Pattern formed by rep rows 1–8.

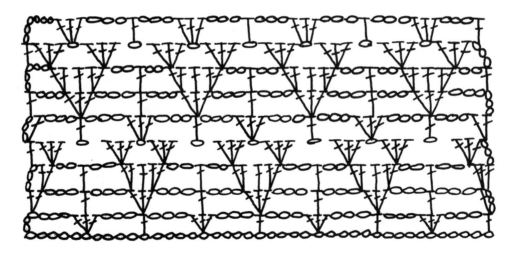

102. Chain multiples of 8 plus 4.

Row 1: 1 dc in the 5th ch, * ch 2, 1 dc in the 3rd ch, ch 2, 1 dc in the 3rd ch and the 2 chs following, rep from *, ending row with 2 dc, 1 in each of the last 2 chs, ch 3 and turn.
Row 2: 2 dc in the 2nd dc, * ch 1, 1 dc in the next dc, ch 1, 2 dc in the next dc, 1 dc in the next dc and 2 dc in the dc after that, rep from *, ending row with 1 dc in the turning ch, ch 3 and turn.
Row 3: 1 dc in the 2nd dc, 2 dc in the next dc, * ch 1, 2 dc in the next dc, 1 dc in each of the next 3 dc, 2 dc in the next dc, rep from *, ending row with 1 dc in the turning ch, ch 3 and turn.
Row 4: 1 dc in the 2nd dc, * ch 2, 1 dc in the 1-ch, ch 2, 1 dc in the 3rd dc and the 2 dc after that, rep from *, ending row with 1 dc in the turning ch, ch 3 and turn.
Pattern formed by rep rows 1–4.

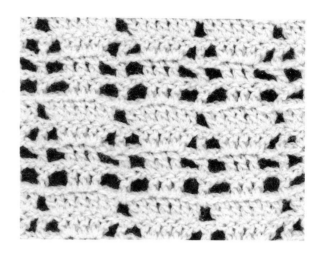

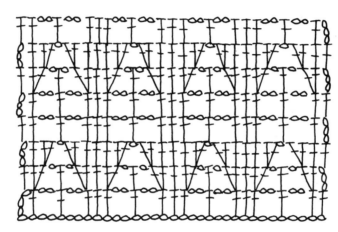

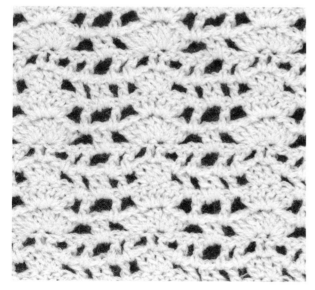

103. Chain multiples of 12 plus 4.

Row 1: 3 dc in the 4th ch, * ch 1, 1 dc in the 5th ch and also in the ch following, ch 1, work 4 dc in the 5th ch, 4 dc in the next ch, rep from *, ending row with 4 dc in the last ch, ch 3 and turn.
Row 2: 2 dc in the 1st dc, * ch 1, 1 dc in the 1st 1-ch, ch 2, 1 dc in the 1-ch after the 2 dc, ch 1, 3 dc in the 4th dc, 3 dc in the next dc, rep from *, ending row with 3 dc in the turning ch, ch 3 and turn.
Row 3: 1 dc in the 1st dc, * ch 1, 1 dc in the 1-ch, ch 1, 2 dc in the 2-ch, ch 1, 1 dc in the 1-ch, 2 dc in the 3rd dc, 2 dc in the next dc, rep from *, ending row with 2 dc in the turning ch, ch 4 and turn.
Row 4: * 1 dc in the 1-ch, ch 1, 1 dc in the next 1-ch, ch 2, 1 dc in the next 1-ch, ch 1, 1 dc in the next ch, ch 1, 1 dc in the 2nd dc, 1 dc in the next dc, ch 1, rep from *, ending row with 1 dc in the turning ch, ch 3 and turn.
Pattern formed by rep rows 1–4.

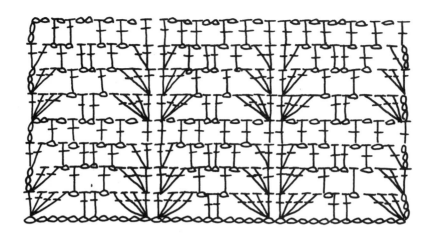

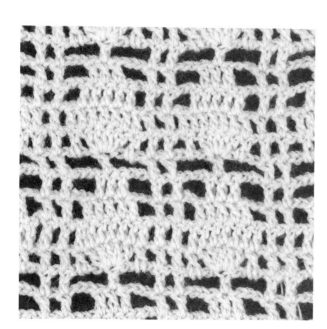

104. Chain multiples of 12 plus 4.

Row 1: 1 dc in 7th ch, * 5 dc in 3rd ch, 1 dc in 3rd ch, ch 1, 1 dc in 2nd ch, ch 1, 1 dc in 2nd ch, ch 1, 1 dc in 2nd ch, rep from *, ending row with last set, 1 ch and 1 dc, ch 5 and turn.

Row 2: sk 1st dc, * dc in the next dc, 1 dc in each of the next 5 dc, 1 dc in the next dc, ch 1, 1 dc, ch 1 and 1 dc, ch 1, rep from *, ending row with 1 ch and 1 dc, ch 5 and turn.

Row 3: sk 1st dc, * dc in 2nd dc and in the 4 next dc, ch 2, 1 dc in the 2nd dc, 1 ch and 1 dc in the next dc, ch 2, rep from *, ending row with 2 chs and 1 dc in the turning ch, ch 6 and turn.

Row 4: sk 1st dc, * dc in 2nd dc, 1 dc in each of the next 2 dc, ch 3, 1 dc in 2nd dc, ch 1, 1 dc in next dc, ch 3 and rep from *, row ending with 3 chs and 1 dc in the turning ch, ch 7 and turn.

Row 5: sk 1st dc, * dc in 2nd dc, ch 4, 1 dc in the next dc, ch 1, 1 dc in next dc, ch 4 and rep from *, row ending with 4 chs and 1 dc in the turning ch, ch 4 and turn.

Row 6: Same as row 1, except that the single dc are worked in the ch, the 5 dc are worked in the single dc.

Pattern formed by rep rows 1–5.

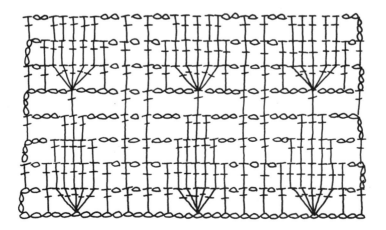

105. Chain multiples of 16 plus 4.

Row 1: 1 dc in the 5th ch, ch 1, 1 dc in the 2nd ch, ch 1, 1 dc in the 2nd ch, * 3 dc in the 3rd ch, ch 1, 3 dc in the ch just used, 1 dc in the 3rd ch, ch 1 and 1 dc in the 2nd ch 5 times, rep from *, ending row with 1 extra dc in the last ch, ch 3 and turn.

Row 2: Same as row 1, ch 3 and turn.

Row 3: 3 dc in the 1st dc, * dc in the 2nd dc, ch 1, dc in the dc, ch 1, dc in 3rd dc, ch 1, dc in next dc, ch 1, dc in 3rd dc, ch 1, dc in dc, 3 dc in 2nd 1-ch, ch 1, 3 dc in same 1-ch, rep from *, ending row with 4 dc in the turning ch.

Row 4: Same as row 3, except dc worked in dc, 6 dc shell worked in 1-ch between sides of the shell of row below.

Pattern formed by rep rows 1–4.

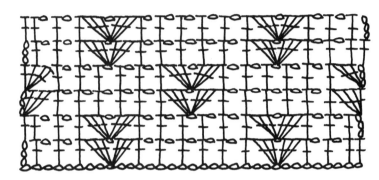

• 9 •
Shells—Symmetrical

106. Chain multiples of 8 plus 4.

Row 1: 1 dc in the 5th ch and all the way across, ch 3 and turn.
Row 2: 1 dc in the 3rd dc, * ch 1, 1 dc in the same ch, 5 dc in the 4th dc, 1 dc in the 4th dc, rep from *, ending row with last set of dc, 1 dc in the turning ch, ch 3 and turn.
Row 3: Same as row 1, 1 dc in each dc and in each ch.
Pattern formed by rep rows 1–2.

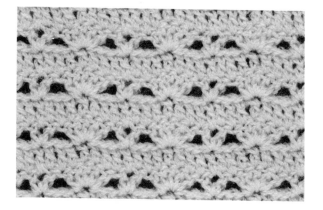

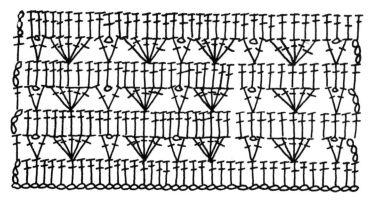

107. Chain multiples of 6 plus 4.

Row 1: 1 dc in the 5th ch and in each ch all across the row, ch 1 and turn.
Row 2: 1 sc in the 1st dc, * ch 2, 1 dc in the 3rd dc, ch 2, 1 sc in the 3rd dc, rep from *, ending row with 2 chs and 1 sc in the last dc, ch 3 and turn.
Row 3: 2 dc in the sc, * 1 sc in the dc, 5 dc in the sc, rep from *, ending row with 3 dc in the sc, ch 1 and turn.
Row 4: 1 sc in the 1st dc, * ch 2, 1 dc in the sc, ch 2, 1 sc in the 3rd dc, rep from *, ending row with 1 sc in the turning ch, ch 3 and turn.
Pattern formed by rep rows 1–4.

108. Chain multiples of 8 plus 5.

Row 1: 1 dc in the 5th ch and all the way across the row, ch 1 and turn.
Row 2: 1 sc in the 1st dc, * ch 1, 1 dc in the 4th dc, rep 3 additional times in the same ch; ch 1, 1 sc in the 4th dc, rep from *, ending row with 1 sc in the last dc, ch 6 and turn.
Row 3: * 1 sc in the 3rd 1-ch, ch 3, 1 dc in the next sc, ch 3, rep from *, ending row with 1 dc in the last sc, ch 3 and turn.
Pattern formed by rep rows 1–3.

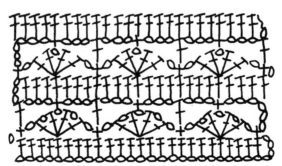

109. Chain multiples of 8 plus 5.

Row 1: 1 dc in the 7th ch, * ch 1, 1 dc in the 2nd ch, rep from *, ending row with 1 ch and 1 dc, ch 3 and turn.

Row 2: 3 dc in the 2nd dc, * ch 2, 3 dc in the same dc, 1 dc in the 2nd dc, 3 dc in the 2nd dc, rep from *, ending row with 1 dc in the turning ch after completion of the last set, ch 6 and turn.

Row 3: * 1 sc in the 2-ch, ch 3, 1 dc in the 4th dc, ch 3, rep from *, ending row with 1 dc in the turning ch after completion of the last set, ch 4 and turn.

Row 4: * 1 dc in the 3-ch, ch 1, 1 dc in the sc, ch 1, 1 dc in the 3-ch, ch 1, 1 dc in the dc, ch 1, rep from *, ending row with 1 ch and the last dc in the turning ch, ch 3 and turn.

Row 5: 1 dc in each ch and in each dc all across the row, ending with 2 dc in the turning ch, ch 4 and turn.

Pattern formed by rep rows 1–5.

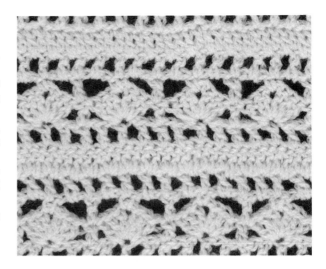

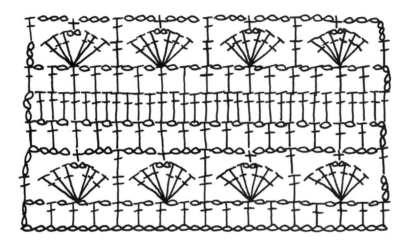

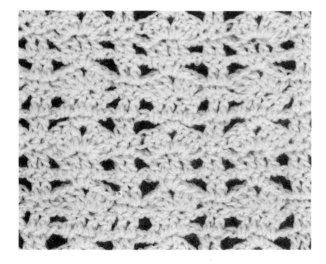

110. Chain multiples of 10 plus 5.

Row 1: 1 dc in the 9th ch and in the 3 chs following, * ch 2, 1 dc in the 3rd ch and the ch following, ch 2, 1 dc in the 3rd ch and the 3 chs following, rep from *, ending row with 1 dc in the last ch, ch 1 and turn.

Row 2: 1 sc in the 1st dc, * 3 dc in the 2nd dc, ch 2, 3 dc in the next dc, sc in the 2nd dc and in the next dc, rep from *, ending row with 1 sc in the turning ch, ch 6 and turn.

Row 3: * 1 sc in the 1st of the 2-ch, 1 sc in the last 2-ch, ch 3, 1 dc in the sc and in the sc after that, ch 3, rep from *, ending row with 1 dc in the last sc, ch 5 and turn.

Row 4: Same as row 1 except that the dc are worked in the last ch before the sc, in the 2 sc and in the 1st ch after the sc.

Pattern formed by rep rows 1–3.

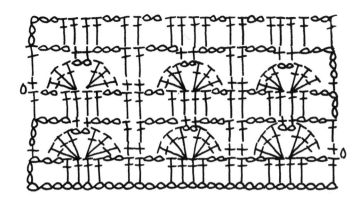

111. Chain multiples of 11 plus 6.

Row 1: 1 dc in the 9th ch, 1 dc in each of the next 4 chs, * ch 2, 1 dc in the 3rd ch, 1 dc in the next ch, ch 2, 1 dc in the 3rd ch and in each of the next 4 chs, rep from *, ending row with 2 chs and 1 dc in the last ch, ch 1 and turn.
Row 2: 1 sc in 1st dc, 1 sc in the 1st ch, * 3 dc in the 3rd dc, ch 1, 3 dc in the same dc, 1 sc in the 2nd ch, 1 sc in each of the next 2 dc, 1 sc in the 1st ch after the 2 dc, rep from *, ending row with 2 sc, ch 3 and turn.
Row 3: 1 dc in the 2nd sc, * ch 3, 1 sc in the 1-ch, ch 3, 1 dc in each of the next 4 sc, rep from *, ending row with 3 chs and 2 dc, ch 5 and turn.
Pattern formed by rep rows 1–3.

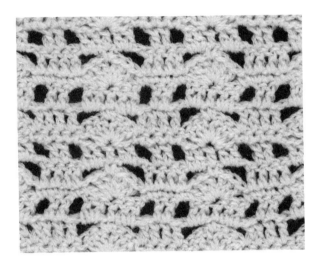

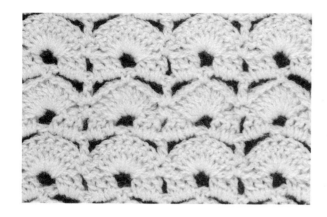

112. Chain multiples of 8 plus 1.

Row 1: 1 sc in 2nd ch, * 9 dc in 4th ch, 1 sc in 4th ch, rep from *, ending row with 1 sc, ch 6.
Row 2: * 1 sc in 5th dc, ch 3, 1 dc in sc, ch 3, rep from *, ending row with 1 dc in the sc, ch 3 and turn.
Row 3: * 3 dc in the 3-ch, ch 1, rep from *, ending row with 1 extra dc, ch 1 and turn.
Row 4: Same as row 1 except that the 9 dc are formed in the sc directly above the 1st sets.
Pattern formed by rep rows 1–3.

113. Chain multiples of 13 plus 5.

Row 1: 1 dc in the 5th ch and in each ch all across the row, ch 3 and turn.
Row 2: 1 dc in the 2nd dc, * ch 3, 1 dc in the 4th dc and in each of the next 2 dc, ch 3, 1 dc in the 4th dc and in each of the next 3 dc, rep from *, ending row with 2 dc, 1 in the last dc and 1 in the turning ch, ch 4 and turn.
Row 3: 3 dc in the 1st dc, * 1 dc in the 3rd ch, 1 dc in each of the next 3 dc, 1 dc in the ch following the 3 dc, ch 5 and turn, attach the last ch in the space between the 1st of the 5 dc and the dc before, work 7 sc along the ch, attaching the last sc to the 1st ch formed, 3 dc in the 2nd dc, ch 1, 1 dc in the same dc, 1 dc in the next dc, ch 1, 3 dc in the same dc, rep from *, ending row with 3 dc, 1 ch and 1 dc all worked in the turning ch, ch 3 and turn.
Row 4: 2 dc in the 1st 1-ch, * ch 2, 1 sc in the 3rd sc, 1 in the next sc and in the sc following that, ch 2, 2 dc in the 1-ch, ch 2, 2 dc in the next 1-ch, rep from *, ending row with 3 dc in the turning ch, ch 3 and turn.
Row 5: Same as row 1, except that the dc is worked in every stitch and in every ch, ch 3 and turn.
Pattern formed by rep rows 1–4.

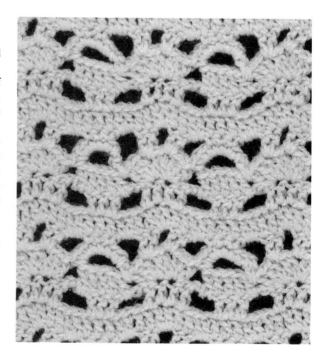

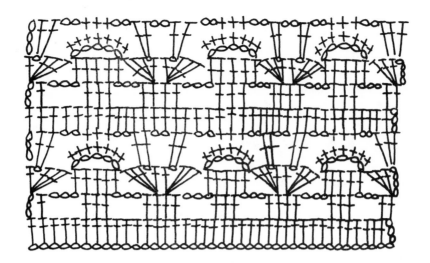

114. Chain multiples of 8 plus 4.

Row 1: 1 dc in the 5th ch, * ch 2, 1 dc in the 3rd ch and 1 in the ch after that, rep from *, ending row with 2 dc in the last 2 chs, ch 1 and turn.
Row 2: 1 sc in the 1st dc, ch 2, * 1 sc in the 2-ch, ch 3, rep from *, ending row with 2 chs and 1 sc in the turning ch, ch 3 and turn.
Row 3: Work 3 dc around the 2-ch, * 1 sc around the 3-ch, work 6 dc around the 3-ch, rep from *, ending row with 3 dc in the last 2-ch, 1 dc in the last sc, ch 3 and turn.
Row 4: 1 dc in the 2nd dc, * ch 2, 2 dc in the sc, ch 2, 1 dc in the 3rd dc and the dc after that, rep from *, ending row with 1 dc in the 3rd dc and in the turning ch, ch 1 and turn.
Row 5: 1 sc in the dc, ch 2, * 1 sc in the 2-ch, ch 3, 1 sc in the next 2-ch, rep from *, ending row with 1 sc in the last 2-ch, ch 2, 1 sc in the turning ch, ch 1 and turn.
Row 6: 1 sc in the 1st sc, * work 6 dc around the 1st 3-ch, 1 sc around the next 3-ch, rep from *, ending row with 1 sc in the sc, ch 3 and turn.
Row 7: 1 dc in the sc, * ch 2, 1 dc in the 3rd dc and in the dc after that, ch 2, 2 dc in the sc, rep from *, ending row with 2 dc in the sc, ch 1 and turn.
Pattern formed by rep rows 1–7.

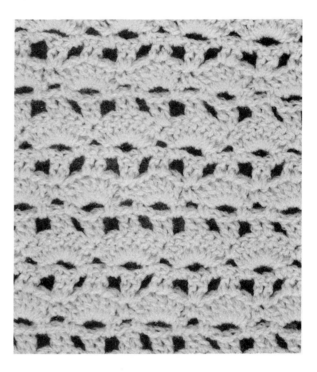

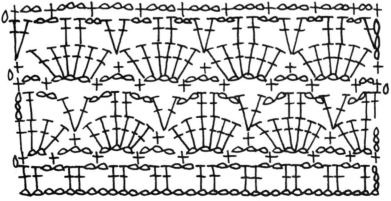

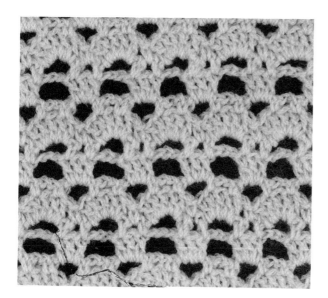

115. Chain multiples of 6 plus 4.

Row 1: 1 dc in the 5th ch, * ch 3, 1 dc in the 4th ch and in the next 2 chs, rep from *, ending row with 2 dc, ch 3 and turn.
Row 2: 1 sc in the 2nd dc, * ch 5, 1 sc in the 1st dc, ch 2, 1 sc in the 2nd dc, rep from *, ending row with 1 sc in the last dc, ch 1, 1 hdc in the turning ch, ch 1 and turn.
Row 3: 1 sc in the 1st hdc, * 5 dc around the 5-ch, 1 sc around the 2-ch, rep from *, ending row with 1 sc in the turning ch, ch 4 and turn.
Row 4: * 1 sc in the 2nd dc, ch 2, 1 sc in the 2nd dc, ch 3, rep from *, ending row with 1 ch and 1 dc in the sc, ch 3 and turn.
Row 5: Same as row 1 except 3 dc worked around the 3-ch.
Pattern formed by rep rows 1–4.

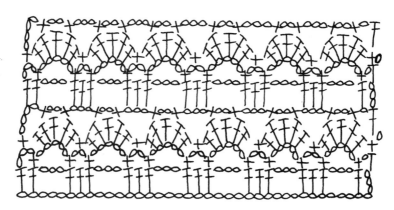

116. Chain multiples of 8 plus 4.

Row 1: 1 dc in the 5th ch, * ch 2, 1 dc in the 3rd ch, ch 2, 1 dc in the 3rd ch, 1 dc in each of the next 2 chs, rep from *, ending the row with 2 dc, ch 5 and turn.
Row 2: * 1 sc in 2-ch, ch 3, 1 sc in the next 2-ch, ch 5, rep from *, ending row with 2 chs and 1 dc, ch 3 and turn.
Row 3: 3 dc in 1st 2-ch, * 1 sc in 3-ch, 7 dc around 5-ch, rep from *, ending row with 4 dc in turning ch, ch 1 and turn.
Row 4: 1 sc in the 1st dc and also in the next dc, * ch 2, 1 dc in the next dc, ch 2, 1 sc in the 3rd dc and also in the next 2 dc, rep from *, ending row with 2 chs and 2 sc, ch 3 and turn.
Row 5: Same as row 1 except dc is worked in the dc, 3 dc worked in the 3 sc.
Pattern formed by rep rows 1–4.

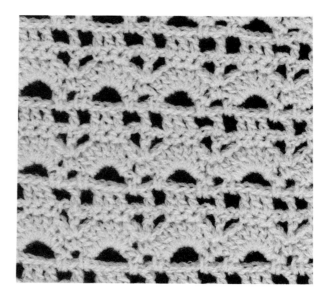

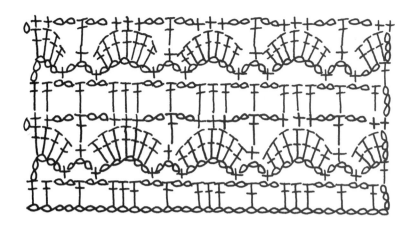

117. Chain multiples of 8 plus 4.

Row 1: 2 dc in the 4th ch, * 1 dc in the 3rd ch, 1 dc in the next ch, 3 dc in the 3rd ch, 3 dc in the next ch, rep from *, ending in 3 dc in the last ch, ch 3 and turn.
Row 2: Sk 1 dc, * 3 dc in the 3rd dc, 3 dc in the next dc, 1 dc in the 3rd dc and 1 dc in the next dc, rep from *, ending row with 1 dc in the turning ch, ch 3 and turn.
Pattern formed by rep rows 1–2.

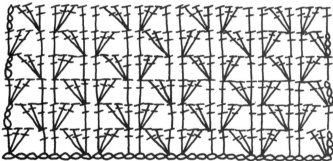

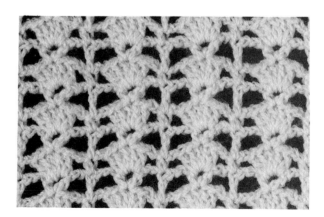

118. Chain multiples of 6 plus 1.

Row 1: 1 sc in 2nd ch, * ch 2, 5 dc in 3rd ch, ch 2, 1 sc in 3rd ch, rep from *, ending row with sc after completion of last set, ch 5 and turn.
Row 2: * 1 dc, 1 ch and 1 dc in middle dc, ch 2, 1 dc in next sc, ch 2 and rep from *, ending row with 2 chs and 1 dc in the last sc.
Row 3: Same as row 1, 5 dc always made around the 1-ch between the 2 dc.
Pattern formed by rep rows 1–2.

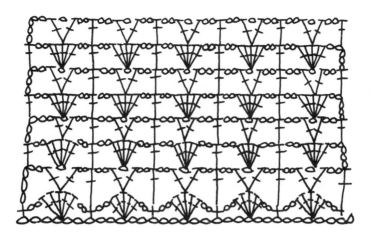

119. Chain multiples of 8 plus 4.

Row 1: 1 dc in the 5th ch and in each ch all across the row, ch 3 and turn.

Row 2: 1 dc in the 2nd dc, * ch 3, 1 sc in the 3rd dc, ch 3, 1 sc in the next dc, ch 3, 1 dc in the 3rd dc and the dc after that, rep from *, ending row with 1 dc in the last dc and 1 in the turning ch, ch 3 and turn.

Row 3: 1 dc in the 2nd dc, * ch 1, 4 dc around the 2nd 3-ch, ch 1, 1 dc in each of the next 2 dc, rep from *, ending row with 1 extra dc in the turning ch, ch 3 and turn.

Row 4: 1 dc in the 2nd dc, * ch 2, 1 dc in the 2nd dc and the dc after that, ch 2, 1 dc in the 2nd dc and the dc after that, rep from *, ending row with 1 dc in the last dc and 1 in the turning ch, ch 3 and turn.

Row 5: Same as row 1 except that the dc are formed in each ch and in each dc all across the row.

Pattern formed by rep rows 1–4.

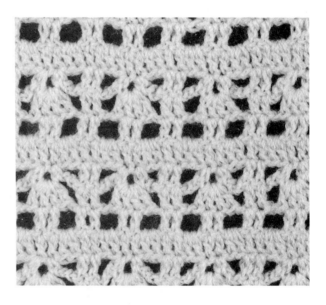

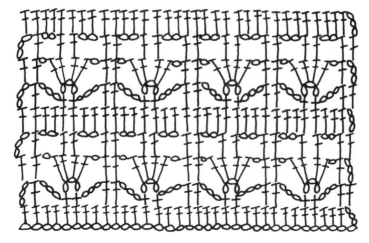

120. Chain multiples of 8 plus 4.

Row 1: 1 dc in the 4th ch, * ch 2, 1 dc in the 4th ch, ch 2, 1 dc in the 4th ch, ch 1, 1 dc in the same ch, rep from *, ending row with 1 dc after the set, ch 5 and turn.

Row 2: * 3 dc in the 1-ch between the 2 sides of the V, ch 2, 1 dc in the dc, ch 2, rep from *, ending row with 2 dc in the turning ch, ch 3.

Row 3: 2 dc in the 1st dc, * ch 1, 1 dc in the dc, ch 1, 5 dc in the 2nd dc, rep from *, ending row with 1 ch and 1 dc in the turning ch, ch 3 and turn.

Row 4: * 7 dc in the middle of the 5 dc, 1 dc in the single standing dc, rep from *, ending row with 4 dc in the turning ch, ch 5 and turn.

Row 5: 1 dc in the 5th dc, * ch 1, 1 dc in the dc just used, ch 2, 1 dc in the 4th dc, ch 2, 1 dc in the 4th dc, rep from *, ending row with 2 dc in the turning ch, ch 3 and turn.

Row 6: 1 dc in the 1st dc, * ch 2, 1 dc in the dc, ch 2, 3 dc in the 1-ch between the 2 sides of the V-stitch, rep from *, ending row with last set and 1 dc in the turning ch, ch 4 and turn.

Row 7: * 5 dc in the middle of the 3 dc, ch 1, 1 dc in the single standing dc, ch 1, rep from *, ending row with 3 dc in the turning ch, ch 3 and turn.

Row 8: 3 dc in the 1st dc, * 1 dc in the single standing dc, 7 dc in the middle of the 5 dc, rep from *, ending row with 1 dc in the turning ch after the last set, ch 3 and turn.

Pattern formed by rep rows 1–8.

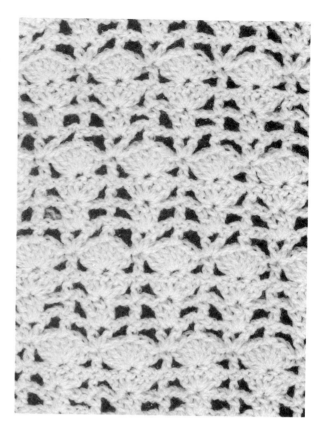

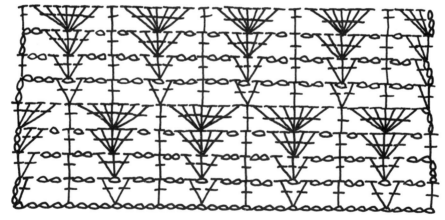

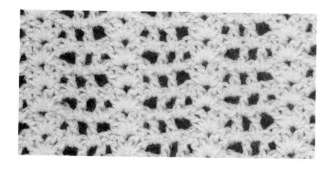

121. Chain multiples of 9 plus 4.

Row 1: 2 dc in 4th ch, * 1 dc in 3rd ch, ch 1, 1 dc in 2nd ch, ch 1, 2 dc in 4th ch, ch 1, 2 dc in same ch as 1st 2 dc, rep from *, ending row with 1 dc, 1 ch and 1 dc, ch 3 and turn.

Row 2: 1 dc in the 1-ch, * ch 1, 2 dc, 1 ch and 2 dc around the ch between the 2 sets of dc, 1 dc in 1st ch after set, ch 1, 1 dc around ch between 2 dc, rep from *, ending row with 3 dc in the turning ch, ch 3 and turn.

Pattern formed by rep rows 1–2.

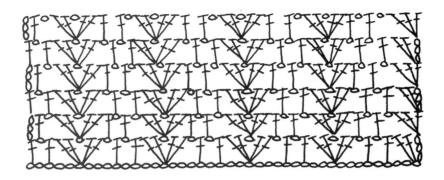

122. Chain multiples of 5 plus 4.

Row 1: 1 sc in the 2nd ch, * ch 3, work 5 dc in the ch just used, 1 sc in the 5th ch, rep from *, ending row with sc after the last set, ch 5 and turn.

Row 2: * work 1 sc in the 5th dc and 1 sc in the top of the 3-ch, ch 3, rep from *, ending row with 1 sc in the last dc and 2 in the turning ch, ch 3 and turn.

Row 3: 1 dc in the 2nd sc and the 1 after that, * ch 3, 1 dc in each sc, rep from *, ending row with 2 chs and 1 dc in the turning ch, ch 3 and turn.

Row 4: 1 dc in the 2-ch, * ch 3, 2 dc in the 3-ch, rep from *, ending row with 3 chs and 1 dc in the turning ch, ch 1 and turn.

Row 5: 1 sc in the 1st dc, * ch 3, 5 dc in the stitch just used, 1 sc in the 2nd dc, rep from *, ending row with last set and 1 sc in the turning ch, ch 5 and turn.

Pattern formed by rep rows 1–4.

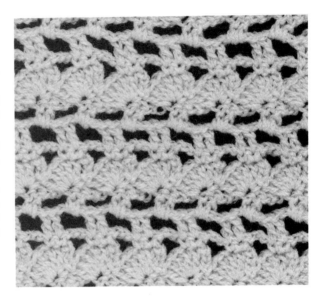

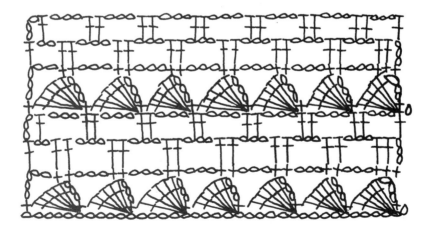

123. Chain multiples of 10 plus 5.

Row 1: 2 dc in the 6th ch, * 2 dc in the 6th ch, ch 2, 1 dc in the ch just used, ch 1, 1 dc in the 2nd ch, ch 1, 1 dc in the 2nd ch, ch 2, 2 dc in the ch just used, rep from *, ending row with 2 dc, 2 ch and 1 dc in the same ch, ch 5 and turn.

Row 2: 2 dc in the 1st dc, * 2 dc in the 3rd dc of the next set, ch 2, 1 dc in the dc just used, ch 1, dc in the next dc, ch 1, dc in the next dc, ch 2, 2 dc in the dc just used, rep from *, ending row with 2 dc, 2 chs and 1 dc in the turning ch.

Pattern formed by rep rows 1–2.

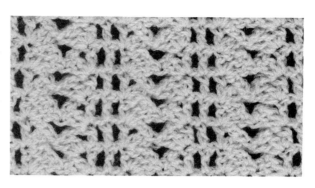

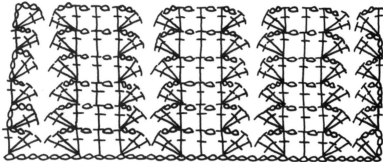

124. Chain 6 plus 6.

Row 1: 1 dc in the 6th ch, * 1 dc in the 5th ch, ch 2, 1 dc in the same ch, 1 dc in the next ch, ch 2, 1 dc in the same ch, rep from *, ending rows with 1 dc, 2 chs and 1 dc, ch 5 and turn.

Row 2: 1 dc in 1st dc, * dc in 3rd dc, ch 2, 1 dc in same dc just used, dc in next dc, ch 2, dc in dc just used, rep from *, ending row with last dc, 2 chs and a dc in turning ch.

Row 3: 1 dc in the 1st 2-ch, * ch 2, 1 dc in the 2-ch, 1 dc in each of the 2 dc, 1 dc in the 2-ch, rep from *, ending row with 2 dc, ch 3 and turn.

Row 4: 1 dc in every ch and in every dc all across the row, ending with 1 in the turning ch, ch 5 and turn.

Row 5: Same as row 1, except that the dc are worked in every 5th and next dc.

Pattern formed by rep rows 1–4.

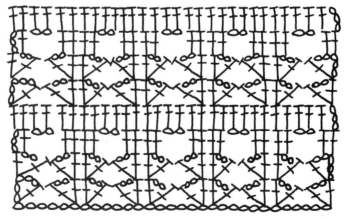

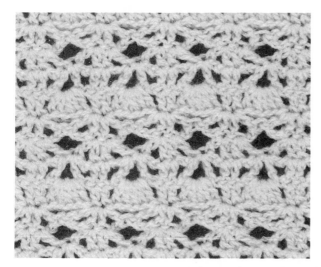

125. Chain multiples of 7 plus 4.

Row 1: 5 dc in the 7th ch, * 1 dc in the 3rd ch, 1 dc in the next ch, 5 dc in the 3rd ch, rep from *, ending row with 1 dc after the last set, ch 5 and turn.

Row 2: 1 dc in the 1st dc, * 1 dc in the 6th dc, ch 2, 1 dc in the same dc, 1 dc in the next dc, ch 2, 1 dc in the same dc, rep from *, ending row with 1 dc, 2 chs, and 1 dc in the turning ch, ch 5 and turn.

Row 3: Same as row 2, ch 4 and turn.

Row 4: * 1 dc in the 2nd dc, ch 2, 1 dc in the next dc, ch 1, 1 dc in the next dc and the dc after that, ch 1, rep from *, ending row with 1 ch and 1 dc, ch 3 and turn.

Row 5: * 5 dc in the 2-ch, 1 dc in the next dc and dc after that, rep from *, ending row with 1 dc in the turning ch after the last set, ch 5 and turn.

Pattern formed by rep rows 1–5.

126. Chain multiples of 9 plus 4.

Row 1: 2 dc in the 7th ch, * ch 1, 2 dc in the same ch, 1 dc in the 3rd ch and also in the next 3 chs, 2 dc in the 3rd ch, rep from *, ending row with last set and 1 dc in the last ch, ch 3 and turn.

Rows 2–3: Same as row 1, ch 3 and turn.

Row 4: 1 dc in the 2nd dc and also in the next 3 dc, * 2 dc between the 2nd and 3rd dc, ch 1, 2 dc in the space just used, 1 dc in each of the next 4 dc, rep from *, ending row with 1 extra dc in the turning ch, after the last set ch 3 and turn.

Rows 5–6: Same as row 4.

Pattern formed by rep rows 1–6.

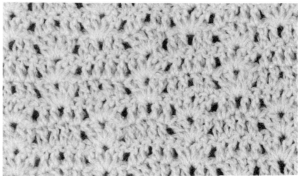

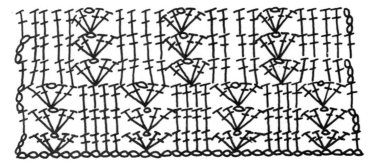

127. Chain multiples of 9 plus 4.

Row 1: 1 dc in 4th ch, * ch 1, 1 sc in 4th ch, ch 1, 2 dc in 4th ch, 2 dc in next ch, rep from *, ending row with 2 dc in last ch, ch 1 and turn.

Row 2: 1 sc in 1st dc, * 1 dc in 1st sc, ch 3, 1 dc in same sc, ch 3, 1 dc in same sc, 1 sc in 2nd dc, 1 sc in next dc, rep from *, ending row with 1 sc in the turning ch, ch 3 and turn.

Row 3: Same as row 1, except 2 dc are worked in each of the 2 sc and 1 sc is worked in the dc.

Pattern formed by rep rows 1–2.

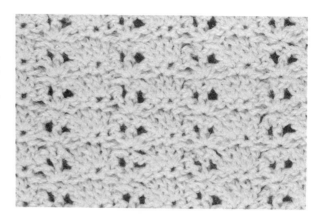

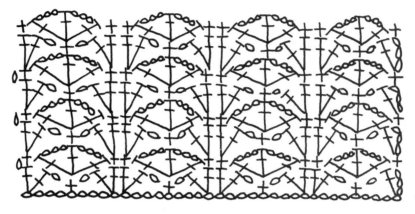

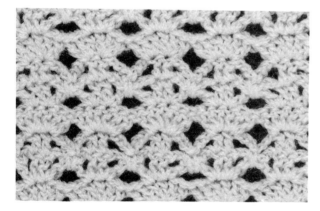

128. Chain multiples of 6 plus 3.

Row 1: 2 dc in the 4th ch, * 6 dc in 6th ch, rep from *, last set should be 3 dc, ch 5 and turn.

Row 2: 1 dc in 1st dc, * dc in 3rd dc, ch 2, dc in dc just used, dc in next dc, ch 2, dc in dc just used, rep from *, last set should be 1 dc, 2 chs, 1 dc in dc just used, dc, 2 chs and 1 dc in the turning ch, ch 6 and turn.

Row 3: Sc between 2nd and 3rd dc, ch 3, * dc in next dc, dc in next dc, ch 3, sc in between next 2 dc, ch 3, rep from *, ending row with 1 dc in the turning ch, ch 3, and turn.

Pattern formed by rep rows 1–3.

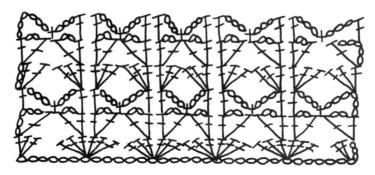

129. Chain multiples of 9 plus 1.

Row 1: 1 sc in 2nd ch, * 1 dc in 4th ch, ch 2, 1 dc in the same ch, 1 dc in next ch, ch 2, 1 dc in the same ch, 1 sc in 4th ch, rep from *, ending row with 1 sc, ch 1 and turn.
Row 2: 1 sc in 1st sc, * 4 dc around 1st 2 chs, 4 dc around next 2 chs, 1 sc in the sc, rep from *, ending row with 1 sc in the end sc, ch 7 and turn.
Row 3: 1 sc in 4th dc, * 1 sc in next dc, ch 7, 1 sc in 4th dc of new group, rep from *, ending row with 3 chs and 1 trc, ch 1 and turn.
Row 4: Same as row 1, except that the 4 dc are worked in the 2 sc.
Pattern formed by rep rows 1–3.

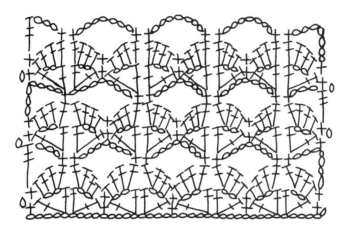

130. Chain multiples of 11 plus 3.

Row 1: 3 dc in the 4th ch, * ch 2, 1 sc in the 5th ch, ch 3, 1 sc in the next ch, ch 2, 3 dc in the 5th ch, ch 1, 3 dc in the ch just used, rep from *, ending row with 4 dc in the 5th and last ch, ch 1 and turn.
Row 2: 1 sc in the 1st dc, * ch 2, 1 dc in each of the 2-chs, ch 2, 1 dc in each of the next 2-chs, ch 2, 1 sc in the 1-ch, rep from *, ending row with 1 sc in the turning ch, ch 3 and turn.
Row 3: Same as row 1 with the exception that the shell (3 dc, 1 ch, 3 dc) should be made in the sc of the row below.
Pattern formed by rep rows 1–2.

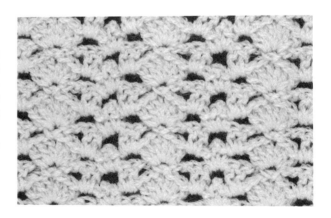

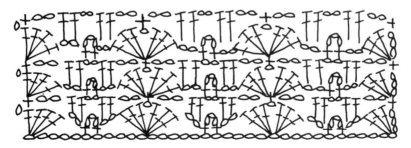

131. Chain multiples of 12 plus 4.

Row 1: 1 dc in the 5th ch and the ch after that, * ch 2, 1 dc in the 5th ch, ch 5, 1 dc backwards 2 chs, ch 2, 1 dc in the 3rd ch and the 4 chs after that, rep from *, ending row with 1 dc in each of the last 3 chs, ch 3 and turn.

Row 2: 1 dc in the 2nd and the next dc, * ch 1, 5 sc around the 5-ch, ch 1, 1 dc in each of the 5 dc, rep from *, ending row with 1 dc in each of the last 2 dc and 1 in the turning ch, ch 7 and turn.

Row 3: 1 dc in the 2nd dc, * ch 2, 1 dc in each of the 5 sc, ch 2, 1 dc in the 4th dc, ch 5, 1 dc backwards in the 2nd dc, rep from *, ending row with 2 dc in the turning ch, ch 3 and turn.

Row 4: 1 dc in the 2nd dc, form 1 sc in the top of the ch and 2 around the dc, * ch 1, 1 dc in each of the 5 dc, ch 1, 1 sc in each of the 5-chs, rep from *, ending row with 1 ch and 3 sc around the turning ch, ch 7 and turn.

Row 5: 1 dc in the 1st sc, * ch 2, 1 dc in the 4th dc, ch 5, 1 dc backwards 2 dc, ch 2, 1 dc in the 4th sc, ch 5, 1 dc backwards in the 2nd sc, rep from *, ending row with 1 dc in the last sc, ch 2, and 1 trc in the same sc, ch 1 and turn.

Row 6: 1 sc in the trc, 1 sc in the 2-ch, * ch 4, 3 sc around the 5-ch, rep from *, ending row with 2 sc in the turning ch, ch 3 and turn.

Pattern formed by rep rows 1–6.

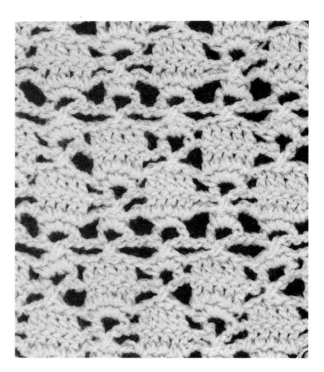

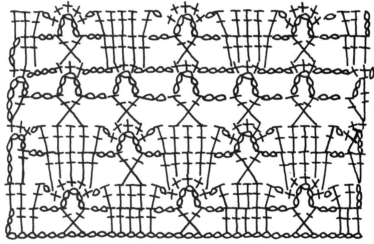

· 10 ·
Shells—Overall Patterns

132. Chain multiples of 6 plus 1.

Row 1: 1 sc in the 2nd ch and in the 3rd ch, * ch 4, 1 sc in the 5th ch, 1 sc in the next ch, rep from *, ending row with 2 sc, ch 3 and turn.

Row 2: * 2 dc around the 4-ch, ch 2, 2 dc around the same 4-ch, rep from *, ending row with 1 dc in the last sc after completion of the last set, ch 5 and turn.

Row 3: * 1 sc in the 1st ch, 1 sc in the next ch, ch 4, rep from *, ending row with 2 chs and 1 dc in the turning ch, ch 4 and turn.

Row 4: 2 dc around the 2-ch, * 2 dc around the 4-ch, ch 2, 2 dc around the same 4-ch, rep from *, ending row with 2 dc, 1 ch and 1 dc, ch 1 and turn.

Pattern formed by rep rows 1–4.

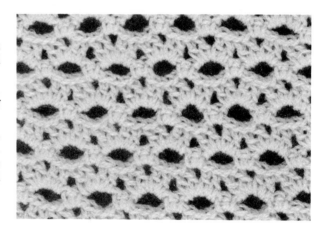

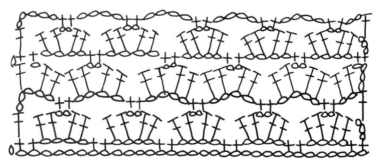

133. Chain multiples of 10 plus 3.

Row 1: 1 dc in the 5th ch, * 1 dc in the 4th ch, ch 3, 1 dc in the ch just used, dc in the next ch, ch 3, 1 dc in the ch just used, dc in the 4th ch, dc in the next ch, rep from *, ending row with a dc in each of the last 2 chs, ch 4 and turn.

Row 2: 1 dc in the 3rd dc, * 3 dc in the 3-ch, sk 2 dc, 3 dc in the next 3 ch, 1 dc in the next dc, ch 2, 1 dc in the 3rd dc, rep from *, finishing with 1 ch and 1 dc in the turning ch, ch 3 and turn. Pattern formed by rep rows 1–2.

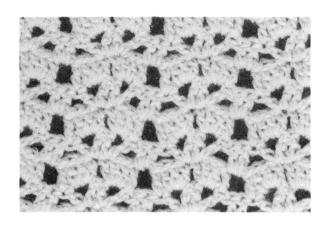

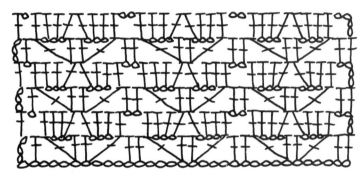

134. Chain multiples of 4 plus 4.

Row 1: 1 dc in the 7th ch, * ch 3, 1 dc in the ch just used, 1 dc in the 4th ch, rep from *, ending row after last set with 1 dc, ch 3 and turn.

Row 2: * 4 dc around the 3-ch, ch 1, rep from *, ending row after last set with 1 dc in the turning ch, ch 4 and turn.

Row 3: 1 dc in 1st dc, * 1 dc in the 1st ch, ch 3, 1 dc in the same ch, rep from *, ending row with 1 dc, 1 ch and 1 dc in the turning ch, ch 3 and turn.

Row 4: 2 dc in the 1st ch, ch 1, * 4 dc around the 3-ch, ch 1, rep from *, ending row with 3 dc in the turning ch, ch 4 and turn. Pattern formed by rep rows 1–4.

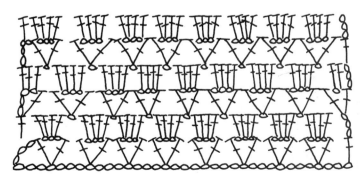

Shells—Overall Patterns 123

135. Chain multiples of 6 plus 4.

Row 1: 5 dc in the 7th ch, * ch 1, 5 dc in the 6th ch, rep from *, ending row after the last set with 1 dc in the 3rd ch after the last set, ch 4 and turn.
Row 2: 1 dc in the 1st dc, * 1 dc in the 3rd dc, 1 dc in the 1st ch, ch 3, 1 dc in the same ch, rep from *, ending row with 1 dc, 1 ch and 1 dc in the turning ch, ch 3 and turn.
Row 3: 2 dc in the 1st 1-ch, * ch 1, 5 dc in the 3-ch, rep from *, ending row with 3 dc in the turning ch, ch 3 and turn.
Row 4: * 1 dc in the 1-ch, ch 3, 1 dc in the same 1-ch, 1 dc in the 3rd dc, rep from *, ending row with 1 dc in the turning ch after the last set, ch 3 and turn.
Pattern formed by rep rows 1–4.

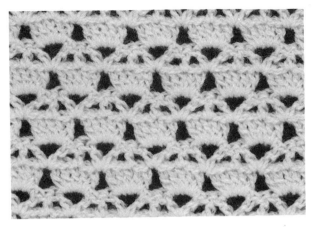

136. Chain multiples of 10 plus 5.

Row 1: 7 dc in the 10th ch, * ch 1, 1 dc in the 5th ch, ch 1, 7 dc in the 5th ch, rep from *, ending row with 1 ch and 1 dc, ch 4 and turn.
Row 2: 1 dc in the 1st dc, * ch 1, 1 dc in the 3rd dc and also in the next 2 dc, ch 1, 1 dc in the 3rd dc, ch 3, 1 dc in the dc just used, rep from *, ending row with 1 dc, 1 ch and 1 dc in the turning ch, ch 3 and turn.
Row 3: 3 dc in the 1st 1-ch, * ch 1, 1 dc in the middle of the 3 dc, ch 1, 7 dc around the 3-ch, rep from *, ending row with 4 dc in the turning ch, ch 3 and turn.
Row 4: 1 dc in the 2nd dc, ch 1, 1 dc in the 3rd dc, ch 3, 1 dc in the same dc, ch 1, 1 dc in the 3rd dc and in the next 2 dc, rep from *, ending row with 2 dc, 1 in the last dc and 1 in the turning ch, ch 4 and turn.
Pattern formed by rep rows 1–4.

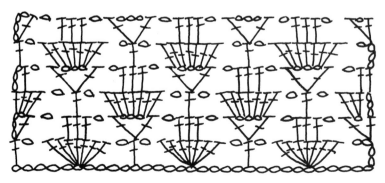

137. Chain multiples of 7 plus 4.

Row 1: 3 dc in the 7th ch, * ch 2, 3 dc in the same ch, 3 dc in the 7th ch, rep from *, ending row with last set and 1 dc in the 3rd ch, ch 3 and turn.
Row 2: * 5 dc around the 2-ch, ch 2, 5 dc around the 2-ch, ch 2, rep from *, ending row with last set and 1 dc in the turning ch, ch 4 and turn.
Row 3: 3 dc in the 1st dc, * 3 dc in the 2-ch, ch 2, 3 dc in the same 2-ch, rep from *, ending row with 3 dc, 1 ch and 1 dc in the turning ch, ch 3 and turn.
Row 4: 2 dc in the 1-ch, * ch 2, 5 dc in the 2-ch, rep from *, ending row with 3 dc in the turning ch, ch 3 and turn.
Pattern formed by rep rows 1–4.

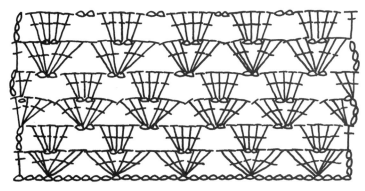

138. Chain multiples of 7 plus 4.

Row 1: 1 dc in 5th ch, * ch 2, 1 dc in 7th ch, ch 3, 1 dc in ch just used for last dc, rep from *, ending after last set with 1 dc in 7th ch, 1 ch and 1 dc in the same ch, ch 3 and turn.
Row 2: 3 dc in the 1st ch, * 8 dc around 3-ch, rep from *, ending row with 5 dc in turning ch, ch 4 and turn.
Row 3: Same as row 1 except that 2 dc should be worked in 4th dc of the set.
Pattern formed by rep rows 1–2.

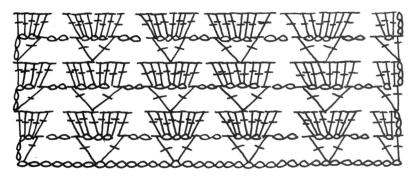

139. Chain multiples of 8 plus 4.

Row 1: 1 dc in 5th ch, * ch 5, 1 dc in 6th ch, 1 dc in next ch and the 1 after, rep from *, ending row with 2 dc, ch 3 and turn.
Row 2: * 9 dc around 5-ch, rep from *, ending row after last set with 1 dc, ch 5 and turn.
Row 3: * 1 dc in 4th dc and in the next 2 dc, ch 5, rep from *, ending row with 2 ch and 1 dc, ch 3 and turn.
Row 4: 4 dc in 2-ch, * 9 dc around 5-ch, rep from *, ending row with 5 dc in the turning ch, ch 3 and turn.
Pattern formed by rep rows 1–4.

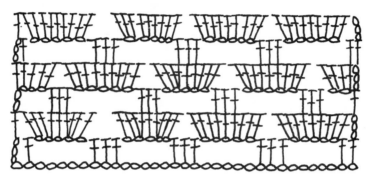

140. Chain multiples of 7 plus 4.

Row 1: 2 dc in 8th ch, * ch 1, 3 dc in the ch just used, ch 1, 2 dc in ch just used, 2 dc in 7th ch, rep from *, ending row after last set with 1 dc in 4th ch, ch 3 and turn.
Row 2: * 1 dc, 1 ch and 2 dc in 1st ch, ch 2, 2 dc, 1 ch and 1 dc in next ch, rep from *, ending row after last set with 1 dc, ch 3 and turn.
Row 3: Rep row 1, except that all sets are worked in the middle 2 chs of the set below.
Pattern formed by rep rows 1–2.

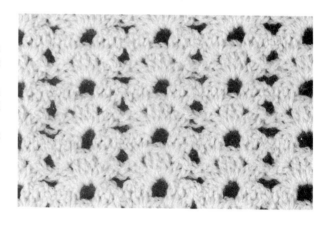

141. Chain multiples of 10 plus 3.

Row 1: 2 dc in the 4th ch, * 1 dc in the 3rd ch, 1 dc in each of the next 4 chs, 2 dc in the 3rd ch, ch 1, 2 dc in the ch just used, rep from *, ending row with 3 dc in the last ch, ch 3 and turn.
Row 2: 2 dc in the 1st dc, * ch 3, 1 sc in the middle of the 5 dc, ch 3, 2 dc in the 1-ch, ch 1, 2 dc in the 1-ch just used, rep from *, ending row with 3 dc in the turning ch, ch 3 and turn.
Row 3: 1 dc in 2nd and next dc, * 2 dc in the sc, ch 1, 2 dc in the same 1-ch, 1 dc in each of the next 2 dc, 1 dc in the 1-ch and 1 dc in each of the next 2 dc, rep from *, ending row with 1 dc in each of the last 2 dc and 1 in the turning ch, ch 1 and turn.
Row 4: 1 sc in the 1st dc, * ch 3, 2 dc in the 1-ch, ch 1, 2 dc in the same 1-ch, ch 3, 1 sc in the middle of the 5 dc, rep from *, ending row with 1 sc in the turning ch, ch 3 and turn.
Pattern formed by rep rows 1–4.

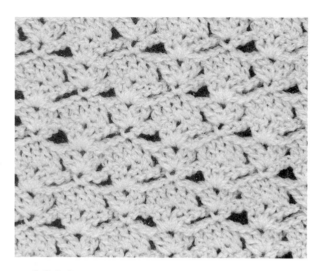

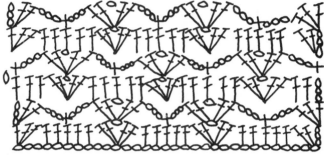

142. Chain multiples of 5 plus 3.

Row 1: 1 dc in 5th ch, * ch 2, 1 dc in 3rd ch, 1 dc in next ch, 1 dc in next ch, rep from *, ending row with 1 dc in 3rd ch from last dc, 1 dc in next ch, ch 1 and turn.
Row 2: 1 sc in 1st dc, * 5 dc around the 2 chs, 1 sc in 2nd (middle) dc, rep from *, ending row with 1 sc in turning ch of row below, ch 4 and turn.
Row 3: * 1 dc in 2nd dc of set, 1 dc in the next dc, 1 dc in next dc, ch 2, rep from *, ending row with 1 ch and 1 dc in sc, ch 3 and turn.
Row 4: 2 dc in the dc, * 1 sc in 2nd dc (middle stitch), 5 dc around 2-ch, rep from *, ending row with 3 dc in turning ch of row below, ch 3 and turn.
Pattern formed by rep rows 1–4.

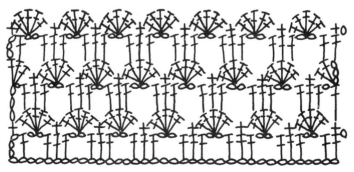

143. Chain multiples of 6 plus 1.

Row 1: 1 sc in 2nd ch, * 7 dc in 3rd ch, 1 sc in 3rd ch, rep from *, ending row with sc, ch 4 and turn.

Row 2: 1 dc in 2nd dc, * 1 dc in each of next 4 dc, 1 dc in 2nd dc of set, rep from *, ending row with 1 trc in last sc, ch 3 and turn.

Row 3: 3 dc in trc, * 1 sc in the 3rd dc, 7 dc in the space between the 3rd and next dc, rep from *, ending row with 4 dc in turning ch of row below, ch 3 and turn.

Row 4: 1 dc in 2nd dc, 1 dc in next dc, * 1 dc in 2nd dc of set and in each of the next 4 dc, rep from *, ending row with 1 dc in each of the last 2 dc of the row and 1 in the turning ch, ch 1 and turn.

Pattern formed by rep rows 1–4.

144. Chain multiples of 8 plus 4.

Row 1: 1 dc in the 3rd ch, * ch 3, 1 sc in the 4th ch, ch 3, 3 dc in the 4th ch, rep from *, ending row with 2 dc in the 4th and last ch, ch 1 and turn.

Row 2: 1 sc in the 1st dc, * ch 3, 1 dc around the middle of the 3-ch, 1 dc in the middle of the next 3-ch, ch 3, 1 sc in the 2nd dc, rep from *, ending row with 3 chs and 1 sc in the turning ch, ch 3 and turn.

Pattern formed by rep rows 1–2.

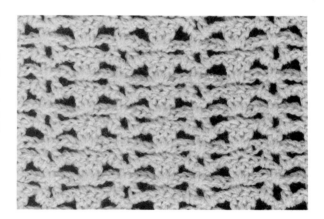

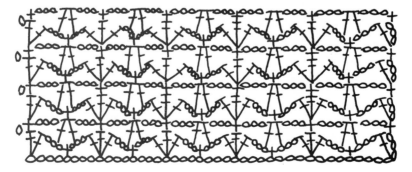

145. Chain multiples of 6 plus 4.

Row 1: 1 dc in the 5th ch and in the next 4 after that, * ch 1, 1 dc in the 2nd ch and in the next 4 chs after that, rep from *, ending row with 5 dc and 1 extra in the last ch, ch 3 and turn.

Row 2: 1 dc in the 1st dc, * ch 2, 1 sc in the 3rd dc, ch 2, 3 dc in the 1-ch, rep from *, ending row with 2 chs and 2 dc in the turning ch, ch 3 and turn.

Row 3: 1 dc in the 2nd dc, 1 dc in the 1st ch, * ch 1, 1 dc in the last ch before the 3 dc, 1 dc in each of the 3 dc, 1 dc in the ch afterwards, rep from *, ending row with 3 dc, ch 1 and turn.

Row 4: 1 sc in the 1st dc, * ch 2, 3 dc in the 1-ch, ch 2, 1 sc in the 3rd dc, rep from *, ending row with 2 chs and 1 sc in the turning ch, ch 3 and turn.

Pattern formed by rep rows 1–4.

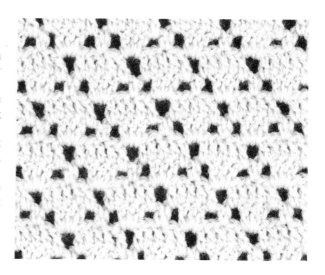

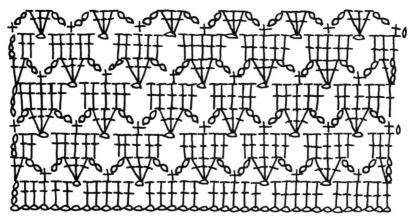

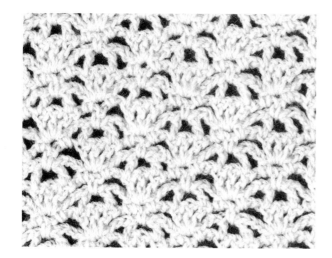

146. Chain multiples of 10 plus 4.

Row 1: 1 dc in the 5th ch, * ch 3, 1 sc in the 3rd ch, ch 1, 1 sc in the 2nd ch, ch 3, 1 dc in the 3rd ch, ch 1, 1 dc in the 2nd ch, rep from *, ending row with 1 sc in each of the last 2 chs, ch 4 and turn.

Row 2: 1 dc in the 1st sc, * ch 3, 1 sc in the 1-ch, ch 3, 1 dc in the next 1-ch, ch 1, 1 dc in the same 1-ch, ch 1, 1 dc in the same 1-ch, rep from *, ending row with 1 sc in the turning ch, ch 1 and turn.

Row 3: 1 sc in the 1st sc, * 1 sc around the 3-ch, ch 3, 1 dc in the 1-ch, ch 1, 1 dc in the 1-ch, ch 3, 1 sc around the next 3-ch, ch 1, rep from *, ending row with 2 dc in the turning ch, ch 1 and turn.

Row 4: 1 sc in the 1st dc, * ch 3, 1 dc in the 1-ch, ch 1, 1 dc in the same 1-ch, ch 1, 1 dc in the same 1-ch, ch 3, 1 sc in the 1-ch, rep from *, ending row with 1 dc, 1 ch and 1 dc in the last sc, ch 3 and turn.

Pattern formed by rep rows 1–4.

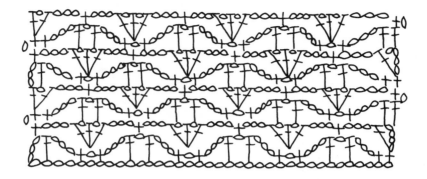

147. Chain multiples of 8 plus 1.

Row 1: 1 sc in the 2nd ch, * ch 3, 3 dc in the 4th ch, ch 3, 1 sc in the 4th ch, rep from *, ending row with 1 sc, ch 4 and turn.
Row 2: * 1 dc in the 1st dc, ch 1, 1 dc in the same dc, ch 1, 1 dc in the next dc, ch 1, 1 dc in the same dc, ch 1, 1 dc in the next dc, ch 1, 1 dc in the same dc, rep from *, ending row with 1 trc in the sc, ch 1 and turn.
Row 3: Same as row 1, except that the 3 dc are formed in the 1-ch between the middle 2 dc, sc in the space between the sets.
Pattern formed by rep rows 1–2.

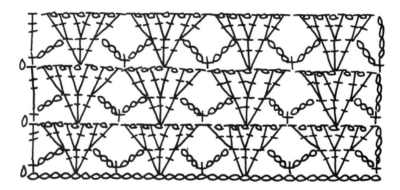

148. Chain multiples of 8 plus 6.

Row 1: 1 sc in the 8th ch, * ch 5, 1 sc in the 5th ch, ch 5, 1 sc in the 3rd ch, rep from *, ending row with 1 sc, ch 2 and 1 dc in the 2nd ch, ch 1 and turn.
Row 2: 1 sc in the 1st dc, * 9 dc around the 1st 5-ch, 1 sc around the middle of the next 5-ch, rep from *, ending row with last set of 9 dc and 1 sc in the turning ch, ch 5 and turn.
Row 3: * 1 sc in the 4th dc, ch 5, 1 sc in the 3rd dc, ch 2, 1 dc in the sc, ch 2, rep from *, ending row with 2 ch and 1 dc in the last sc, ch 3 and turn.
Row 4: 4 dc in the 2-ch, * 1 sc around the 5-ch, 4 dc in the next 2-ch, 1 dc in the dc and 4 dc around the next 2-ch, rep from *, ending row with 5 dc in the turning ch, ch 5 and turn.
Pattern formed by rep rows 1–4.

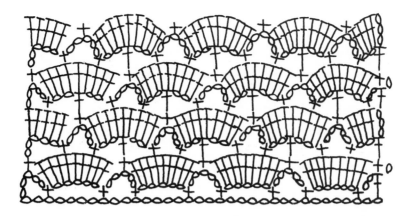

149. Chain multiples of 8 plus 7.

Row 1: Begin 1 dc in the 7th ch, * begin 2nd dc in the 4th ch, finish off the 2 stitches together, ch 5, begin 1 dc in the same ch, rep from *, ending row with 2 dc worked together, 2 chs and 1 trc in the same ch, ch 1 and turn.

Row 2: 1 sc in the trc, * work 7 dc around the 1st 5-ch, 1 sc around the next 5-ch, rep from *, ending row with last set and 1 sc in the turning ch, ch 6 and turn.

Row 3: Same as row 1, except that 1 set is worked in the 1-ch and the next set worked in the 4th dc, ch 1 and turn.

Pattern formed by rep rows 1–2.

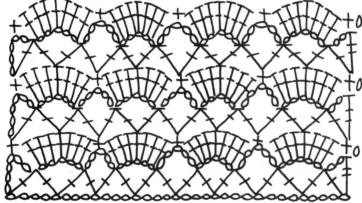

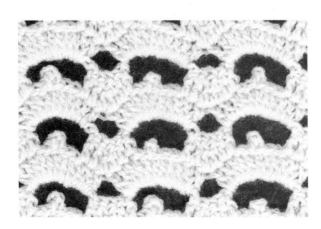

150. Chain multiples of 11 plus 1.

Row 1: 1 sc in the 2nd ch, ch 3, 1 sc in the 3rd ch, and in the next 4 chs, * ch 8, 1 sc in the 7th ch, sc in each of the next 4 chs, rep from *, ending row with 3 chs and 1 sc in the last ch, ch 3 and turn.

Row 2: 5 dc around the 3-ch, * 6 dc around the 8-ch, 1 picot, 5 dc around the 8-ch, rep from *, ending the row with 6 dc in the last 3 chs, ch 6 and turn.

Row 3: 1 dc in the 4th dc, * 1 dc in the next dc, finish off 2 dc together in the next 2 dc, 1 dc in the next dc and the 1 after that, ch 8, 1 dc in the 6th dc, rep from *, ending row with 3 chs and 1 dc in the turning ch, ch 3 and turn.

Pattern formed by rep rows 1–3.

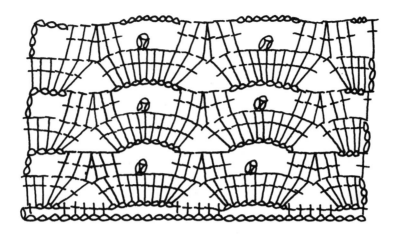

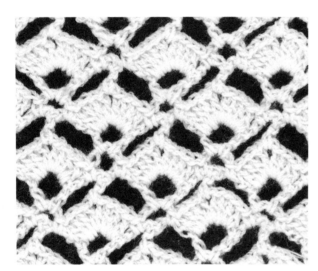

151. Chain multiples of 13 plus 5.

Row 1: 1 dc in the 4th ch, * ch 4, 1 dc in the 6th ch, ch 4, 1 dc in the 6th dc, ch 4, 1 dc in the same ch, rep from *, ending row with 4 chs and 1 dc in the 6th and last ch, ch 5 and turn.

Row 2: * 1 sc around the 4-ch, 4 dc around the next 4-ch, ch 2, 4 dc around the same 4-ch, 1 sc around the next 4-ch, ch 4, rep from *, ending row with 4 dc in the turning ch and 1 trc, ch 7 and turn.

Row 3: * 1 dc around the 4-ch, ch 4, 1 dc around the same 4-ch, ch 4, 1 dc around the 2-ch, ch 4, rep from *, ending row with 1 dc, 1 ch and 1 dc in the turning ch, ch 4 and turn.

Row 4: 4 dc in the 1-ch, * 1 sc around the 1st 4-ch, ch 4, 1 sc around the next 4-ch, 4 dc around the next 4-ch, ch 2, 4 dc around the same 4-ch, rep from *, ending row with 1 sc in the turning ch, 2 chs and 1 dc in the turning ch.

Pattern formed by rep rows 1–4.

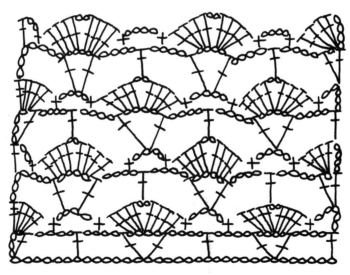

◆ *11* ◆
Shells and Chains

152. Chain multiples of 3 plus 3.

Row 1: 1 sc in the 4th ch, * ch 3, 1 sc in the 3rd ch, rep from *,
ending row with last sc, ch 3 and turn.
Row 2: 2 dc in the 1st sc, * 1 sc around the middle of the 3-ch, 3 dc
in the next sc, rep from *, ending row with 2 dc in the last sc, ch 1
and turn.
Row 3: Same as row 1, except that the sc is worked in the middle
dc.
Pattern formed by rep rows 1–2.

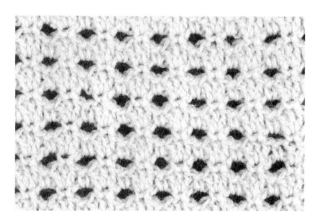

153. Chain multiples of 4 plus 1.

Row 1: 1 sc in 2nd ch, * ch 5, 1 sc in 4th ch, rep from *, ending row with 1 sc in last ch, ch 3 and turn.
Row 2: 2 dc in 1st sc, * 1 sc around the middle of the 5-ch, 2 dc in next sc, ch 1, 2 dc in the same sc, rep from *, ending row with 3 dc in the end sc, ch 1 and turn.
Row 3: Same as row 1, except that the sc is made in the 1-ch.
Pattern formed by rep rows 1–2.

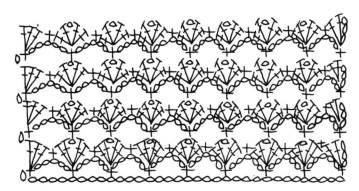

154. Chain multiples of 4 plus 1.

Row 1: 1 sc in the 2nd ch, ch 5, * 1 sc in the 4th ch, ch 5, rep from *, ending row with 1 sc, ch 4 and turn.
Row 2: * 5 dc around the middle of the 5-ch, rep from *, ending row after last set with 1 trc, ch 1 and turn.
Row 3: Same as row 1, but sc worked between the 2 sets.
Pattern formed by rep rows 1–2.

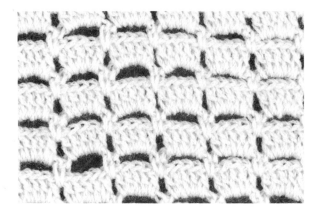

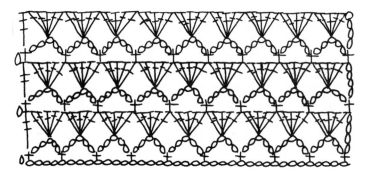

155. Chain multiples of 5 plus 4.

Row 1: 2 dc in the 4th ch, * 2 dc in the 5th ch, ch 3, 2 dc in the same ch, rep from *, ending row with 3 dc in the last ch, ch 5 and turn.
Row 2: * 1 dc between the sets, ch 4, rep from *, ending row with 2 chs and 1 dc in the turning ch, ch 3 and turn.
Row 3: * 2 dc in the 2nd dc, ch 3, 2 dc in the same dc, rep from *, ending row with 1 dc in the turning ch after the last set, ch 7 and turn.
Row 4: * 1 dc between the sets, ch 4, rep from *, ending row with 4 chs and 1 dc in the turning ch.
Pattern formed by rep rows 1–4.

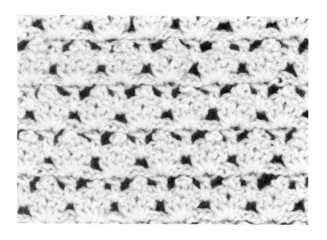

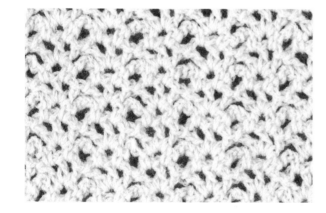

156. Chain multiples of 5 plus 3.

Row 1: 1 dc in the 7th ch, * ch 2, 1 dc in the same ch, ch 2, 1 dc in the same ch, 1 dc in the 5th ch, rep from *, ending row with 1 hdc in the 3rd and final ch, ch 4 and turn.
Row 2: * 1 sc in the 2-ch, ch 3, 1 sc in the next 2-ch, ch 4, rep from *, ending row with 1 hdc in the turning ch, ch 3 and turn.
Row 3: Same as row 1, except that the dc are worked in the 3-ch.
Pattern formed by rep rows 1–2.

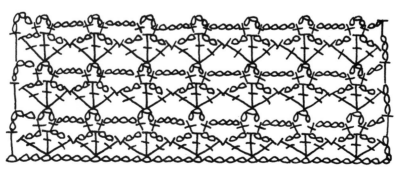

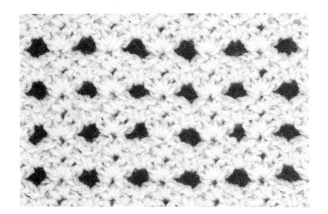

157. Chain multiples of 5 plus 4.

Row 1: 2 dc in the 7th ch, * ch 1, 2 dc in the same ch, 2 dc in the 5th ch, rep from *, ending row with last set and 1 dc in the 3rd and last ch, ch 1 and turn.
Row 2: 1 sc in the 1st dc, * 1 sc before the next set, ch 2, 1 sc in the 1-ch, ch 3, 1 sc in the same 1-ch, ch 2, rep from *, ending row with 2 sc in the turning ch, ch 3 and turn.
Row 3: Same as row 1, except that the 2 dc and the ch are worked in the 3-ch.
Pattern formed by rep rows 1–2.

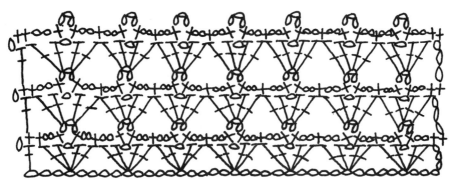

158. Chain multiples of 12 plus 1.

Row 1: 1 sc in the 2nd ch, * ch 5, 1 sc in the 4th ch, rep from *, ending row with 2 chs and 1 dc in the 2nd ch, ch 1 and turn.
Row 2: 1 sc in the 1st dc, * 7 dc around the next 5-ch, 1 sc around the middle of the next 5-ch, ch 5, 1 sc around the next 5-ch, rep from *, ending row after last set with 2 chs and 1 trc in the sc, ch 1 and turn.
Row 3: Same as row 1, except that the sc are worked in the 2nd dc and the 4th dc and around the middle of the 5-ch between the shells.
Pattern formed by rep rows 1–2.

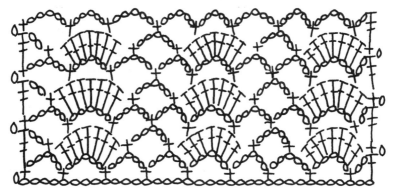

159. Chain multiples of 16 plus 6.

Row 1: 1 sc in the 8th ch, * ch 5, 1 sc in the 4th ch, rep from *, ending row with last sc, 2 chs and 1 dc in the 2nd ch, ch 1 and turn.

Row 2: 1 sc in the dc, * ch 5, 1 sc around the middle of the 5-ch, ch 5, 1 sc around the middle of the next 5-ch, 8 dc around the next 5-ch, 1 sc around the next 5-ch, rep from *, ending row with 1 sc in the turning ch, ch 5 and turn.

Row 3: 1 sc around the 5-ch, * ch 4, 1 dc in the 2nd dc and in the next 5 dc, ch 4, 1 sc around the 5-ch, ch 5, 1 sc around the 5-ch, rep from *, ending row with last sc, 2 chs and 1 dc in the sc, ch 1 and turn.

Row 4: 1 sc in the 1st dc, * ch 5, 1 sc around the 5-ch, ch 5, 1 sc around the middle of the 4-ch, ch 3, 1 dc in the 2nd dc and the 3 dc after that, ch 3, 1 sc around the 4-ch, rep from *, ending row with last sc in the turning ch, ch 5 and turn.

Row 5: * 1 sc around the 5-ch, ch 5, 1 sc in the 3-ch, ch 3, 1 dc in the 2nd dc, 1 dc in the next dc, ch 3, 1 sc in the 3-ch, ch 5, 1 sc in the 5-ch, ch 5, rep from *, ending row with last sc, 2 chs and 1 dc in the sc, ch 1 and turn.

Row 6: 1 sc in the dc, * 8 dc in the 5-ch, 1 sc around the 5-ch, ch 5, 1 sc in the last ch, ch 5, 1 sc in the 5-ch, rep from *, ending row with 4 dc in the turning ch, ch 3 and turn.

Row 7: 1 dc in the 2nd and next dc, * ch 4, 1 sc in the 5-ch, ch 5, 1 sc in the 5-ch, ch 4, 1 dc in the 2nd dc and the 5 dc after that, rep from *, ending row with last set, 1 ch and 1 dc in the sc, ch 5 and turn.

Row 8: 1 sc in the 1-ch, * ch 3, 1 dc in the 2nd dc and the 3 after that, ch 3, 1 sc in the 4-ch, ch 5, 1 sc in the 5-ch, ch 5, 1 sc in the 4-ch, rep from *, ending row with 1 dc in the last dc and 1 in the turning ch, ch 6 and turn.

Row 9: * 1 sc in the 3-ch, ch 5, 1 sc in the 5-ch, ch 5, 1 sc in the 5 ch, ch 5, 1 sc in the 3-ch, ch 3, 1 dc in the 2nd dc and the dc after that, ch 3, rep from *, ending row with last set, 2 chs and 1 dc, ch 1 and turn.

Pattern formed by rep rows 1–9.

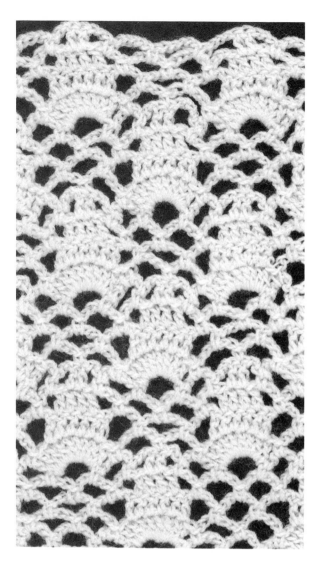

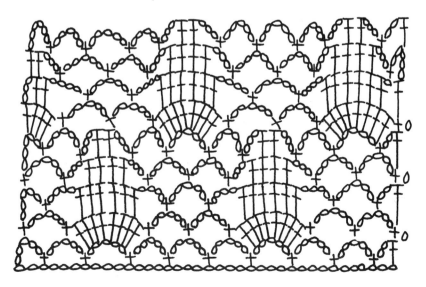

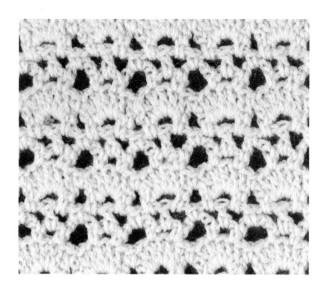

160. Chain multiples of 6 plus 6.

Row 1: 1 sc in the 8th ch, * ch 3, 1 sc in the 3rd ch, ch 5, 1 sc in the 3rd ch, rep from *, ending row with last set of 3 chs, 1 sc, 2 chs and 1 dc in the 2nd ch, ch 1 and turn.
Row 2: 1 sc in the 1st dc, * ch 2, 1 dc in the 3-ch, ch 2, 1 sc around the 5-ch, rep from *, ending row with 1 sc in the turning ch, ch 5 and turn.
Row 3: 1 sc around the 2-ch, * ch 3, 1 sc around the next 2-ch, ch 5, 1 sc around the next 2-ch, rep from *, ending row with 2 chs and 1 dc, ch 1 and turn.
Row 4: 1 sc in the 1st dc, * 5 dc around the 3-ch, 1 sc around the middle of the 5-ch, rep from *, ending row with last set and 1 sc, ch 5 and turn.
Row 5: Same as row 1, except that the sc are formed in the 2nd and the 4th dc of the set of 5.
Pattern formed by rep rows 1–4.

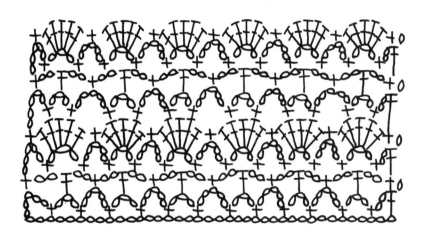

'161. Chain multiples of 14 plus 4.

Row 1: 2 dc in the 4th ch, * 1 dc in the 3rd ch, ch 7, 1 dc in the 8th ch, 5 dc in the 3rd ch, rep from *, ending row with last set and 3 dc in the last ch.
Row 2: 2 dc in the 1st dc, * 1 dc in the 3rd dc, ch 7, 1 dc in the next dc, 5 dc in the middle of the 5 dc, rep from *, ending row with 3 dc in the turning ch, ch 3 and turn.
Row 3: 2 dc in the 1st dc, * 1 dc in the 3rd dc, ch 3, 1 sc all around the 3 rows of chs below, gather them and finish off the sc, ch 3, 1 dc in the next dc, 5 dc in the middle of the 5 dc, rep from *, ending row with 3 dc in the turning ch, ch 3 and turn.
Row 4: 2 dc in the 1st dc, * 1 dc in the 3rd dc, ch 7, 1 dc in the next dc, 5 dc in the middle of the 5 dc, rep from *, ending row with 3 dc in the turning ch, ch 3 and turn.
Pattern formed by rep rows 1–4.

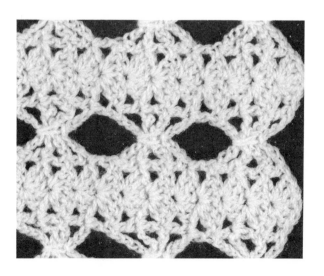

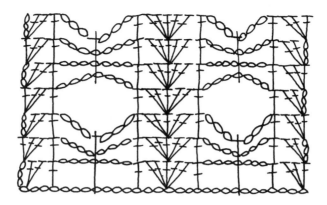

162. Chain multiples of 8 plus 1.

Row 1: 1 sc in 2nd ch, * ch 5, 1 sc in the 4th ch, rep from *, ending row with 1 sc, ch 4 and turn.

Row 2: * 1 sc around the middle of the 3rd ch, ch 3, rep from *, ending row after last set with 1 ch and 1 dc, ch 3 and turn.

Row 3: 2 dc around 1st 1-ch, * 1 sc around the middle of the 3-ch, 5 dc around the next 3-ch, rep from *, ending row after last sc, with 3 dc around turning ch, ch 4 and turn.

Row 4: 1 dc in 2nd dc, ch 1, 1 dc in next dc, ch 1, * 1 sc in sc, ch 1, 1 dc in next dc, ch 1, dc in dc, ch 1, dc in dc, ch 1, dc in dc, ch 1 and dc in last dc, ch 1, rep from *, ending row with 3 dc, spaced between chs in the last 2 dc and the turning ch, ch 5 and turn.

Row 5: 1 sc in 2nd dc, * ch 5, 1 sc in 2nd dc of the new set, ch 5, 1 sc in the 2nd dc of the set, rep from *, ending row with 2 chs and 1 dc in the turning ch, ch 1 and turn.

Row 6: 1 sc in 1st dc, ch 3, * 1 sc in the middle of the 5-ch, ch 3, rep from *, ending row with 3 chs and 1 sc in the turning ch, ch 2 and turn.

Row 7: 5 dc around 1st 3-ch, * 1 sc around next 3-ch, 5 dc around next 3-ch, rep from *, ending row with 1 sc and 1 dc, ch 3 and turn.

Row 8: 1 dc in 1st dc, * ch 1, 1 sc in sc, ch 1, 1 dc in 1st dc, 1 ch, 1 dc in next dc, 1 ch, 1 dc in next dc, 1 ch, 1 dc in next dc, ch 1, 1 dc in next dc, rep from *, row ending with dc, ch 1 and turn.

Pattern formed by rep rows 1–8.

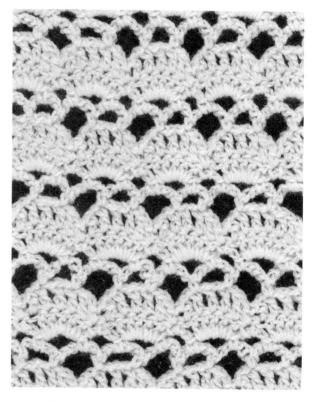

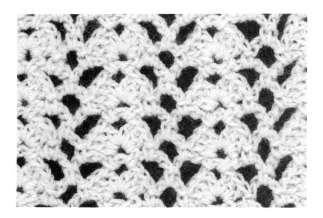

163. Chain multiples of 12 plus 1.

Row 1: 1 sc in the 2nd ch, * ch 4, 1 sc in the 4th ch, rep from *, ending row with 1 sc in the turning ch, ch 4 and turn.
Row 2: * 1 sc in the middle of the 4-ch, 3 dc in the next 4-ch, ch 3, 3 dc around the same 4-ch, 1 sc in the middle of the next 4-ch, ch 4, rep from *, ending row with 1 sc, 1 ch and 1 dc in the last sc, ch 1 and turn.
Row 3: Same as row 1, except sc worked in the 1st ch of the 3-ch and the last ch of the 3-ch and in the middle of the 4-ch.
Pattern formed by rep rows 1–2.

164. Chain multiples of 12 plus 4.

Row 1: 2 dc in 4th ch, * ch 3, 1 sc in 4th ch, ch 5, 1 sc in 4th ch, ch 3, 2 dc in 4th ch, ch 1, 2 dc in ch just used, rep from *, ending row with 3 dc in the last ch, ch 3 and turn.
Row 2: 2 dc in the 1st dc, * 1 dc around the 1st 3-ch, ch 3, 1 sc around the next 5-ch, ch 3, 1 dc around the 3-ch, 2 dc, 1 ch and 2 dc around the 1-ch between the 2 dc of the row below, rep from *, ending row with 3 dc in turning ch, ch 3 and turn.
Row 3: Same as row 1, but the sc should be made just after the dc, ch 5 and the next sc should be made just before the double ch.
Pattern formed by rep rows 1–2.

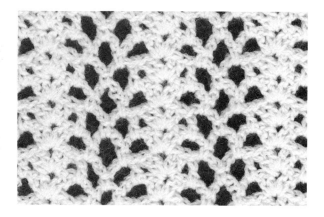

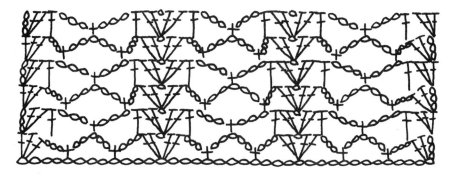

165. Chain multiples of 8 plus 4.

Row 1: 1 sc in the 6th ch, * ch 3, 1 sc in the 4th ch, rep from *, ending row with 1 ch and 1 hdc, ch 1.

Row 2: 1 sc in the hdc, * ch 1, 1 dc in the 1st 3-ch, ch 1, 1 dc in the same 3-ch, ch 1, 1 dc in the same 3-ch, ch 1, 1 dc in the same 3-ch, ch 1, 1 sc in the next 3-ch, rep from *, ending row with last set and 1 sc in the turning ch, ch 4 and turn.

Row 3: Same as row 1, except that the 1st sc is worked in the 2nd 1-ch and the 2nd sc is worked in the 2nd 1-ch.

Pattern formed by rep rows 1–2.

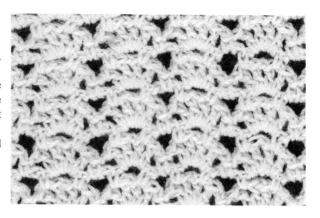

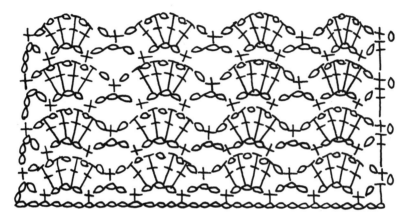

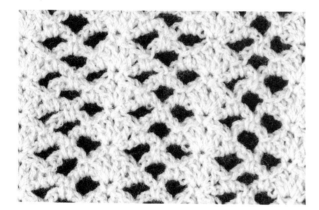

166. Chain multiples of 8 plus 1.

Row 1: 1 sc in the 2nd ch, * ch 5, 1 sc in the 4th ch, rep from *, ending row with last set, ch 6 and turn.

Row 2: * 1 sc around the middle of the 5-ch, 2 dc in the next sc, ch 1, 2 dc in the same sc, 1 sc around the middle of the 5-ch, ch 5, rep from *, ending row with last set, 1 sc around the middle of the 5-ch, ch 2 and 1 trc in the sc, ch 1 and turn.

Pattern formed by rep rows 1–2.

Shells—Overall Patterns 141

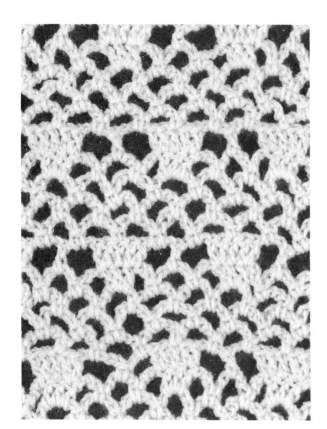

167. Chain multiples of 12 plus 5.

Row 1: 1 sc in the 7th ch, * ch 5, 1 sc in the 4th ch, ch 3, 3 dc in the 4th ch, ch 3, 1 sc in the 4th ch, rep from *, ending row with 2 ch and 1 hdc in the 2nd ch, ch 6 and turn.

Row 2: * 1 dc around the middle of the 5-ch, ch 3, 2 dc in the 1st dc, 1 dc in the next dc, 2 dc in the next dc, ch 3, rep from *, ending row with 3 chs and 1 dc in the turning ch, ch 4 and turn.

Row 3: * 1 sc in the 3-ch, ch 5, 1 sc in the next 3-ch, ch 5, 1 sc in the 3rd dc, ch 5, rep from *, ending row with 1 sc in the turning ch, ch 2, 1 hdc in the turning ch, ch 1 and turn.

Row 4: 1 sc in the hdc, * ch 5, 1 sc around the next 5-ch, rep from *, ending row with 1 sc in the turning ch, ch 5 and turn.

Row 5: * 1 sc around the 5-ch, ch 5, rep from *, ending row with 1 sc around the last 5-ch, ch 2, 1 dc in the last sc, ch 1 and turn.

Row 6: 1 sc in the dc, * ch 3, 3 dc in the next 5-ch, ch 3, 1 sc around the next 5-ch, ch 5, 1 sc in the next 5-ch, rep from *, ending row with last set, 3 chs and 1 sc in the turning ch, ch 4 and turn.

Row 7: * 2 dc in the 1st dc, 1 dc in the next dc, 2 dc in the next dc, ch 3, 1 dc around the middle of the 5-ch, ch 3, rep from *, ending row with 1 ch and 1 dc in the sc, ch 1 and turn.

Row 8: 1 sc in the 1st dc, * ch 5, 1 sc in the 3rd dc, ch 5, 1 sc around the 3-ch, ch 5, 1 sc around the next 3-ch, rep from *, ending row with last 5-ch and a sc in the turning ch, ch 5 and turn.

Pattern formed by rep rows 1–8.

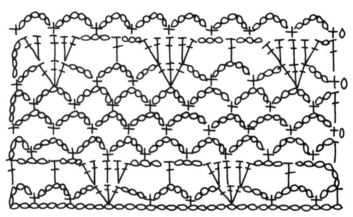

168. Chain multiples of 6 plus 2.

Row 1: 2 dc in the 6th ch, * ch 2, 2 dc in the same ch, 2 dc in the 6th ch, rep from *, ending row with 1 dc in the 3rd ch after the last set, ch 1 and turn.

Row 2: 1 sc in the 1st dc, * ch 3, 1 dc in the 2-ch, ch 3, 1 sc between the 2 sets of dc, rep from *, ending row with 1 sc, ch 4 and turn.

Pattern formed by rep rows 1–2.

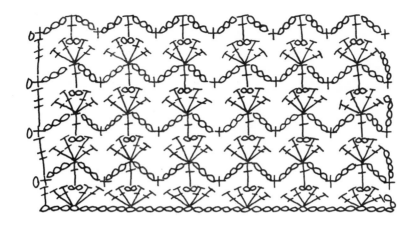

169. Chain multiples of 17 plus 1.

Row 1: 1 sc in 2nd ch, * ch 5, 1 sc in 5th ch, 1 dc in 3rd ch, ch 1, 1 dc in same ch, ch 1, 1 dc in same ch, 1 sc in the 3rd ch, 1 dc in the 3rd ch, ch 1, 1 dc in the same ch, ch 1, 1 dc in the same ch, 1 sc in the 3rd ch, rep from *, ending row with 5 chs and 1 sc, ch 5 and turn.

Row 2: * 1 sc around the middle of the 5-ch, ch 5, 1 sc in the middle of the 3 dc, 1 dc in the next sc, ch 1, 1 dc in the same sc, ch 1, 1 dc in the same stitch, 1 sc in the same dc, ch 5, rep from *, ending row with 2 chs and 1 dc in the turning ch, ch 1 and turn. Pattern formed by rep rows 1–2.

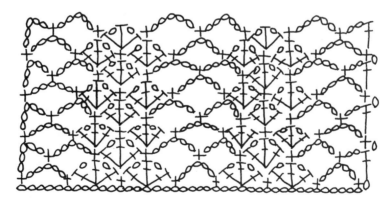

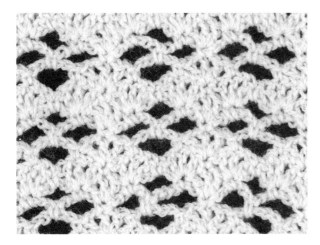

170. Chain multiples of 8 plus 1.

Row 1: 1 sc in the 2nd ch, * ch 5, 1 sc in the 4th ch, rep from *, ending row with last set, ch 5 and turn.

Row 2: * 1 sc around the middle of the 5-ch, 1 dc in the sc, ch 1, 1 dc in the same sc, ch 1, 1 dc in the same ch, 1 sc around the middle of the next 5-ch, ch 5, rep from *, ending row with 3 chs and 1 dc, ch 1 and turn.

Row 3: 1 sc in the 1st dc, * 1 dc in the next sc, ch 1, 1 dc in the same sc, ch 1, 1 dc in the same sc, 1 sc in the 2nd dc, rep from *, ending row with 1 sc after the last set, ch 5 and turn.

Row 4: 1 sc in the 2nd dc, * 1 dc in the 1st sc, ch 1, 1 dc in the same sc, ch 1, 1 dc in the same sc, 1 sc in the 2nd dc, ch 5, 1 sc in the 2nd dc, rep from *, ending row with 2 chs and 1 dc, ch 1 and turn.
Pattern formed by rep rows 1–4.

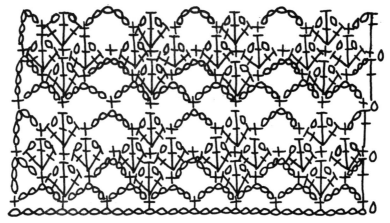

171. Chain multiples of 12 plus 1.

Row 1: 1 sc in 2nd ch, * ch 7, 1 sc in 6th ch, rep from *, ending row with 1 sc, ch 8 and turn.

Row 2: 1 dc in 2nd sc, * ch 5, 1 dc in next sc, rep from *, ending row with 1 dc in the last sc, ch 6 and turn.

Row 3: * 1 sc around chs from 2 rows underneath, having a gathering effect, ch 3, 1 dc in dc, ch 3, rep from *, ending row with 1 dc in turning ch, ch 1 and turn.

Row 4: * 1 sc in 1st dc, 5 dc in the sc, 1 sc in dc, ch 2, 1 dc in the sc, ch 2, rep from *, ending row with 1 sc in turning ch.
Pattern formed by rep rows 1–4.

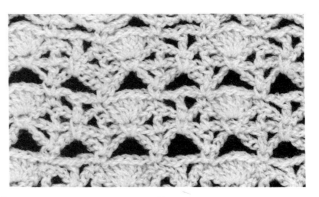

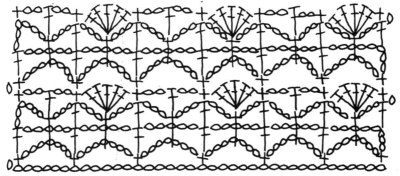

· *12* ·
Shells—Staggered

172. Chain multiples of 8 plus 1.

Row 1: 1 sc in 1st ch, * ch 4, sc in 4th ch, ch 3, 2 dc in same ch as the sc, 1 sc in 4th ch, rep from *, ending with 1 sc in last ch, ch 5 and turn.

Row 2: * 1 sc in the top of the next ch, ch 3, 2 dc in the top of the sc just formed—1 sc in the middle of the 4-ch in row below, ch 4, rep from *, ending row with 1 sc in the middle of the 4-ch, 2 chs, 1 dc in sc, ch 1 and turn.

Pattern formed by rep rows 1–2.

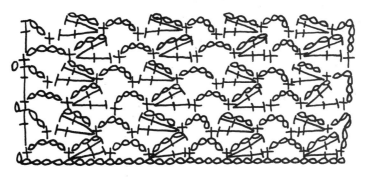

173. Chain multiples of 7 plus 5.

Row 1: 2 dc in the 5th ch, * ch 2, 1 sc in the 4th ch, ch 2, 1 trc and 2 dc in the 3rd ch, rep from *, ending row with 2 chs and 1 sc, ch 4 and turn.
Row 2: 2 dc in the sc, * ch 2, 1 sc in the top of the 2-ch, ch 2, 1 trc and 2 dc in the sc, rep from *, ending row with 2 chs and 1 sc in the turning ch, ch 4 and turn.
Pattern formed by rep rows 1–2.

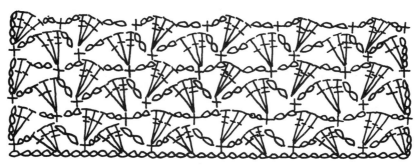

174. Chain multiples of 14 plus 7.

Row 1: 1 sc in the 10th ch, * ch 3, 3 dc in the same ch, 1 dc in the 4th ch, 3 dc in the 4th ch, ch 3, 1 sc in the same ch, ch 3, 1 dc in the 3rd ch, ch 3, 1 sc in the 3rd ch, rep from *, ending row with 1 dc in the 4th ch after the group, ch 1 and turn.
Row 2: 1 sc in the dc, ch 3, 1 sc in the top of the 3-ch, * ch 3, 1 sc in the dc, ch 3, 1 sc in the top of the 3-ch, rep from *, ending row with 1 sc in the turning ch, ch 6 and turn.
Pattern formed by rep rows 1–2.

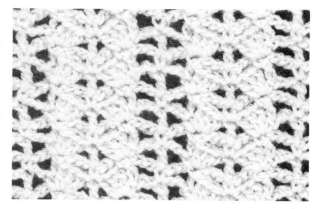

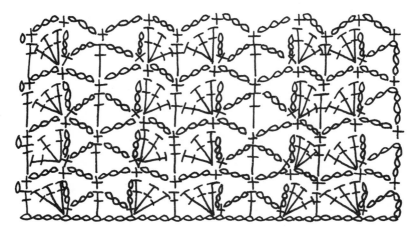

175. Chain multiples of 12 plus 4.

Row 1: 3 dc in the 4th ch, * 4 dc in the 6th ch, ch 4, 1 sc in the 3rd ch, ch 4, 4 dc in the 3rd ch, rep from *, ending row with 4 chs and 1 dc in the last ch, ch 8 and turn.
Row 2: * 1 sc in the 1st sc, ch 5, work 4 dc in the 1st dc, 4 dc in the 7th dc, ch 5, rep from *, ending row with last set, ch 7 and turn.
Row 3: * 1 sc between the 2 sets of 4 dc, ch 4, work 4 dc in the 4th dc, 4 dc in the next dc, ch 4, rep from *, ending row with 4 dc in the turning ch, ch 3 and turn.
Row 4: 3 dc in the 1st dc, * 4 dc in the 7th dc, ch 5, 1 sc in the sc, ch 5, 4 dc in the next dc, rep from *, ending row with 5 chs and 1 dc in the turning ch, ch 3 and turn.
Pattern formed by rep rows 1–4.

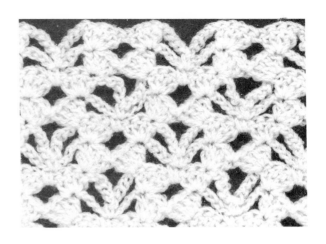

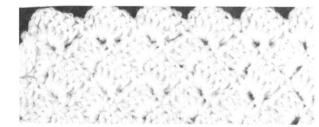

176. Chain multiples of 4 plus 1.

Row 1: 1 sc in the 2nd ch, * ch 2, 4 dc in the sc, 1 sc in the 4th ch, rep from *, ending row with 1 sc, ch 3 and turn.
Row 2: 2 dc in the 1st sc, * 1 sc in the top of the next 2-ch, ch 2, 4 dc in the sc just formed, rep from *, ending row with 1 sc in the turning ch, ch 3.
Pattern formed by rep rows 1–2.

Shells—Staggered 147

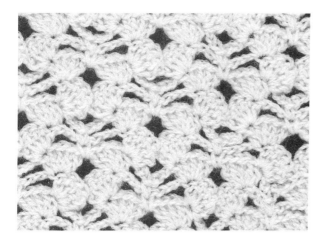

177. Chain multiples of 12 plus 1.

Row 1: 1 sc in 2nd ch, * ch 3, 5 dc in the 3rd ch, 5 dc in the 6th ch, ch 3, 1 sc in the 3rd ch, rep from *, ending row with 3 chs and 1 sc in the last ch, ch 1 and turn.
Row 2: 1 sc in the 1st sc, * ch 3, 5 dc in the 1st dc, 5 dc in the 9th dc, ch 3, 1 sc in the sc, rep from *, ending row with 3 chs and 1 sc in the last sc, ch 2 and turn.
Row 3: 5 dc in the 1st dc, * ch 3, 1 sc between the 2 sets of 5 dc, ch 3, 5 dc in the 5th dc, 5 dc in the next dc, rep from *, ending row with 5 dc in the last dc and 1 dc in the last sc, ch 3 and turn.
Row 4: 5 dc in the 5th dc, * ch 3, 1 sc in the next sc, ch 3, 5 dc in the next dc, rep from *, ending row with 5 dc in the 9th dc and 1 trc in the turning ch, ch 1 and turn.
Pattern formed by rep rows 1–4.

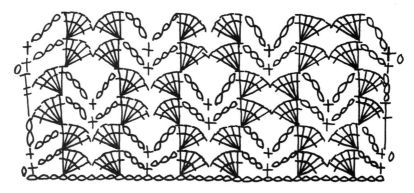

178. Chain multiples of 5 plus 4.

Row 1: 4 dc in the 7th ch, * ch 3, 1 dc in the same ch, 4 dc in the 5th ch, rep from *, ending row after last set with 1 dc, ch 3 and turn.
Row 2: * 4 dc in the 3-ch, ch 3, 1 dc in the same ch, rep from *, ending row after last set with 1 dc, ch 3 and turn.
Pattern formed by rep rows 1–2.

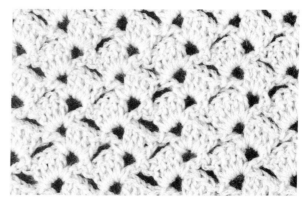

179. Chain multiples of 8 plus 4.

Row 1: 1 dc in the 4th ch, 4 dc in the 4th ch, * ch 3, 1 dc in the ch just used, dc in the 4th ch, ch 1, 1 dc in the ch just used, 4 dc in the 4th ch, rep from *, ending row with last set and 2 dc in the 4th and last chs, ch 3 and turn.

Row 2: 1 dc in the 1st dc, * 4 dc around the 3-ch, ch 3, 1 dc in the 3-ch just used, 1 dc in the next 1-ch, ch 1, 1 dc in the 1-ch just used, rep from *, ending row with 2 dc in the turning ch, ch 3 and turn.

Pattern formed by rep rows 1–2.

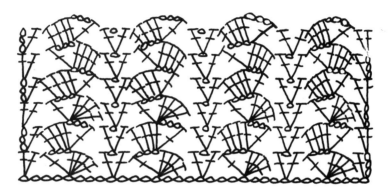

· *13* ·
Shells—Small Lace Patterns

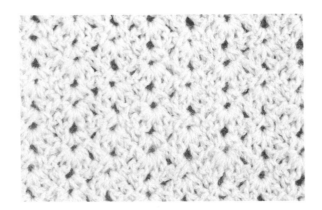

180. Chain multiples of 8 plus 4.

Row 1: 2 dc in the 4th ch, * 1 sc in the 4th ch, ch 3, 1 sc in the same ch, 2 dc in the 4th ch, ch 2, 2 dc in the same ch, rep from *, ending row with 3 dc in the end ch, ch 3 and turn.

Row 2: 1 sc in the 1st dc, * 2 dc in the 3-ch, ch 2, 2 dc in the same 3-ch, 1 sc in the 2-ch, ch 3, 1 sc in the 2-ch, rep from *, ending row with 1 ch and 1 hdc in the turning ch, ch 3 and turn.

Pattern formed by rep rows 1–2.

181. Chain multiples of 8 plus 1.

Row 1: 1 sc in the 2nd ch, * ch 2, 5 dc in the 4th ch, ch 2, 1 sc in the 4th ch, rep from *, ending row after the last set with a sc, ch 5 and turn.

Row 2:* 1 sc in the 1st dc, ch 3, 1 sc in the next dc, ch 3, 1 sc in the 2nd dc, ch 3, 1 sc in the last dc of the set, ch 5 and turn, rep from *, ending row with 2 chs and 1 dc in the sc, ch 3 and turn.

Row 3: 2 dc in the 1st dc, * ch 2, 1 sc around the middle of the 2nd 3-ch, ch 2, 5 dc around the middle of the 5-ch, rep from *, ending row with 3 dc in the turning ch, ch 5 and turn.

Row 4: 1 sc in the 2nd dc, ch 3, 1 sc in the next dc, * ch 5, 1 sc in the next dc, ch 3, 1 sc in the next dc, ch 3, 1 sc in the 2nd dc, ch 3, 1 sc in the next dc, rep from *, ending row with 2 chs and 1 dc in the turning ch.

Pattern formed by rep rows 1–4.

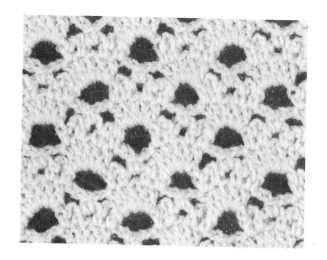

182. Chain multiples of 12 plus 6.

Row 1: 1 dc in the 5th ch, * 1 sc in the 4th ch and in the next 4th ch, 1 dc in the 4th ch, ch 2, 1 dc in the same dc, ch 2, 1 dc in the same ch, rep from *, ending row with 1 dc, 2 chs and 1 dc in the same ch, ch 3 and turn.

Row 2: 4 dc around the 2-ch, * 1 sc in the 2nd sc and in the next 2 sc, 4 dc around the next 2-ch, 1 dc in the dc, 4 dc around the next 2-ch, rep from *, ending row with 5 dc around the turning ch, ch 1 and turn.

Row 3: 1 sc in the 1st and next 2 dc, * 1 dc in the 2nd sc, ch 2, 1 dc in the same sc, ch 2, 1 dc in the same ch, 1 sc in the 3rd dc and the next 4 dc, rep from *, ending row with 2 sc in the last 2 dc and 1 in the turning ch, ch 1 and turn.

Row 4: 1 sc in the 1st and 2nd sc, * 4 dc around the 2-ch, 1 dc in the dc, 4 dc around the 2-ch, 1 sc in the 2nd sc and the next 2 after that, rep from *, ending row with sc in the last 2 sc.

Pattern formed by rep rows 1–4.

Shells—Small Lace Patterns 151

183. Chain multiples of 12 plus 5.

Row 1: 1 sc in the 8th ch, * 1 dc in the 4th ch, ch 2, 1 dc in the same ch, ch 2, 1 dc in the same ch, ch 2, 1 dc in the same ch, 1 sc in the 4th ch, ch 5, 1 sc in the 4th ch, rep from *, ending row with last set, 1 sc in the 4th ch, ch 2 and 1 dc in the 2nd ch, ch 4 and turn.
Row 2: 1 sc in the 2-ch, * 3 dc in the 2-ch, ch 2, 3 dc in the next 2-ch, ch 2, 3 dc in the next 2-ch, 1 sc in the 5-ch, ch 3, 1 sc in the same 5-ch, rep from *, ending row with last set, 1 sc in the turning ch, 1 ch and 1 hdc, ch 4 and turn.
Row 3: 1 dc in the 1-ch, ch 2, 1 dc in the same 1-ch, * 1 sc in the 2-ch, ch 5, 1 sc in the next 2-ch, 1 dc in the 3-ch, ch 2, 1 dc in the same 3-ch, ch 2, 1 dc in the same 3-ch, ch 2, 1 dc in the same 3-ch, rep from *, ending row with 1 dc in the turning ch, ch 2, 1 dc in the same turning ch, ch 1 and work last dc in the turning ch, ch 3 and turn.
Row 4: 1 dc in the 1-ch, ch 2, 3 dc in the 2-ch, * 1 sc in the 5-ch, ch 3, 1 sc in the same 5-ch, 3 dc in the 2-ch, ch 2, 3 dc in the next 2-ch, ch 2, 3 dc in the next 2-ch, rep from *, ending row with 3 dc in the 2-ch, ch 2 and 2 dc in the turning ch, ch 5 and turn.
Pattern formed by rep rows 1–4.

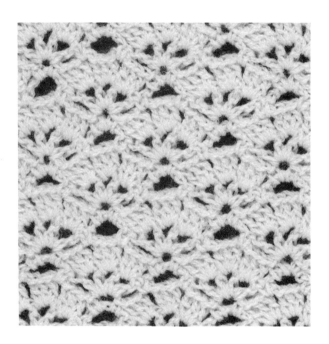

184. Chain multiples of 9 plus 5.

Row 1: 1 sc in the 7th ch, * 5 dc in the 3rd ch, 1 sc in the 3rd ch, ch 3, 1 sc in the 3rd ch, rep from *, ending row with 1 sc, 1 ch and 1 dc in the 2nd ch, ch 1 and turn.
Row 2: 1 sc in the 1st dc, * 1 dc in the dc, 1 dc in the next dc, ch 3, 1 sc in the next dc, ch 3, 1 dc in the next dc and the dc after that, 1 sc around the 3-ch, rep from *, ending row with 1 sc in the turning ch, ch 3 and turn.
Row 3: 2 dc in the 1st sc, * 1 sc around the 3-ch, ch 3, 1 sc around the next 3-ch, 5 dc in the next sc, rep from *, ending row with 3 dc in the sc, ch 1 and turn.
Row 4: 1 sc in the 1st dc, * ch 3, 1 dc in the next dc, 1 dc in the dc after that, 1 sc around the middle of the 3-ch, 1 dc in the next dc and the dc after that, ch 3, 1 sc in the next dc, rep from *, ending row with 3 chs and 1 sc in the turning ch, ch 4 and turn.
Pattern formed by rep rows 1–4.

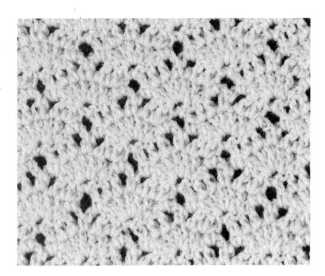

185. Chain multiples of 14 plus 4.

Row 1: 3 dc in the 5th ch, * 1 sc in the 4th ch, 5 dc in the 3rd ch, 1 sc in the 3rd ch, 7 dc in the 4th ch, rep from *, ending row with 4 dc in the 4th and last ch, ch 4 and turn.
Row 2: 1 dc in the 2nd dc, ch 1, 1 dc in the next dc, ch 1, 1 dc in the next dc, * ch 2, 1 sc in the 3rd dc, ch 2, 1 dc in the dc after the sc, ch 1 and dc in the next dc 6 times, rep from *, ending row with 1 dc in the turning ch, ch 3 and turn.
Row 3: Form a total of 6 dc in the next ch, dc, ch, dc, ch and dc, * ch 2, 1 dc in each dc and in each ch all across the set (totalling 13), rep from *, ending row with 2 dc in the turning ch, ch 3 and turn.
Row 4: 2 dc in the 1st dc, 1 sc in the 3rd dc, * 7 dc around the 2-ch, 1 sc in the 4th dc, 5 dc in the 3rd dc, 1 sc in the 3rd dc, rep from *, ending row with 3 dc in the turning ch, ch 1 and turn.
Row 5: 1 sc in the 1st dc, * ch 2, 1 dc in the next dc, ch 1 and dc in the dc 6 times, ch 2, 1 sc in the 3rd dc, rep from *, ending row with 1 sc in the turning ch, ch 3 and turn.
Row 6: * 1 dc in each dc and in each ch (totalling 13), ch 2, rep from *, ending row with 1 dc in the sc, ch 3 and turn.
Pattern formed by rep rows 1–6.

Shells—Small Lace Patterns 153

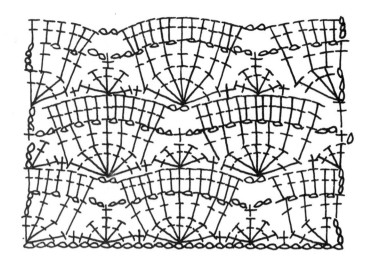

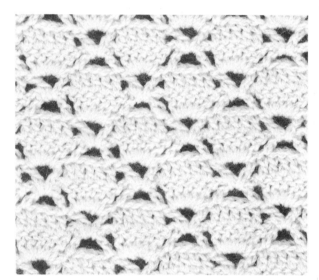

186. Chain multiples of 10 plus 4.

Row 1: 1 dc in 5th ch, 1 dc in next ch, * 1 dc in 3rd ch, ch 3, 1 dc in ch just used, 1 dc in 3rd ch and 1 dc in each of the next 4 chs, rep from *, ending row with 3 dc in each of the last 3 chs, ch 3 and turn.

Row 2: 1 dc in 3rd dc, * ch 2, 5 dc around the 3-ch, ch 2, begin 1 dc in the 1st dc and begin 2nd dc in 4th dc, then finish off both dc together, rep from *, ending row with 1 dc in dc and 1 dc in the turning ch, finished together, ch 4 and turn.

Row 3: 1 dc in the top of the 1st inverted V, * 1 dc in each of the next 5 dc, 1 dc in the top of the inverted V, ch 3, 1 dc in the same top of the inverted V as the 1st dc, rep from *, ending row with 1 dc, 1 ch and 1 more dc in the turning ch, ch 3 and turn.

Row 4: 2 dc in the 1-ch, * ch 2, begin 1 dc in 1st of the 5 dc, begin 2nd dc in 4th dc and finish off the 2 dc together, rep from *, ending row with 3 dc in the turning ch, ch 3 and turn.

Pattern formed by rep rows 1–4.

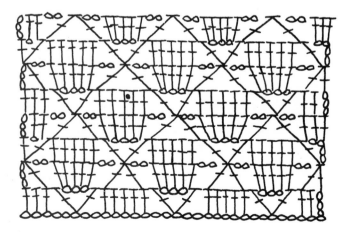

187. Chain multiples of 10 plus 1.

Row 1: 1 sc in the 2nd ch and 1 sc in the next ch, * ch 1, 1 dc in the 4th ch, ch 3, 1 dc in the ch just used, ch 1, 1 sc in the 4th ch and in the 2 chs following, rep from *, ending row with sc in the last 2 chs, ch 3 and turn.
Row 2: * 1 dc in the 1st dc, ch 1, 5 dc around the 3-ch, ch 1, 1 dc in the next dc, rep from *, ending row with 1 dc in the sc after the last set, ch 4 and turn.
Row 3: 1 dc in the 2nd dc, * ch 1, 1 sc in the 2nd dc and sc in the next 2 dc, ch 1, 1 dc in the 2nd dc, ch 3, 1 dc in the next dc, rep from *, ending row with 1 dc, 1 ch and 1 dc in the turning ch.
Row 4: 2 dc in the 1st 1-ch, * ch 1, 1 dc in the next dc, 1 dc in the next dc, ch 1, 5 dc around the 3-ch, rep from *, ending row with 3 dc in the turning ch, ch 1 and turn.
Pattern formed by rep rows 1–4.

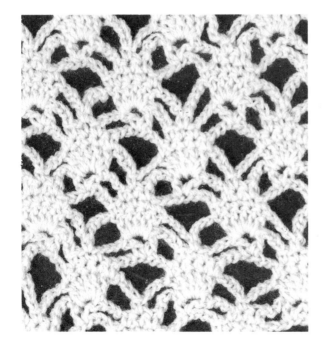

188. Chain multiples of 10 plus 1.

Row 1: 1 sc in the 2nd ch and the ch after that, * ch 3, 1 dc in the 4th ch, ch 2, 1 dc in the ch just used, ch 3, 1 sc in the 4th ch and in the 2 chs following, rep from *, ending row with sc in the last 2 chs, ch 1 and turn.
Row 2: 1 sc in the 1st sc, * ch 4, 5 dc around the 2-ch, ch 4, 1 sc in the 2nd sc, rep from *, ending row with 1 sc in the last sc, ch 7 and turn.
Row 3: * 1 sc in each of the 5 dc, ch 7, rep from *, ending row with 3 chs and 1 trc in the last sc, ch 3 and turn.
Row 4: 1 dc in the trc, * ch 3, 1 sc in the 2nd sc and the 2 sc following, ch 3, 1 dc around the middle of the 7-ch, ch 2, 1 dc around the same ch, rep from *, ending row with 2 dc in the turning ch, ch 3 and turn.
Row 5: 2 dc in the 1st dc, * ch 4, 1 sc in the 2nd sc, ch 4, 5 dc around the 2-ch, rep from *, ending row with 3 dc in the turning ch, ch 1 and turn.
Row 6: 1 sc in each of the next 3 dc, * ch 7, 1 sc in each of the next 5 dc, rep from *, ending row with 3 sc, the last 1 in the turning ch, ch 1 and turn.
Pattern formed by rep rows 1–6.

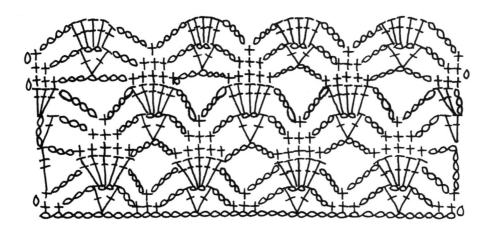

189. Chain multiples of 10 plus 4.

Row 1: 1 dc in the 5th ch, * ch 3, 1 sc in the 3rd ch, 1 sc in each of the next 2 chs, ch 3, 1 dc in the 3rd ch and in each of the 2 chs following, rep from *, ending row with 1 dc in each of the last 2 chs, ch 3 and turn.

Row 2: 2 dc in the 2nd dc, * ch 1, work 1 triple X-stitch in the 3rd sc, ch 1, trc backwards 2 sc, ch 1, 2 dc in the 1st dc, 1 dc in the next dc and 2 dc in the next dc, rep from *, ending row with 1 dc in the turning ch, ch 1 and turn.

Row 3: 1 sc in each of the 1st 2 dc, * ch 3, 3 dc in the 1-ch between the 2 sides of the X, ch 3, 1 sc in the 2nd dc and the 2 dc following, rep from *, ending row with 1 sc in the last dc and 1 sc in the turning ch, ch 2 and turn.

Row 4: 1 dc in the 2nd sc, ch 3, 1 dc in the dc just formed, * ch 1, 2 dc in the next dc, 1 dc in the next dc, 2 dc in the next dc, ch 1, work 1 triple X-stitch in the 3rd sc, ch 1, trc backwards 2 sc, rep from *, ending row with 1 triple X-stitch in the last 2 sc, ch 3 and turn.

Pattern formed by rep rows 1–4.

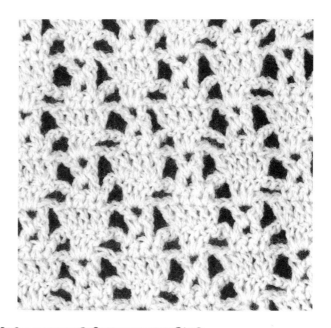

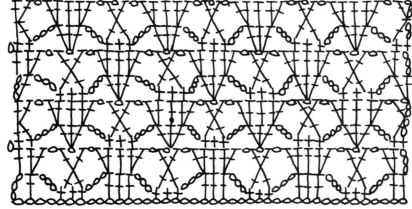

190. Chain multiples of 10 plus 4.

Row 1: 2 dc in the 5th ch, * ch 3, 1 sc in the 4th ch, ch 3, 2 dc in the 4th ch, 1 dc in the next ch, 2 dc in the ch following, rep from *, ending row with 2 dc in the second to the last ch, 1 dc in the last ch, ch 3 and turn.
Row 2: 1 dc in the 2nd dc, 1 dc in the next dc, * 2 dc in the 1st ch, ch 1, 2 dc in the last ch before the dc, 1 dc in each of the next 5 dc, rep from *, ending row with 2 dc in the last ch before the dc, 1 dc in each dc and 1 dc in the turning ch, ch 3 and turn.
Row 3: 1 dc in the 2nd dc and 1 dc in the next dc, * ch 3, 1 sc in the 1-ch, ch 3, 1 dc in the 3rd dc and in the next 4 dc, rep from *, ending row with 1 dc in the 3rd and next dc and 1 in the turning ch, ch 6 and turn.
Row 4: * 1 sc in the 1st ch, 5 dc in the sc, 1 sc in the last ch, ch 3, 1 dc in the 3rd dc, ch 3, rep from *, ending row with 3 chs and 1 dc in the turning ch, ch 3 and turn.
Pattern formed by rep rows 1–4.

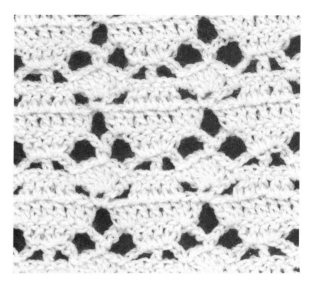

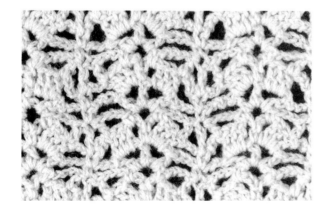

191. Chain multiples of 10 plus 1.

Row 1: 1 sc in 2nd ch, * ch 3, 1 dc in 5th ch, ch 3, 1 dc in same ch, ch 3, 1 dc in same ch, ch 3, 1 sc in 5th ch, rep from *, ending row with sc, ch 1 and turn.
Row 2: * sc in sc, ch 3, 3 dc in 2nd 3-ch, ch 3, 1 dc in dc, ch 3, 3 dc around next 3-ch, ch 3, rep from *, ending row with 1 sc, ch 3 and turn.
Row 3: * 1 dc in 1st dc, ch 3, 1 sc in the top of the 3-ch, ch 3, 1 sc in the top of the 3-ch, ch 3, 1 dc in the 3rd dc, 1 dc in the sc, rep from *, ending row with 1 dc in the sc, ch 1 and turn.
Pattern formed by rep rows 1–3.

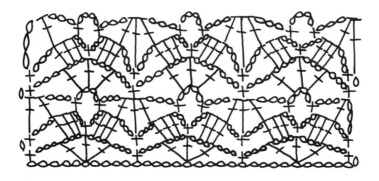

192. Chain multiples of 10 plus 4.

Row 1: 1 dc in the 5th ch and 1 dc in the ch after that, * ch 3, 1 sc in the 3rd ch, ch 3, 1 dc in the 3rd ch and also in the 4 chs following, rep from *, ending row with 3 dc, ch 3 and turn.

Row 2: 1 dc in the 2nd dc, * ch 3, 1 sc around the middle of the 3-ch, ch 3, 1 sc around the middle of the next 3-ch, ch 3, 1 dc in the 2nd dc and the 2 dc after that, rep from *, ending row with 2 dc, the last in the turning ch, ch 6 and turn.

Row 3: * 1 sc around the 3-ch, ch 3, 1 sc around the middle of the 3-ch, ch 3, 1 sc around the middle of the next 3-ch, ch 3, 1 dc in the 2nd dc, ch 3, rep from *, ending row with 1 dc in the turning ch, ch 3 and turn.

Row 4: 1 dc in the 1st dc, * ch 3, 1 sc in the middle of the 2nd 3-ch, ch 3, 1 sc around the middle of the next 3-ch, ch 3, work 3 dc in the dc, rep from *, ending row with 2 dc in the turning ch, ch 3 and turn.

Row 5: 2 dc in the 2nd dc, * ch 3, 1 sc in the middle of the 2nd 3-ch, ch 3, 2 dc in the 1st dc, 1 dc in the next dc, 2 dc in the next dc, rep from *, ending row with 2 dc and 1 dc in the turning ch, ch 1 and turn.

Row 6: 1 sc in each of the next 3 dc, * ch 2, 1 dc in the sc, ch 2, 1 sc in each of the next 5 dc, rep from *, ending row with 3 sc, the last in the turning ch, ch 1 and turn.

Row 7: 1 sc in the 1st sc, * ch 3, 1 dc around each of the 2-ch, 1 dc in the dc, 2 dc in the 2-ch, ch 3, 1 sc in the 3rd sc, rep from *, ending row with 3 chs and a sc in the sc, ch 5 and turn.

Row 8: 1 sc around the middle of the 3-ch, * ch 3, 1 dc in the 2nd dc and the 2 dc after that, ch 3, 1 sc around the middle of the next 3-ch, ch 3, 1 sc around the middle of the next 3-ch, rep from *, ending row with 1 sc around the 3-ch, ch 1 and 1 trc in the sc, ch 1 and turn.

Row 9: 1 sc in the 1st dc, * ch 3, 1 sc around the 3-ch, ch 3, 1 dc in the 2nd dc, ch 3, 1 sc around the 3-ch, ch 3, 1 sc around the 3-ch, rep from *, ending row with 1 sc in the turning ch, ch 5 and turn.

Row 10: 1 sc in the 3-ch, * ch 3, 3 dc in the dc, ch 3, 1 sc in the 3-ch, ch 3, 1 sc in the next 3-ch, rep from *, ending row with 1 sc, 1 ch and 1 trc in the sc, ch 1 and turn.

Row 11: 1 sc in the dc, * ch 3, 2 dc in the 1st dc, 1 dc in the next dc, 2 dc in the next dc, ch 3, 1 sc in the 2nd 3-ch, rep from *, ending row with 3 chs and 1 sc in the turning ch, ch 6 and turn.

Row 12: * 1 sc in each of the 5 dc, ch 2, 1 dc in the sc, ch 2, rep from *, ending row with 2 chs and 1 trc in the last sc.

Pattern formed by rep rows 1–12.

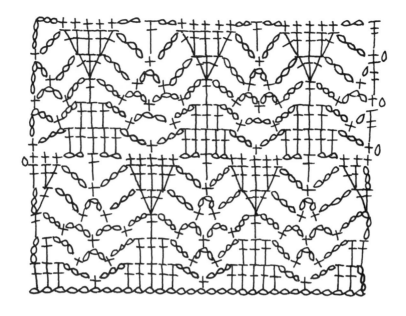

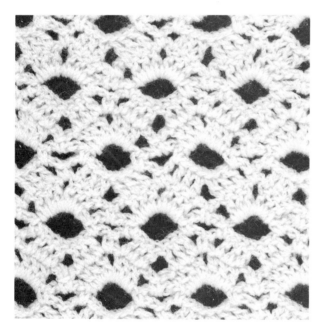

193. Chain multiples of 20 plus 5.

Row 1: 1 sc in the 8th ch, * ch 5, 1 sc in the 5th ch, rep from *, ending row with 2 chs and 1 hdc in the 3rd ch, ch 3 and turn.

Row 2: Work 3 dc around the 2-ch, * ch 2, 1 sc around the 5-ch, ch 2, work 3 dc in the next 5-ch, ch 2, work 3 dc in the same 5-ch, rep from *, ending row with 4 dc in the turning ch, ch 1 and turn.

Row 3: 1 sc in the 1st dc, * ch 3, work 1 dc in each of the next 3 dc, 3 dc worked 1 each in each of the next 3 dc, ch 3, 1 sc around the next 2-ch, rep from *, ending row with dc in the last 3 dc, ch 3 and 1 sc in the turning ch, ch 5 and turn.

Row 4: * 1 sc in the space between the top of the 3-ch and the dc, ch 5, 1 sc in between the next 3-ch and the dc, ch 5, rep from *, ending row with last sc, 2 chs and 1 dc in the last sc, ch 1 and turn.

Row 5: 1 sc in the dc, * ch 2, 3 dc in the 5-ch, ch 2, 3 dc in the same 5-ch, ch 2, 1 sc around the 5-ch, rep from *, ending row with sc in the turning ch, ch 3 and turn.

Row 6: * 1 dc in each of the 1st 3 dc, ch 3, 1 sc in the 2-ch, ch 3, 3 dc, 1 in each of the next 3 dc, rep from *, ending row with last set and 1 extra dc in the last sc, ch 5 and turn.

Pattern formed by rep rows 1–6.

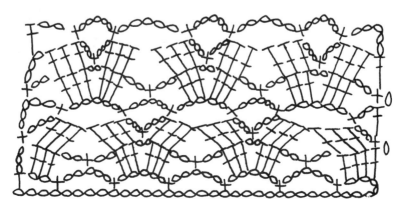

194. Chain multiples of 18 plus 4.

Row 1: 1 dc in the 5th ch and the 3 chs after that, * ch 2, 1 dc in the 5th ch, ch 1, 1 dc in the same ch, ch 1, 1 dc in the same ch, ch 1, 1 dc in the same ch, ch 2, 1 dc in the 5th ch and in the 8 chs following, rep from *, ending row with 5 dc, ch 3 and turn.

Row 2: 1 dc in the 2nd dc and in the 3 dc after that, * ch 2, 1 sc in the 1-ch, ch 3, 1 sc in the dc, 1 sc in the next 1-ch, ch 3, 1 sc in the next dc, 1 sc in the next 1-ch, ch 3, 1 sc in the next dc, ch 2, 1 dc in the next dc and the next 8 dc after that, rep from *, ending row with 4 dc and 1 in the turning ch, ch 3 and turn.

Row 3: 1 dc in the 2nd dc and the 3 following, rep row 1, all of the 4 dc in the lace section are worked in the middle of the middle 3-ch, ch 3 and turn.

Row 4: Same as row 2, ch 3 and turn.

Row 5: 1 dc, 1 ch and 1 dc in the 1st dc, * ch 2, 1 dc in the 2nd to the last dc, 1 dc in the next dc, 1 dc in the 2-ch, 1 in each of the 3-chs, 1 in the 2-ch, and 1 in each of the next 2 dc, ch 2, 1 dc and 1 ch 3 times, plus 1 extra dc in the same dc, rep from *, ending row with 1 dc, 1 ch and 2 dc in the turning ch, ch 3 and turn.

Row 6: 1 sc in the 2nd dc and the 1-ch, ch 3, 1 sc in the dc, ch 2, * 1 dc in each of the next 9 dc, ch 2, 1 sc in the 1-ch, ch 3, 1 sc in the dc, 1 sc in the 1-ch, ch 3, 1 sc in the dc, 1 sc in the 1-ch, ch 3, 1 sc in the last dc, ch 2, rep from *, ending row with 1 sc in the 1-ch, ch 3, 1 sc in the dc, ch 1, 1 hdc in the turning ch, ch 3 and turn.

Row 7: 1 dc in the 1-ch, ch 1, 1 dc in the 1-ch, * ch 2, 1 dc in each dc, ch 2, 1 dc and 1 ch in the middle 3-ch, 3 times, plus 1 dc in the same 3-ch, rep from *, ending row with 1 dc, 1 ch and 2 dc in the turning ch, ch 3 and turn.

Row 8: Same as row 6.

Pattern formed by rep rows 2–8.

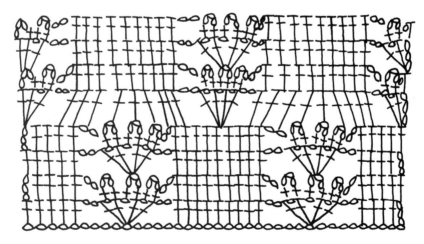

195. Chain multiples of 21 plus 4.

Row 1: 3 dc in the 6th ch, 3 dc in the 3rd ch, 3 dc in the 3rd ch, * ch 13, 3 dc in the 6th ch, 3 dc in the 3rd ch, rep 3 dc in the 3rd ch 4 more times, rep from *, ending row with 1 extra dc in the 2nd ch, ch 3 and turn.

Row 2: 1 dc in the 1st dc, 3 dc between the 2 sets of 3 dc, 3 dc in the space between the next 3 dc, * ch 6, 1 sc around the middle of the 1 3-ch, ch 6, work 3 dc together between the sets of 3 dc 5 times, rep from *, ending row with 2 dc in the turning ch, ch 3 and turn.

Row 3: 3 dc in the space between the 1st and 2nd sets of dc and between the next sets, * ch 6, 1 sc in the last ch before the sc, 1 in the sc and 1 in the 1st ch of the set of the next 6 chs, ch 6, rep 3 dc between the sets of 3 dc 4 times, rep from *, ending row with 1 dc in the turning ch, ch 3 and turn.

Row 4: 1 dc in the 1st dc, 3 dc between the sets, * ch 6, 1 sc around the last of the 6-ch, 1 sc in the next 3 sc, 1 sc in the 1st of the next 6-ch, ch 6, 3 dc in the space between the sets 3 times, rep from *, ending row with 2 dc in the turning ch, ch 3 and turn.

Row 5: 3 dc between 2 sets of dc, *, ch 6, 1 sc in the last of the 6-ch, 1 sc in each of next 5 sc, 1 sc in the 1st ch of the next 6, 3 dc between the 1st 2 sets, 3 dc between the next 2 sets, rep from *, ending row with 3 dc between last 2 sets, 1 dc in last ch, ch 3 and turn.

Row 6: 1 dc in the 1st dc, ch 6, 1 sc in the last of the 6-ch, 1 sc in each of the next 7 sc, 1 sc in the 1st ch of the next set, ch 6, 3 dc between the 2 sets, rep from *, ending row with 2 dc in the turning ch, ch 3 and turn.

Row 7: Same as row 5, except that the sc are worked into the 2nd sc, 3 dc added in 1st and last ch.

Row 8: Same as row 4, except that the sc are worked into the 2nd sc, 3 dc added in 1st and last ch.

Row 9: Same as row 3, except that the sc are worked into the 2nd sc.

Row 10: Same as row 2, except that the sc are worked into the 2nd sc.

Row 11: Same as row 1, except that the sc are worked into the 2nd sc.

Pattern formed by rep rows 1–11.

196. Chain multiples of 8 plus 4.

Row 1: 2 dc in the 7th ch, * ch 5, 2 dc in the next ch, 1 dc in the 3rd ch and the next ch, 2 dc in the 3rd ch, rep from *, ending row after last set with 1 dc in the last ch, ch 3 and turn.

Row 2: 1 dc in 2nd dc and in the next dc, * 2 sc in the 5-ch, 1 dc in each of the next 6 dc, rep from *, ending row with 1 dc in the turning ch, ch 3 and turn.

Pattern formed by rep rows 1–2.

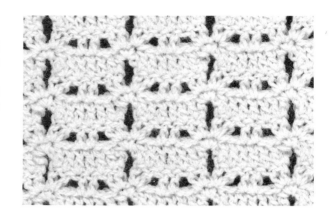

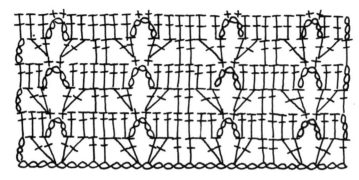

· *14* ·
Fantail Shells

197. Chain multiples of 6 plus 1.

Row 1: 1 sc in the 2nd ch, * 1 dc in the 3rd ch, ch 1, 1 dc in the same ch, ch.1, 1 dc in the same ch, ch 1, 1 dc in the same ch, ch 1, 1 dc in the same ch, 1 sc in the 3rd ch, rep from *, ending row after the last set with a sc, ch 5 and turn.
Row 2: * 1 sc in the 2nd 1-ch, ch 1, 1 sc in the next 1-ch, ch 2, 1 dc in the sc, ch 2, rep from *, ending row with 2 chs and 1 dc in the sc, ch 1 and turn.
Row 3: Same as row 1, except that the 5 dc are all worked in the 1-ch.
Pattern formed by rep rows 1–2.

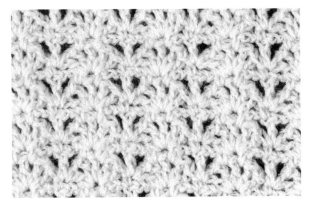

198. Chain multiples of 8 plus 1.

Row 1: 1 sc in the 2nd ch, * 9 dc in the 4th ch, 1 sc in the 4th ch, rep from *, ending row with set and sc in the last ch, ch 3 and turn.

Row 2: 1 dc in the sc, * ch 2, 1 sc in the 5th dc, ch 2, 1 dc in the sc, ch 1, 1 dc in the same sc, rep from *, ending row with 2 dc in the sc, ch 3 and turn.

Row 3: 4 dc in the 1st dc, * 1 sc in the sc, 9 dc in the 1-ch between the 2 sides of the V-stitch, rep from *, ending row with 5 dc in the turning ch, ch 1 and turn.

Row 4: 1 sc in the 1st dc, * ch 2, 1 dc in the sc, ch 1, 1 dc in the sc, ch 2, 1 sc in the 5th dc, rep from *, ending row with 1 sc in the turning ch, ch 1 and turn.

Pattern formed by rep rows 1–4:

199. Chain multiples of 10 plus 1.

Row 1: 1 sc in the 2nd ch, * 12 dc in the 5th ch, 1 sc in the 5th ch, rep from *, ending row with 1 sc, ch 8 and turn.

Row 2: * 1 sc in between the 6th and the 7th dc, ch 4, 2 dc in the sc, ch 4, rep from *, ending row with 2 dc in the last sc, ch 1 and turn.

Pattern formed by rep rows 1–2.

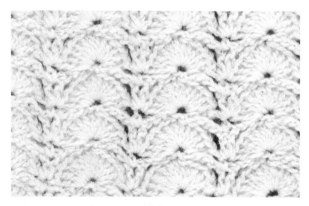

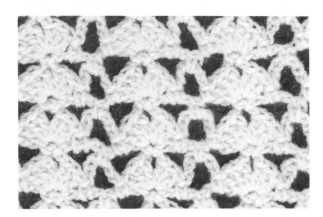

200. Chain multiples of 10 plus 4.

Row 1: 3 dc in the 4th ch, * 1 sc in 4th ch, ch 7, 1 sc in 2nd ch, 3 dc in 4th ch, ch 3, 3 dc in same ch, rep from *, ending row with 3 dc, 1 ch and 1 dc in last ch, ch 1 and turn.
Row 2: 1 sc in 1st dc, * ch 4, 1 sc in the middle of the 7-ch, ch 4, 1 sc around the middle of the 3-ch, rep from *, ending row with 1 sc, ch 4 and turn.
Pattern formed by rep rows 1–2.

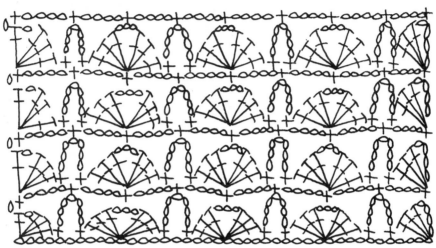

· *15* ·
Shells—Triple Crochet

201. Chain multiples of 6 plus 6.

Row 1: 1 trc in the 7th ch, * 1 trc in the next ch, 1 trc in the next ch, ch 3, trc in the ch following the last trc, 1 trc in the 3rd ch, rep from *, ending row with 1 trc after the last set in the 2nd and last ch, ch 4 and turn.
Row 2: * work 3 trc in the 3-ch, ch 3, 1 trc in the same 3-ch, rep from *, ending row with 1 trc in the turning ch, ch 4 and turn.
Pattern formed by rep rows 1–2.

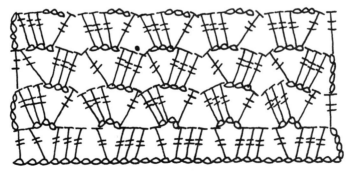

202. Chain multiples of 10 plus 1.

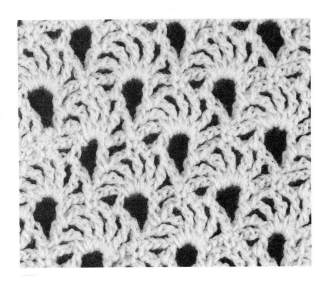

Row 1: 1 sc in 2nd ch, * ch 1, 1 trc in the 5th ch, ch 2, 1 trc in the same ch, ch 2, trc in same ch, ch 2, trc in the same ch, ch 2, trc in the same ch, ch 1, 1 sc in the 5th ch, rep from *, ending row with 3 trc, interspaced with the chs, ch 1 and turn.
Row 2: * sc in 1st trc, ch 3, 1 dc around the 2nd group of 2-ch, ch 2, 1 dc around next 2-ch, ch 3, rep from *, ending row with 1 ch and 1 trc in the sc, ch 7 and turn.
Row 3: 1 trc in the trc, * ch 2, 1 trc in same trc, ch 1, 1 sc in the sc, ch 1, 1 trc in the next 2-ch, ch 2, 1 trc in the same stitch, ch 2, 1 trc in the same stitch, ch 2, 1 trc in the same stitch, rep from *, ending row with 1 sc after the last set, ch 5 and turn.
Row 4: * 1 dc in the 1st 2-ch, ch 3, 1 sc in the 3rd trc, ch 3, 1 dc in the 2nd 2-ch, ch 2, rep from *, ending row with 3 chs and 1 sc, ch 1 and turn.
Pattern formed by rep rows 1–4.

• *16* •
Shells—Large Lace Patterns

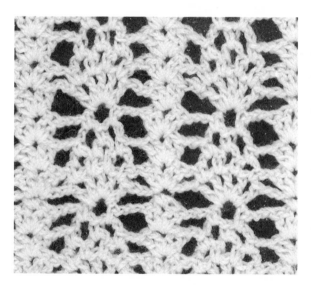

203. Chain multiples of 12 plus 1.

Row 1: 1 sc in the 2nd ch, * ch 3, 1 dc in the 6th ch, ch 1 and dc in the same ch 4 times, ch 3, 1 sc in the 6th ch, rep from *, ending row with 1 dc and 1 ch in the 6th ch, dc, ch and dc in the ch just used, ch 3 and turn.
Row 2: 1 sc in the 1-ch, ch 3, 1 sc in the next 1-ch, * ch 1, 2 dc in the sc, ch 1, 2 dc in the same sc, ch 1, 1 sc in the 1-ch, 3 times ch 3, sc in the last 1-ch, rep from *, ending row with 3 dc in the sc, ch 3 and turn.
Row 3: 2 dc in the 1st dc, * ch 2, 1 sc in the 1st 3-ch, ch 3, sc in the next 3-ch, ch 3, sc in the next 3-ch, ch 2, 2 dc in the 2nd 1-ch, ch 1, 2 dc in the same 1-ch, rep from *, ending row with sc in the turning ch, ch 4 and turn.
Row 4: 1 sc in the 3-ch, * ch 3, 2 dc in the 1-ch, ch 1, 2 dc in the same 1-ch, ch 3, 1 sc in the 3-ch, ch 3, 1 sc in the next 3-ch, rep from *, ending row with 3 dc in the turning ch, ch 1 and turn.
Pattern formed by rep rows 1–4.

204. Chain multiples of 14 plus 4.

Row 1: 1 dc in the 4th ch, * ch 2, 1 sc in the 3rd ch, 1 dc in the 4th ch, ch 1, 1 dc in the same ch, ch 1, 2 more sets of dc followed by a ch in the same ch, 1 dc in the same ch, 1 sc in the 4th ch, ch 2, 1 dc in the 3rd ch, ch 1, 1 dc in the same ch, rep from *, ending row with 3 dc spaced with 2 chs in the last ch, ch 1 and turn.

Row 2: 1 sc in the 1st dc, * 1 sc in the 1-ch, ch 3, 1 sc in the same 1-ch, 1 sc in the next 1-ch, ch 3, 1 sc in the same ch, ch 3, 1 sc in the 1-ch between the 2 sides of the V-stitch, ch 3, 1 sc in the same 1-ch, ch 3, 1 sc in the 1-ch, ch 3, 1 sc in the 1-ch, 1 sc in the next 1-ch, ch 3, 1 sc in the same 1-ch, rep from *, ending row with 1 sc in the turning ch, 1 ch and 1 hdc in the turning ch, ch 3 and turn.

Row 3: 1 dc in the hdc, * ch 3, 1 sc in the 3rd 3-ch, ch 3, 1 sc in the next 3-ch, ch 3, 1 dc in the 3rd 3-ch, ch 1, 1 dc in the same 3-ch, rep from *, ending row with 1 sc, 1 ch and 1 hdc in the last sc.

Row 4: Same as row 1, except that 1 sc, 3 chs and 1 sc are worked in the 1-ch, and the 5 dc spaced with the 1-ch are worked in the middle of the 3-ch.

Pattern formed by rep rows 1–3.

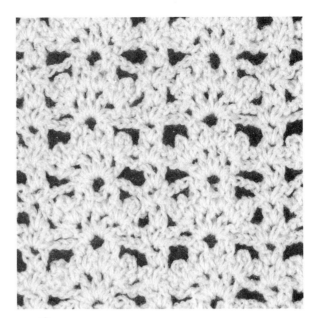

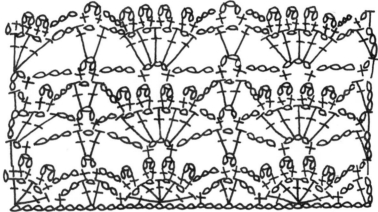

205. Chain multiples of 14 plus 4.

Row 1: 1 dc in the 5th ch, * ch 3, 1 sc in the 4th ch, ch 4, 1 sc in the 4th ch, ch 3, 1 dc in the 4th ch and in the 2 chs following, rep from *, ending row with 1sc, 1 ch and 1 hdc in the 2nd ch, ch 3 and turn.

Row 2: 1 dc in the 1st hdc, 2 dc in the 1-ch, * ch 3, 1 sc in the 1st dc, ch 2, and 1 sc in the 2nd dc, ch 3, 7 dc around the 4-ch, rep from *, ending row with 1 sc in the last dc and 1 in the turning ch, ch 3 and turn.

Row 3: 1 dc in the 2nd sc, * work 1 dc and 1 ch in each of the next 6 dc, 1 dc in the next dc, 3 dc in the 2-ch, rep from *, ending row with 4 dc spaced with 1 ch in between each, ch 4 and turn.

Row 4: 1 sc in the 1-ch, ch 3, 1 sc in the 1-ch, ch 3, 1 sc in the 1-ch, * ch 4, 1 sc in the 1-ch, ch 3, 5 times, 1 sc in the next 1-ch, rep from *, ending row with last set, 2 chs, and 1 hdc in the turning ch, ch 3 and turn.

Row 5: Same as row 1, except that the sc are worked in every other 3-ch.

Pattern formed by rep rows 1–4.

206. Chain multiples of 10 plus 6.

Row 1: 1 sc in the 8th ch, * ch 5, 1 sc in the 4th ch, ch 6, 1 sc in the 6th ch, rep from *, ending row with 2 chs and 1 dc, ch 1 and turn.
Row 2: 1 sc in the dc, * 11 dc in the 5-ch, 1 sc in the middle of the 6-ch, rep from *, ending row with 1 sc in the turning ch, ch 3 and turn.
Row 3: * 1 dc in the 3rd dc of the set, ch 1, dc in the next dc and 1 ch 5 times, dc in the next dc, rep from *, ending row with 1 trc in the last sc, ch 1 and turn.
Row 4: 1 sc in the trc, * ch 1, sc in the next 1-ch, ch 3, 5 times, sc in the next 1-ch, ch 1, sc between the 2 sets, rep from *, ending row with 1 sc in the turning ch, ch 6 and turn.
Row 5: Same as row 1, except that the sc are worked in the 2nd 3-ch and the 2nd 3-ch.
Pattern formed by rep rows 1–4.

207. Chain multiples of 9 plus 1.

Row 1: 1 sc in the 2nd ch, * ch 3, 1 sc in the 4th ch, ch 7, sc in next ch, ch 3, 1 sc in the 4th ch, rep from *, ending row with 1 sc in the last ch, ch 1 and turn.
Row 2: 1 sc in the sc, * work 13 dc around the 7-ch, 1 sc in the next sc, rep from *, ending row with the last sc, ch 5 and turn.
Row 3: * 1 dc in the 6th dc of the set, ch 3, 1 dc in the next dc, ch 3, 1 dc in the next dc, rep from *, ending row with last set and 1 trc in the last sc, ch 3 and turn.
Row 4: * 3 dc around the next 3-ch, ch 3, 3 dc around the next 3-ch, rep from *, ending row after last set with 1 dc in the turning ch, ch 6 and turn.
Row 5: * 1 sc in the 3-ch, 1 sc in the same 3-ch, ch 3, 1 dc between the 2 sets of 3 dc, ch 3, rep from *, ending row with dc in the turning ch, ch 1 and turn.
Pattern formed by rep rows 1–4.

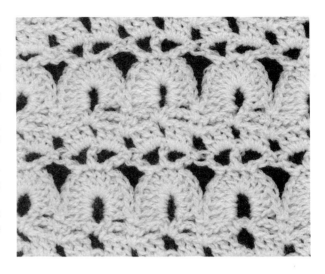

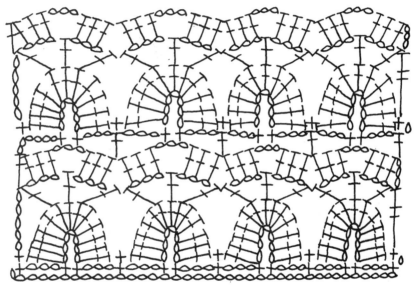

208. Chain multiples of 12 plus 1.

Row 1: 1 sc in the 2nd ch, * ch 5, 1 sc in the 4th ch, rep from *, ending row with sc, ch 5 and turn.
Row 2: * 1 sc around the middle of the 5-ch, work 8 dc around the next 5-ch, 1 sc around the next 5-ch, ch 5, rep from *, ending row with 1 sc around the last 5-ch, ch 2 and 1 dc in the sc, ch 1 and turn.
Row 3: 1 sc in the dc, * 1 dc in the 1st dc, ch 3 and slip 3rd ch into 1st (picot), rep 7 times, 1 dc in the last dc, 1 sc in the 5-ch, rep from *, ending row after last set with 1 sc in the turning ch, ch 8 and turn.
Row 4: Same as row 1, except that the sc are worked in the 3rd and the 2nd picot.
Pattern formed by rep rows 1–3.

Shells—Large Lace Patterns 171

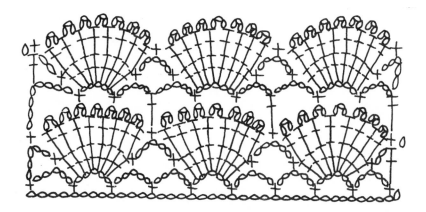

209. Chain multiples of 14 plus 5.

Row 1: 1 dc in the 7th ch, * ch 2, 1 dc in the 3rd ch and in the 4 chs following, turn and ch 7, attach the last ch between the dc and the 2-ch leading into it, turn again and work 1 sc around the ch, 1 hdc, 5 dc, 1 hdc and 1 sc, ch 2, 1 dc in the 3rd ch, ch 1, 1 dc in the 2nd ch, ch 1, 1 dc in the 2nd ch, rep from *, ending row with 1 dc, 1 ch and 1 dc, ch 9 and turn.

Row 2: 1 trc in the 2nd dc, * ch 2, 1 sc in the 1st dc, ch 5, 1 sc in the last of the 5 dc, ch 2, 1 trc in the next dc, ch 5, 1 trc in the next dc, ch 5, 1 trc in the next dc, rep from *, ending row with last trc, 5 chs and a trc in the turning ch, ch 7 and turn.

Row 3: * 1 sc around the 5-ch, ch 5, 1 sc around the next 5-ch, ch 5, 1 sc in the next 5-ch, ch 5, 1 sc in the next 5-ch, rep from *, ending row with 2 chs and 1 trc in the turning ch, ch 3 and turn.

Row 4: Work 2 dc in the 2-ch, * ch 2, 1 sc around the 5-ch, ch 5, 1 sc around the next 5-ch, ch 2, work 5 dc around the 5-ch, rep from *, ending row with 3 dc in the turning ch, ch 4 and turn.

Row 5: Same as row 1, except that the 5 dc are worked around the 5-ch, and there is 1 dc worked in the 1st dc, 1 ch and 1 dc worked in the 2nd dc, ch 1 and 1 dc in the last of the 5 dc.

Pattern formed by rep rows 1–4.

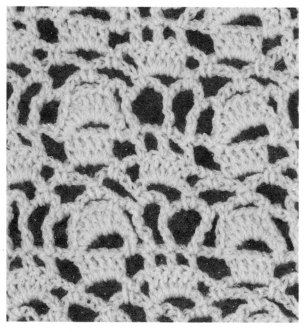

210. Chain multiples of 15 plus 4.

Row 1: 2 dc in the 4th ch, * ch 7, 1 sc in the 6th ch, ch 3, 1 sc in the 3rd ch, ch 7, 2 dc in the 6th ch, ch 1, 2 dc in the same ch, rep from *, ending row with 3 dc in the 6th ch, ch 3 and turn.

Row 2: 2 dc in the 1st dc, * ch 3, 1 sc around the middle of the 7-ch, ch 5, 1 sc in the middle of the next 7-ch, ch 3, 2 dc in the 1-ch, ch 1, 2 dc in the same 1-ch, rep from *, ending row with 3 dc in the turning ch, ch 3 and turn.

Row 3: 2 dc in the 1st dc, * work 11 trc around the 5-ch, 2 dc in the 1-ch, ch 1, 2 dc in the same 1-ch, rep from *, ending row with 3 dc in the turning ch, ch 3 and turn.

Row 4: 2 dc in the 1st dc, * ch 2, 1 sc in the 1st trc, ch 3, 1 sc in the 2nd trc, ch 3, 1 sc in the 2nd trc, ch 3, 1 sc in the 2nd trc, ch 3, 1 sc in the 2nd trc, ch 3, 1 sc in the 2nd trc, ch 2, 2 dc in the 1-ch, ch 1, 2 dc in the same 1-ch, rep from *, ending row with 3 dc in the turning ch, ch 3 and turn.

Row 5: 2 dc in the 1st dc, * ch 3, 1 sc in the 1st 3-ch, ch 3, 1 sc in the next 3-ch, ch 3, 1 sc in the next 3-ch, ch 3, 1 sc in the next 3-ch, ch 3, 1 sc in the next 3-ch, ch 3, 2 dc in the 1-ch, ch 1, 2 dc in the same 1-ch, rep from *, ending row with 3 dc in the turning ch, ch 3 and turn.

Row 6: 2 dc in the 1st dc, * ch 4, 1 sc in the 1st 3-ch, ch 3, 1 sc in the next 3-ch, ch 3, 1 sc in the next 3-ch, ch 3, 1 sc in the next 3-ch, ch 4, 2 dc in the 1-ch, ch 1, 2 dc in the same 1-ch, rep from *, ending row with 3 dc in the turning ch, ch 3 and turn.

Row 7: 2 dc in the 1st dc, * ch 5, 1 sc in the 1st 3-ch, ch 3, 1 sc in the next 3-ch, ch 3, 1 sc in the next 3-ch, ch 5, 2 dc in the 1-ch, ch 1, 2 dc in the same 1-ch, rep from *, ending row with 3 dc in the turning ch, ch 3 and turn.

Row 8: 2 dc in the 1st dc, * ch 7, 1 sc in the 3-ch, ch 3, 1 sc in the 3-ch, ch 7, 2 dc in the 1-ch, ch 1, 2 dc in the same 1-ch, rep from *, ending row with 3 dc in the turning ch, ch 3 and turn.
Pattern formed by rep rows 1–8.

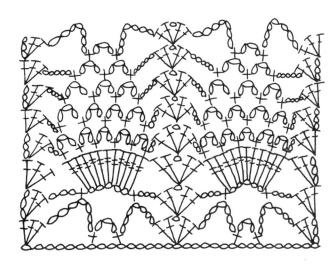

· *17* ·
Stitch—Finished Together

211. Chain multiples of 2 plus 4.

Row 1: Work 2 dc together in the 4th and 2nd ch, * ch 1, work 2 dc together in the ch just used and the 2nd ch, rep from *, ending row with 2 dc in the 2nd and last ch, ch 3 and turn.
Row 2: Work 2 dc together between the 1st 2 dc and in the 1st 1-ch, * ch 1, work 2 dc together before and after the 2 dc worked together in the row below, rep from *, ending row with 1 extra dc in the turning ch, ch 3 and turn.
Pattern formed by rep rows 1–2.

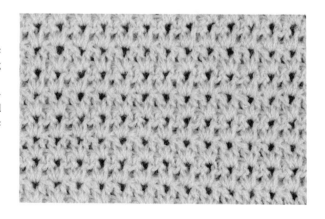

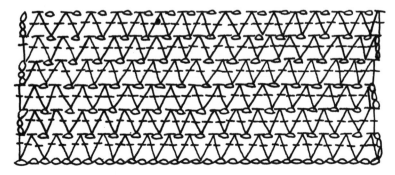

212. Chain multiples of 2 plus 6.

Row 1: 1 dc in the 7th ch, * ch 1, 1 dc in the 2nd ch, rep from *, ending row with last dc, ch 3 and turn.
Row 2: Work 2 dc together in 1st and 2nd dc, ch 1, form 1st part of 2 dc worked together in the dc just used, finishing it up with the 2nd part in the next dc, rep from *, ending row with 2 dc in the turning ch, ch 4 and turn.
Pattern formed by rep rows 1–2.

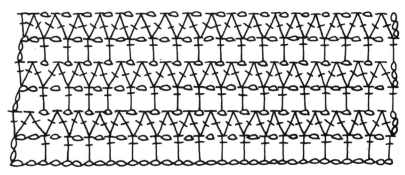

213. Chain multiples of 8 plus 5.

Row 1: 1 dc in 7th ch, * ch 1, begin 1 dc in next ch, begin 2nd dc in 2nd ch, then finish off both dc together, ch 1, 1 dc in next ch, ch 1, 1 dc in 2nd ch, ch 1, 1 dc in 2nd dc, rep from *, ending row with 1 dc, 1 ch and 1 dc, ch 3 and turn.
Row 2: 1 dc in 1st dc, * ch 1, begin 1 dc in next ch, finish it off with 2nd dc begun in next ch, ch 1, 1 dc in 1st dc, ch 1, 1 dc in next dc, ch 1, 1 dc in next dc, rep from *, ending row with 1·dc, 1 ch and 1 dc, ch 4 and turn.
Pattern formed by rep rows 1–2.

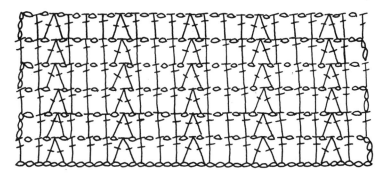

214. Chain multiples of 10 plus 1.

Row 1: 1 sc in the 2nd ch and the ch after that, * ch 3, 1 sc in the 4th ch and the ch after that, rep from *, ending row with 1 sc in each of the last 2 chs, ch 3 and turn.

Row 2: 1 dc in the 2nd sc, * ch 3, 1 dc in the next sc, 1 dc in the next sc, ch 1, work 2 dc together in the sc just used and the next sc, ch 1, 1 dc in the sc just used, 1 dc in the next sc, rep from *, ending row with 1 dc in each of the last 2 sc, ch 1 and turn.

Row 3: * 1 sc in the dc, sc in next dc, ch 3 and rep from *, ending row with 1 sc in the last dc and in the turning ch, ch 3 and turn.

Row 4: 1 dc in the 2nd sc, * ch 1, work 2 dc together in the sc just used and the next sc, ch 1, 1 dc in the sc just used, and 1 dc in the next sc, ch 3, 1 dc in the next sc, 1 dc in the next sc, rep from *, ending row with regular set, ch 1 and turn.

Pattern formed by rep rows 1–4.

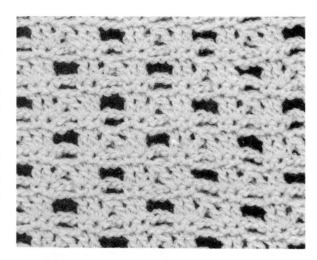

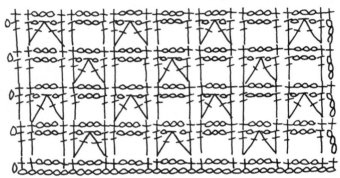

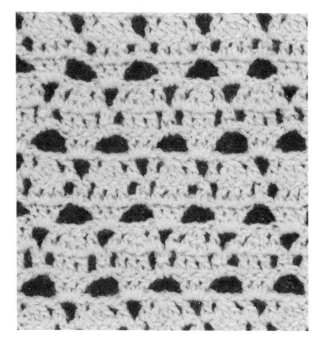

215. Chain multiples of 6 plus 4.

Row 1: 1 dc in the 5th ch, * ch 3, 1 dc in the 4th ch and the 2 chs after that, rep from *, ending row with 1 dc in each of the last 2 chs, ch 3 and turn.

Row 2: 1 dc in the 2nd dc, * ch 3, 1 sc around the 3-ch, ch 3, 1 dc in each of the next 3 dc, rep from *, ending row with 1 dc in last dc in the turning ch, ch 2 and turn.

Row 3: 1 dc in the 2nd dc, ch 1, * 1 dc around the 1st of the 3-ch, ch 2, 1 dc around the last of the next 3-ch, ch 1, finish 3 dc together in the next 3 dc, ch 1, rep from *, ending row with 2 dc finished together in the last dc and the turning ch, ch 4 and turn.

Row 4: * work 3 dc in the 2-ch, ch 3, rep from *, ending row with last set, 1 single ch and a dc in the turning ch, ch 1 and turn.

Row 5: 1 sc in the 1st dc, * ch 3, 1 dc in each of the 3 dc, ch 3, 1 sc around the 3-ch, rep from *, ending row with 3 chs and 1 sc in the turning ch, ch 4 and turn.

Row 6: 1 dc in the last of the 3-ch, * ch 1, work 3 dc together in the next 3 dc, ch 1, 1 dc in the beginning of the next 3-ch, ch 2, 1 dc in the last of the next 3-ch, rep from *, ending row with last set, 1 ch and 1 trc in the last sc.

Pattern formed by rep rows 1–6.

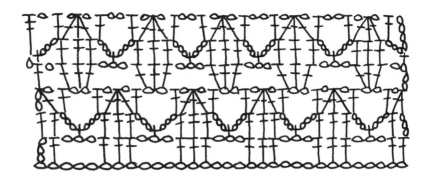

216. Chain multiples of 12 plus 5.

Row 1: 1 dc in the 7th ch, * ch 1, 1 dc in the 2nd ch, rep from *, ending row with 1 dc in the last ch, ch 3 and turn.

Row 2: Work 3 trc in the 1st dc, * 1 dc in the 2nd dc, ch 1, dc in the next dc, ch 1, dc in the next dc, work 7 trc in the 2nd dc, rep from *, ending row with 4 trc in the turning ch, ch 3 and turn.

Row 3: Finish 3 trc together in the 2nd and next 2 trc, * ch 3, dc in the dc, ch 1, dc in the dc, ch 1, dc in the dc, ch 3, finish 7 trc together in the next 7 trc, rep from *, ending row with 3 trc finished together and 1 dc in the turning ch, ch 4 and turn.

Row 4: * 1 dc in the 3-ch, ch 1, 1 dc in the dc, ch 1, dc in the dc, ch 1, dc in the dc, ch 1, 1 dc in the 3-ch, ch 1, 1 dc in the top of the 7 trc finished together, ch 1 and rep from *, ending row with 1 dc in the turning ch, ch 4 and turn.

Row 5: Sk 1st dc, * dc in the dc, ch 1, rep from *, ending row with 1 dc in the turning ch, ch 4 and turn.

Row 6: 1 dc in the 2nd dc, * 7 trc in the 2nd dc, 1 dc in the 2nd dc, ch 1, 1 dc in the 2nd dc, ch 1 and 1 dc in the next dc, rep from *, ending row with 1 dc in the turning ch, ch 4 and turn.

Row 7: 1 dc in the 2nd dc, * ch 3, work 7 trc together in the next 7 trc, ch 3, 1 dc in the next dc, ch 1, dc in the dc, ch 1, dc in the dc, rep from *, ending row with dc in the turning ch, ch 4 and turn.

Row 8: Dc in the 2nd dc, * ch 1, dc in the 3-ch, ch 1, dc in the top of 7 trc finished together, ch 1, dc in the 3-ch, ch 1, dc in the dc, ch 1, dc in the dc, ch 1, dc in the dc, rep from *, ending row with dc in the turning ch.

Pattern formed by rep rows 1–8.

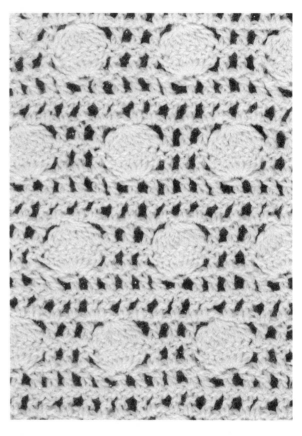

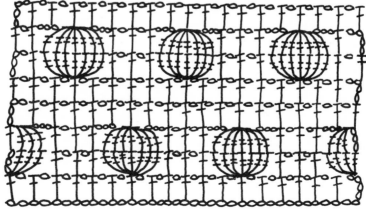

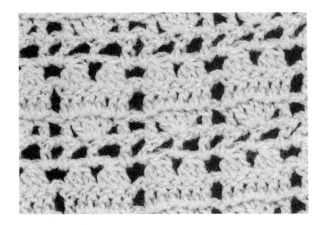

217. Chain multiples of 9 plus 6.

Row 1: 1 dc in the 9th ch, * ch 2, 1 dc in the 3rd ch, rep from *, ending row with 1 dc in the last ch, ch 5 and turn.
Row 2: 1 dc in the 2nd dc, * 4 dc in the next dc, 1 dc in the next dc, ch 2, dc in the next dc, rep from *, ending row after last set with 2 chs and 1 dc in the turning ch, ch 5 and turn.
Row 3: 1 dc in the 2nd dc, * 1 dc in each of the next 5 dc, ch 2, 1 dc in the next dc, rep from *, ending row with last set, 2 chs and 1 dc in the turning ch, ch 5 and turn.
Row 4: Sk 1st dc, * finish 3 dc together in the next 3 dc, ch 2, finish 3 dc together in the next 3 dc, ch 3, rep from *, ending row with 2 chs and 1 dc in the turning ch, ch 5 and turn.
Pattern formed by rep rows 1–4.

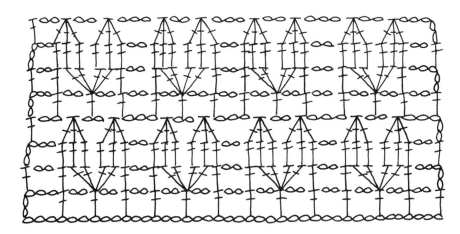

218. Chain multiples of 10 plus 1.

Row 1: 1 sc in the 2nd ch and the ch after that, * ch 3, 1 dc in the 5th ch, ch 1, 1 dc backwards 2 chs, ch 3, 1 sc in the 3rd ch, ch 1, 1 sc in the 2nd ch, rep from *, ending row with 1 sc in each of the last 2 chs, ch 3 and turn.
Row 2: 2 dc in the 1st sc, * ch 3, 1 sc in the 1-ch, ch 3, 5 dc in the next 1-ch, rep from *, ending row with 3 dc in the last sc, ch 3 and turn.
Row 3: Finish 2 dc together in the 2nd and next dc, * ch 4, 1 sc in the 3-ch, ch 1, 1 sc in the next 3-ch, ch 4, finish 5 dc together in the next 5 dc, rep from *, ending row with 3 dc finished together in the last 2 dc and the turning ch, ch 1 and turn.
Row 4: 1 sc in the top of the 3 dc finished together, * 1 sc in the 1st of the 4-ch, ch 3, 1 dc in the 2nd sc, ch 1, 1 dc backwards in the previous sc, ch 3, 1 sc in the last of the next 4-ch, ch 1, rep from *, ending row with 1 sc in the last of the 4-ch and 1 in the turning ch, ch 3 and turn.
Pattern formed by rep rows 1–3.

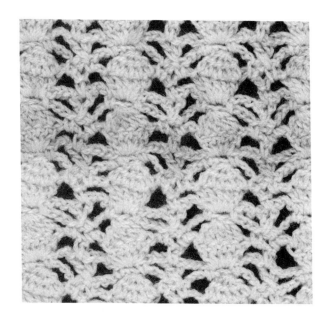

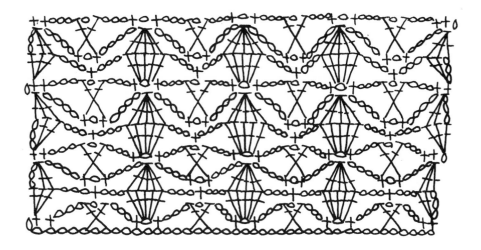

219. Chain multiples of 9 plus 4.

Row 1: 1 dc in the 5th ch, * ch 1, 1 dc in the 3rd ch, ch 3, 1 dc in the ch just used, ch 1, finish 2 dc together in the 2nd ch and the 4th ch, rep from *, ending row with 2 dc finished together in the last 2 chs, ch 4 and turn.

Row 2: Sk 2 dc finished together, * 1 dc in the next dc, 2 dc in the 3-ch, 1 dc in the next dc, ch 2, 1 dc in the top of the 2 dc finished together, ch 2 and rep from *, ending row with 1 dc in the turning ch, ch 4 and turn.

Row 3: 1 dc in the dc, * ch 1, finish 2 dc together in the next dc and the 3rd dc, ch 1, 1 dc in the next dc, ch 3, 1 dc in the dc just used, rep from *, ending row with 1 dc, 1 ch and 1 dc in the turning ch, ch 3 and turn.

Row 4: Sk 1st dc, dc in next dc, * ch 2, 1 dc in the top of the 2 dc finished together, ch 2, 1 dc in the next dc, 2 dc in the 3-ch, 1 dc in the dc, rep from *, ending row with 2 dc in the turning ch, ch 3 and turn.

Pattern formed by rep rows 1–4.

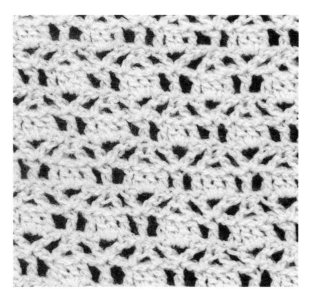

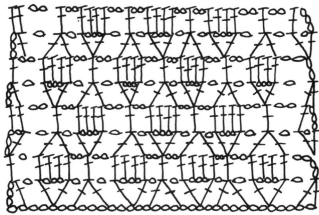

220. Chain multiples of 7 plus 1.

Row 1: 1 sc in the 2nd ch, * 6 dc in the 3rd ch, 1 sc in the 3rd ch and the ch after that, rep from *, ending row with sc, ch 5 and turn.
Row 2: * 1 sc in the 3rd dc and the next dc, ch 2, 1 dc in each of the 2 sc, ch 2, rep from *, ending row with 2 chs and 1 dc in the last sc, ch 5 and turn.
Row 3: * work 2 dc together in the 2 sc, ch 2, 1 dc in each of the next 2 dc, ch 2, rep from *, ending row with 1 dc in the turning ch, ch 1 and turn.
Row 4: 1 sc in each ch and stitch all across the row, including 1 extra in the turning ch, ch 1 and turn.
Pattern formed by rep rows 1–4.

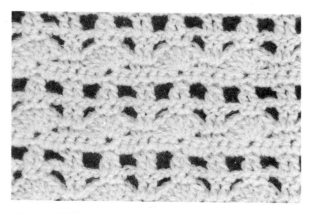

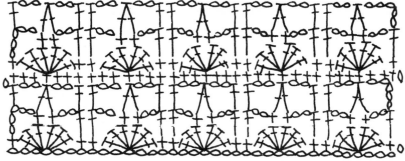

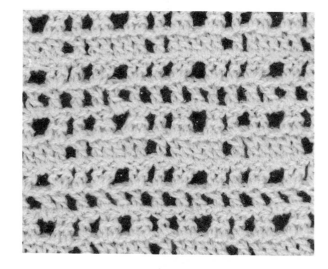

221. Chain multiples of 8 plus 5.

Row 1: 1 dc in the 7th ch, * ch 1, 1 dc in the 2nd ch, rep from *, ending row with last dc, ch 4 and turn.
Row 2: 2 dc in the 2nd dc, * ch 1, 2 dc in the 2nd dc, ch 1, 1 dc in the next dc, ch 1, 2 dc in next dc, rep from *, ending row after the last set and 1 ch and 1 dc in the turning ch, ch 4 and turn.
Row 3: 1 dc in the 2nd dc, * 1 dc in the next dc, 1 dc in the ch and 1 dc in each of the dc, ch 1, 1 dc in the dc, ch 1, 1 dc in the next dc, rep from *, ending row with 1 ch and 1 dc in the last ch, ch 4 and turn.
Row 4: Begin 1 dc in the 2nd dc, begin the 2nd dc in the next dc, finish the 2 together, * ch 3, finish the next 2 dc together in the 2nd and the next dc, ch 1, 1 dc in the next dc, ch 1, finish 2 dc together in the 2nd and next dc, rep from *, ending row with 1 ch and 1 dc in the turning ch, ch 4 and turn.
Pattern formed by rep rows 1–4.

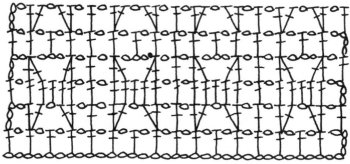

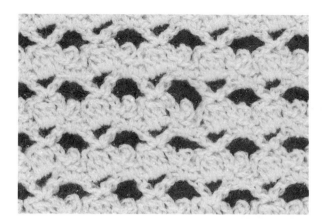

222. Chain multiples of 6 plus 3.

Row 1: 1 dc in the 4th ch, ch 2, * 1 sc in the next ch, 1 sc in the ch after that, 1 picot, 1 sc in the next ch, ch 2, work 3 dc together in the next 3 chs, ch 3, rep from *, ending row with 2 dc finished together in the last 2 chs, ch 5 and turn.

Row 2: 1 dc in the top of the 2 dc finished together, * ch 1, 1 dc in the top of the 3 dc finished together, ch 3, 1 dc in the spot just used, rep from *, ending row with 1 dc, 1 ch and 1 dc in the turning ch, ch 2 and turn.

Row 3: Same as row 1, except that the 3 dc finished together should be worked in the 3-ch and the sc are worked in the top of the dc and the sc with the picot should be worked in the 1-ch.

Pattern formed by rep rows 1–2.

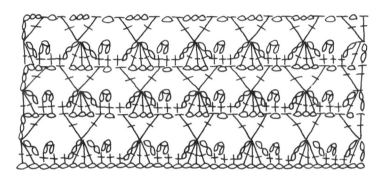

223. Chain multiples of 10 plus 4.

Row 1: 1 dc in the 4th ch, * ch 5, 1 sc in the 5th ch, ch 5, 3 dc in the 5th ch, rep from *, ending row with 2 dc in the last ch, ch 3 and turn.

Row 2: 1 dc in the 2nd dc, * ch 5, 1 sc in the sc, ch 5, 1 dc in each of the next 3 dc, rep from *, ending row with 1 dc.in the last dc and 1 in the turning ch, ch 3 and turn.

Row 3: 1 dc in the 2nd dc, * ch 5, 1 dc in the sc, ch 5, finish 3 dc together in the next 3 dc, rep from *, ending row with 2 dc finished together in the last dc and the turning ch, ch 1 and turn.

Row 4: 1 sc in the top of the 2 dc finished together, * ch 5, 3 dc in the next dc, ch 5, 1 sc in the top of the 3 dc finished together, rep from *, ending row with 1 sc in the top of the last dc and the turning ch, ch 1 and turn.

Row 5: * 1 sc in the sc, ch 5, 1 dc in each of the 3 dc, ch 5, rep from *, ending row with sc in the last sc, ch 8 and turn.

Row 6: * finish 3 dc together in the next 3 dc, ch 5, 1 dc in the sc, ch 5, rep from *, ending row with 1 dc in the last sc, ch 3 and turn.

Pattern formed by rep rows 1–6.

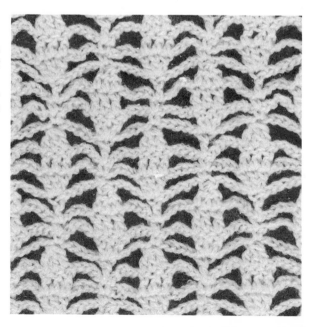

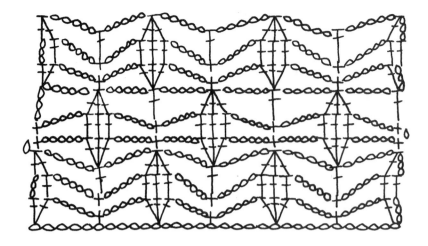

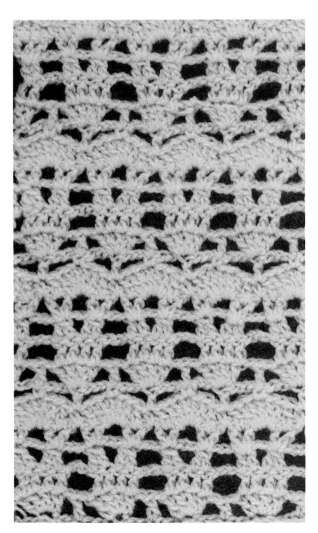

224. Chain multiples of 8 plus 5.

Row 1: 4 dc in 9th ch, * ch 1, 1 dc in 4th ch, ch 1, 4 dc in 4th ch, rep from *, ending row with 1 ch and 1 dc after last set, ch 4 and turn.

Row 2: * 1 dc in each of the next 4 dc, ch 3, rep from *, ending row after last set with 1 ch and a dc in the turning ch, ch 4 and turn.

Row 3: * begin 1 dc in 1st dc, begin 2nd dc in next dc, finish together, ch 2, rep same process of finishing the 2 dc together in next 2 dc, ch 3, rep from *, ending row after last set with 1 ch and 1 dc, ch 3 and turn.

Row 4: * 1 dc in 1st inverted 2 dc, ch 1, 1 dc in same dc, ch 2, rep 1 dc, 1 ch, 1 dc in top of inverted 2 dc, ch 1, rep from *, ending row with 1 dc in turning ch immediately following last set, ch 1 and turn.

Row 5: 1 sc in 1st dc, * 1st dc in 1st ch, 5 dc in 2-ch, 1 dc in next 1-ch, 1 sc in next 1-ch, rep from *, ending row with 1 sc after last set, ch 6 and turn.

Row 6: * 1 sc in 4th dc, ch 3, 1 dc in sc, ch 3, rep from *, ending row with 1 dc, ch 3 and turn.

Row 7: 1 dc in 1st dc, * ch 1, 1 dc in sc, ch 1, 4 dc in next dc, rep from *, ending row with 2 dc in turning ch, ch 3 and turn.

Row 8: 1 dc in 2nd dc, * ch 3, 1 dc in each of next 4 dc, rep from *, ending row with 2 dc, ch 3 and turn.

Row 9: * 1 dc in 1st dc, finish together with a 2nd dc in 2nd dc, ch 3, finish 2 dc together in next 2 dc, ch 2, rep from *, ending row with 2 dc finished together and 1 dc, ch 3 and turn.

Row 10: * 1 dc, 1 ch, 1 dc in 2nd dc, ch 1, 1 dc, 1 ch, 1 dc finished in dc worked together, ch 2, rep from *, ending last set with 1 more dc in the turning ch, ch 3 and turn.

Row 11: 2 dc in the 1st dc, 1 dc in 1-ch between 1st 2 dc, * 1 sc, 1 dc in 1-ch between 1st 2 dc, 5 dc in 2-ch, 1 dc in 1-ch, rep from *, ending row with 3 dc in turning ch, ch 1 and turn.

Row 12: 1 sc in 1st dc, * ch 3, 1 dc in sc, ch 3, 1 sc in 4th dc, rep from *, ending row with sc.

Pattern formed by rep rows 1–12.

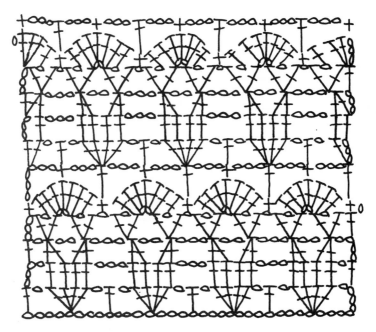

225. Chain multiples of 14 plus 4.

Row 1: 1 dc in the 5th ch and in the 6 chs following, * 3 dc in the next ch, ch 3, 1 sc in the 3rd ch, ch 3, 3 dc in the 3rd ch, 1 dc in the next ch and the 6 chs after that, rep from *, ending row with series of 8 dc, ch 3 and turn.

Row 2: 1 dc in the 2nd dc and in each of the 6 dc after that, * ch 2, finish 6 dc together 1 in each of the next 6 dc, ch 4, 1 dc in each of the next 7 dc, rep from *, ending row with 8 dc, the last in the turning ch, ch 3 and turn.

Row 3: 1 dc in the 2nd dc and the 6 dc following, * ch 1, 3 dc in the top of the 6 dc worked together, ch 3, 3 dc worked together in the same spot, ch 1, 1 dc in each of the 7 dc, rep from *, ending row with 8 dc, the last in the turning ch, ch 3 and turn.

Row 4: 1 dc in the 2nd dc and the next 6 dc, * finish 3 dc together in the next 3 dc, ch 2, 1 sc in the 3-ch, ch 2, work 3 dc together in the next 3 dc, 1 dc in each of the next 7 dc, rep from *, ending row with 1 dc in the turning ch, ch 3 and turn.

Row 5: Sk 1 dc, * 3 dc in the next dc, ch 3, 1 sc in the 3rd dc, ch 3, 3 dc in the 3rd dc, 1 dc in the top of the 3 dc worked together, 1 dc in each of the 2 chs, 1 dc in the sc, 1 dc in each of the 2 chs, 1 dc in the top of the 3 dc finished together, rep from *, ending row with last set and 1 dc in the turning ch, ch 5 and turn.

Row 6: Sk 1st dc, * finish 6 dc together, 1 in each of the next 6 dc, ch 4, 1 dc in each of the 7 dc, ch 2, rep from *, ending row with 4 chs and 1 dc in the turning ch, ch 4 and turn.

Row 7: * 3 dc in the top of the 6 dc worked together, ch 3, 3 dc in the same spot, 1 dc in each of the next 7 dc, ch 1, rep from *, ending row with 1 ch and 1 dc in the turning ch, ch 3 and turn.

Row 8: Sk 1st dc, * finish 3 dc together in the next 3 dc, ch 2, 1 sc in the 3-ch, ch 2, finish 3 dc together in the next 3 dc, 1 dc in each of the next 7 dc, rep from *, ending row with 1 dc in the turning ch.

Pattern formed by rep rows 1–8.

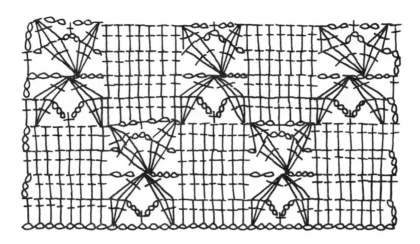

226. Chain multiples of 10 plus 4.

Row 1: 1 dc in the 5th ch and in the 4 chs following, * 1 dc in the 3rd ch, ch 3, 1 sc in the same ch used for the dc, ch 3, 1 dc in the same ch as the dc and the sc, 1 dc in the 3rd dc and in the 4 chs following, rep from *, ending row with 1 dc in the last ch, ch 3 and turn.

Row 2: 1 dc in the 2nd dc and the following 4 dc, * ch 2, begin 1 dc in the 1st 3-ch, begin the 2nd dc in the 2nd 3-ch, finish off together, ch 2, 1 dc in each of the 5 dc, rep from *, ending row with 5 dc in the dc and 1 dc in the turning ch, ch 3 and turn.

Row 3: Same as row 1.

Row 4: Same as row 2, ch 3 and turn.

Row 5: 1 dc in the 4th dc, * ch 3, 1 sc in the same dc, ch 3, 1 dc in the same dc, 1 dc in each of the 2 chs, 1 dc in the top of the 2 dc finished together, 1 dc in each of the 2 chs, 1 dc in the 3rd dc, rep from *, ending row with last set and 1 extra dc in the turning ch, ch 5 and turn.

Row 6: * begin 1 dc in the 1st 3-ch, begin 2nd dc in the next 3-ch, finish off together, ch 2, 1 dc in each of the 5 dc, ch 2, rep from *, ending row with last set 2 ch and 1 extra dc in the turning ch, ch 3 and turn.

Row 7: Same as row 5.

Row 8: Same as row 6.

Pattern formed by rep rows 1–8.

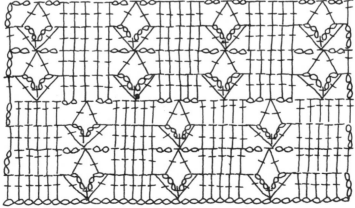

· 18 ·
Inverted Shells

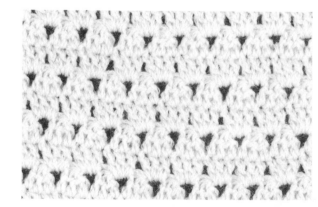

227. Chain multiples of 3 plus 4.

Row 1: 1 dc in the 4th ch, * 3 dc in the 3rd ch, rep from *, ending row with 2 dc in the last ch, ch 3 and turn.

Row 2: * dc in the 2nd dc, * ch 2, finish off 3 dc together in the next 3 dc, rep from *, ending row with 1 dc in the last dc and 1 in the turning ch, ch 3 and turn.

Row 3: * 3 dc in the 2-ch, rep from *, ending row with last set and 1 in the turning ch, ch 4 and turn.

Row 4: Sk 1st dc, * work 3 dc together in the next 3 dc, ch 2, rep from *, ending row after last set with 1 ch and 1 dc in the turning ch, ch 3 and turn.

Pattern formed by rep rows 1–4.

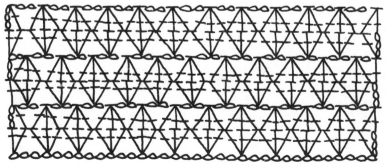

228. Chain multiples of 6 plus 4.

Row 1: 4 dc in the 8th ch, * ch 1, 1 dc in the 3rd ch, ch 1, 4 dc in the 3rd ch, rep from *, ending row with 1 ch and 1 dc in the last ch, ch 5 and turn.
Row 2: Sk 1 dc, * finish off the next 4 dc together, in the next 4 dc, ch 2, 1 dc in the dc, ch 2, rep from *, ending row with 1 dc in the turning ch, ch 3 and turn.
Row 3: 1 dc in the 1st dc, * ch 1, 1 dc in the top of the 4 dc finished together, ch 1, 4 dc in the dc, rep from *, ending row with 2 dc in the turning ch, ch 3 and turn.
Row 4: 1 dc in the 2nd dc, * ch 2, 1 dc in the dc, ch 2, finish off 4 dc together in the next 4 dc, rep from *, ending row with 2 dc finished together in the last dc and the turning ch, ch 4 and turn.
Pattern formed by rep rows 1–4.

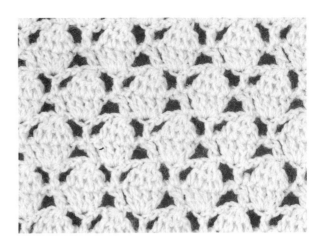

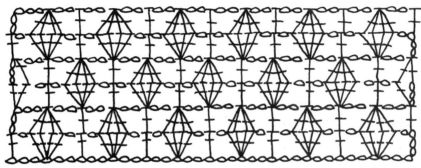

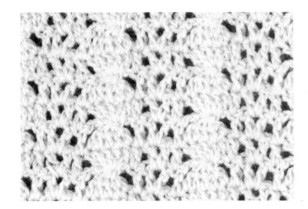

229. Chain multiples of 10 plus 4.

Row 1: 5 dc in the 7th ch, * 1 dc in the 3rd ch, 1 dc in the 2nd ch, ch 1, 1 dc in the ch just used, 1 dc in the 2nd ch, 5 dc in the 3rd ch, rep from *, ending row with last set and 1 dc in the 3rd and last ch, ch 5 and turn.
Row 2: Sk 1 dc, * work 5 dc together in the next 5 dc, ch 2, 1 dc in the dc, 1 dc in the 1-ch, ch 1, 1 dc in the 1-ch just used, dc in the dc, ch 2, rep from *, ending row with 1 dc in the turning ch, ch 3 and turn.
Pattern formed by rep rows 1–2.

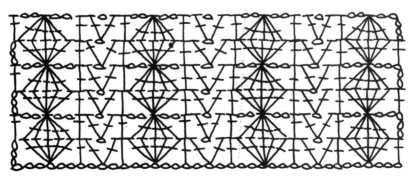

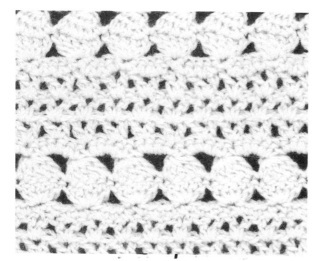

230. Chain multiples of 15 plus 4.

Row 1: 1 dc in the 6th ch, ch 1 and 1 dc in the same ch, * 1 dc in the 3rd ch, ch 1 and 1 dc in the same ch, rep from *, ending row with last set and 1 dc in the 2nd ch after that, ch 3 and turn.
Row 2: Same as row 1, ch 3 and turn.
Row 3: Same as row 1, ch 1 and turn.
Row 4: 1 sc in the 1st dc and in each dc and ch all across the row, ch 3 and turn.
Row 5: Work 5 dc in the 4th sc, * work 5 dc in the 5th sc, rep from *, ending row with the last set and 1 additional dc in the last sc, ch 5 and turn.
Row 6: Sk the 1st dc, * work 5 dc together in the next 5 dc, ch 4, rep from *, ending row after last set with 1 dc in the turning ch, ch 1 and turn.
Row 7: 1 sc in each stitch all the way across the row.
Pattern formed by rep rows 1–7.

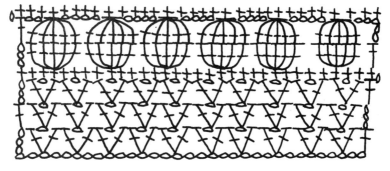

231. Chain multiples of 10 plus 3.

Row 1: 1 dc in the 4th ch, * 4 dc in the 5th ch, ch 3, 4 dc in the ch just used, 1 dc in the 5th ch, ch 1, 1 dc in the ch just used, rep from *, ending row with 2 dc in the 5th ch, ch 3 and turn.
Row 2: 1 dc in the 1st dc, * ch 3, finish off 8 dc together, 1 in each of the 8 dc of the set, ch 5, 1 dc in the 1-ch, ch 1, dc in the same 1-ch, rep from *, ending row with 2 dc in the turning ch, ch 3 and turn.
Pattern formed by rep rows 1–2.

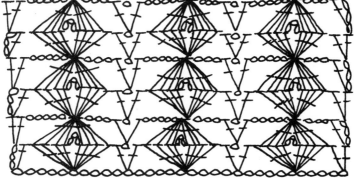

Inverted Shells 187

232. Chain multiples of 8 plus 4.

Row 1: 3 dc in the 4th ch, * 1 sc in the 4th ch, 7 dc in the 4th ch, rep from *, ending row with 4 dc in the 4th and end ch, ch 1 and turn.

Row 2: 1 sc in the 1st dc, * ch 2, finish 3 dc together in the next 3 dc, along with 1 dc in the sc and 3 dc in the next 3 dc, ch 4, 1 sc in the next dc, rep from *, ending row with 4 chs and 1 sc in the turning ch, ch 3 and turn.

Row 3: Same as row 2, except that the 7 dc are worked in the sc and the sc is worked in the top of the 7 dc worked together.

Pattern formed by rep rows 1–2.

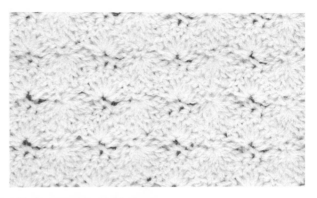

233. Chain multiples of 8 plus 1.

Row 1: 1 sc in the 2nd ch, * work 7 dc in the 4th ch, 1 sc in the 4th ch, rep from *, ending row with last set and a sc, ch 3 and turn.

Row 2: Work 3 relief dc together, from the front around the base of the 1st 3 dc, * ch 4, 1 sc in the next dc, ch 2, work 6 relief dc from the front around the base of the next 6 dc, rep from *, ending row with the last 3 relief dc finished together and 1 dc in the last sc, ch 3 and turn.

Row 3: 3 dc in the 1st dc, * 1 sc in the sc, 7 dc in the last ch before the 6 dc finished together, rep from *, ending row with 4 dc in the turning ch, ch 1 and turn.

Row 4 1 sc in the 1st dc, * ch 3, 1 dc in the sc, ch 3, 1 sc in the 4th dc, rep from *, ending row with 3 chs and 1 sc in the turning ch, ch 1 and turn.

Pattern formed by rep rows 1–4.

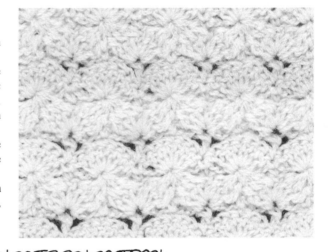

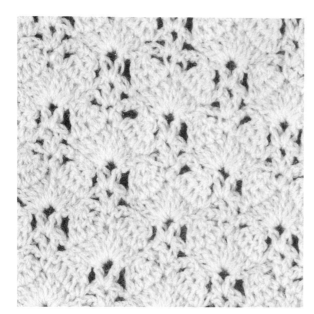

234. Chain multiples of 12 plus 4.

Row 1: 1 dc in the 4th ch, * ch 1, 4 dc in the 6th ch, ch 2, 4 dc in the ch just used, ch 1, 1 dc in the 6th ch, ch 1, 1 dc in the ch just used, rep from *, ending row with 2 dc in the 6th and last ch, ch 3 and turn.

Row 2: 1 dc in the 1st dc, * finish 4 dc together in the 4 dc of the set, ch 4, 1 sc in the 2-ch, ch 3, work 4 dc together in the next 4 dc, ch 1, 1 dc in the 1-ch between the sides of the V-stitch, ch 1, 1 dc in the same 1-ch, rep from *, ending row with 2 dc in the turning ch, ch 3 and turn.

Row 3: 4 dc between the 1st 2 dc, * ch 1, 1 dc in the sc, ch 1, 1 dc in the same sc, ch 1, 4 dc in the 1-ch, ch 2, 4 dc in the same 1-ch, rep from *, ending row with 5 dc in the turning ch, ch 1 and turn.

Row 4: 1 sc in the 1st dc, * ch 4, work 4 dc together in the next 4 dc, ch 1, 1 dc in the 1-ch between the sides of the V-stitch, ch 1, 1 dc in the 1-ch just used, finish 4 dc together in the set of 4 worked together, rep from *, ending row with 1 sc in the turning ch, ch 3 and turn.

Pattern formed by rep rows 1–4.

235. Chain multiples of 11 plus 4.

Row 1: 1 dc in the 5th ch, * ch 3, 5 dc in the 5th ch, ch 3, 2 dc finished together in the 5th and next ch, rep from *, ending row with 2 dc finished together in the 5th and next ch, ch 1 and turn.

Row 2: 1 sc in the 1st dc, * ch 3, 1 dc in each of the next 3 dc, ch 3, 1 dc in the dc just used and in the next 2 dc, ch 3, 1 sc in the top of the 2 dc worked together, rep from *, ending row with 3 chs and 1 sc in the turning ch, ch 4 and turn.

Row 3: * work 3 dc together in the 1st, 3 dc, ch 3, 1 sc in the 3-ch, ch 5, 1 sc in the same 3-ch, ch 3, finish 3 dc together in the next 3 dc, rep from *, ending row with 1 trc after the last set in the sc, ch 3 and turn.

Row 4: Same as row 1, except for the 5 dc worked in the 5-ch.

Pattern formed by rep rows 1–3.

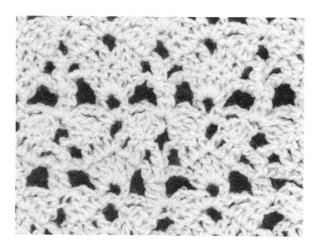

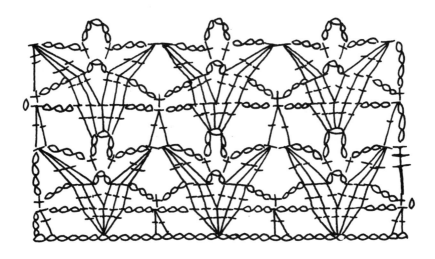

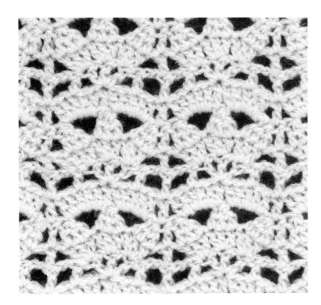

236. Chain multiples of 12 plus 4.

Row 1: 1 dc in the 5th ch and in each ch all across the row, ch 5 and turn.

Row 2: 1 dc in the 4th dc, * 1 dc in the 3rd dc, ch 1, 1 dc in the dc just used, ch 1, 1 dc in the dc just used, 1 dc in the 3rd dc, ch 2, 1 dc in the 3rd dc, ch 2, 1 dc in the 3rd dc, rep from *, ending row with 1 dc in the turning ch, ch 4 and turn.

Row 3: Sk 1st dc, * work 3 dc in the 2nd dc, work 3 dc in the next dc, work 3 dc in the next dc, ch 1, 1 dc in the 2nd dc, ch 1, rep from *, ending row with 1 ch and 1 dc in the turning ch, ch 3 and turn.

Row 4: Sk 1st dc, * work 3 dc together in the next 3 dc, ch 4, work 3 dc together in the next 3 dc, ch 4, work 3 dc together in the next 3 dc, 1 dc in the next dc, rep from *, ending row with 1 dc in the turning ch, ch 3 and turn.

Row 5: Same as row 1, except that a dc is worked in each ch and stitch.

Pattern formed by rep rows 1–4.

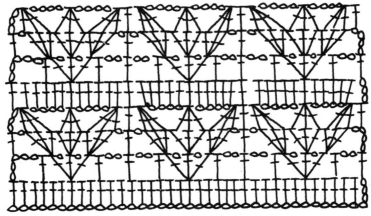

237. Chain multiples of 10 plus 8.

Row 1: 1 dc in the 14th ch, * ch 4, 1 dc in the 5th ch, rep from *, ending row with last dc, ch 3 and turn.
Row 2: * work 7 dc in the 2nd dc, ch 2, rep from *, ending row with last set, 1 ch and 1 dc, ch 4 and turn.
Row 3: * 1 dc in each of the 1st 3 dc of the set of 7, ch 2, 3 dc in the last 3 dc of the set of 7, ch 2, rep from *, ending row with last set, 1 ch and 1 dc in the turning ch, ch 3 and turn.
Row 4: * finish off 3 dc worked together in the 1st, 2nd and 3rd dc of the set, ch 3, 1 dc around the 2-ch, ch 3, finish off 3 dc worked together in the next 3 dc, ch 1 and rep from *, ending row with 1 dc in the turning ch after the last set, ch 7 and turn.
Row 5: * 1 dc in the single standing dc, ch 4, 1 dc in the 1-ch between the 2 groups of 3 dc finished together, ch 4, rep from *, ending row with 1 dc in the turning ch, ch 3 and turn.
Row 6: 3 dc in the 1st dc, * ch 2, 7 dc in the 2nd dc, rep from *, ending row with 4 dc in the turning ch, ch 3 and turn.
Row 7: * work 1 dc in the last 3 dc of the set, ch 2, work each of 1 dc in the 1st 3 dc, ch 2, rep from *, ending row with 3 dc and 1 dc in the turning ch, ch 6 and turn.
Row 8: * work 3 dc together in the last 3 dc of the set, ch 1, work 3 dc together in the next 3 dc, ch 3, 1 dc in the 2-ch, ch 3, rep from *, ending row with 3 dc worked together, ch 3 and 1 dc worked in the turning ch, ch 7 and turn.
Pattern formed by rep rows 1–8.

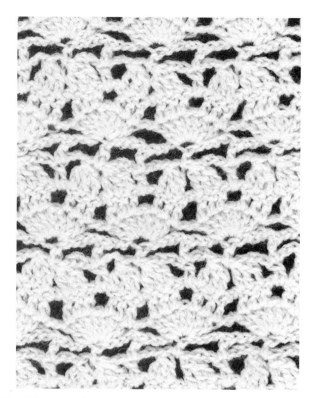

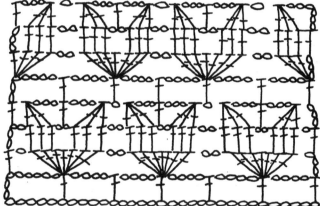

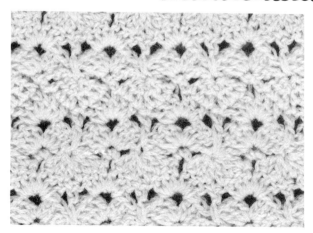

238. Chain multiples of 8 plus 4.

Row 1: 3 dc in the 8th ch, * ch 3, 3 dc in the ch just used, 3 dc in the 8th ch, rep from *, ending row with 1 dc in the 3rd ch after the last set, ch 3 and turn.
Row 2: * 3 dc in the 3-ch, ch 3, 3 dc in the same 3-ch, 1 dc all the way down to the 4th ch of the row below, rep from *, ending row with 1 dc in the turning ch, ch 3 and turn.
Row 3: Sk 1st dc, finish 3 dc together in the next 3 dc, * ch 3, 1 sc in the 3-ch, ch 3, finish 6 dc together, 3 in the next 3 dc, sk the dropped dc and use the next 3 dc, rep from *, ending row with 3 dc finished together in the last 3 dc and form 1 dc in the turning ch, ch 3 and turn.
Row 4: Same as row 1, except that the dc are worked in the sc.
Pattern formed by rep rows 1–3.

Inverted Shells 191

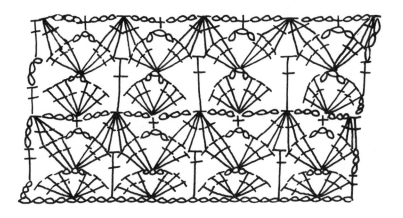

239. Chain multiples of 10 plus 10.

Row 1: 1 dc in the 12th ch, * ch 4, 1 dc in the 5th ch, rep from *, ending row with last dc, ch 4 and turn.

Row 2: Sk 1st dc, * 7 dc in the next dc, ch 2, rep from *, ending row with 1 ch and 1 dc in the turning ch, ch 3 and turn.

Row 3: Sk 1st dc, * 1 dc in each of the next 3 dc, ch 2, 1 dc in the 2nd dc and the 2 dc after that, ch 2, rep from *, ending row with last set and 1 dc in the turning ch, ch 3 and turn.

Row 4: Sk 1st dc, * finish 3 dc together in the next 3 dc, ch 3, 1 dc in the 2-ch, ch 3, finish 3 dc together in the next 3 dc, ch 1, rep from *, ending row with 1 dc in the turning ch, ch 7 and turn.

Row 5: Same as row 1, except that the dc are formed in the single standing dc and the 1-ch.

Pattern formed by rep rows 1–4.

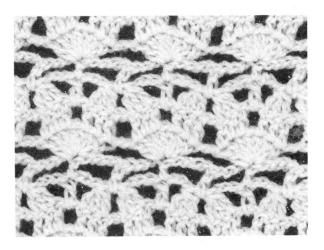

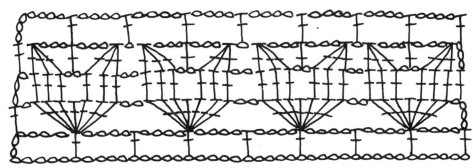

· *19* ·
Wraparound Stitch

240. Chain multiples of 3 plus 4.

Row 1: 2 dc in the 5th ch, * 3 dc in the 3rd ch, rep from *, ending row with 2 dc in the last ch, ch 3 and turn.

Row 2: 1 dc in the 2nd dc, 1 dc in the next dc, * 1 dc worked back around the middle of the 1st dc, 1 dc in the 2nd dc and the one after, rep from *, ending row after the last set with 1 dc, ch 3 and turn.

Row 3: Same as row 1, except that the 3 dc are worked between the sets.

Pattern formed by rep rows 1–2.

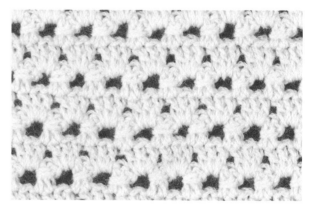

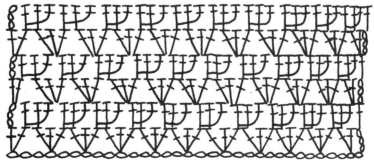

241. Chain multiples of 6 plus 4.

Row 1: 1 dc in the 5th ch and the ch after, * work 2 dc finished together around the middle of the 1st dc, 1 dc in the 3rd ch, ch 1, 1 dc in the same ch, 1 dc in the 2nd ch and the ch after that, rep from *, ending row with 1 dc in the 2nd ch after completion of the last set, ch 3 and turn.

Row 2: 1 dc in the 2 dc finished together and 1 dc in each of the next 2 dc, * 1 dc in the 1-ch, ch 1, 1 dc in the same 1-ch, 1 dc in the top of the 2 dc finished together, 1 dc in each of the next 2 dc, rep from *, ending row with 1 extra dc in the turning ch, ch 3 and turn.

Pattern formed by rep rows 1–2.

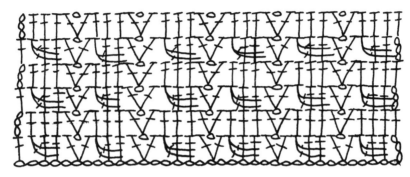

242. Chain multiples of 3 plus 4.

Row 1: 1 dc in the 5th ch, 1 dc in the ch after that, work 1 dc back around the middle of the 1st dc, * 1 dc in the 2nd ch, 1 dc in the next ch, work 1 dc back around the 1st dc of the set, rep from *, ending row with 1 extra dc in the turning ch, ch 3 and turn.

Row 2: * 1 dc in the top of the dc worked across the 1st 2 dc, 1 dc in the next dc and 1 dc in the next dc, rep from *, ending row with 1 dc in the turning ch, ch 3 and turn.

Pattern formed by rep rows 1–2.

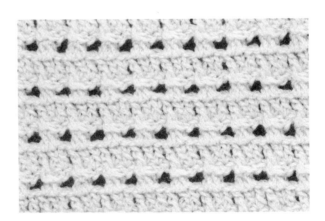

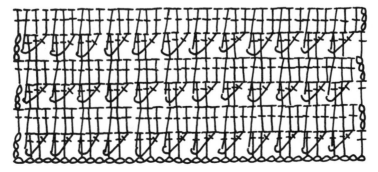

243. Chain multiples of 3 plus 4.

Row 1: 1 dc in the 6th ch, * 1 dc in the next ch, 1 dc backwards in the ch before the last 2 dc, 1 dc in the 2nd ch, rep from *, ending row with 1 dc after the last set, ch 3 and turn.
Row 2: 1 dc in the top of each dc, the last one in the turning ch, ch 3 and turn.
Pattern formed by rep rows 1–2.

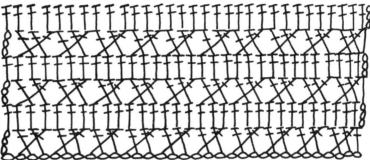

244. Chain multiples of 11 plus 4.

Row 1: 1 dc in the 6th ch and 1 in the next ch, * 1 dc backwards in the ch before the 1st dc, 1 dc in the 2nd ch and the ch after that, 1 dc backwards in the ch before the 1st dc, ch 2, 1 dc in the 3rd ch, ch 2, 1 dc in 4th ch and 1 in the next ch, rep from *, ending row with 1 dc, ch 1 and 1 dc in the 2nd ch, ch 4 and turn.
Rows 2–3: Same as row 1, except dc always worked in the dc, ch 3 and turn.
Row 4: Same as row 1, except dc always worked in the dc, ch 5 and turn.
Row 5: 1 dc in the 4th dc, * ch 2, 1 dc in the 1st ch and 1 dc in the next ch, 1 dc backwards in the last dc, 1 dc in the 1st ch and 1 dc in the next ch, 1 dc backwards in the dc, ch 2, 1 dc in the 3rd dc, rep from *, ending row with last set and 1 extra dc, worked together with the last set in the turning ch, ch 2 and turn.
Rows 6–8: Same as row 5.
Pattern formed by rep rows 1–5.

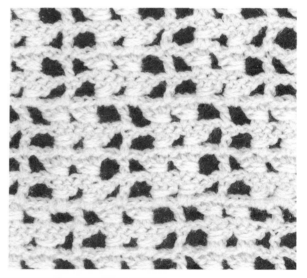

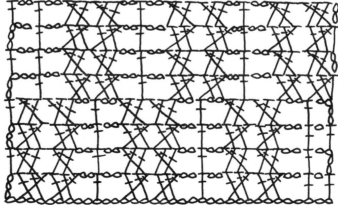

245. Chain multiples of 6 plus 6.

Row 1: 1 dc in the 9th ch, * ch 2, finish 2 dc together around the middle of the dc just made, together with 1 dc in the 3rd ch, ch 2, 1 dc in the 3rd ch, rep from *, ending row with last set, ch 1 and turn.
Row 2: 1 sc in the 1st dc, * ch 2, 1 sc in the dc, rep from *, ending row with a sc in the turning ch, ch 5 and turn.
Row 3: Work 2 dc together around the turning ch, together with 1 dc in the sc, * ch 2, 1 dc in the sc, ch 2, work 2 dc around the middle of the dc just made, together with 1 dc in the sc, rep from *, ending row with 1 dc in the last sc, ch 1 and turn.
Row 4: * work 1 sc in the dc, ch 2, rep from *, ending row with 1 sc in the turning ch, ch 5 and turn.
Pattern formed by rep rows 1–4.

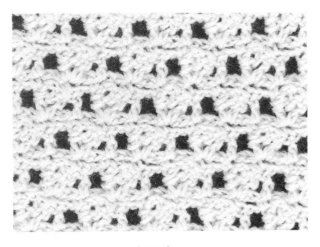

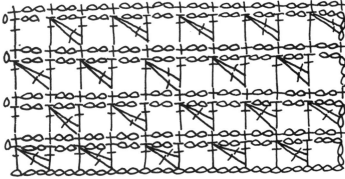

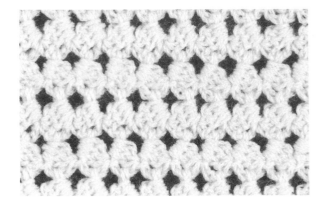

246. Chain multiples of 3 plus 4.

Row 1: 1 dc in the 5th ch, * ch 3, finish off 3 dc together, worked around the middle of the 1st dc, 1 dc in the 3rd ch, rep from *, ending row with last set, ch 4 and turn.
Row 2: * 1 dc around the middle of the 3-ch, ch 3, work 3 dc around the middle of the dc just formed, finish together with 1 dc in 3-ch, rep from *, ending row with 1 dc after the last set in the turning ch.
Pattern formed by rep rows 1–2.

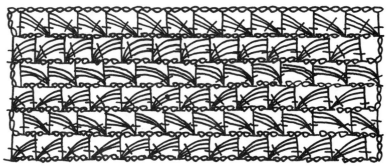

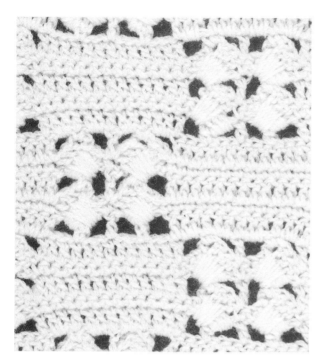

247. Chain multiples of 24 plus 4.

Row 1: 1 dc in the 5th ch and in the 11 chs following, * ch 3, 1 sc in the 3rd ch, ch 3, 1 dc in the 3rd ch, ch 3, 1 sc in the 3rd ch, ch 3, 1 dc in the 3rd ch and in the 12 chs following, rep from *, ending row with last dc, ch 1 and turn.

Row 2: * 1 sc in each dc all across row, work 3 dc in the 2nd 3-ch, ch 3, work 3 dc backwards in the 1st ch, 1 sc in the dc, work 3 dc in the 2nd 3-ch, ch 3, work 3 dc backwards in the 1st 3-ch, rep from *, ending row with sc over the dc and 1 sc in the turning ch, ch 3 and turn.

Row 3: Same as row 1, ch 1 and turn.

Row 4: Same as row 2, ch 3 and turn.

Row 5: * dc in each sc, ch 2, 1 sc in the top of the 3-ch, ch 2, 1 dc in the sc, ch 2, 1 sc in the 3-ch, ch 2, rep from *, ending row with dc in the sc, ch 6 and turn.

Row 6: Sk 1 dc, * 1 sc in the 3rd dc, ch 3, 1 dc in the 3rd dc, ch 3, 1 sc in the 3rd dc, ch 3, 1 dc in the last dc, 1 dc in each of the 2 chs, the sc, the 2-ch, the dc, the 2-ch, the sc, the 2-ch and the 1st dc, rep from *, ending row with 3 chs and 1 dc in the turning ch.

Rows 7–10: Rep rows 2–5, keeping in mind that the patterns are worked alternatively; the order is switched like a checkerboard. Pattern formed by rep rows 1–10.

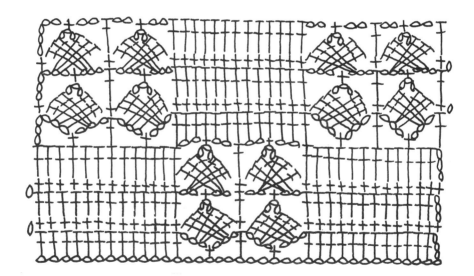

• 20 •
Staggered Square

248. Chain multiples of 8 plus 4.

Row 1: 1 dc in 5th ch and in the next ch, * 1 dc in 3rd ch, ch 3, 3 dc
around the dc just made (perpendicular angles), 1 dc in 3rd ch
and in each of next 2 chs, rep from *, ending row with 3 dc, ch 3
and turn.

Row 2: 1 dc in 2nd dc and in the next dc, * ch 2, 1 sc in the top of
the ch, ch 2, 1 dc in each of the next 3 dc, rep from *, ending row
with 3 dc, 2 in the dc and 1 in the turning ch, ch 3 and turn.

Row 3: Same as row 1, except that the base dc for the square
formation are worked in the sc.

Pattern formed by rep rows 1–2.

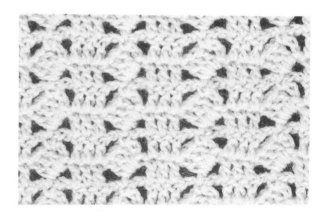

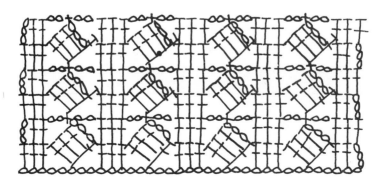

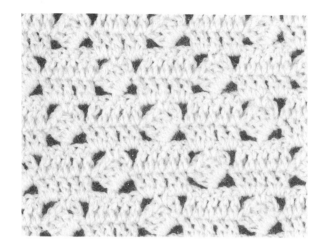

249. Chain multiples of 10 plus 4.

Row 1: 1 dc in the 7th ch, * ch 3, 3 dc perpendicular around the dc, 1 dc in the 3rd dc and in the next 4 chs, 1 dc in 3rd ch, rep from *, ending row with 1 dc after the last set, ch 5 and turn.
Row 2: 1 sc in the top of the ch, * ch 2, 1 dc in each of the 5 dc, ch 2, 1 sc in the top of the ch, rep from *, ending row with 1 dc after the last set, ch 3 and turn.
Row 3: * 1 dc in each of the 1st 2-ch, 1 dc in the sc, 1 dc in each of the next 2-ch, 1 dc in the 3rd dc, ch 3, 3 dc perpendicular to the dc, rep from *, ending row with last set, ch 3 and turn.
Row 4: 1 dc in the 2nd dc, * 1 dc in each of the next 4 dc, ch 2, 1 sc in the top of the ch, ch 2, 1 dc in next dc, rep from *, ending row with 3 dc in the 5 dc and 1 dc in the turning ch, ch 3 and turn.
Pattern formed by rep rows 1–4.

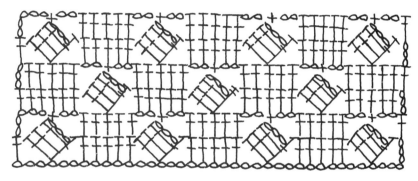

250. Chain multiples of 4 plus 1.

Row 1: 1 sc in the 2nd ch, * ch 5, 1 sc in the 4th ch, rep from *, ending row with last sc, ch 4 and turn.
Row 2: * 1 sc around the 5-ch, ch 3, rep from *, ending row with last sc, 1 ch and 1 dc in the sc, ch 3 and turn.
Row 3: 2 dc in the dc, * 1 sc in the sc, ch 2, 2 dc in the same sc, rep from *, ending row with 1 sc in the last sc, ch 2, begin 1 dc in the single ch and 1 in the turning ch, finish off the 2 together, ch 1 and turn.
Row 4: 1 sc in the dc, * ch 2, 2 dc around the 2-ch, 1 sc in the space between the 2-ch and the dc, rep from *, ending row with 1 sc in the turning ch, ch 5 and turn.
Row 5: * 1 sc in the 2nd dc, ch 5, rep from *, ending row with last sc, 2 chs and 1 dc in the sc, ch 1 and turn.
Row 6: 1 sc in the dc, * ch 5, 1 sc in the middle of the 5-ch, rep from *, ending row with last sc in the turning ch, ch 4 and turn.
Row 7: * 1 sc in the middle of each 5-ch, ch 3, rep from *, ending row with 1 sc, ch 1 and 1 dc in the sc, ch 3 and turn.
Pattern formed by rep rows 1–7.

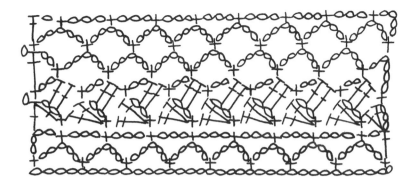

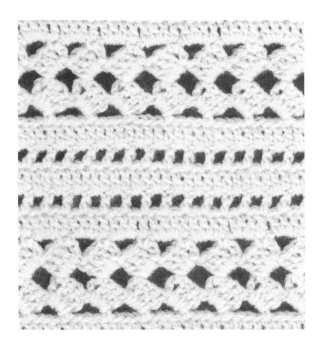

251. Chain multiples of 4 plus 4.

Row 1: 1 dc in the 5th ch and in every ch all across the row, ch 4 and turn.
Row 2: Sk 1 dc, 1 dc in the 3rd dc, * ch 1, 1 dc in the 2nd dc, rep from *, ending row with 1 ch and 1 dc in the turning ch, ch 3 and turn.
Row 3: 1 dc in each ch and each dc all across the row, ch 4 and turn.
Row 4: Sk 1 dc, * 1 dc in the 3rd dc, ch 1 and rep from *, ending row with last set, ch 3 and turn.
Row 5: 1 dc in every ch and every dc all across row, ch 2 and turn.
Row 6: 1 dc in the 5th dc, * ch 3, 3 dc around the 1st dc, 1 dc in the 4th dc, rep from *, ending row after last set with 1 dc in the turning ch, ch 4 and turn.
Row 7: * 1 dc in the top of the 3-ch, ch 3, 3 dc around the 1st dc, rep from *, ending row with 1 trc in the turning ch, ch 4 and turn.
Row 8: * 1 sc in the top of the 3-ch, ch 3, rep from *, ending row with 1 sc, 1 ch and 1 dc in the turning ch, ch 3 and turn.
Row 9: Dc in every ch and every dc.
Pattern formed by rep rows 1–8.

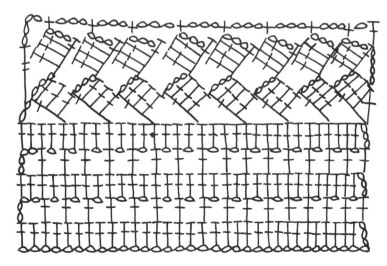

252. Chain multiples of 6 plus 4.

Row 1: 1 dc in the 7th ch, ch 1, * 1 dc in the 2nd ch, ch 1, rep from *, ending row with last set, ch 1.
Row 2: * 1 sc in the dc, ch 1, rep from *, ending row with 1 sc in the turning ch, ch 3 and turn.
Row 3: * 1 dc in the 2nd ch, ch 3, work 3 dc around the dc, 1 dc in the 2nd sc, rep from *, ending row with last set and 1 dc in the sc, ch 5 and turn.
Row 4: * 1 sc in the top ch, ch 2, 1 dc in the dc, ch 2, rep from *, ending row with dc in the turning ch, ch 4 and turn.
Row 5: Same as row 1, except that the dc are worked in the dc and 1 each in the 2-ch.
Pattern formed by rep rows 1–4.

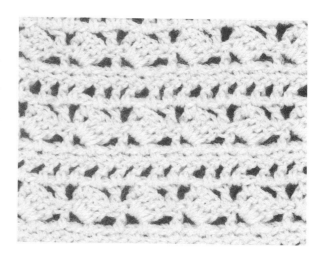

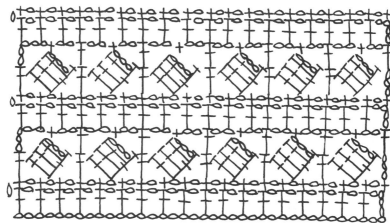

253. Chain multiples of 6 plus 5.

Row 1: 1 dc in the 6th ch, * ch 1, 1 dc in the 2nd ch, rep from *, ending row with the last set, ch 4 and turn.
Row 2: Same as row 1, ch 3 and turn.
Row 3: * 1 dc in the 2nd 1-ch, ch 3, work 3 dc around the dc, 1 dc in the 2nd dc, rep from *, ending row with last dc in the turning ch, ch 5 and turn.
Row 4: * 1 sc in the top of the 3-ch, ch 2, 1 dc in the dc, ch 2, rep from *, ending row with 2 chs and 1 dc in the turning ch, ch 4 and turn.
Row 5: Same as row 1, except that the dc are worked in the dc and in the 2-ch.
Pattern formed by rep rows 1–4.

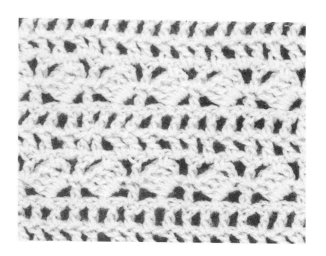

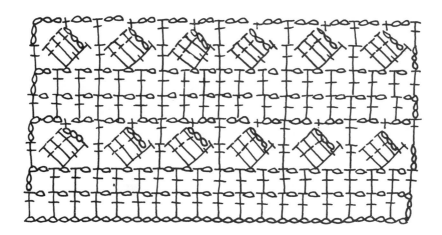

254. Chain multiples of 5 plus 4.

Row 1: 1 dc in 7th ch, * ch 3, 3 dc around the dc at a perpendicular angle, 1 dc in 5th ch, rep from *, ending row after last set with 1 dc at row's end, ch 3 and turn.
Row 2: * 1 picot, ch 2, 1 sc at the end of the ch, ch 2, rep from *, ending row with 1 picot and 1 dc, ch 6.
Row 3: * 1 sc in sc, ch 7, rep from *, ending row with 3 chs and 1 dc in turning ch, ch 3 and turn.
Row 4: 2 dc in dc, * 1 dc around the middle of the 7-ch, ch 3, 3 dc around and perpendicular to the dc, rep from *, ending row with last set having 2 instead of 3 dc around 1st dc and 1 dc around the turning ch, ch 1 and turn.
Row 5: 1 sc in dc, 1 picot, ch 2, * 1 sc in top of the ch, ch 2, 1 picot, 2 ch, rep from *, ending row with 1 sc in the turning ch, ch 1 and turn.
Row 6: * 1 sc in sc, ch 7, 1 sc in sc, ch 7, rep from *, ending row with 3 chs and 1 dc in the turning ch, ch 3.
Pattern formed by rep rows 1–6.

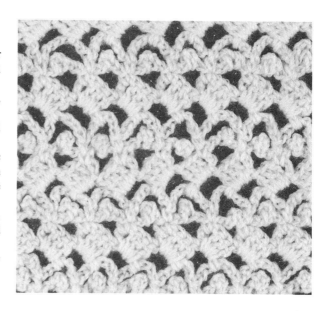

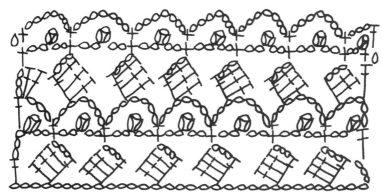

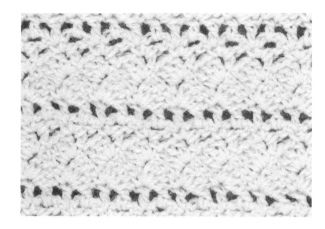

255. Chain multiples of 4 plus 4.

Row 1: 3 dc in 4th ch, * 1 sc in 4th ch, ch 3, 3 dc in the sc, rep from *, ending row in sc, ch 3 and turn.

Row 2: 2 dc in 1st sc, * 1 sc in top ch, ch 3, 3 dc around the ch, rep from *, ending row with 1 sc,.ch 1 and turn.

Row 3: 1 sc in 1st sc, ch 3, * 1 dc back into sc, 1 sc in the top of the ch, ch 3, rep from *, ending row with 1 sc in the turning ch, ch 4 and turn.

Row 4: * 1 dc in 3-ch, 1 ch, 1 dc in the sc, ch 1, rep from *, ending row with 1 dc in the end sc, ch 3 and turn.

Row 5: Same as row 1, except that the 3 dc are worked in every other dc.

Pattern formed by rep rows 1–4.

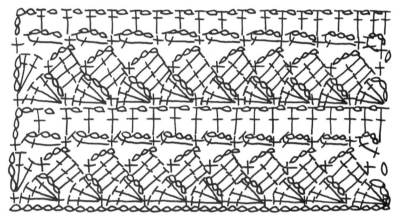

256. Chain multiples of 10 plus 3.

Row 1: 1 dc in the 4th ch, * ch 3, 1 sc in the 5th ch, ch 3, 3 dc in the same ch, 1 dc in the 5th ch, ch 1, 1 dc in the ch just used, rep from *, ending row with 2 dc in the last ch, ch 3 and turn.

Row 2: 1 dc in the 1st dc, * ch 3, 1 sc in the top of the 3-ch, ch 3, 3 dc around the 1st 3-ch of row below, forming a perpendicular angle, 1 dc, 1 ch and 1 dc in the 1-ch of the row below, rep from *, ending row with 2 dc in the turning ch, ch 3 and turn.

Pattern formed by rep rows 1–2.

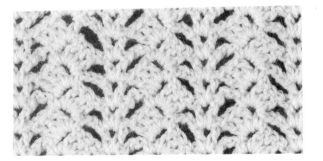

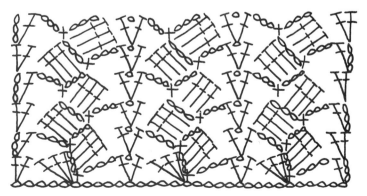

257. Chain multiples of 10 plus 6.

Row 1: 1 sc in the 9th ch, * ch 2, 3 dc in the 5th ch, ch 1, 3 dc in the ch just used, ch 2, 1 sc in the 5th ch, rep from *, ending row with sc, 2 chs and 1 dc in the 3rd and last ch, ch 6 and turn.
Row 2: * 1 sc in the sc, ch 1, turn, work 4 sc backwards along the ch, ch 1 and turn, 1 sc in each of the 4 sc, ch 1 and turn, 1 sc in each of the 4 sc, ch 1 and turn, 1 sc in each of the 4 sc, 3 dc in the 1-ch, ch 1, 3 dc in the 1-ch, ch 3, rep from *, ending row after last set with 1 dc in the turning ch, ch 5 and turn.
Row 3: Same as row 1, except that the sc are worked in the top of the corner of the sc square.
Pattern formed by rep rows 1–2.

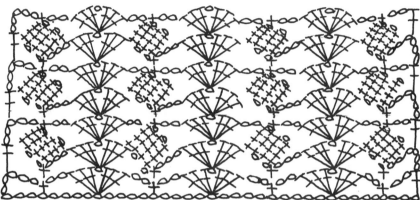

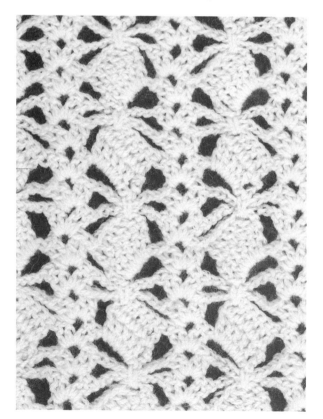

258. Chain multiples of 12 plus 4.

Row 1: 2 dc in the 4th ch, * ch 8, 2 dc in the 12th ch, ch 2, 2 dc in the same ch, rep from *, ending row with 3 dc in the 12th and last ch, ch 3 and turn.
Row 2: 2 dc in the 1st dc, * ch 4, 1 sc worked around the middle of the 2 chs below, ch 4, 2 dc in the 2-ch, ch 2, 2 dc in the 2-ch, rep from *, ending row with 3 dc in the turning ch, ch 3 and turn.
Row 3: 2 dc in the 1st dc, * ch 5, 1 sc in the sc, ch 3, work 5 dc around the 5-ch, ch 3 and turn, 1 dc in the 2nd dc, the 3 dc after that and 1 in the turning ch, 2 dc in the 2-ch, ch 2, 2 dc in the same 2-ch, rep from *, ending row after last set with 3 dc in the turning ch, ch 3 and turn.
Row 4: Work 2 dc in the 1st dc, * ch 8, 2 dc in the 2-ch, ch 2, 2 dc in the same 2-ch, rep from *, ending row with 3 dc in the turning ch, ch 3 and turn.
Row 5: 2 dc in the 1st dc, * ch 8, 2 dc in the 2-ch, ch 2, 2 dc in the same 2-ch, rep from *, ending row with 3 dc in the turning ch, ch 3 and turn.
Row 6: 2 dc in the 1st dc, * ch 5, work 1 sc around the middle of the 2 chs below, ch 3, work 5 dc around the 5-ch, ch 3, 1 dc in the 2nd dc, the next 3 dc and 1 in the turning ch, 2 dc in the 2-ch, ch 2, 2 dc in the same 2-ch, rep from *, ending row with last set and 3 dc in the turning ch, ch 3 and turn.
Row 7: Rep row 1, ch 3 and turn.
Row 8: Rep row 1, ch 3 and turn.
Pattern formed by rep rows 1–8.

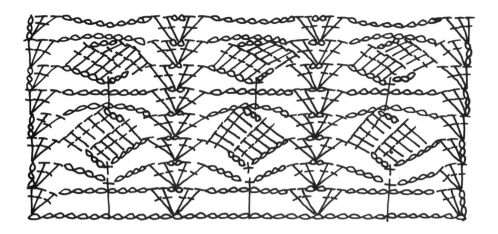

259. Chain multiples of 16 plus 4.

Row 1: 1 dc in the 5th ch, * 1 dc in the 3rd ch, ch 3, work 3 dc around the last dc made so they are perpendicular, 1 dc in the 4th ch and in the next ch, rep from *, ending row with 2 dc, ch 3 and turn.

Row 2: 1 dc in the 2nd dc, * ch 3, 1 sc in the top of the 3-ch, 3 dc in the next dc, 3 dc in the next dc, 1 sc in the top of the 3-ch, ch 3, 1 dc in each of the next 2 dc, rep from *, ending row with 2 dc, the last of which is in the turning ch, ch 3 and turn.

Row 3: 1 dc in the 2nd dc, * 1 dc in the sc, ch 3, 3 dc worked around the dc just made, work 3 dc together in the next 3 dc, work 3 dc together in the next 3 dc, 1 dc in the next sc, ch 3, 3 dc around the dc just formed, 1 dc in each of the next 2 dc, rep from *, ending row with 2 dc, the last of which is in the turning ch, ch 3 and turn.

Row 4: 1 dc in the 2nd dc, * ch 3, 1 sc in the top of the 3-ch, ch 3, 1 dc in the top of the 3 dc worked together, 1 dc in the top of the next 3 dc worked together, ch 3, 1 sc in the top of the 3-ch, ch 3, 1 dc in the top of each of the next 2 dc, rep from *, ending row with the dc in last dc and 1 in the turning ch, ch 3 and turn.

Pattern formed by rep rows 1–4.

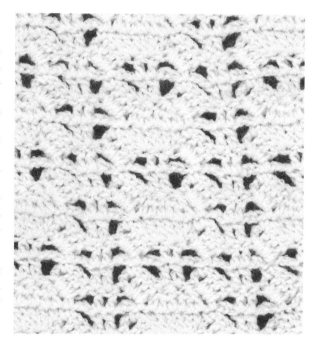

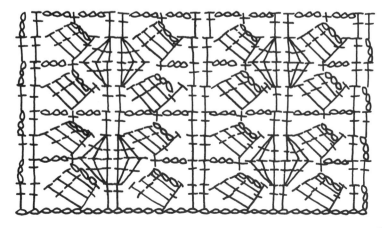

21
Y-Stitch

260. Chain multiples of 6 plus 1.

Row 1: 1 sc in the 2nd ch, * ch 3, 1 sc in the 4th ch, rep from *,
ending row with 3 chs and 1 sc, ch 4 and turn.
Row 2: * 1 Y-stitch around the middle of the 3-ch (1 trc, 2 dc
worked in the middle of the trc), ch 1, rep from *, ending row
with trc in the end sc, ch 1 and turn.
Row 3: Same as row 1, but sc worked in the 1-ch.
Pattern formed by rep rows 1–2.

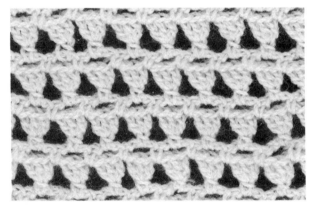

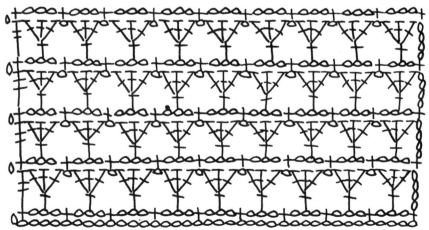

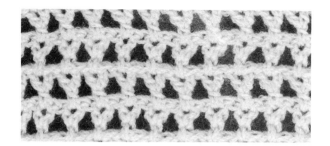

261. Chain multiples of 3 plus 5.

Row 1: * Y-stitch (wrap yarn around hook twice, follow through as with a trc, ch 1, 1 dc through the middle of the trc), rep process into 3rd ch, rep from *, ending row with trc in the 2nd ch after the last set, ch 4 and turn.

Row 2: Same as row 1, but the Y-stitch to be formed in the ch between the 2 loops in the ch of the Y below.

Pattern formed by rep rows 1–2.

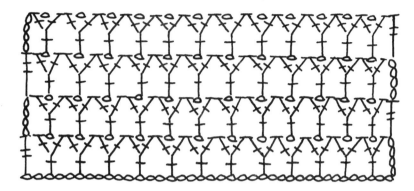

262. Chain multiples of 4 plus 5.

Row 1: 1 dc in the 7th ch, * ch 1, 1 dc in 2nd ch, rep from *, ending row with last set, ch 3 and turn.

Row 2: 1 dc in 1st ch, 1 dc in dc, * ch 1, 1 dc in dc, 1 dc in the ch, 1 dc in the dc, rep from *, ending row with 1 ch and 1 dc, ch 4 and turn.

Row 3: 1 dc in 2nd dc, * ch 1, 1 dc in 2nd dc, ch 1, 1 dc in next dc, rep from *, ending row with 1 dc in the turning ch, ch 4 and turn.

Row 4: Sk 1st dc, * 1 Y-stitch in next dc (trc in dc, work 2 dc in the middle of the trc), 1 trc in next dc, rep from *, ending row with 1 trc in the turning ch, ch 4 and turn.

Row 5: Same as row 1, except that the dc are worked in the middle loop of the Y-stitch and in the trc.

Pattern formed by rep rows 1–4.

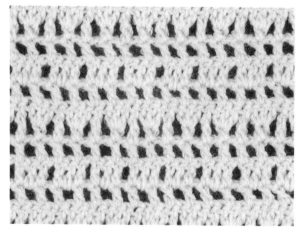

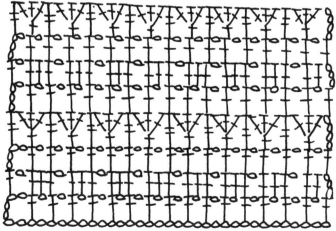

· 22 ·
X-Stitch

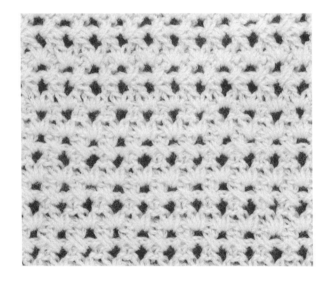

263. Chain multiples of 3 plus 4.

Row 1: 1 dc in the 7th ch, * ch 1, 1 dc backwards 2 chs, 1 dc in the 3rd ch, rep from *, ending row with 1 dc in the ch after the last set, ch 2 and turn.

Row 2: 1 dc in the 1-ch, * ch 2, finish 2 dc together in the 1-ch just used and the next 1-ch, rep from *, ending row with 2 dc finished together in the last 1-ch and the turning ch, ch 2 and turn.

Row 3: 1 dc in the 2-ch, ch 1, 1 dc backwards in the 2 dc finished together, * 1 dc in the next 2-ch, ch 1, 1 dc backwards in the last 2-ch, rep from *, ending row with 2 dc finished together, 1 in the last 2-ch and 1 in the turning ch, ch 3 and turn.

Row 4: Finish 2 dc together in the 1st 2 dc finished together and the 1-ch, * ch 2, begin 2 dc finished together in the 1-ch just used and the next 1-ch, rep from *, ending row with 2 dc finished together in the last 1-ch and the turning ch, ch 3 and turn.

Pattern formed by rep rows 1–4.

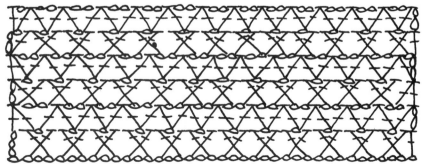

264. Chain multiples of 2 plus 4.

Row 1: 1 dc in the 6th ch, 1 dc backwards 1 ch, * 1 dc in the 2nd ch, 1 dc backwards in the 1st ch, rep from *, ending row with 1 extra dc in the last ch, ch 3 and turn.
Row 2: Sk 1 dc, * 1 dc in 2nd dc, 1 dc backwards in last dc, rep from *, ending row with 1 dc in last dc, 1 in the turning ch, ch 3 and turn.
Pattern formed by rep rows 1–2.

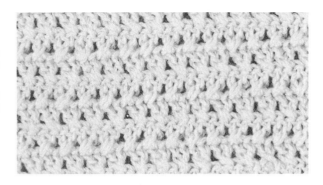

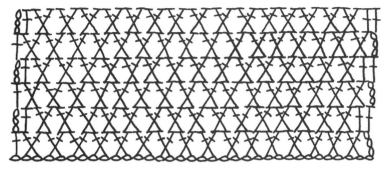

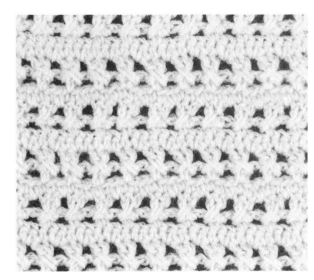

265. Chain multiples of 6 plus 1.

Row 1: 1 sc in the 2nd ch and all the way across the row, ch 1 and turn.
Row 2: 1 sc in the 1st sc, * ch 2, 1 sc in the 3rd sc, rep from *, ending row with 2 chs and 1 sc in the last sc, ch 3 and turn.
Row 3: 1 dc in the 1st 2-ch, * ch 1, 1 dc in the 2nd 2-ch, 1 dc backwards in the 1st 2-ch, rep from *, ending row with 1 ch and 1 dc in the sc, ch 1 and turn.
Row 4: 1 sc in each dc and in each ch all across the row, ending with the last sc in the sc, ch 1 and turn.
Row 5: 1 sc in the 1st sc, * ch 2, 1 sc in the 3rd sc, rep from *, ending row with 2 chs and 1 sc in the sc, ch 3 and turn.
Row 6: 1 dc in the 1st ch, * ch 1, 1 dc in the 2-ch after the sc, 1 dc in the 2-ch before the sc, rep from *, ending row with 1 ch and 1 dc in the sc, ch 1 and turn.
Row 7: 1 sc in each ch and each dc.
Pattern formed by rep rows 1–7.

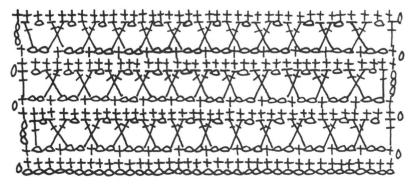

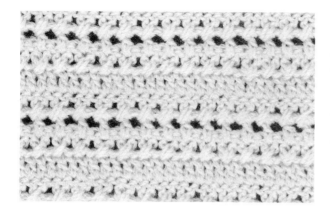

266. Chain multiples of 2 plus 4.

Row 1: 1 dc in 5th ch and all across row in each ch, ch 3 and turn.
Row 2: 1 dc in 3rd dc, 1 dc backwards 1 dc forming an X, * 1 dc in 2nd dc, 1 dc in 1st dc, rep from *, ending row with 1 dc in turning ch, ch 3 and turn.
Row 3: * 1 dc between 2 sides of the X, ch 1 and rep from *, ending row with 1 ch and 1 dc in the turning ch, ch 3 and turn.
Row 4: Sk 1 dc * 1 dc in the ch after the next dc, 1 dc in the ch before the same dc, rep from *, ending row with 1 dc in turning ch.
Pattern formed by rep rows 1–4.

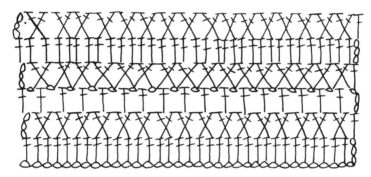

267. Chain multiples of 2 plus 6

Row 1: 1 dc in the 7th ch, * ch 1, 1 dc in the 2nd ch, rep from *, ending row with dc, ch 3 and turn.
Row 2: Sk 1st dc, * work 1 dc in the 1-ch following the next dc, ch 1, work 1 dc backwards in the last 1-ch, rep from *, ending row with 1 dc in turning ch, ch 3 and turn.
Row 3: 1 dc in the 2nd dc, * ch 1, 1 dc in the top of the next dc, rep from *, ending row with 1 extra dc in the turning ch, ch 3 and turn.
Row 4: 1 dc in the top of the 3rd dc, * ch 1, 1 dc backwards in the last dc, dc in the 2nd dc, rep from *, ending row with dc in the turning ch, ch 4 and turn.
Pattern formed by rep rows 1–4.

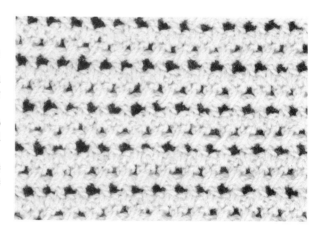

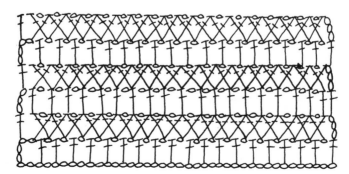

268. Chain multiples of 6 plus 4.

Row 1: 1 dc in 6th ch, go backwards, 1 dc in the ch before, * 1 dc in ch after X-stitch, ch 2, 1 dc in 3rd ch, 1 dc in 2nd ch backwards, 1 dc in 1st ch, rep from *, ending row with 2 chs and 1 dc, ch 3 and turn.

Row 2: * 1 dc in 2nd ch backwards, 1 dc in 1st ch, 1 dc in dc, ch 2, 1 dc in dc, after X-stitch, rep from *, ending row with 2 chs and 1 dc, ch 3 and turn.

Pattern formed by rep rows 1–2.

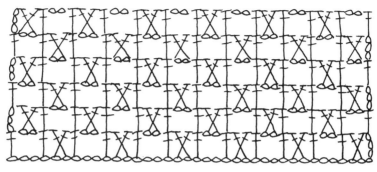

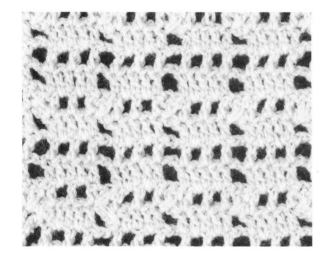

269. Chain multiples of 7 plus 4.

Row 1: 1 dc in 5th ch, 1 dc in next ch, * ch 2, 1 dc in 3rd ch and in 4 chs following, rep from *, ending row with 3 dc in last 3 chs, ch 4 and turn.

Row 2: 1 dc in 3rd dc, * ch 2, 1 dc in 1st dc, ch 1, 1 dc in 2nd dc, ch 1, 1 dc in 2nd dc, rep from *, ending row with 1 dc, 1 ch and 1 dc in the turning ch, ch 3 and turn.

Row 3: 1 dc in 1st ch, 1 dc in 2nd dc, * ch 2, 1 dc in 1st dc, ch, next dc, ch and the next dc, totalling 5 dc, rep from *, ending row with 1 dc in the last dc and 2 in the turning ch, ch 4 and turn.

Row 4: 1 dc in 3rd dc, * 1 dc in 2nd ch, 1 dc back in 1st ch, forming an X, 1 dc in next dc, ch 1, dc in 2nd dc, ch 1, dc in 2nd dc, rep from *, ending row with 1 dc, 1 ch and 1 dc in turning ch, ch 3 and turn.

Pattern formed by rep rows 1–4.

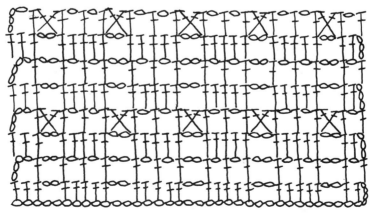

270. Chain multiples of 4 plus 5.

Row 1: 1 dc in the 9th ch, * ch 1, 1 dc back 2 chs, ch 1, 1 dc in the 4th ch, rep from *, ending row with 1 ch and 1 dc in the next ch after finishing the set, ch 2 and turn.

Row 2: Sk 1 dc, * 1 dc in the next dc, ch 1, 1 dc backwards in the dc, ch 1, rep from *, ending row with 1 dc finished together in turning ch after the last X.

Pattern formed by rep rows 1–2.

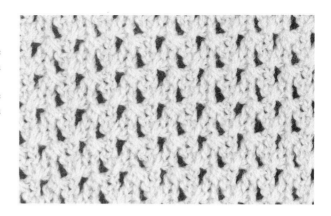

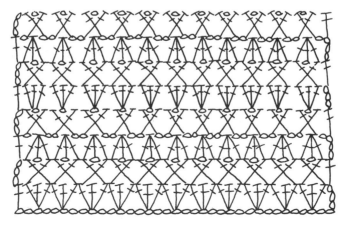

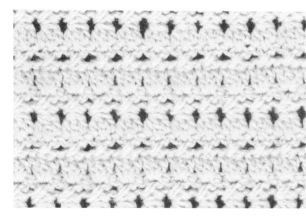

271. Chain multiples of 3 plus 4.

Row 1: 3 dc in the 6th ch, * 3 dc in the 3rd ch, rep from *, ending row with last set and 1 dc in the 2nd ch, ch 3 and turn.

Row 2: Sk 1st dc, * 1 dc in the 3rd dc, ch 1, 1 dc backwards 2 dc, rep from *, ending row after the last set with 1 dc in the turning ch, ch 4 and turn.

Row 3: Sk 1st dc, * work 3 dc together in the dc, the ch and the dc, ch 2, rep from *, ending row with last set and 1 dc in the turning ch, ch 3 and turn.

Row 4: * 1 dc after the 3 dc finished together, ch 1, 1 dc backwards before the 3 dc finished together, rep from *, ending row with 1 dc in the turning ch, ch 3 and turn.

Pattern formed by rep rows 1–4.

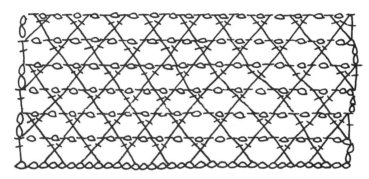

272. Chain multiples of 3 plus 1.

Row 1: 1 sc in the 2nd ch and in each ch all across the row, ch 4 and turn.

Row 2: Work 1 triple cross-stitch in the 2nd and the 4th sc, ch 1 between, * work triple cross-stitch in the next sc and in the 2nd sc, rep from *, ending row with 1 extra trc in the sc, ch 1 and turn.

Row 3: Same as row 1, except 1 sc is worked in each trc and in each ch, ch 4 and turn.

Pattern formed by rep rows 1–2.

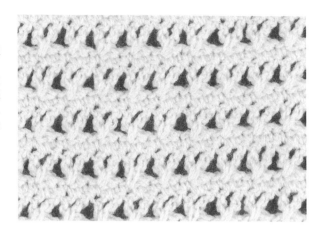

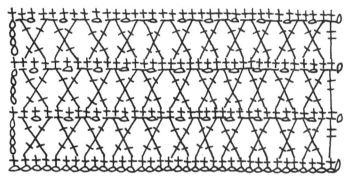

273. Chain multiples of 4 plus 6.

Row 1: Work 1 trc in the 6th ch and the 3rd ch, with 2 chs between, * work 1 trc in the next ch and the 3rd ch, with 2 chs between, rep from *, ending row with last set and 1 trc in the last ch, ch 1 and turn.

Row 2: 1 sc in the 1st trc, * 1 hdc, 1 dc and 1 hdc in the 2-ch, 1 sc between the 2 triple cross-stitches, rep from *, ending row with 1 sc in the turning ch, ch 5 and turn.

Row 3: Same as row 1, except that the sides of the X-stitch are formed in the sc.

Pattern formed by rep rows 1–2.

274. Chain multiples of 6 plus 5.

Row 1: 1 trc in the 8th ch, * ch 1, 1 trc backwards 2 chs, 3 trc in the 2nd ch, 1 trc in the 4th ch, rep from *, ending row with 1 trc in the last ch, ch 4 and turn.
Row 2: Sk 1st trc, * 1 trc in the 3rd trc, ch 1, 1 trc backwards 2 trc, 3 trc in the 1-ch between the 2 sides of the X, rep from *, ending row with 1 trc in the turning ch, ch 4 and turn.
Pattern formed by rep rows 1–2.

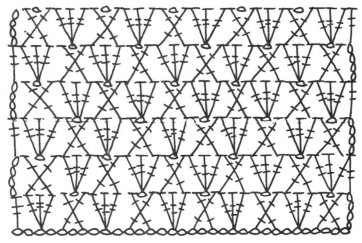

275. Chain multiples of 10 plus 4.

Row 1: 1 dc in the 7th ch, ch 1, 1 dc in the same stitch, ch 1, 1 dc in the same stitch, * 1 dc in the 6th ch, ch 3, 1 dc backwards 2 chs, 1 dc in the 4th ch, ch 1, 1 dc in the same ch, ch 1, 1 dc in the same ch, rep from *, ending row with 1 dc in the last ch after the last set, ch 3 and turn.
Row 2: * 1 dc in the 2nd ch, ch 3, 1 dc back in the 1st ch, 1 dc in the 3-ch, ch 1, 1 dc in the same 3-ch, ch 1, 1 dc in the same 3-ch, rep from *, ending row with 1 dc in the turning ch, ch 3 and turn.
Pattern formed by rep rows 1–2.

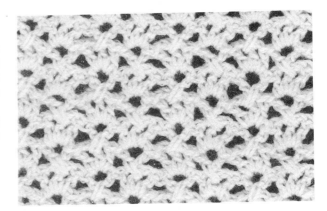

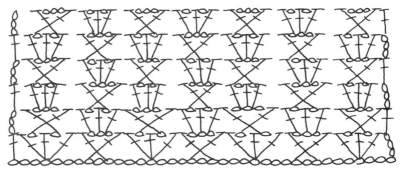

276. Chain multiples of 6 plus 4.

Row 1: 1 dc in the 5th ch, 1 dc in the 3rd ch, * 1 dc in the 4th ch, ch 3, 1 dc backwards in the 2nd ch, 1 dc in the 2nd ch, rep from *, ending row with 1 dc, 1 ch and 1 dc in the 3rd ch, ch 3 and turn.
Row 2: 3 dc in the 1st ch, 1 sc in the 3rd dc, * 7 dc around the 3-ch, 1 sc in the 2nd dc, rep from *, ending row with 4 dc in the turning ch, ch 1 and turn.
Row 3: 1 sc in the 1st dc and also in the 2nd dc, * ch 1, 1 dc in the next sc, ch 1, 1 sc in the 3rd dc and in the 2 dc following that, rep from *, ending row with 1 sc in the last dc and 1 sc in the turning ch, ch 3 and turn.
Row 4: * 1 dc in the 2nd ch, ch 3, 1 dc backwards in the 1st ch, 1 dc in the 2nd sc, rep from *, ending row with last set and then 1 dc in the last sc, ch 1 and turn.
Row 5: 1 sc in the 1st dc, * 7 dc in the 3-ch, 1 sc in the 2nd dc, rep from *, ending row with 7 dc in the last 3 chs and 1 sc in the turning ch, ch 4 and turn.
Row 6: * 1 sc in the 3rd dc, 1 sc in each of the next 2 dc, ch 1, 1 dc in the next sc, ch 1, rep from *, ending row with 1 ch and 1 dc, ch 4 and turn.
Pattern formed by rep rows 1–6.

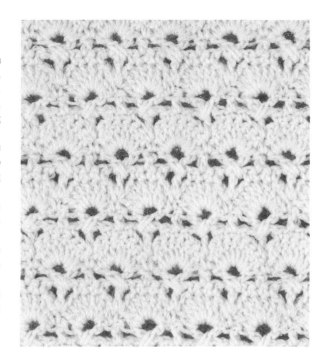

277. Chain multiples of 6 plus 1.

Row 1: 1 sc in 2nd ch, * ch 1, 2 dc in 3rd ch, ch 1, 2 dc in same ch, ch 1, 1 sc in 3rd ch, rep from *, ending row with 1 sc after last set, ch 5 and turn.
Row 2: * 1 sc in 1st ch, ch 2, 1 dc in 1st ch after the sc, ch 1, 1 dc back in the last ch before the sc, ch 2, rep from *, ending row with 2 chs and 1 dc in the sc, ch 1 and turn.
Row 3: Same as row 1, except that the 4 dc are worked in the sc and the X-stitches are worked in the 2 chs around the sc.
Pattern formed by rep rows 1–2.

278. Chain multiples of 8 plus 4.

Row 1: 1 dc in the 5th ch, * ch 1, 1 dc in the 3rd ch, ch 1 and rep 1 dc in the same ch, ch 1, 1 dc in the 3rd ch and the 2 chs after that, rep from *, ending row with 2 dc, ch 3 and turn.

Row 2: Same as row 1, ch 1 and turn.

Row 3: 1 sc in the 1st dc, * ch 1, 2 dc in the 1-ch between the 2 sides of the V-stitch, ch 1, 2 more dc in the same ch, ch 1, 1 sc in the middle of the 3 dc, rep from *, ending row with 1 sc in the turning ch, ch 3 and turn.

Row 4: 1 dc in the sc, * ch 2, 1 sc in the 1-ch between the 2 sets of dc, ch 2, work 1 dc in the 3rd dc 2 rows below, ch 1, work 1 dc backwards in the 1st dc, rep from *, ending row with 2 dc in the sc, ch 3 and turn.

Row 5: 2 dc in the 1st dc, * ch 1, 1 sc in the sc, ch 1, 2 dc in the 1-ch between the 2 sides of the X-stitch, ch 1, 2 dc in the same 1-ch, rep from *, ending row with 3 dc in the turning ch, ch 1 and turn.

Row 6: 1 sc in the 1st dc, * ch 2, 1 dc in the 1-ch after the sc, ch 1, 1 dc backwards in the 1-ch before the sc, ch 2, 1 sc in the 1-ch, rep from *, ending row with sc in the turning ch, ch 3 and turn.

Row 7: Same as row 1, except that the V-stitch is made in the 1-ch between the sides of the X-stitch.

Pattern formed by rep rows 1–6.

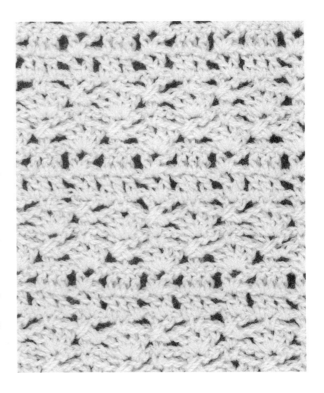

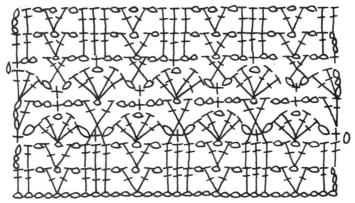

279. Chain multiples of 5 plus 4.

Row 1: 1 dc in the 5th ch and all across the row, ch 5 and turn.
Row 2: Work 1 triple X-stitch in the 2nd and 3rd dc, with 2 chs in between, ch 1, * ch 1, work 1 triple cross-stitch in the 2nd and then the 3rd dc, leaving 2 chs in between, rep from *, ending row with last set and 1 extra trc in the turning ch, ch 3 and turn.
Row 3: * work 4 dc around the 2-ch, ch 1 and rep from *, ending row after the last set with 1 extra dc in the turning ch, ch 3 and turn.
Row 4: 1 dc in the 2nd dc and in the 3 dc after that, * ch 1, 1 dc in each of the 4 dc, rep from *, ending the row with 1 extra dc in the turning ch after the last set, ch 5 and turn.
Row 5: Sk 1st dc, * finish 4 dc together in the next 4 dc, ch 5 and rep from *, ending row with last set, 2 chs and 1 dc in the turning ch, ch 5 and turn.
Row 6: * work 1 trc cross-stitch in the 2nd ch before the set and the 2nd ch after the set, with 2 chs between the 2 sides of the X, ch 1, rep from *, ending row after last set with 1 extra trc in the turning ch, ch 3 and turn.
Row 7: Same as row 1, except that the dc are made in each ch and in each side of the trc, 1 in the turning ch, ch 5 and turn.
Pattern formed by rep rows 1–4.

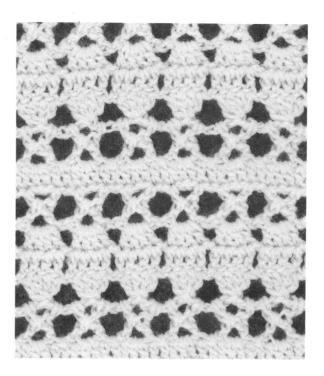

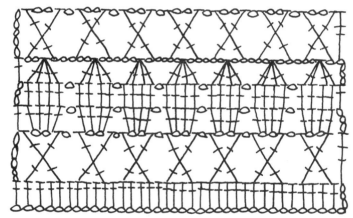

◆ *23* ◆
Picot

280. Chain multiples of 2 plus 2.

Row 1: 1 sc in 5th ch, ch 3, 1 sc in same ch, * 1 sc in 2nd ch, ch 3, 1 sc in same ch, rep from *, ending row after last set with l ch and l hdc in last ch, ch 3 and turn.
Row 2: * 1 dc in 3-ch, ch 1, rep from *, ending row after the last set with dc in the turning ch, ch 3 and turn.
Row 3: Same as row 1, except that the sc, 3 chs and sc are worked in the 1-ch.
Pattern formed by rep rows 1–2.

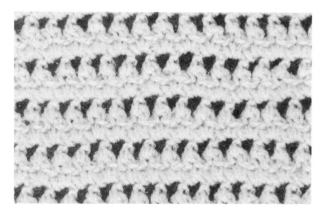

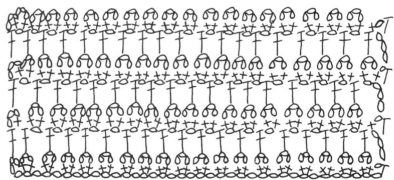

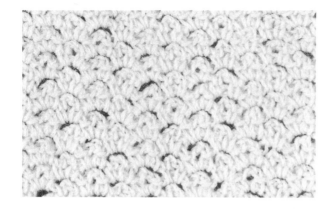

281. Chain multiples of 5 plus 1.

Row 1: 1 sc in the 2nd ch, * ch 5, 1 sc in the 5th ch, rep from *, ending row with 1 sc in the last ch, ch 5 and turn.
Row 2: * 1 sc in the 5-ch, ch 3, 1 sc in the same 5-ch, ch 5, rep from *, ending row with 2 chs and 1 dc in the last sc, ch 5 and turn.
Row 3: * 1 sc in the 5-ch, ch 3, 1 sc in the same 5-ch, ch 5, rep from *, ending row with 1 sc in the turning ch, ch 5 and turn.
Pattern formed by rep rows 2–3.

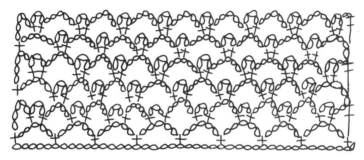

282. Chain multiples of 4 plus 1.

Row 1: 1 sc in the 2nd ch, * 1 picot, 1 sc, 1 sc in the next ch and the 3 chs following, rep from *, ending row with 1 sc in each of the last 2 chs, ch 4 and turn.
Row 2: * finish 2 dc together in the 1st and the 4th sc, ch 3, rep from *, always beginning the 2 stitches finished together with the stitch just used, end row with 2 dc finished together in the 3rd to the last sc and the last sc, ch 1 and turn.
Row 3: 1 sc in the 1st 2 dc finished together, * 2 sc around the 3-ch, 1 picot, 1 sc around the same 3-ch, rep from *, ending row with 2 sc in the turning ch, ch 3 and turn.
Row 4: 1 dc in the 3rd sc, * ch 3, finish 2 dc together in the sc just used and the 4th sc, rep from *, ending row with 1 dc in the last sc, 1 ch and 1 dc in the sc just used, ch 1 and turn.
Pattern formed by rep rows 1–4.

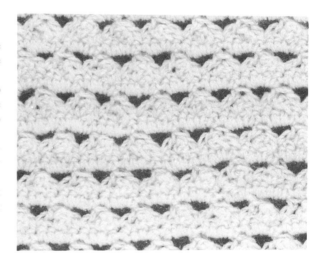

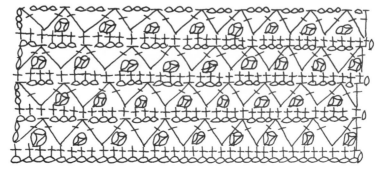

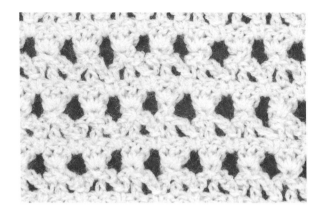

283. Chain multiples of 4 plus 4.

Row 1: 1 picot, * ch 3, 1 sc in 6th ch before picot, ch 3, 1 dc in 2nd ch, 1 picot, ch 3, sc in 2nd ch, rep from *, ending row with 1 dc, ch 3 and turn.

Row 2: 1 dc in 1st dc, * 3 dc in the picot, rep from *, ending row with 2 dc in end picot, ch 4 and turn.

Row 3: Same as row 1, except that the sc is worked between the 2 groups of 3 dc, and the dc is worked in the middle dc.

Pattern formed by rep rows 1–2.

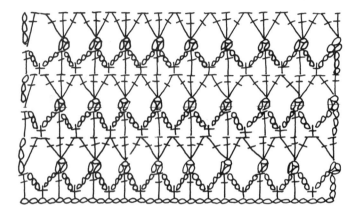

284. Chain multiples of 7 plus 1.

Row 1: 1 sc in 2nd ch, * 5 dc in the 3rd ch, 1 sc in 3rd ch, ch 3 (picot), 1 sc in next ch, rep from * ending row with 1 sc and 7 chs.

Row 2: * 1 sc in 3rd dc, ch 3, 1 sc in same dc, ch 3, 1 dc in the picot, ch 3, rep from *, ending row with 1 trc, ch 1 and turn.

Row 3: Same as row 1, except that 5 dc are worked in the picot (3-chs) and the picot are worked in the dc.

Pattern formed by rep rows 1–2.

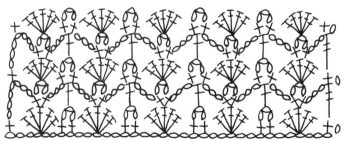

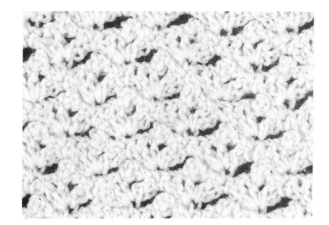

285. Chain multiples of 6 plus 1.

Row 1: 1 sc in the 2nd ch, * ch 7, 1 sc in the 6th ch, rep from *, ending row with 1 sc in the end ch, ch 4 and turn.
Row 2: 1 dc in the single ch, * 1 sc around the middle of the 7-ch, 1 dc in the sc, ch 1, 1 dc in the same sc, 1 picot, ch 1, 1 dc in the same sc, rep from *, ending row with 1 dc, 1 ch and 1 dc in the end sc, ch 6 and turn.
Row 3: * 1 sc in the sc, ch 7, rep from *, ending row with 3 chs and 1 dc in the turning ch, ch 1 and turn.
Row 4: 1 sc in the dc, * 1 dc in the sc, ch 1, 1 dc in the same sc, 1 picot, 1 ch, 1 dc in the sc, 1 sc around the middle of the 7-ch, rep from *, ending row with 1 sc in the turning ch, ch 1 and turn.
Pattern formed by rep rows 1–4.

286. Chain multiples of 5 plus 7.

Row 1: 1 sc in the 9th ch, * 1 picot, ch 3, 1 dc in the 2nd ch and the ch after that, ch 3, 1 sc in the 2nd ch, rep from *, ending row with 1 dc, ch 3 and turn.
Row 2: 1 dc in the 1st of the 3-ch, * ch 1, 1 dc in the last of the next 3-ch, 1 dc in each of the next 2 dc, 1 dc in the 1st of the next 3-ch, rep from *, ending row with 2 dc in the turning ch, ch 6 and turn.
Pattern formed by rep rows 1–2.

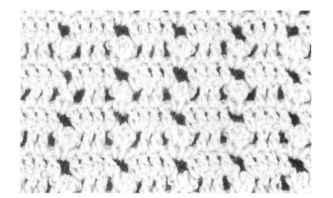

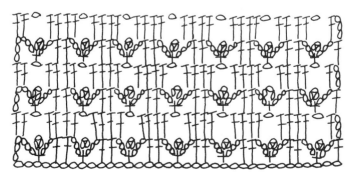

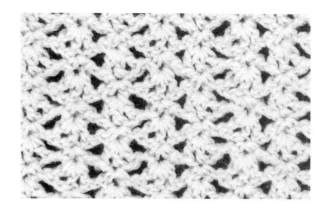

287. Chain multiples of 8 plus 1.

Row 1: 1 sc in the 2nd ch, * ch 1, 1 dc in the 4th ch, ch 1, dc in the same ch, ch 1, 1 dc in the same ch, ch 1, 1 sc in the 4th ch, ch 3, 1 sc in the same ch, rep from *, ending row with 1 dc, 1 ch and 1 dc, ch 1 and turn.
Row 2: 1 sc in the 1st dc, * ch 1, 1 dc in the 3-ch, ch 1, 1 dc in the same ch, ch 1, 1 dc in the same ch, ch 1, 1 sc in the middle dc, ch 3, 1 dc in the same ch, rep from *, ending row with 1 dc, 1 ch and 1 dc in the end sc, ch 1 and turn.
Pattern formed by rep rows 1–2.

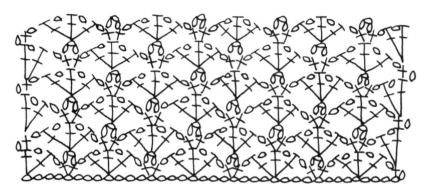

288. Chain multiples of 7 plus 4.

Row 1: 2 dc in 7th ch, ch 2, 2 dc in same ch, * ch 1, 1 picot, ch 1, 2 dc in 7th ch, ch 2, 2 dc in the same ch, rep from *, row ending in 1 dc, ch 3 and turn.
Row 2: Same as row 1, except that the sets of 2 dc and 2 chs are worked around the 2-ch.
Pattern formed by rep row 1.

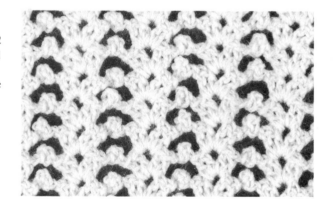

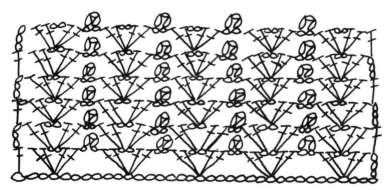

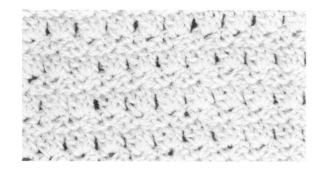

289. Chain multiples of 3 plus 1.

Row 1: 1 sc in the 3rd ch, ch 1, 1 sc in the 2nd ch, ch 2, 1 sc in the ch just used, * ch 2, 1 sc in the 3rd ch, ch 2, 1 sc in the same ch, rep from *, ending row with 1 ch and 1 sc in the ch after the last set, ch 3 and turn.
Row 2: 3 dc in the 2-ch, * 3 dc in the next 2-ch, rep from *, ending row with 1 extra dc in the sc, ch 1 and turn.
Pattern formed by rep rows 1–2.

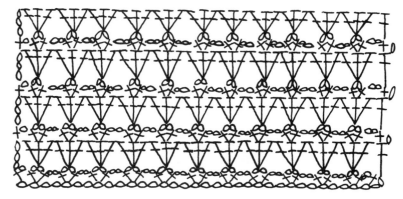

290. Chain multiples of 10 plus 4.

Row 1: 1 dc in 5th ch, * ch 2, 1 dc in 4th ch, ch 2, 1 dc in same ch, ch 2, 1 dc in each of the next 3 chs, rep from *, ending row with 2 dc, ch 3 and turn.
Row 2: 1 dc in 2nd dc, * picot, 7 dc in the 2-ch, 1 picot, 1 dc in each of the next 3 dc, rep from *, ending row with 2 dc (the last in the turning ch), ch 3 and turn.
Row 3: 1 dc in the 2nd dc, * ch 2, 1 dc in the middle of the 7 dc, ch 1, 1 dc in the same dc, ch 2, 1 dc in each of the next 3 dc, rep from *, ending row with 2 dc (the last in the turning ch), ch 3 and turn.
Row 4: Dc in 2nd dc, 1 in each of the 2-ch and 1 in each stitch all the way across the row, ch 3 and turn.
Pattern formed by rep rows 1–4.

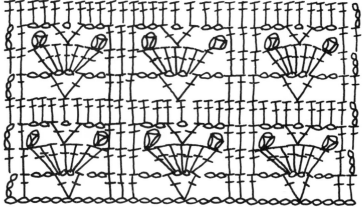

291. Chain multiples of 8 plus 4.

Row 1: 1 dc in the 5th ch, 1 dc in the next ch, * ch 2, 1 sc in the 2nd ch, ch 2, 1 dc in the 2nd ch, 1 dc in each of the next 4 chs, rep from *, ending row with 1 dc in each of the last 3 chs, ch 1 and turn.
Row 2: 1 sc in the 1st dc, * ch 1, 1 dc in the sc, ch 3, 1 dc in the sc just used, ch 1, 1 sc in the 3rd dc, rep from *, ending row with 1 sc in the turning ch, ch 3 and turn.
Row 3: * 3 dc around the 3-ch, 1 picot, 3 dc around the same ch, 1 picot, 3 dc around the same 3-ch, rep from *, ending row with last set, then 1 dc in the end sc, ch 5 and turn.
Row 4: Sk 1 dc, * dc in the 4th dc and next 2 dc, ch 5, rep from *, ending row after last set with 2 chs and 1 dc in the turning ch, ch 3 and turn.
Pattern formed by rep rows 1–4.

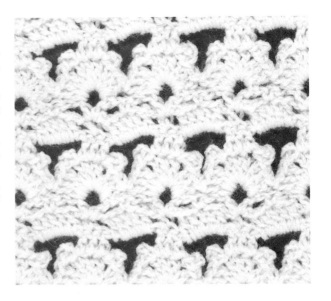

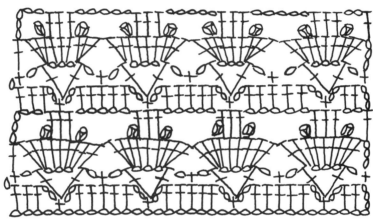

292. Chain multiples of 15 plus 4.

Row 1: 1 dc in the 5th ch and in each ch all across the row, ch 3 and turn.
Row 2: 1 dc in the 2nd dc, * ch 3, 1 sc in the 3rd dc, 1 picot, ch 3, 1 dc in the 3rd dc, ch 3, 1 sc in the 3rd dc, 1 picot, ch 3, 1 dc in the 3rd dc and in the 3 chs following, rep from *, ending row with 2 dc (the last in the turning ch), ch 3 and turn.
Row 3: 1 dc in the 2nd dc, * ch 5, 1 dc in the next dc, ch 5, 1 dc in each of the next 4 dc, rep from *, ending row with 2 dc (the last in the turning ch), ch 3 and turn.
Row 4: Same as row 2, ch 3.
Row 5: Same as row 3, ch 3.
Row 6: Same as row 1, except dc should be worked in the dc and 1 dc should be worked in each 5-ch.
Pattern formed by rep rows 1–5.

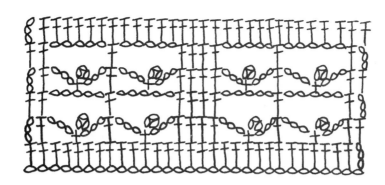

293. Chain multiples of 8 plus 4.

Row 1: 1 dc in the 5th ch and all across the row, ch 3 and turn.
Row 2: 1 dc in the 2nd dc and the dc after that, * ch 2, work 2 dc together in the next dc and the 4th dc, work 1 picot and secure end, work 2nd picot and secure, work 3rd picot and secure, ch 2, 1 dc in the next dc and the 2 dc after that, rep from *, ending row with 2 dc in the dc and 1 in the turning ch, ch 3 and turn.
Row 3: 1 dc in the 2nd dc and the dc after that, * ch 2, 1 sc in the top of the middle picot, ch 2, 1 dc in each of the next 3 dc, rep from *, ending row with 2 dc in the dc and 1 in the turning ch, ch 3 and turn.
Row 4: 1 dc in each ch and stitch all across the row.
Pattern formed by rep rows 1–3.

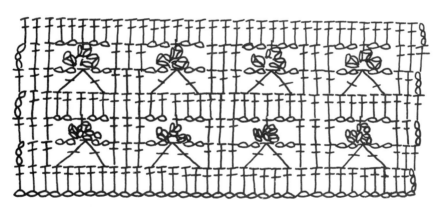

294. Chain multiples of 10 plus 4.

Row 1: 1 dc in the 5th ch and the ch after that, * 1 picot, 1 dc in the 2nd ch, 1 picot, 1 dc in the 2nd ch, 1 picot, 1 dc in the 2nd ch and the 4 chs after that, rep from *, ending row with 1 dc in each of the last 3 chs, ch 3 and turn.
Row 2: Same as row 1, except that the dc are worked in the dc.
Pattern formed by rep row 1.

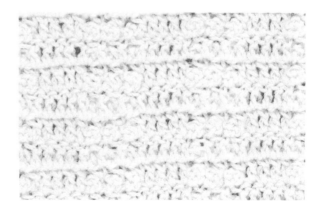

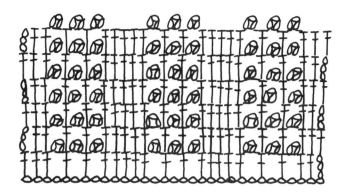

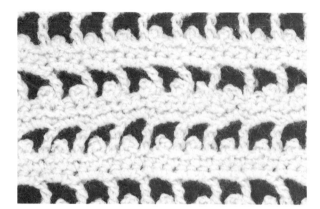

295. Chain multiples of 3 plus 1.

Row 1: Sc in the 2nd ch and in each ch all across the row, ch 1 and turn.
Row 2: Sc in the 1st and 2nd sc, * form 1 picot, 1 sc in each of the next 3 sc, rep from *, ending row with 1 sc in each of the last 2 sc, ch 6 and turn.
Row 3: * 1 trc in the middle of the 3 sc between the 2 picot, ch 2, rep from *, ending row with 1 trc in the last sc, ch 1 and turn.
Row 4: Same as row 1, except that the sc are worked in each ch and each trc.
Pattern formed by rep rows 1–3.

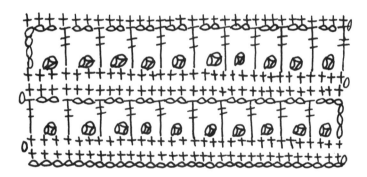

296. Chain multiples of 6 plus 5.
Row 1: 1 trc in the 6th ch, * ch 3, 1 trc in the 4th ch and the 2 chs after that, rep from *, ending row with 1 trc in each of the last 2 chs, ch 1 and turn.
Row 2: 1 sc in the 1st and 2nd trc, * 1 sc in each of the next 2 chs, form 1 picot, 1 sc in the next ch, 1 sc in each of the trc, rep from *, ending row with 1 extra sc in the turning ch, ch 4 and turn.
Pattern formed by rep rows 1–2.

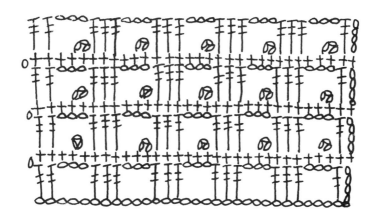

297. Chain multiples of 12 plus 1.

Row 1: 1 sc in the 2nd ch, * ch 5, 1 sc in the 6th ch, rep from *, ending row after last set, ch 3 and turn.

Row 2: * 5 dc around the 5-ch, ch 3, 1 sc around the middle of the 5-ch, ch 3, rep from *, ending row with 5 dc in the 5-ch and 1 extra dc in the sc, ch 3 and turn.

Row 3: Sk 1 dc, * 5 dc, 1 in each of the next 5 dc, ch 3, 1 sc in the sc, ch 3, rep from *, ending row with 5 dc in the dc and 1 dc in the turning ch, ch 3 and turn.

Row 4: Sk 1 dc, 1 dc in the 5 dc * ch 3, 1 sc in the sc, 1 picot, ch 3, 1 dc in each of the next 5 dc, rep from *, ending row with 5 dc in the dc and 1 dc in the turning ch, ch 1 and turn.

Row 5: 1 sc in the 1st dc, ch 5, * 1 sc in the 5th dc, ch 5, 1 sc in the next dc, rep from *, ending row with 5 chs and 1 sc in the turning ch, ch 5 and turn.

Row 6: * 1 sc around the middle of the 5-ch, ch 3, 5 dc around the 5-ch, rep from *, ending row with 1 sc, 2 chs and 1 dc in the sc, ch 5 and turn.

Row 7: * 1 sc in the sc, ch 3, 1 dc in each of the next 5 dc, ch 3, rep from *, ending row with 2 chs and 1 dc in the turning ch, ch 5 and turn.

Row 8: * 1 sc in the sc, 1 picot, ch 3, 1 dc in each of the next 5 dc, ch 3, rep from *, ending row with 2 chs and 1 dc, ch 1 and turn.
Pattern formed by rep rows 1–8.

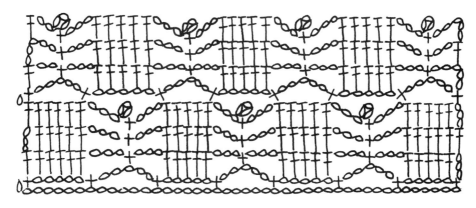

298. Chain 10 plus 4.

Row 1: 1 dc in the 5th and in the next ch, * ch 3, 1 sc in the 3rd ch, ch 3, 1 dc in the 3rd ch and in the 4 chs following, rep from *, ending row with 3 dc, ch 3 and turn.
Row 2: 1 dc in the 2nd and the next dc, * ch 3, 1 sc in the sc, ch 3, 1 sc in the same sc, ch 3, 1 dc in each of the next 5 dc, rep from *, ending row with dc in the dc and 1 in the turning ch, ch 1 and turn.
Row 3: 1 sc in each of the 3 dc, * 1 sc in the 1st ch, ch 3, 1 sc around the last ch before the dc, 1 sc in each of the 5 dc, rep from *, ending row with 3 sc, the last one in the turning ch, ch 1 and turn.
Row 4: 1 sc in the 1st sc, * ch 3, 5 dc around the 3-ch, ch 3, 1 sc in the 4th sc, rep from *, ending row with 3 chs and 1 sc in the sc, ch 1 and turn.
Row 5: 1 sc in the 1st sc, * ch 3, 1 dc in each of the next 5 dc, ch 3, 1 sc in the sc, ch 3, 1 sc in the same sc, rep from *, ending row with 3 chs and 1 sc in the sc, ch 4 and turn.
Row 6: * 1 sc in the last ch before the 5 dc, 1 sc in each of the next 5 dc, 1 sc around the 1st ch just after the dc, ch 3 and rep from *, ending row with 1 ch and 1 dc in the sc, ch 3 and turn.
Pattern formed by rep rows 1–6.

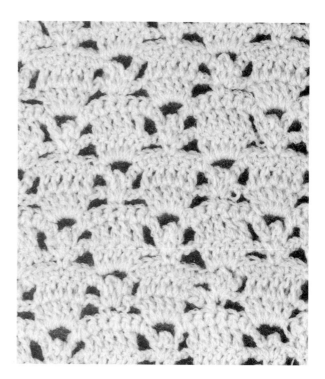

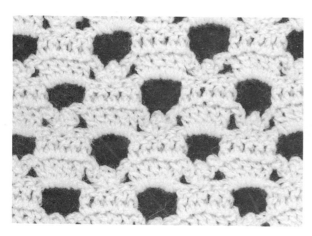

299. Chain multiples of 8 plus 5.

Row 1: 1 dc in the 5th ch, 1 dc in the next ch, * ch 3, 1 sc in the 2nd ch, 1 picot and 1 sc in the ch just used, ch 3, 1 dc in the 2nd ch and the 4 chs after that, rep from *, ending row with 1 dc in each of the last 3 chs, ch 1 and turn.
Row 2: * 1 sc in each of the dc, ch 5, rep from *, ending row with 1 sc in each of the last 2 dc and 1 in the turning ch, ch 1 and turn.
Row 3: 1 sc in the 1st sc, * ch 3, 5 dc around the 5-ch, ch 3, 1 sc in the 3rd sc, 1 picot, 1 sc in the same sc, rep from *, ending row with 3 chs and 1 sc in the last sc, ch 5 and turn.
Row 4: * 1 sc in each of the dc, ch 5, rep from *, ending row with 2 chs and 1 dc in the last sc, ch 3 and turn.
Pattern formed by rep rows 1–4.

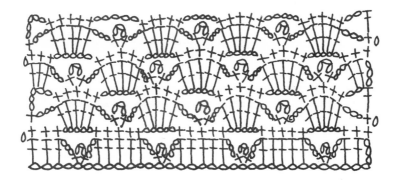

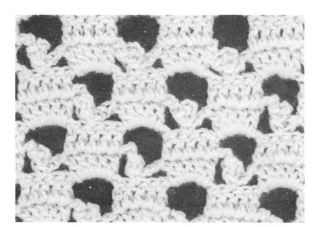

300. Chain multiples of 10 plus 4.

Row 1: 1 dc in 5th ch, * and in the next 4 chs, ch 3, 1 sc in the 3rd ch, ch 4, slip end of the ch into the beginning of the ch, ch 3, 1 dc in 3rd ch, rep from *, ending row with 6 dc (1 each in the last 6 chs), ch 3 and turn.

Row 2: 1 dc in 2nd dc and in the next 4 dc, * ch 5, 1 dc in each of the next 5 dc, rep from *, ending row with 5 in the dc and 1 in the turning ch, ch 6 and turn.

Row 3: Same as row 1, except that the order is switched, ch and picot are formed over the dc, with the picot formed in the 3rd and middle dc, 5 dc are formed around the 5-ch.

Pattern formed by rep rows 1–2, with design alternated for the next 2 rows.

301. Chain multiples of 4 plus 4.

Row 1: 1 dc in the 6th ch, * 1 dc in the same ch, 1 picot, 1 dc in the same ch, ch 2, 1 dc in the 4th ch, rep from *, ending row with 1 dc after the last set, ch 1 and turn.

Row 2: 1 sc in the 1st dc, * ch 5, 1 sc in the 2-ch, rep from *, ending row with 1 sc in the turning ch, ch 3 and turn.

Row 3: 1 sc around the 5-ch, * ch 3, 1 sc around the 5-ch, rep from *, ending row with 1 ch and 1 hdc in the sc, ch 3 and turn.

Row 4: 1 dc in the 1-ch and in every sc and ch all across the row, ending with 2 dc in the turning ch, ch 3 and turn.

Pattern formed by rep rows 1–4.

Picot 229

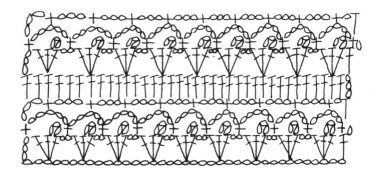

302. Chain multiples of 7 plus 3.

Row 1: 1 dc in the 4th ch, * ch 1, work 2 dc together in the 2nd ch and the 3rd ch after that, ch 4 and attach end ch to 1st ch, ch 1, 4 dc in the 2nd ch, rep from *, ending row with 2 dc in the 2nd ch, ch 3 and turn.

Row 2: 2 dc in the 2nd dc, * 1 sc in the top of the 4-ch, 2 dc in the 1st of the 4 dc, ch 2, 2 dc in the last of the 4 dc, rep from *, ending row with 2 dc in the last dc and 1 in the turning ch, ch 2 and turn.

Row 3: Sk 1 dc, 1 dc in the next dc, * ch 1, 4 dc in the sc, ch 1, finish 2 dc together in the 2nd dc and the next dc, ch 4, attach the end ch back to the 1st ch, rep from *, ending row with 2 dc finished together in the last dc and the turning ch, ch 3 and turn.

Row 4: * 2 dc in the 1st of the 4 dc, ch 2, 2 dc in the last of the 4 dc, 1 sc in the top of the 4-ch, rep from *, ending row with 1 dc in the turning ch, ch 3 and turn.

Pattern formed by rep rows 1–4.

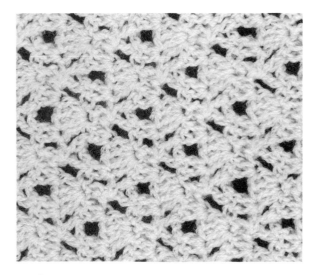

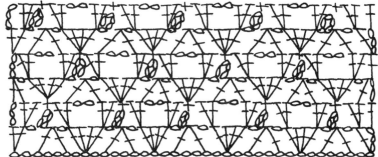

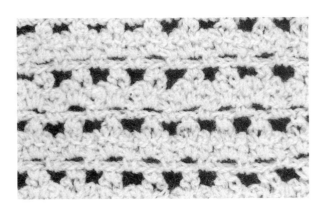

303. Chain multiples of 6 plus 6.

Row 1: 1 sc in the 8th ch, * 1 picot, make another picot, sc in the next ch, 1 picot, 1 sc in the next ch, ch 5, 1 sc in the 4th ch, rep from *, ending row with 2 chs and 1 dc in the 2nd ch, ch 1 and turn.

Row 2: 1 sc in the dc, * ch 9, 1 sc in the 5-ch, rep from *, ending row with sc in the turning ch, ch 5 and turn.

Row 3: Same as row 1, except that the sc and picot are worked in the 9-ch.

Pattern formed by rep rows 1–2.

304. Chain multiples of 4 plus 1.

Row 1: 1 sc in the 2nd ch, * ch 3, 1 sc in the 4th ch, rep from *, ending row with last set, ch 1 and turn.
Row 2: 1 sc in the 1st sc, * ch 3, 1 sc around the 3-ch, ch 5, 1 sc in the same 3-ch, ch 3, 1 sc in the sc, rep from *, ending row after last set with a sc in the last sc, ch 4 and turn.
Row 3: * 1 sc in the 5-ch, ch 3, rep from *, ending row with 1 sc in the last 5-ch, ch 1, 1 dc in the sc, ch 1 and turn.
Row 4: Same as row 1, except that 1 sc is always worked in the middle of the 3-ch.
Pattern formed by rep rows 1–3.

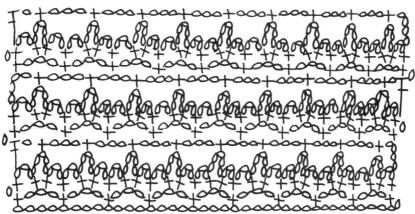

305. Chain multiples of 11 plus 5.

Row 1: 1 dc in the 5th ch, * ch 3, 1 sc in the 4th ch, ch 3, 1 sc in the next ch, ch 3, 1 sc in the next ch, ch 3, 1 sc in the next sc, ch 3, 1 dc in the 4th ch, ch 2, 1 dc in the same ch, rep from *, ending row with 1 sc, 3 chs, 1 sc in the next ch, 1 ch and 1 hdc in the next and last ch, ch 4 and turn.
Row 2: 1 dc in the 1-ch, * ch 3, 1 sc in the 2-ch, ch 3, 1 sc in the same 2-ch, ch 3, 1 sc in the same 2-ch, ch 3, 1 dc in the middle of the middle 3-ch, ch 2, 1 dc in the same 3-ch, rep from *, ending row with 1 sc, 3 chs, 1 sc, 1 ch and 1 hdc in the turning ch, ch 4 and turn.
Pattern formed by rep rows 1–2.

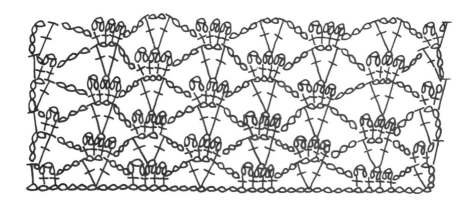

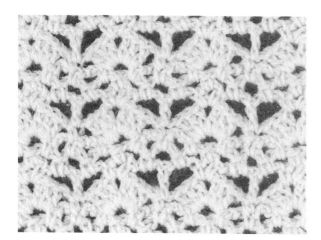

306. Chain multiples of 8 plus 1.

Row 1: 1 sc in the 2nd ch, * ch 1, 3 dc in the 4th ch, ch 2, 3 dc in the same ch, ch 1, 1 sc in the 4th ch, rep from *, ending row after the last set, ch 6 and turn.
Row 2: * 1 sc in the 2-ch, ch 3, 1 sc in the 2-ch, ch 3, 1 dc in the sc, ch 3, rep from *, ending row with 1 dc in the last sc, ch 3 and turn.
Row 3: * 1 sc in the 3-ch, ch 3, 1 sc in the next 3-ch, ch 3, 1 sc in the next 3-ch, ch 3, rep from *, ending row with 1 sc around the last ch, ch 1 and 1 hdc in the turning ch, ch 1 and turn.
Row 4: 1 sc in the hdc, * ch 3, 1 sc around the 3-ch, ch 3, 1 sc around the next 3-ch, ch 3, 1 sc around the next 3-ch, rep from *, ending row after the last set, ch 1 and turn.
Pattern formed by rep rows 1–4.

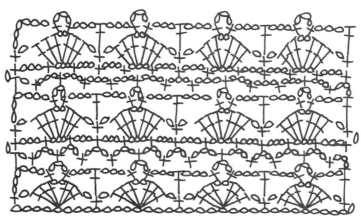

307. Chain multiples of 6 plus 1.

Row 1: 1 sc in the 2nd ch, * ch 6, attach the last ch into the 4th ch, 1 dc in the sc just used, 1 picot, 1 dc in ch just used, 1 picot, 1 dc in same ch, 1 picot, 1 dc in the same ch, 1 picot, 1 sc in the 6th ch, rep from *, ending row after last set with 1 sc, ch 8 and turn.
Row 2: * 1 sc in the top of the 3-ch, ch 5, rep from *, ending row with the last sc in the turning ch, ch 1 and turn.
Row 3: Same as row 1, except that the sc is worked in the sc.
Pattern formed by rep rows 1–2.

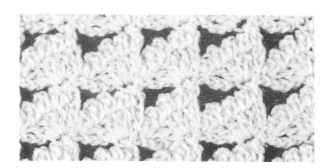

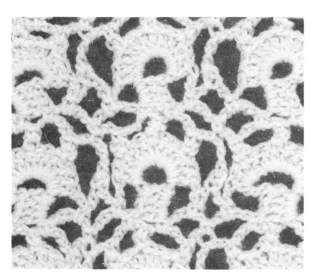

308. Chain multiples of 12 plus 1.

Row 1: 1 sc in the 2nd ch, * ch 5, 1 sc in 4th ch, ch 11, 4 dc around the beginning part of the ch, 1 sc in the 4th ch, ch 5, 1 sc in the 4th ch, rep from *, row ending with 5 chs and 1 sc, ch 3 and turn.
Row 2: 1 picot in turning ch, * ch 2, 3 dc in the end of the ch configuration, 1 picot, 3 more dc in same ch configuration, 1 picot, 3 dc in same place, 1 picot, 3 dc in same place, ch 2, 1 sc around the middle of the 5-ch, ch 3, 1 picot, rep from *, ending row with 2 chs, 1 picot and 1 dc in the end sc, ch 7 and turn.
Row 3: Sk 1st picot, 1 sc in next picot, * 1 sc in 1st picot, ch 5, 1 sc in next picot, ch 5, 1 sc in next picot, ch 2, 1 trc in the next picot, ch 2, rep from *, ending row after last set with 2 chs and 1 trc, ch 1 and turn.
Row 4: Same as row 1, but 1st sc around the middle of the 5-ch, next sc in the middle of the next 5-ch, next sc in the trc.
Pattern formed by rep rows 1–3.

· *24* ·
Puff Stitch

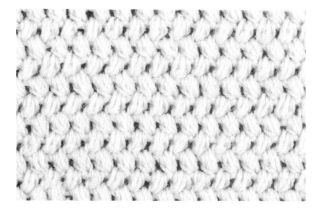

309. Chain multiples of 2 plus 3.

Row 1: Work 3-looped puff stitch in the 5th ch, * ch 1, work 3-looped puff stitch in the 2nd ch, rep from *, ending row with 1 dc in the ch after the last puff stitch, ch 4 and turn.
Row 2: Work 3-looped puff stitch in the 1-ch, * ch 1, work 3-looped puff stitch in the 1-ch, rep from *, ending row with 1 ch and 1 dc in the turning ch, ch 3 and turn.
Pattern formed by rep rows 1–2.

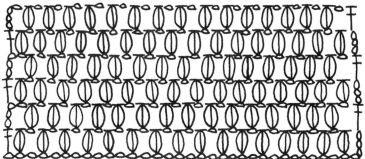

310. Chain multiples of 4 plus 4.

Row 1: 1 hdc in the 7th ch, * ch 1, 1 hdc in the 2nd ch, rep from *, ending row with last set, ch 3 and turn.
Row 2: * 1 hdc in the 1-ch, ch 1, work a 5-looped puff stitch in the next 1-ch, ch 1, rep from *, ending row with last set and 1 hdc in the turning ch, ch 4 and turn.
Row 3: 1 hdc in the 1-ch, ch 1, rep from *, ending row with 1 hdc in the turning ch, ch 3 and turn.
Row 4: * work a 5-looped puff stitch in the next 1-ch, ch 1, 1 hdc in next 1-ch, ch 1, rep from *, ending row with puff stitch 1 ch and 2 hdc in the turning ch, ch 4 and turn.
Pattern formed by rep rows 1–4.

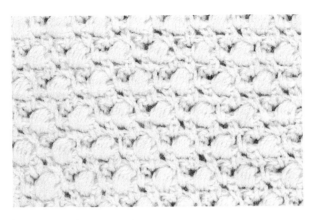

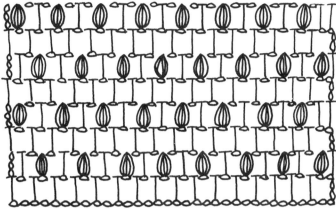

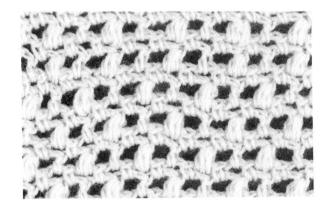

311. Chain multiples of 6 plus 1.

Row 1: 1 sc in the 2nd ch, * ch 2, 1 sc in the 3rd ch, rep from *, ending row with last sc, ch 3 and turn.
Row 2: * work a 3-looped puff stitch in the 1st 2-ch, ch 2, 1 hdc in the next 2-ch, ch 2, rep from *, ending row with 1 ch after the last puff stitch and 1 hdc in the last sc, ch 1 and turn.
Row 3: 1 sc in the 1st hdc, * ch 2, 1 sc around the 2-ch, rep from *, ending row with 2 chs and 1 sc in the turning ch, ch 3 and turn.
Row 4: * 1 hdc in the 1st 2-ch, ch 2, work a 3-looped puff in the next 2-ch, ch 2, rep from *, ending row with 1 hdc in the last 2-ch, ch 1 and 1 hdc in the sc, ch 1 and turn.
Pattern formed by rep rows 1–4.

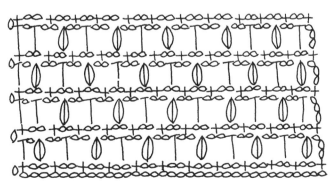

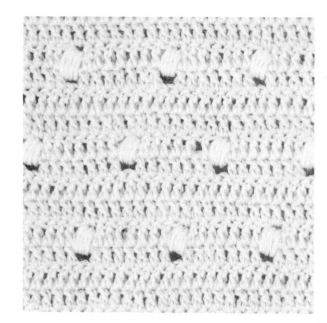

312. Chain multiples of 8 plus 4.

Row 1: 1 dc in the 5th ch and the 2 chs following, * ch 1, 1 dc in the 2nd ch and the 6 chs following, rep from *, ending row with 4 dc, ch 3 and turn.

Row 2: 1 dc in the 2nd dc and the 2 dc after that, * work a 5-looped puff around the 1-ch, 1 dc in each of the next 7 dc, rep from *, ending row with 4 dc, the last in the turning ch, ch 3 and turn.

Rows 3–4: 1 dc in each dc and in each puff, ch 3 and turn.

Row 5: 1 dc in the 2nd dc and in the next 6 dc, * ch 1, 1 dc in the 2nd dc and the next 6 dc, rep from *, ending row with 7 dc and 1 in the turning ch, ch 3 and turn.

Row 6: 1 dc in the 2nd dc and in the next 6 dc, * work a 5-looped puff stitch around the 1-ch, 1 dc in the next dc and in the 6 dc after that, rep from *, ending row with 7 dc and 1 extra in the turning ch, ch 3 and turn.

Rows 7–8: Work 1 dc in each stitch and in the turning ch, ch 3 and turn.

Pattern formed by rep rows 1–8.

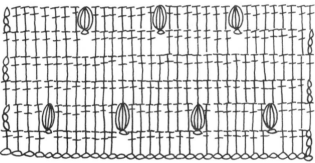

313. Chain multiples of 8 plus 4.

Row 1: 1 sc in the 2nd ch and in each ch all the way across the row, ch 3 and turn.

Row 2: 1 dc in the 2nd sc, * ch 1, 1 dc in the 2nd sc, rep from *, ending row with 1 dc in the turning ch, ch 1 and turn.

Row 3: 1 sc in each ch and in each dc all the way across the row, ch 3 and turn.

Row 4: * 1 dc in the 2nd sc, ch 1, work a 4-looped puff in the next sc, work 1 dc in the next sc, ch 1, dc in the 2nd sc, ch 1, dc in the 2nd sc, ch 1, rep from *, ending row with 1 dc in the last sc, ch 1 and turn.

Row 5: 1 sc in each stitch and ch all the way across the row, ch 3 and turn.

Row 6: Sk 1st sc, * 1 dc in the 2nd sc, ch 1, rep from *, ending row with 1 dc in the sc, ch 1 and turn.

Row 7: 1 sc in each stitch all across the row, ch 3 and turn.

Row 8: Sk 1st sc, * dc in the next sc, ch 1, 1 dc in the 2nd sc, ch 1, 1 dc in the 2nd sc, ch 1, work 4-looped puff stitch in the next sc, dc in the next sc, ch 1, rep from *, ending row with 1 dc in the last sc, ch 1 and turn.

Pattern formed by rep rows 1–8.

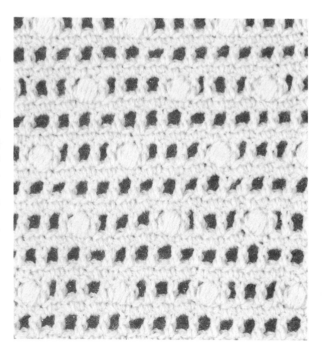

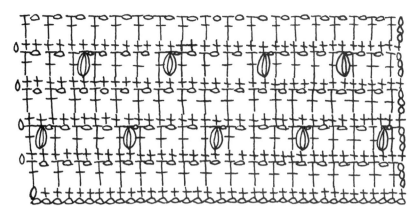

314. Chain multiples of 8 plus 4.

Row 1: 1 dc in the 5th ch, * 1 dc in each of the next 2 chs, work a 3-looped puff stitch in the next ch, 1 dc in each of the next 3 chs, ch 1, 1 dc in the 2nd ch, rep from *, ending row with last set and 1 extra dc, ch 4 and turn.
Row 2: * 1 dc in the 3rd dc, the dc after that, the puff and the 2 dc after that, ch 1, 1 dc in the 1-ch, ch 1, rep from *, ending row with 5 dc, 1 ch and 1 dc in the turning ch, ch 3 and turn.
Row 3: * 1 dc in the 1-ch, ch 1, 1 dc in the 2nd dc and the 2 dc after that, ch 1, 1 dc in the 1-ch, 1 dc in the dc, rep from *, ending row with 1 dc in the 1-ch and 1 in the turning ch, ch 3 and turn.
Row 4: 1 dc in the 2nd dc, * 1 dc in the 1-ch, ch 1, 1 dc in the 2nd dc, ch 1, 1 dc in the 1-ch, 1 dc in each of the next 3 dc, rep from *, ending row with 3 dc, the last of which is in the turning ch, ch 3 and turn.
Row 5: 1 dc in the 2nd dc, 1 dc in the next dc, 1 dc in the 1-ch, * ch 1, 1 dc in the 1-ch, 1 dc in each of the 2 dc, work a 3-looped puff in the next dc, 1 dc in each of the next 2 dc and 1 dc in the 1-ch, rep from *, ending row with 4 dc, the last of which is in the turning ch, ch 3 and turn.
Row 6: 1 dc in the 2nd and 3rd dc, * ch 1, 1 dc in the 1-ch, ch 1, 1 dc in the 2nd dc, the dc after that, the puff stitch and the 2 dc after that, rep from *, ending row with 3 dc, the last of which is worked in the turning ch, ch 3 and turn.
Row 7: 1 dc in the 2nd dc, * ch 1, 1 dc in the 1-ch, 1 dc in the dc, 1 dc in the 1-ch, ch 1, 1 dc in the 2nd dc and the 2 dc after that, rep from *, ending row with 2 dc, the last of which is in the turning ch, ch 4 and turn.

Row 8: * 1 dc in the 1-ch, 1 dc in each of the next 3 dc, 1 dc in the 1-ch, ch 1, 1 dc in the 2nd dc, ch 1, rep from *, ending row with 1 ch and 1 dc in the turning ch, ch 3 and turn.
Pattern formed by rep rows 1–8.

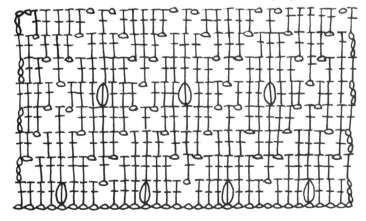

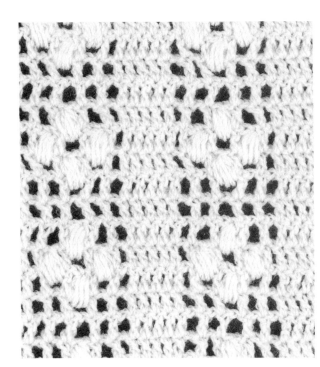

315. Chain multiples of 14 plus 4.

Row 1: 1 dc in the 5th ch and the 3 chs following, * ch 1 , 1 dc in the 2nd ch 5 times, 1 dc in the next 4 chs, rep from *, ending row with 5 dc, ch 3 and turn.
Row 2: Same as row 1, ch 3 and turn.
Row 3: 1 dc in the 2nd dc and the 3 following, * ch 1, 1 dc in the next dc, ch 1, 1 dc in the next dc, work a 4-looped puff stitch in the next ch, 1 dc in the next dc, ch 1, 1 dc in the next dc, ch 1, 1 dc in the next dc, 1 dc in each of next 4 dc, rep from *, ending row with 5 dc, the last in the turning ch, ch 3 and turn.
Row 4: 1 dc in the 2nd dc and also in the next 3 dc, * ch 1, 1 dc in the next dc, work a 4-looped puff stitch in the next 1-ch, 1 dc in the next dc, ch 1, 1 dc in the next dc, work a 4-looped puff stitch in the next ch, 1 dc in the next dc, ch 1, 1 dc in the next dc and in the next 4 dc, rep from *, ending row with 5 dc, the last in the turning ch, ch 3 and turn.
Row 5: 1 dc in the 2nd dc and the next 3 dc, * ch 1, 1 dc in the next dc, ch 1, 1 dc in the next dc, work a 4-looped puff stitch in the next 1-ch, 1 dc in the next dc, ch 1, 1 dc in the next dc, ch 1, 1 dc in the next dc, 1 dc in each of the next 4 dc, rep from *, ending row with 5 dc, the last in the turning ch, ch 3 and turn.
Pattern formed by rep rows 1–5.

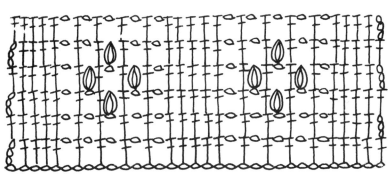

316. Chain multiples of 10 plus 5.

Row 1: 1 dc in the 7th ch, * ch 1, 1 dc in the 2nd ch, rep from *, ending row with last dc, ch 4 and turn.
Row 2: Same as row 1, ch 4 and turn.
Row 3: 1 dc in the 2nd dc, * ch 2, begin 3-looped puff in the next dc, begin 2nd 3-looped puff stitch in the 2nd dc, finish off both puff stitches together, ch 4, 1 dc in the next dc, ch 1, 1 dc in the next dc, rep from *, ending row with 1 dc in the turning ch, ch 4 and turn.
Row 4: 1 dc in the 2nd dc, * work 3-looped puff stitch in the top of the 2 puff stitches, ch 3, work another 3-looped puff stitch in the same place as the 1st puff stitch, ch 2, 1 dc in the dc, ch 1, 1 dc in the dc, rep from *, ending row with 1 dc in the turning ch, ch 4 and turn.
Pattern formed by rep rows 1–4.

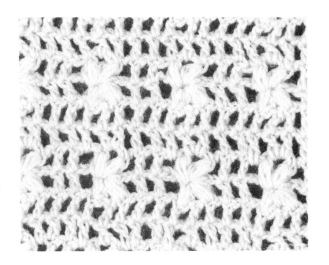

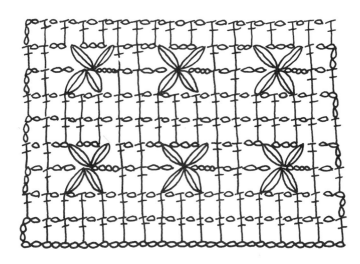

317. Chain multiples of 12 plus 4.

Row 1: 1 dc in the 7th ch, ch 1, dc in the 2nd ch, ch 1, 1 dc in the 2nd ch, * work a 3-looped puff stitch in the 3rd ch, ch 3, work a 3-looped puff in the ch just used, ch 1, 1 dc in the 3rd ch, ch 1, dc in the 2nd ch, ch 1, dc in the 2nd ch, ch 1, dc in the 2nd ch, rep from *, ending row with last dc, ch 4 and turn.

Row 2: * work 3-looped puff in the 3-ch, ch 3, work 3-looped puff in the same 3-ch, 1 dc in the next dc, ch 1, dc in the dc, ch 1, dc in the dc, ch 1, dc in the dc, ch 1, rep from *, ending row with 1 dc in the turning ch, ch 4 and turn.

Row 3: Same as row 1, ch 3 and turn.

Row 4: * 3-looped puff stitch in the 3-ch, ch 3, 3-looped puff in the same 3-ch, ch 1, 3-looped puff in the 1-ch, ch 3, 3-looped puff in the same 1-ch, ch 1, 3-looped puff in the 2nd 1-ch, ch 3, 3-looped puff in the same 1-ch, ch 1, rep from *, ending row with dc in the turning ch.

Row 5: Same as row 1, except that the dc is worked above the puff stitch.

Pattern formed by rep rows 1–4.

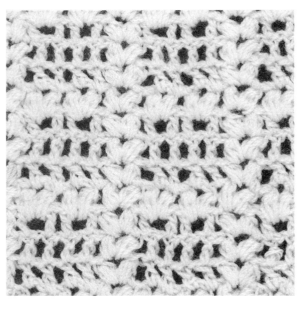

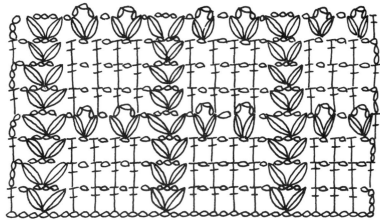

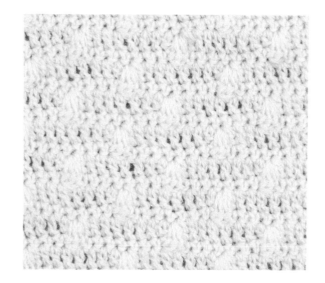

318. Chain multiples of 8 plus 4.

Row 1: 1 sc in the 2nd ch and in each ch all across the row, ch 3 and turn.
Row 2: 1 dc in the 2nd sc and in each sc all across the row, ch 1 and turn.
Row 3: 1 sc in each of the 1st 3 dc, work a 3-looped puff in relief around the base of the 4th dc of the row below, * work sc in the next 7 dc, work a 3-looped puff in relief around the base of the next dc, rep from *, ending row with 3 sc, ch 3 and turn.
Row 4: 1 dc in the 2nd sc and all the way across the row, including puff, ch 1 and turn.
Row 5: * 1 sc in the 1st dc and in each of the next 6 dc, work a 3-looped puff around the base of the next dc, rep from *, ending row with last sc, ch 3 and turn.
Row 6: 1 dc in the 2nd sc and in each sc and puff all across the row, ch 1 and turn.
Pattern formed by rep rows 1–6.

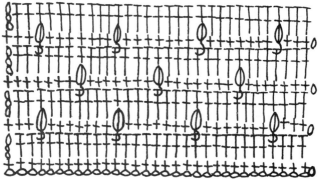

319. Chain multiples of 6 plus 1.

Row 1: 1 sc in the 2nd ch, * ch 3, work a 3-looped puff stitch in the 3rd ch, ch 3, 1 sc in the 3rd ch, rep from *, ending row with 1 sc after the last puff stitch and 3 chs, ch 7 and turn.
Row 2: 1 sc in the 3-ch, ch 3, * work a 3-looped puff stitch around the next 3-ch, ch 3, 1 sc in the next 3-ch, ch 3, rep from *, ending row with a 3-looped puff and 1 trc in the sc, ch 1 and turn.
Pattern formed by rep rows 1–2.

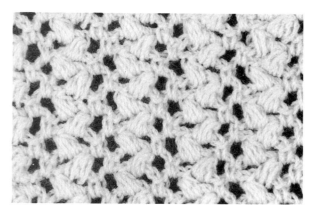

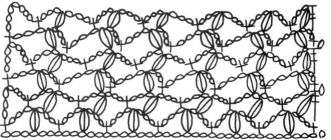

320. Chain multiples of 8 plus 6.

Row 1: 1 sc in the 8th ch, * ch 4, 1 sc in the 4th ch, rep from *, ending row with last sc, 2 chs and 1 dc in the 2nd and last ch, ch 5 and turn.
Row 2: * 1 sc in the 4-ch, ch 3, work a 3-looped puff stitch in the next 4-ch, ch 3, rep from *, ending row with sc in the turning ch, ch 5 and turn.
Row 3: * 1 sc in the 3-ch, ch 4, rep from *, ending row with last sc, 2 chs and 1 sc in the turning ch, ch 5 and turn.
Row 4: * work a 3-looped puff stitch in the 4-ch, ch 3, 1 sc around the 4-ch, ch 3, rep from *, ending row with the last sc, ch 3 and a 2-looped puff stitch in the turning ch, ch 5 and turn.
Pattern formed by rep rows 1–4.

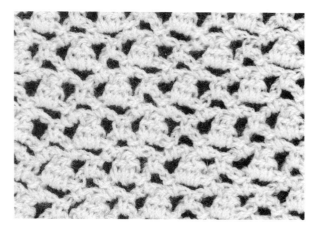

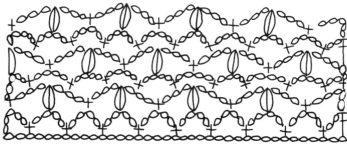

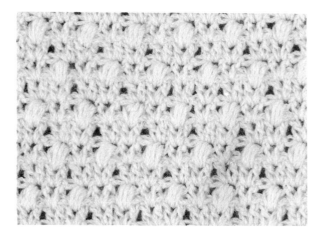

321. Chain multiples of 4 plus 4.

Row 1: 2 dc in the 6th ch, * 2 dc in the 2nd ch, rep from *, ending row with last set and 1 extra dc in the 2nd ch, ch 3 and turn.
Row 2: * work a 4-looped puff stitch in the middle of the 2 dc worked in the same ch, work 2 dc in the middle of the next 2 dc worked together in the same stitch, rep from *, ending row with last set and 1 extra dc in the turning ch, ch 3 and turn.
Row 3: * 2 dc in the top of the puff stitch, 2 dc in the top of the 2 dc, rep from *, ending row with last set and 1 extra dc in the turning ch, ch 3 and turn.
Row 4: * 2 dc in between the 1st 2 dc, work 4-looped puff stitch in the middle of the next 2 dc worked in the same stitch, rep from *, ending row with 1 extra dc in the turning ch, ch 3 and turn.
Pattern formed by rep rows 1–4.

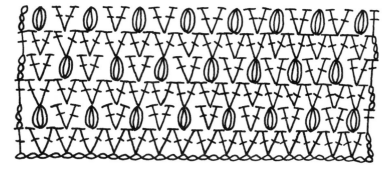

322. Chain multiples of 6 plus 1.

Row 1: 1 sc in 2nd ch, * ch 3, 1 dc in 3rd ch, ch 1, 1 dc in same ch, ch 3, 1 sc in 3rd ch, rep from *, ending row with 1 sc, ch 6 and turn.
Row 2: * 1 sc in 1st 1-ch, ch 3, 3-looped puff stitch in sc, ch 3, rep from *, ending row with 1 dc, ch 1 and turn.
Row 3: Same as row 1, V-stitch worked in sc.
Pattern formed by rep rows 1–2.

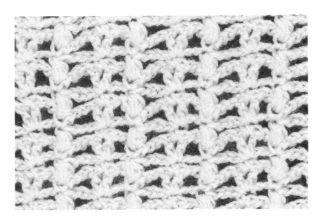

323. Chain multiples of 8 plus 6.

Row 1: Work 3-looped puff in the 7th ch, * ch 3, 1 sc in the 4th ch, ch 3, work 3-looped puff in the 4th ch, ch 5, work 3-looped puff in the ch just used, rep from *, ending row with last puff, 2 chs and 1 trc in the ch just used, ch 1 and turn.
Row 2: 1 sc in the trc, * ch 2, 3 dc in the sc, ch 2, 1 sc in the 5-ch, rep from *, ending row with 1 sc in the turning ch, ch 1 and turn.
Row 3: * sc in the sc, ch 3, work 3-looped puff in the 2nd dc, ch 5, work 3-looped puff in the same dc, ch 3, rep from *, ending row with sc in the last sc, ch 3 and turn.
Row 4: 1 dc in the 1st sc, * ch 2, 1 sc in the 5-ch, ch 2, 3 dc in the sc, rep from *, ending row with 2 dc in the last sc, ch 6 and turn.
Pattern formed by rep rows 1–4.

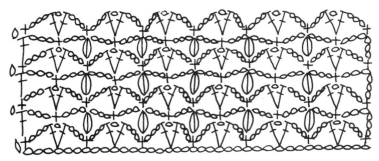

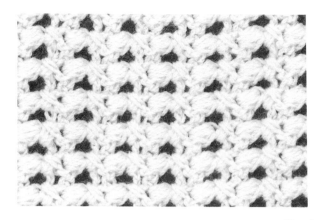

324. Chain multiples of 3 plus 4.

Row 1: 1 dc in 7th ch, ch 1, 1 dc backwards in 2nd ch, * 1 dc in 3rd ch, ch 1, 1 dc backwards in the 2nd ch, rep from *, ending row after last set with 1 dc, ch 5 and turn.

Row 2: 4-looped puff stitch in the middle of the 1st X, around the 1-ch, * ch 3, 4-looped puff stitch in the 1-ch in the middle of the next X, rep from *, ending row after last set with 1 dc in the turning ch, ch 3 and turn.

Row 3: Same as row 1, except that the X is formed around each puff stitch.

Pattern formed by rep rows 1–2.

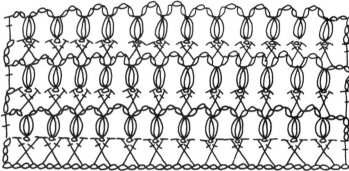

325. Chain multiples of 3 plus 4.

Row 1: 1 dc in the 6th ch, * ch 2, finish 2 dc together in the ch just used and the 3rd ch, rep from *, ending row after last set with 1 ch and 1 dc in the ch just used, ch 4 and turn.

Row 2: * work a 3-looped puff stitch in the top of the 2 dc finished together, ch 3, rep from *, ending row after last set with 1 dc in the turning ch, ch 3 and turn.

Row 3: Same as row 1, except that the dc are worked on either side of the puff stitch.

Pattern formed by rep rows 1–2.

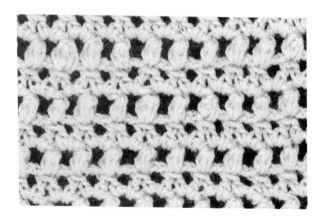

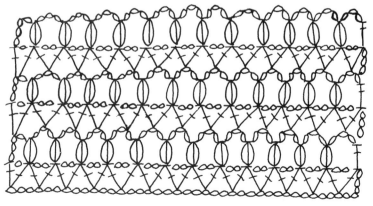

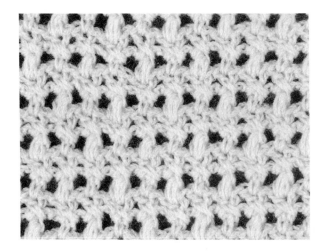

326. Chain multiples of 6 plus 4.

Row 1: 1 dc in the 4th ch, * 1 dc in the 4th ch, ch 1, 1 dc backwards 2 chs, rep from *, ending row with 2 dc in the 2nd ch, ch 1 and turn.

Row 2: 1 sc in the 1st dc, * ch 2, work a 3-looped puff stitch in the next 1-ch, ch 4, 1 sc in the next 1-ch, rep from *, ending row with 1 sc in the turning ch, ch 4 and turn.

Row 3: 1 dc in the sc, * 1 dc in the 2-ch after the puff, ch 1, 1 dc backwards in the 4-ch, 1 dc after the sc in the 4-ch, ch 1, 1 dc backwards in the 2-ch before the sc, rep from *, ending row with 2 dc in the last sc, ch 2 and turn.

Row 4: 1 dc in the 1st dc, * ch 4, 1 sc in the 1-ch, ch 2, work a 3-looped puff in the next 1-ch, rep from *, ending row with 2 chs and a 2-looped puff stitch in the turning ch, ch 3 and turn.

Pattern formed by rep rows 1–4.

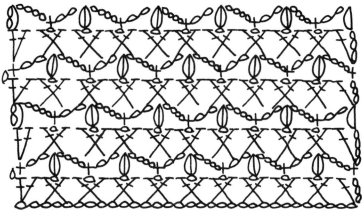

327. Chain multiples of 3 plus 4.

Row 1: 1 dc in the 6th ch, 1 dc backwards in the ch before, * 1 dc in the next ch, 1 dc in the 2nd ch, 1 dc backwards 1 ch, rep from *, ending row with 1 dc after the last X, ch 1 and turn.

Row 2: 1 sc in the 1st dc, * ch 2, 3-looped puff stitch between the 2 sides of the X, ch 4, 1 sc in the dc, rep from *, ending row with 4 chs and 1 sc in the turning ch, ch 5 and turn.

Row 3: * 1 dc in ch after puff stitch, 1 dc back before 1st puff stitch, 1 trc in the sc, rep from *, ending row with 1 trc, ch 1 and turn.

Pattern formed by rep rows 1–3.

328. Chain multiples of 8 plus 4.

Row 1: 1 dc in the 5th ch and dc in each of the next 3 chs, * ch 3, 1 sc in the 2nd ch, ch 3, 1 dc in the 2nd ch and in each of the next 4 chs, rep from *, ending row with 5 dc, ch 1 and turn.

Row 2: * 1 sc in each of the 5 dc, ch 1, work a 3-looped puff in the sc, ch 2, rep from *, ending row with 5 sc, the last in the turning ch, ch 3 and turn.

Row 3: Same as row 1.

Row 4: Same as row 2, ch 6 and turn.

Row 5: Sk 1st sc, * sc in 2nd sc, ch 3, dc in 2nd sc, 1 dc in 2-ch, 1 dc in puff stitch, 1 dc in 1-ch, dc in sc, ch 3, rep from *, ending row with last set, 1 dc in the last sc, ch 1 and turn.

Row 6: 1 sc in the 1st dc, * ch 1, work a 3-looped puff stitch in the sc, ch 2, 1 sc in each of the next 5 dc, rep from *, ending row with 1 sc in the turning ch, ch 6 and turn.

Row 7: Same as row 5.

Row 8: Same as row 6.

Pattern formed by rep rows 1–8.

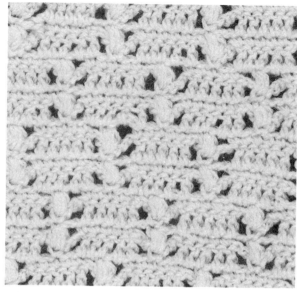

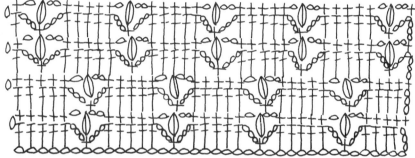

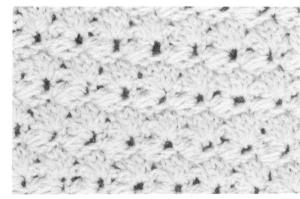

329. Chain multiples of 4 plus 1.

Row 1: 1 sc in the 2nd ch, * ch 4, work a 3-looped puff stitch in the sc, 1 sc in the 4th ch, rep from *, ending row with last set and sc, ch 3 and turn.

Row 2: 2 dc in the 1st sc, * 4 dc in the sc, rep from *, ending row with 2 dc in the last sc, ch 1 and turn.

Row 3: Same as row 1, except that the sc are worked in the 3rd dc of the group.

Pattern formed by rep rows 1–2.

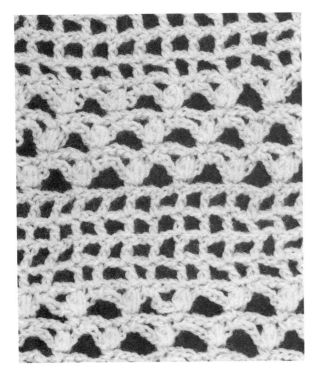

330. Chain multiples of 5 plus 6.

Row 1: 1 dc in 9th ch, * ch 2, 1 dc in the 3rd ch, rep from *, ending row with 2 chs and 1 dc, ch 5 and turn.
Rows 2–3: Same as row 1, ch 5 and turn on 4th row.
Row 4: Same as row 1, except ch 1 and turn.
Row 5: Sk 1 dc, 1 sc in 1st dc, * ch 7, 1 sc in 2nd dc, rep from *, ending row with 1 sc, ch 5 and turn.
Row 6: * 1 sc in the middle of the 7-ch, ch 2, 3-looped puff stitch in next sc, ch 2, rep from *, ending row with 2 chs, 1 dc in the last sc, ch 6 and turn.
Row 7: * 1 sc in the sc, ch 7, rep from *, ending row with 3 chs and 1 dc in the turning ch, ch 6 and turn.
Row 8: 1 sc in the 1st dc, * ch 2, 1 puff stitch in the 1st sc, ch 2, 1 sc in the middle of the 7-ch, rep from *, ending row with 1 sc in the turning ch, ch 1 and turn.
Row 9: * 1 sc in 1st sc, ch 7, rep from *, ending row with 1 sc in the last sc, ch 5 and turn.
Row 10: 1 sc around the middle of the 7-ch, ch 2, a 3-looped puff in the next sc, ch 2, rep from *, ending row with 1 dc in the sc, ch 5 and turn.
Row 11: Same as row 1, except that the dc are placed in the sc and in the puff stitches.
Pattern formed by rep rows 1–10.

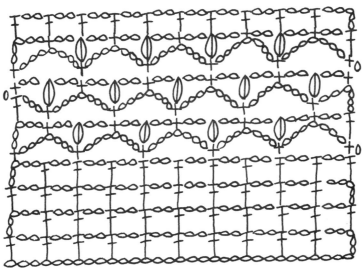

331. Chain multiples of 9 plus 6.

Row 1: 1 sc in the 10th ch, * ch 3, 1 sc in the 3rd ch, ch 3, 1 dc in the 3rd ch, ch 3, 1 sc in the 3rd ch, rep from *, ending row with the dc, ch 1 and turn.
Row 2: 1 sc in the dc, * ch 3, work 3-looped puff stitch in the 2nd 3-ch, ch 3, 1 sc in the next dc, rep from *, ending row with 1 sc in the turning ch, ch 6 and turn.
Pattern formed by rep rows 1–2.

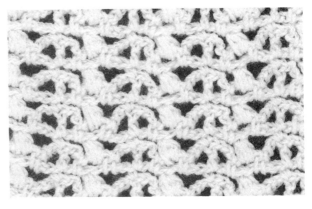

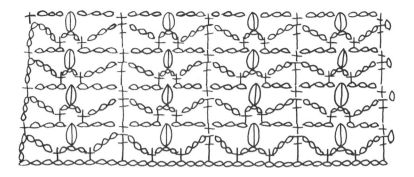

332. Chain multiples of 8 plus 1.

Row 1: 1 sc in the 2nd ch, * ch 3, 1 dc in the 4th ch, ch 3, 1 dc in the same ch, ch 3, 1 sc in the 4th ch, rep from *, ending row with 1 sc, ch 5 and turn.

Row 2: * work 3-looped cluster in the 3-ch between the 2 sides of the V-stitch, ch 2, work another 3-looped puff stitch in the 3-ch, ch 2, work another 3-looped puff stitch in the same 3-ch, ch 4, rep from *, ending row with 2 chs and 1 dc in the last sc, ch 4 and turn.

Row 3: * work a 3-looped puff stitch in the 2-ch, ch 2, work another 3-looped puff stitch in the same 2-ch, ch 2, work a 3-looped puff stitch in the next 2-ch, ch 2, work a 3-looped puff stitch in the same 2-ch, ch 2, rep from *, ending row with 1 ch and 1 dc in the turning ch, ch 4 and turn.

Row 4: * 1 dc in the 2-ch, ch 1, rep from *, ending row with 1 dc in the turning ch, ch 4 and turn.

Row 5: 1 dc in the 1st dc, * ch 3, 1 sc in the 2nd dc, ch 3, 1 dc in the 2nd dc, ch 3, 1 dc in the dc just used, rep from *, ending row with 1 dc, 1 ch and 1 dc in the turning ch, ch 3 and turn.

Row 6: 1 dc in the 1st dc, ch 2, work 3-looped puff stitch in the 1-ch, * ch 4, work 3-looped puff in the 3-ch between the 2 sides of the V-stitch, ch 2, 3-looped puff in the 3-ch, ch 2, work 3-looped puff in the 3-ch, rep from *, ending row with 2 chs and 2-looped puff in the turning ch, ch 4 and turn.

Row 7: Work 3-looped puff in the 2-ch, ch 2, work 3-looped puff in the same 2-ch, * ch 2, work 3-looped puff in the next 2-ch, ch 2, work another 3-looped puff in the same 2-ch, ch 2, work 3-looped puff in the next 2-ch, ch 2, work another 3-looped puff in the same 2-ch, rep from *, ending row with 1 dc in the turning ch, ch 4 and turn.

Row 8: * 1 dc in the 2-ch, ch 1, rep from *, ending row with 1 dc in the turning ch.

Pattern formed by rep rows 1–8.

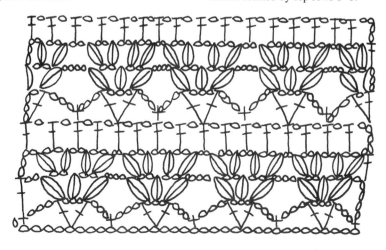

333. Chain multiples of 4 plus 3.

Row 1: 1 dc in the 3rd ch, * ch 3, work 3-looped puff in the 4th ch, rep from *, ending row with a 2-looped puff, ch 4 and turn.
Row 2: Picot, * ch 1, 1 dc in the top of the puff stitch, ch 1, 1 picot, rep from *, ending row with 1 dc in the turning ch, ch 4 and turn.
Row 3: * 1 picot, ch 1, 1 dc in the dc, ch 1, rep from *, ending row with 1 dc in the turning ch, ch 2 and turn.
Pattern formed by rep rows 1–3.

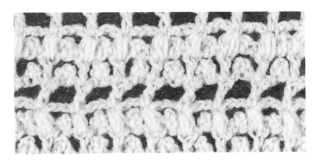

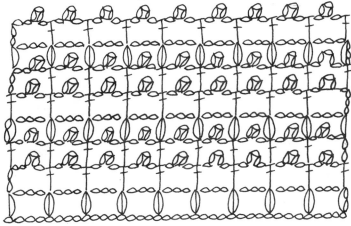

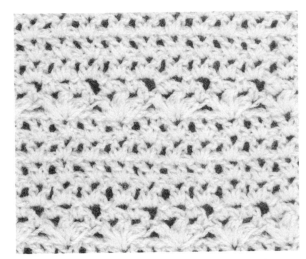

334. Chain multiples of 6 plus 4.

Row 1: 1 dc in the 4th ch, * 1 dc in the 3rd ch, ch 1, 1 dc in the same ch, rep from *, ending row with 2 dc in the 3rd and last ch, ch 3 and turn.
Rows 2–4: Same as row 1, ch 3 and turn.
Row 5: 1 dc in the 1st dc, ch 3, work 2-looped puff stitch in the same dc, * work 2-looped puff stitch in the 2nd 1-ch, ch 3, work 2-looped puff stitch in the same 1-ch, ch 3, work 2-looped puff stitch in the same 1-ch, rep from *, ending row with 2 2-looped puff stitches (interspaced with 3-ch) between the last dc and the turning ch, ch 1 and turn.
Row 6: 1 sc in the 1st puff, 1 sc in the 3-ch, * ch 3, 1 sc in the next 3-ch, ch 3, 1 sc in the next 3-ch, rep from *, ending row with 1 extra sc in the turning ch, ch 3 and turn.
Row 7: Same as row 1, except that 1 V-stitch is made in each 3-ch.
Pattern formed by rep rows 1–6.

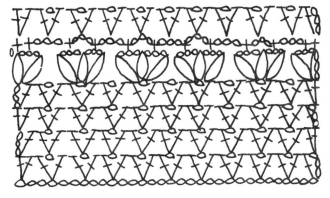

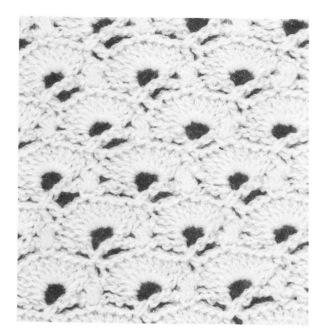

336. Chain multiples of 6 plus 4.

Row 1: 1 sc in the 5th ch, * ch 3, 1 sc in the 3rd ch, rep from *, ending row with last set, 1 ch and 1 hdc in the 2nd ch, ch 1 and turn.

Row 2: 1 sc in the hdc, * 7 dc around the 1st 3-ch, 1 sc around the 2nd 3-ch, rep from *, ending row with last set, sc in the turning ch, ch 6 and turn.

Row 3: * 1 sc in the 4th dc, ch 3, work a 3-looped puff in the sc, ch 3, rep from *, ending row with last sc, ch 3 and 1 dc in the sc, ch 4 and turn.

Row 4: * 1 sc around the middle of the 3-ch, ch 3, rep from *, ending row with last sc around the 3-ch, ch 1 and 1 hdc in the turning ch, ch 3 and turn.

Row 5: 3 dc in the 1-ch, * 1 sc in the 3-ch, work 7 dc in the next 3-ch, rep from *, ending row after last set with 4 dc in the turning ch, ch 1 and turn.

Row 6: 1 sc in the 1st dc, * ch 2, work a 3-looped puff in the sc, ch 2, 1 sc in the 4th dc, rep from *, ending row with 2 chs and 1 sc in the turning ch, ch 3 and turn.

Pattern formed by rep rows 1–6.

335. Chain multiples of 10 plus 1.

Row 1: 1 sc in the 2nd ch, * ch 3, 1 dc in the 6th ch, ch 5, 1 dc backwards 2 ch, ch 3, 1 sc in the 4th ch after the 1st dc, rep from *, ending row with 1 sc, ch 3 and turn.

Row 2: * 11 dc in the 5-ch, work a 3-looped puff stitch in the 1st sc, ch 1, rep from *, ending row after last set with 1 dc in the last sc, ch 2 and turn.

Row 3: Sk 1st dc, 1 hdc in the 2nd dc, ch 4, 1 hdc in the hdc just made, * ch 3, 1 sc in the 4th dc, ch 3, 1 dc in the 2nd dc of the next set, ch 5, 1 dc backwards in the 2nd to the last dc of the previous set, rep from *, ending row with 1 dc formed in the turning ch, ch 2, 1 dc formed backwards in the 2nd to the last dc of the previous set, ch 3 and turn.

Row 4: 5 dc in the 2-ch of the 1st X-stitch, * work a 3-looped puff stitch in the sc, ch 1, work 11 dc around the next 5-ch, rep from *, ending row with 6 dc around the turning ch, ch 1 and turn.

Pattern formed by rep rows 1–4.

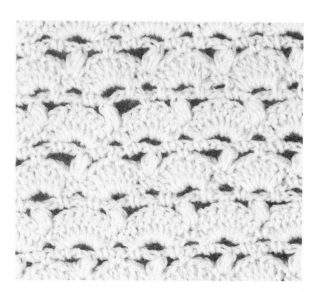

337. Chain multiples of 3 plus 4.

Row 1: 1 dc in the 5th ch and in every ch all across the row, ch 1 and turn.
Row 2: 1 sc in the 1st dc, * ch 4, work a 3-looped puff in the sc, 1 sc in the 3rd dc, rep from *, ending row with 1 sc in the turning ch, ch 4 and turn.
Row 3: 3 dc in the 1st 4-th, * 3 dc in the next 4-ch, rep from *, ending row with last set and 1 trc in the sc, ch 2 and turn.
Row 4: * 1 dc in the 2nd dc, 1 dc in the next dc, 1 dc backwards in the 1st dc, rep from *, ending row with 1 extra dc in the turning ch after the last set.
Pattern formed by rep rows 1–4.

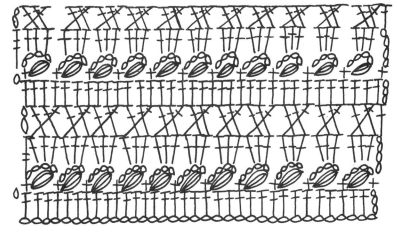

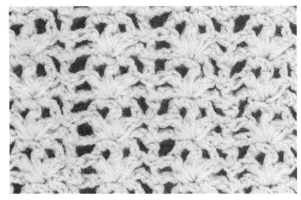

338. Chain multiples of 8 plus 4.

Row 1: 2-looped puff stitch in the 8th ch, * ch 3, a 2-looped puff stitch in the same ch, ch 3, 1 puff stitch in the same ch, ch 1, 1 dc in the 4th ch, a 2-looped puff stitch in the 4th ch, rep from *, ending row with 1 ch and 1 dc in the 4th ch, ch 6 and turn.
Row 2: * 1 sc in the 3-ch between the 1st and 2nd puff stitches, ch 1, 1 sc in between the next 2 puff stitches, ch 3, 1 dc in the dc, ch 3, rep from *, ending row with 3 chs, and 1 dc in the turning ch, ch 3 and turn.
Row 3: Same as row 2, except that the puff stitches are worked in the 1-ch.
Pattern formed by rep rows 1–2.

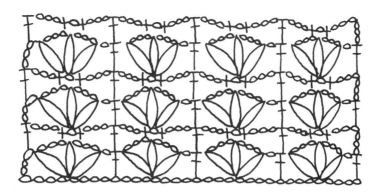

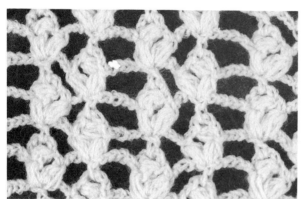

339. Chain multiples of 10 plus 4.

Row 1: 3-looped puff stitch in the 6th ch, * ch 4, 3-looped puff stitch in the top of the 1st puff, ch 1, 3-looped puff in the same ch as the 1st puff, ch 4, 1 dc in the 5th ch, ch 3, 3-looped puff stitch in the 5th ch, rep from *, ending row after last set with 1 dc, 1 ch and 1 dc, ch 3 and turn.

Row 2: 3-looped puff stitch in the 2nd dc, * ch 4, 3-looped puff stitch in the top of the 1st puff, ch 1, 3-looped puff in the same dc as the 1st puff, ch 4, 1 dc in the top of the ch around the puff stitch, ch 3, 3-looped puff stitch in the next dc, rep from *, ending row with 1 ch and 1 dc in the turning ch, ch 3 and turn. Pattern formed by rep rows 1–2.

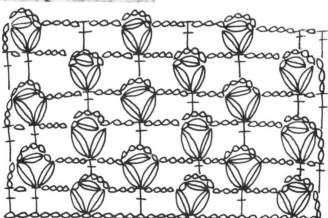

340. Chain multiples of 8 plus 5.

Row 1: 1 dc in the 8th ch, * ch 1, 1 dc in the 2nd ch, rep from *, ending row with last set, ch 4 and turn.

Row 2: 1 dc in the 2nd dc, * ch 1, a 3-looped puff worked around the base of the next dc, worked from the front, ch 1, dc in the next dc, ch 1, dc in the next dc, ch 1, dc in the dc, rep from *, ending row with 1 dc in the turning ch, ch 4 and turn.

Pattern formed by rep rows 1–2.

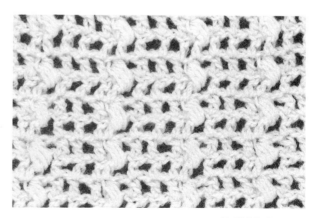

Puff Stitch 251

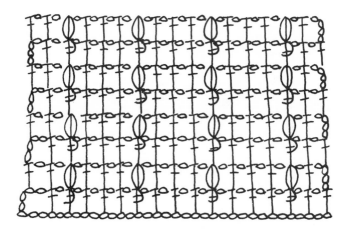

· 25 ·
Cluster Stitch—with Double and Single Crochet and Chains

341. Chain multiples of 10 plus 1.

Row·1: 1 sc in the 2nd ch and all the chs across the row.
Row 2: 1 sc in the 1st and next 2 sc, * ch 3, a 2-looped cluster in the 3rd sc, ch 3, 1 sc in the 3rd sc and the 4 sc following, rep from *, ending row with sc in the last 3 sc, ch 1 and turn.
Row 3: 1 sc in each of the 3 sc, * 1 sc in each of the 3-ch and the cluster, the 3-ch afterwards, and in each of the 5 sc, rep from *, ending row with sc in the last 3 sc, ch 6 and turn.
Row 4: * 1 sc in the 2nd sc around the ch, 1 sc in each of the next 4 sc, ch 3, work 2-looped cluster in the 3rd of the 5 sc, ch 3, rep from *, ending row with 3 chs and 1 dc in the last sc, ch 1 and turn.
Pattern formed by rep rows 1–4.

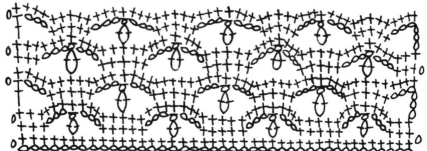

342. Chain multiples of 2 plus 1.

Row 1: 1 sc in the 2nd ch and in each ch all across the row, ch 3 and turn.
Row 2: * 3-looped cluster in the 2nd sc, ch 1, rep from *, ending row with 1 dc in the sc, ch 1 and turn.
Row 3: Same as row 1, except that the sc is worked in each ch and each cluster.
Pattern formed by rep rows 1–2.

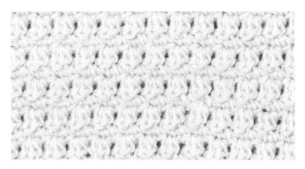

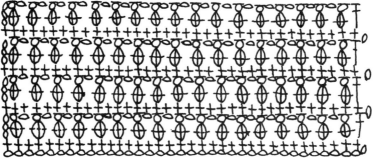

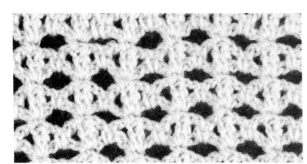

343. Chain multiples of 4 plus 1.

Row 1: 1 sc in the 2nd ch, * ch 2, 2-looped cluster in the 2nd ch, ch 2, 1 sc in the 2nd ch, rep from *, ending row with 1 sc in the turning ch, ch 5 and turn.
Row 2: * 1 sc in the top of the 1st cluster, ch 5, rep from *, ending row with 2 chs and 1 dc in the sc.
Pattern formed by rep rows 1–2.

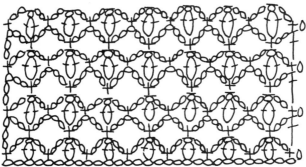

344. Chain multiples of 10 plus 1.

Row 1: 1 sc in the 2nd ch, * ch 5, work 4-looped cluster in the 5th ch, ch 5, 1 sc in the 5th ch, rep from *, ending last set with 1 sc, ch 7.
Row 2: * 4-looped cluster in the ch just before the cluster of the row below, ch 5, 1 sc around the 5-ch, ch 5, rep from *, ending row with 3 chs and 1 trc in the sc, ch 1 and turn.
Pattern formed by rep rows 1–2.

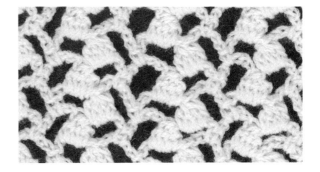

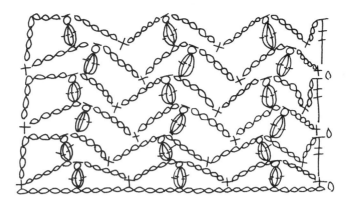

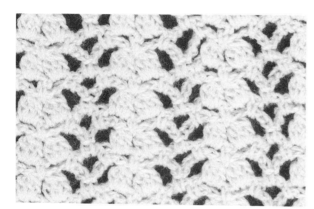

345. Chain multiples of 9 plus 1.

Row 1: 1 sc in the 2nd ch, * ch 3, 1 sc in the 3rd ch, rep from *, ending row with 1 sc, ch 3 and turn.
Row 2: * work 3-looped cluster in the next 3-ch, ch 5, work 1 sc in the next 3-ch, ch 4, work a 3-looped cluster in the next 3-ch, rep from *, ending row after the last cluster with 1 dc in the sc, ch 1 and turn.
Pattern formed by rep rows 1–2.

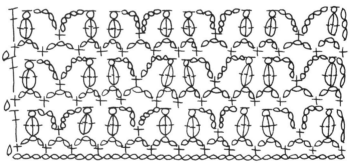

346. Chain multiples of 8 plus 1.

Row 1: 1 sc in the 2nd ch, * ch 3, work a 3-looped cluster in the 4th ch, ch 3, 1 sc in the 4th ch, rep from *, ending row with 3 chs and 1 dc in the last ch, ch 1 and turn.
Row 2: 1 sc in the dc, * ch 3, 1 sc in the sc, ch 3, 1 sc in the top of the cluster, rep from *, ending row with 3 chs and 1 sc in the sc, ch 6 and turn.
Row 3: * 1 sc in the sc, ch 3, work a 3-looped cluster in the sc, ch 3, rep from *, ending row with 3 chs and 1 sc in the sc, ch 1 and turn.
Row 4: 1 sc in the sc, * ch 3, 1 sc in the top of the cluster, ch 3, 1 sc in the sc, rep from *, ending row with 1 sc in the turning ch, ch 1 and turn.
Pattern formed by rep rows 1–4.

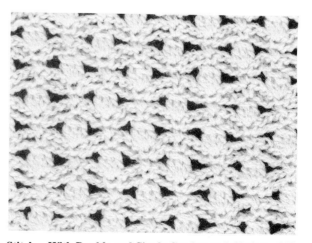

Cluster Stitch—With Double and Single Crochet and Chains 255

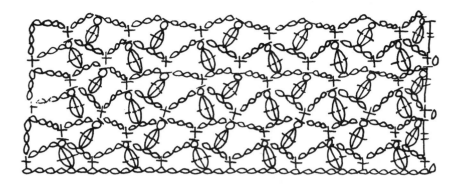

347. Chain multiples of 6 plus 1.

Row 1: 1 sc in the 2nd ch, * ch 3, a 3-looped cluster in the 2nd ch, ch 3, 1 sc in the 4th ch, rep from *, ending row with 1 sc after the last set, ch 7 and turn.
Row 2: * 1 sc in the top of the cluster, ch 3, work 3-looped cluster around the 3-ch, ch 3, rep from *, ending row with 3-looped cluster in the last ch and 1 dc in the last sc, ch 1 and turn.
Row 3: Same as row 1, except that the sc is always worked in the top of the cluster and the cluster worked around the 3-ch.
Pattern formed by rep rows 1–2.

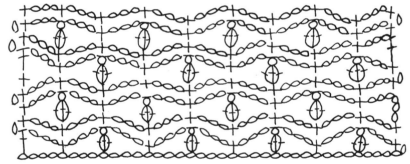

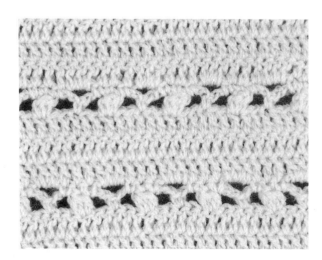

348. Chain multiples of 6 plus 4.

Row 1: 1 dc in the 5th ch and in each ch all across the row, ch 3 and turn.
Row 2: Work a 3-looped cluster in the 2nd dc, * ch 3, 1 sc in the 3rd dc, ch 3, work a 3-looped cluster in the 3rd dc, rep from *, ending row with 1 cluster in the last dc and 1 dc in the turning ch, ch 1 and turn.
Row 3: Work 1 sc in the dc, the cluster and the 1st ch after the cluster, * ch 3, work 1 sc in the ch before the cluster, 1 in the cluster and 1 in the ch after the cluster, rep from *, ending row with 3 sc, the last 1 in the turning ch, ch 3 and turn.
Row 4: 1 dc in each ch and each sc, the last in the sc, ch 3 and turn.
Row 5: Same as row 4.
Pattern formed by rep rows 1–4.

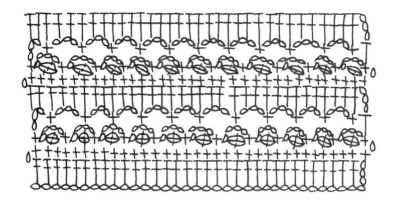

349. Chain multiples of 3 plus 4.

Row 1: 1 dc in the 5th ch and in every ch all across the row, ch 1 and turn.

Row 2: 1 sc in the 1st dc and in every dc all across the row, ch 1 and turn.

Row 3: 1 sc in the 1st sc, * ch 3, 3-looped cluster in the sc just formed, 1 sc in the 3rd sc, rep from *, ending row with last set and 1 sc in the sc, ch 3 and turn.

Row 4: * 1 sc around the 3-ch, ch 3, rep from *, ending row with 1 sc in the 3-ch, 1 hdc in the sc, ch 3 and turn.

Row 5: Dc all the way across, 1 in each sc and 2 in every ch.
Pattern formed by rep rows 1–5.

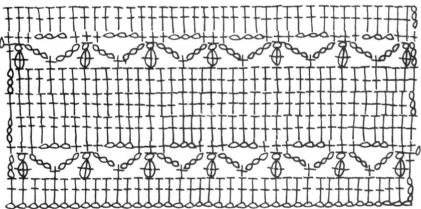

350. Chain multiples of 5 plus 6.

Row 1: 3-looped cluster in 7th ch, * 1 dc in the 3rd ch and in the ch following, ch 2, 3-looped cluster in the next ch, rep from *, ending row after last cluster with 1 dc in the 3rd ch, ch 5 and turn.

Row 2: 3-looped cluster in the top of the cluster, * 1 dc in each of the next 2 dc, ch 2, 3-looped cluster in the cluster, rep from *, ending row after last set with 1 dc in the turning ch, ch 5 and turn.
Pattern formed by rep rows 1–2.

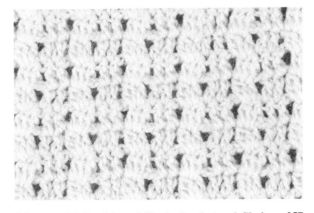

Cluster Stitch—With Double and Single Crochet and Chains   257

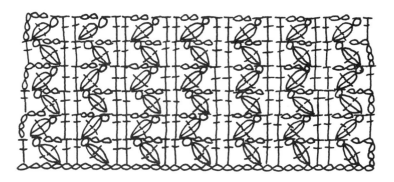

351. Chain multiples of 12 plus 5.

Row 1: 1 dc in 7th ch, * 2-looped cluster in 3rd ch, ch 3, 1 sc in next ch, ch 2, 2-looped cluster in next ch, 1 dc in 3rd ch, ch 1, 1 dc in 2nd ch, ch 1, 1 dc in 2nd ch, rep from *, ending row with 1 dc, ch 4 and turn.
Row 2: 1 dc in 2nd dc, * ch 3, 1 trc in sc between the 2 clusters, ch 3, 1 dc in 1st dc, 1 ch, 1 dc in dc, 1 ch and 1 dc in dc, rep from *, ending row with 1 dc, in the turning ch, ch 4 and turn.
Row 3: Same as row 1, clusters worked into ch nearest the trc.
Pattern formed by rep rows 1–2.

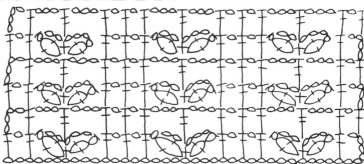

352. Chain multiples of 6 plus 5.

Row 1: 1 dc in the 7th ch, * ch 1, 1 dc in the 2nd ch, rep from *, ending row after the last set, ch 1 and turn.
Row 2: 1 sc in the 1st dc, * ch 1, 1 sc in the next dc, rep from *, ending row with 1 ch and 1 sc in the ch, ch 3 and turn.
Row 3: * Work a 3-looped cluster in 2nd 1-ch, ch 1, 1 dc in the same 1-ch, work a 3-looped cluster in the same 1-ch, ch 1, 1 dc in the 2nd sc, work 3-looped cluster in the 2nd 1-ch, rep from *, ending row with last set, 1 ch and 1 dc in the sc, ch 1 and turn.
Row 4: 1 sc in the 1st dc, * ch 1, 1 sc in the 1st cluster, ch 3, 1 sc in the next ch, ch 1, 1 sc in the next dc, rep from *, ending row with 1 ch and 1 sc in the turning ch, ch 4 and turn.
Pattern formed by rep rows 1–4.

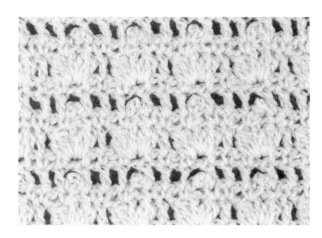

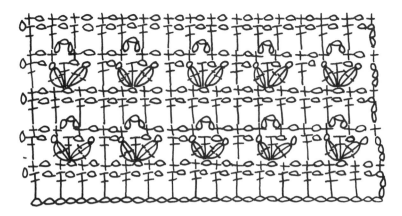

353. Chain multiples of 8 plus 6.

Row 1: Work a 3-looped cluster in 10th ch, * ch 1, work a 3-looped cluster in same ch, ch 2, 1 dc in 4th ch, ch 2, a 3-looped cluster in 4th ch, rep from *, ending row with 1 dc, ch 5 and turn.
Row 2: Same as row 1, ch 3 and turn.
Row 3: 3-looped cluster in 1st dc, * ch 2, 1 dc in 1-ch between 2 clusters of row below, ch 2, a 3-looped cluster in dc, ch 1, a 3-looped cluster in same dc, rep from *, ending row with a 3-looped cluster and 1 dc, ch 5 and turn.
Pattern formed by rep rows 1–3.

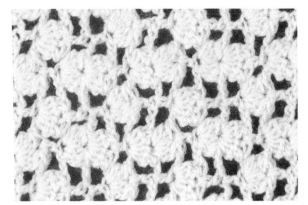

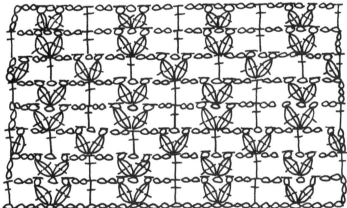

354. Chain multiples of 14 plus 5.

Row 1: 1 dc in the 7th ch, * together with a 3-looped cluster in the 2nd ch, ch 3, work a 3-looped cluster in the same ch, together with 1 dc in the 2nd ch, ch 1, and 1 dc in the 2nd ch 5 times, rep from *, ending row with 1 ch and 1 dc in the last ch, ch 4 and turn.
Row 2: 1 dc in the 2nd dc, * ch 1, 1 dc in the 3-ch, ch 1, 1 dc in the next dc, ch 1, 1 dc in the next dc together with a 3-looped cluster in the next dc, ch 3, a 3-looped cluster in the same dc combined with 1 dc in the next dc, ch 1, 1 dc in the dc, ch 1, 1 dc in the dc, rep from *, ending row with regular set, ch 4 and turn.
Pattern formed by rep rows 1–2.

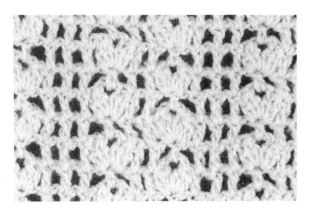

Cluster Stitch—With Double and Single Crochet and Chains   259

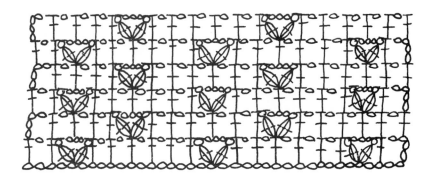

355. Chain multiples of 4 plus 1.

Row 1: 1 sc in the 2nd ch and in every ch all across the row, ch 1 and turn.
Row 2: 1 sc in the 1st sc, * ch 3, work a 2-looped cluster in the sc, just formed, 1 sc in the 4th ch, rep from *, ending row with a sc after the last set, ch 6 and turn.
Row 3: * 1 dc in the sc after the cluster, ch 3, rep from *, ending row after the last set with 1 dc in the sc, ch 1 and turn.
Pattern formed by rep rows 1–3.

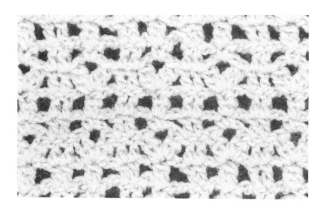

356. Chain multiples of 7 plus 4.

Row 1: Work 2-looped cluster in the 7th ch, * ch 3, 2-looped cluster in the same ch, 1 dc in the 3rd ch, 1 dc in the next ch, 2-looped cluster in the 3rd ch, rep from *, ending row with 1 dc in the 3rd ch after the last set, ch 6 and turn.
Row 2: * 1 sc around the 3-ch, ch 3, 1 dc in the dc and in the dc after that, ch 3, rep from *, ending row with 3 chs and 1 dc in the turning ch, ch 5 and turn.
Row 3: * work 2-looped cluster in the sc, ch 2, 1 dc in the dc and in the dc following, ch 3, rep from *, ending row with 2 chs and 1 dc in the turning ch, ch 3 and turn.
Pattern formed by rep rows 1–3.

357. Chain multiples of 23 plus 5.

Row 1: 1 dc in 7th ch, * ch 1, 1 dc in 2nd ch, ch 1, 2-looped cluster stitch in 3rd ch, ch 1, 2-looped cluster in same ch, 4 dc in the 3rd ch, ch 1, 1 dc in same ch, 2-looped cluster in 6th ch, ch 1, 2-looped cluster in same ch, ch 1, 1 dc in 3rd ch, ch 1, 1 dc in 2nd ch, ch 1, 1 dc in 2nd ch, ch 1, 1 dc in 2nd ch, rep from *, ending row after last set with 1 dc, ch 3 and turn.

Row 2: * 2-looped cluster in 1-ch, ch 1, 2-looped cluster in same ch, ch 1, 1 dc in next dc 5 times, ch 1, 2-looped cluster in 1-ch, ch 1, 2-looped cluster in same ch, 4 dc in next 1-ch, ch 1, 1 dc in same 1-ch, rep from *, ending row with ch and dc, ch 4 and turn.
Pattern formed by rep rows 1–2.

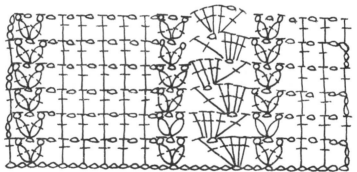

358. Chain multiples of 18 plus 7.

Row 1: 1 sc in the 10th ch, * ch 2, 2-looped cluster in the 3rd ch, ch 2 and 1 dc in the same ch, ch 2, 1 dc in the 3rd ch, ch 2, 2-looped cluster in the same ch, ch 2, 1 sc in the 3rd ch, ch 3, 1 dc in the 3rd ch, ch 2, 1 dc in the 3rd ch, ch 3, 1 sc in 3rd ch, rep from *, ending row with 3 chs and 1 dc in the last ch, ch 5 and turn.
Pattern formed by rep row 1.

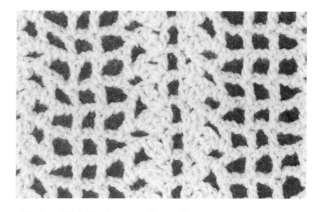

Cluster Stitch—With Double and Single Crochet and Chains   261

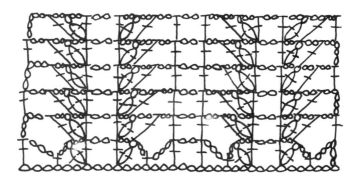

359. Chain multiples of 4 plus 4.

Row 1: 1 dc in 5th ch, * 1 dc in next ch, 1 dc in next ch, ch 1, 1 dc in 2nd ch, rep from *, ending row after last set with 1 additional dc in last ch, ch 2 and turn.
Row 2: 3-looped cluster stitch in 3rd dc, ch 4, 3-looped cluster stitch in the same dc, * 3-looped cluster stitch in middle dc of the next set, ch 4, 3-looped cluster in same dc, rep from *, ending row with 1 dc in turning ch, ch 3 and turn.
Row 3: * 3 dc around 4-ch between the 3-looped clusters, ch 1, rep from *, ending row with 1 dc in turning ch, ch 2 and turn.
Pattern formed by rep rows 1–3.

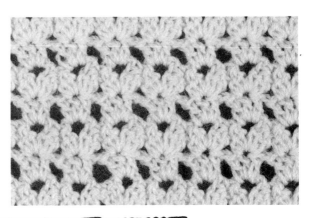

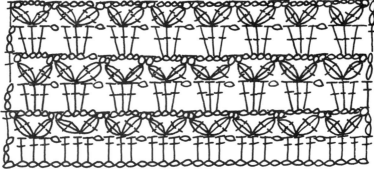

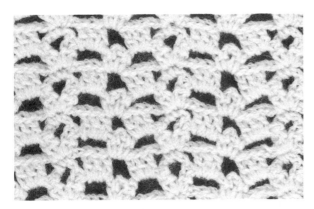

360. Chain multiples of 13 plus 6.

Row 1: 2-looped cluster in the 5th ch, * ch 4, 1 sc in the 6th ch, ch 3, 1 sc in the next ch, ch 3, 2-looped cluster in 6th ch, ch 4, 1 2-looped cluster in the same ch, rep from *, ending row with 2-looped cluster in the last ch, ch 2, 1 dc in the same ch, ch 1 and turn.
Row 2: 1 sc in the 1st dc, * ch 2, 3 dc around the 3-ch, ch 2, 3 dc around the 3-ch, ch 2, 1 sc around the 4-ch, rep from *, ending row with 2 chs and 1 sc in the turning ch, ch 5 and turn.
Pattern formed by rep rows 1–2.

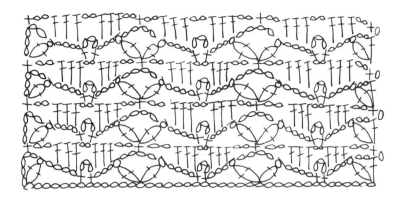

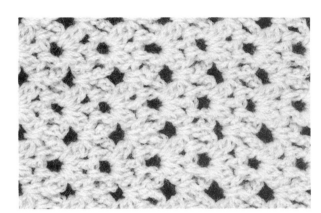

361. Chain multiples of 5 plus 4.

Row 1: 2-looped cluster in 4th ch, * 2-looped cluster in 5th ch, ch 1, 1 dc in the same ch, ch 1, 2-looped cluster in the same ch, rep from *, ending row with 2-looped cluster, 1 ch and 1 dc, ch 3 and turn.

Row 2: * 1 dc in next 1-ch, ch 3, 1 sc between the 2 clusters of the 2 sets, ch 3, 1 dc in the next 1-ch, ch 1, rep from *, ending row with 2 dc in the turning ch, ch 4 and turn.

Row 3: Same as row 1, except that the 2-looped clusters are worked in the single chs.

Pattern formed by rep rows 1–2.

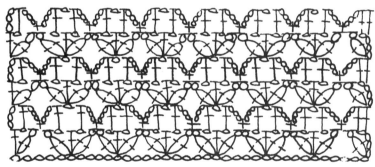

362. Chain multiples of 6 plus 3.

Row 1: 1 dc in 6th ch, * ch 1, 1 dc in same ch, ch 3, 1 dc in same ch, ch 1, 1 dc in same ch, 1 dc in 6th ch, rep from *, row ending with 1 dc in 3rd ch after last set, ch 3 and turn.

Row 2: * 3-looped cluster in 3-ch, ch 3, 3-looped cluster in the same 3-ch, ch 1, rep from *, ending row with 1 dc in turning ch, ch 5 and turn.

Row 3: * 1 dc around the 3-ch, ch 2, 1 dc in the 1-ch, ch 2, rep from *, ending row with 2 chs and 1 dc in the turning ch, ch 2 and turn.

Row 4: Same as row 1, except that the 4 dc are made in every other dc.

Pattern formed by rep rows 1–3.

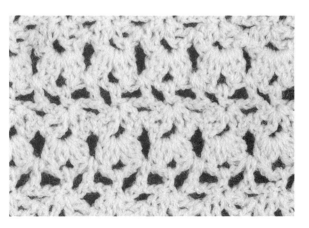

Cluster Stitch—With Double and Single Crochet and Chains 263

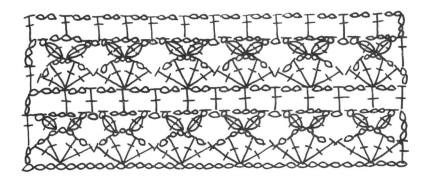

363. Chain multiples of 4 plus 5.

Row 1: 1 dc in the 7th ch, * ch 1, 1 dc in the 2nd ch, rep from *, ending row with the last set, ch 4 and turn.
Row 2: Same as row 1, ch 2 and turn.
Row 3: Work 2-looped cluster in the 1st dc, * ch 4, work 3-looped cluster backwards in the ch, finished together with 3-looped cluster worked in the 2nd dc, rep from *, ending row with last set, ch 4 and turn.
Row 4: * 1 dc around the middle of the 4-ch, ch 1, 1 dc around the top of the 2-cluster, ch 1, rep from *, ending row with a dc in the turning ch, ch 4 and turn.
Row 5: Same as row 4, ch 4 and turn.
Pattern formed by rep rows 1–5.

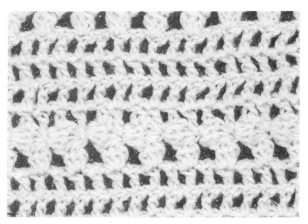

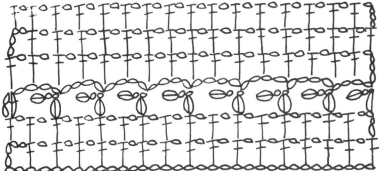

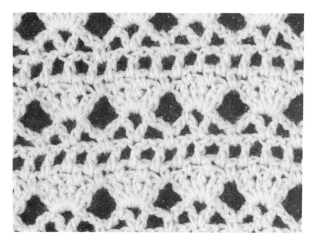

364. Chain multiples of 6 plus 1.

Row 1: 1 sc in the 2nd ch, * ch 2, 1 dc in the 3rd ch, ch 2, 1 dc in the same ch, ch 2, 1 sc in the 3rd ch, rep from *, ending row with last set, ch 4 and turn.
Row 2: * work 2-looped cluster in the 2-ch between the 2 sides of the V-stitch, ch 1, work 2-looped cluster in the same 2-ch, ch 2, work 3rd 2-looped cluster in the same 2-ch, ch 1, rep from *, ending row after last set with 1 trc in the turning ch, ch 1 and turn.
Row 3: 1 sc in the trc, * ch 1, 1 sc between the clusters, ch 1, 1 sc between the clusters, ch 1, 1 sc in the ch between the 2 sets, rep from *, ending row with last sc in the turning ch, ch 3 and turn.
Row 4: * 1 dc in the next 1-ch, ch 1, rep from *, ending row with 1 dc in the last ch and 1 extra dc in the sc, ch 1 and turn.
Pattern formed by rep rows 1–4.

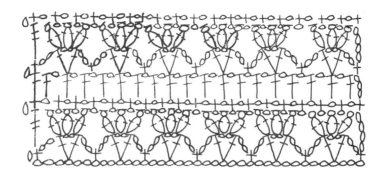

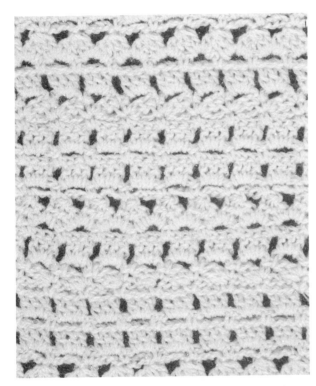

365. Chain multiples of 4 plus 1.

Row 1: 1 sc in the 2nd ch, * ch 4, 2-looped cluster stitch in the sc, 1 sc in the 4th ch, rep from *, ending row with last set and 1 sc in the 4th ch, ch 3 and turn.

Row 2: * 3 dc around the 4-ch, ch 1, rep from *, ending row after last set with 1 dc in the sc, ch 1 and turn.

Row 3: 1 sc in the dc, * ch 3, 1 sc between the 2 sets of 3 dc, rep from *, ending row after last set, ch 3 and turn.

Row 4: 2-looped cluster in the 1st 3-ch, * ch 4, 2-looped cluster in ch just used, finished together with 2-looped cluster in the next 3-ch, rep from *, ending row with 2-looped cluster and 1 dc finished together in the last 3-ch and sc, ch 1 and turn.

Row 5: 1 dc in the 1st dc, * ch 3, 1 sc in the top of the 2-looped cluster, rep from *, ending row with 1 sc in the last cluster, ch 3 and turn.

Row 6: * 3 dc in the middle of the 3-ch, ch 1, rep from *, ending row after last set with 1 dc in the sc, ch 1 and turn.

Row 7: 1 sc in the 1st dc, * ch 3, 1 sc between the 2 sets of 3 dc, ending row after last set with 1 sc in the turning ch, ch 3 and turn.

Row 8: * 3 dc around the 3-ch, ch 1, rep from *, ending row with 1 dc in the sc, ch 1 and turn.

Row 9: 1 sc in the 1st dc, * ch 3, 1 sc in the 1-ch, rep from *, ending in 1 sc in the turning ch, ch 1 and turn.

Pattern formed by rep rows 1–9.

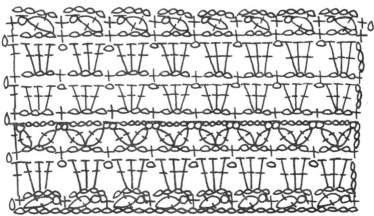

Cluster Stitch—With Double and Single Crochet and Chains 265

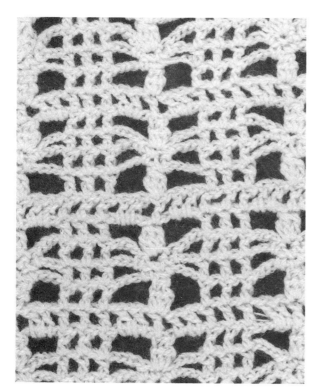

366. Chain multiples of 16 plus 5.

Row 1: 1 dc in the 7th ch, * 1 ch, 1 dc in the 2nd ch, rep from *, ending row with last dc, ch 4 and turn.

Row 2: 1 dc in the 2nd dc, ch 1, 1 dc in the next dc, * ch 5, a 3-looped cluster in the 3rd dc, ch 5, 1 dc in the 3rd dc, ch 1, 1 dc in the next dc, ch 1, 1 dc in the next dc, rep from *, ending row with 1 dc in the turning ch, ch 4 and turn.

Row 3: 1 dc in the 2nd dc, ch 1, 1 dc in the next dc, * ch 4, 1 sc in the last ch before the cluster, 1 sc in the ch just after the cluster, ch 4, 1 dc in the next dc, ch 1, 1 dc in the next dc, ch 1, 1 dc in the next dc, rep from *, ending row with 1 dc in the turning ch, ch 4 and turn.

Row 4: 1 dc in the 2nd dc, ch 1, 1 dc in the next dc, * ch 4, 1 sc in the last ch before the sc, 1 sc between the 2 sc, 1 sc in the ch just after the sc, ch 4, 1 dc in the dc, ch 1, 1 dc in the dc, ch 1, 1 dc in the dc, rep from *, ending row with 1 dc in the turning ch, ch 4 and turn.

Row 5: 1 dc in the 2nd dc, ch 1, 1 dc in the next dc, * ch 5, work a 3-looped cluster in the 2nd sc, ch 5, 1 dc in the next dc, ch 1, 1 dc in the next dc, ch 1, 1 dc in the next dc, rep from *, ending row with 1 dc in the turning ch, ch 4 and turn.

Row 6: Same as row 1, except that 2 dc are worked in each 5-ch and 1 in the top of the cluster.

Pattern formed by rep rows 1–5.

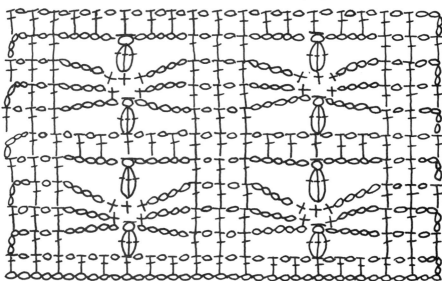

367. Chain multiples of 4 plus 5.

Row 1: 1 dc in the 7th ch, * ch 1, 1 dc in the 2nd ch, rep from *, ending row after last set, ch 1 and turn.

Row 2: * 1 sc in the dc, ch 5, work a 4-looped cluster in the sc, just formed, rep from *, ending row with last sc in the turning ch, ch 4 and turn.

Row 3: * 1 hdc around the middle of the 5-ch, ch 1, 1 dc in the sc, ch 1, rep from *, ending row with 1 ch and 1 dc in the sc, ch 4 and turn.

Pattern formed by rep rows 1–3.

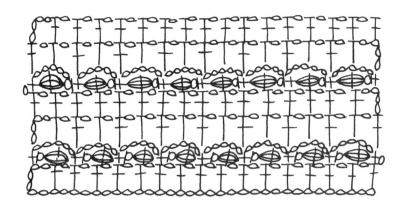

368. Chain multiples of 8 plus 4.

Row 1: 1 dc in the 5th ch, * 2 dc in the 3rd ch, ch 1, 2 dc in the same ch, 1 dc in the 3rd ch, ch 1, 1 dc in the 2nd ch, rep from *, ending row with 1 dc in each of the last 2 chs, ch 3 and turn.

Row 2: Same as row 1, ch 3 and turn.

Row 3: Same as row 2, ch 3 and turn.

Row 4: Sk 1st dc, * finish 3 dc together in the next 3 dc, ch 2, work 3-looped cluster in the 1-ch, ch 2, finish 3 dc together in the next 3 dc, ch 1, rep from *, ending row with last set and 1 dc in the turning ch, ch 3 and turn.

Row 5: 2 dc in the 1st dc, * 1 dc in the 2-ch, ch 1, 1 dc in the next 2-ch, 2 dc in the 1-ch, ch 1, 2 dc in the same 1-ch, rep from *, ending row with 3 dc in the turning ch, ch 3 and turn.

Row 6: Same as row 5, ch 3 and turn.

Row 7: Same as row 6, ch 3 and turn.

Row 8: Sk 1st dc, * finish 3 dc together in the next 3 dc, ch 1, finish 3 dc together in the next 3 dc, ch 2, work 3-looped cluster in the 1-ch, ch 2, rep from *, ending row with 2 chs and 1 dc in the turning ch.

Pattern formed by rep rows 1–8.

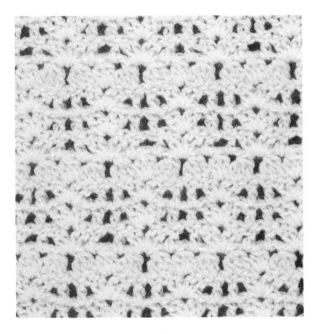

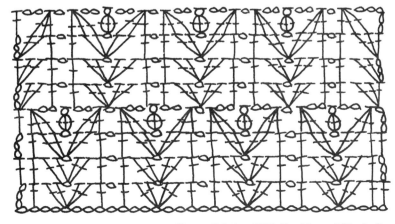

Cluster Stitch—With Double and Single Crochet and Chains 267

369. Chain multiples of 24 plus 4.

Row 1: 1 dc in the 5th ch and in each ch all across the row, ch 7 and turn.

Row 2: Work 3-looped cluster in the 3rd dc, * ch 1, 3-looped cluster in the 4th dc, ch 1, 3-looped cluster in the 4th dc, ch 4, 1 dc in the 2nd dc, 1 ch 6 times, dc in 2nd dc, ch 4, 3-looped cluster in the 2nd dc, rep from *, ending row with 1 dc in the turning ch, ch 7 and turn.

Row 3: * 1 sc in the top of the 1st cluster, 1 sc in the top of the next cluster and the 1 after that, ch 4, 1 dc in each dc with a ch 6 times, dc in last dc, ch 4, rep from *, ending row with 4 chs and 1 dc in the turning ch, ch 4 and turn.

Row 4: * work 3-looped cluster in the 1st sc, ch 3, 3-looped cluster in the next sc, ch 3, 3-looped cluster in the next sc, ch 1, 1 dc in each dc with a ch in between, ch 1, rep from *, ending row with dc in the turning ch, ch 3 and turn.

Row 5: * 1 dc in the 1-ch, 1 in the cluster, 3 dc in the 3-ch, 1 in the cluster, 3 in the 3-ch, 1 in the cluster, 1 in the 1-ch and then 1 in each dc and in each ch, rep from *, ending row with 2 dc in the turning ch, ch 4 and turn.

Row 6: 1 dc in the 3rd dc, * ch 1, 1 dc in the 2nd dc 5 times, ch 4, work a 3-looped cluster in the 2nd dc, ch 1, work a 3-looped cluster in the 4th dc, ch 1, a 3-looped cluster in the 4th dc, ch 4, 1 dc in the 2nd dc, ch 1, dc in 2nd dc, rep from *, ending row with 1 dc in the turning ch, ch 4 and turn.

Row 7: * 1 dc in each dc, ch 1 in between, ch 4, 1 sc in each of the 3 clusters, ch 4, rep from *, ending row with 1 dc in the turning ch, ch 4 and turn.

Row 8: * 1dc in each dc, interspaced with a ch, ch 1, work a 3-looped cluster in the 1st sc, ch 3, a 3-looped cluster in the 2nd sc, ch 3, a 3-looped cluster in the next sc, ch 1, rep from *, ending row with 1 dc in the turning ch, ch 3 and turn.

Pattern formed by rep rows 1–8.

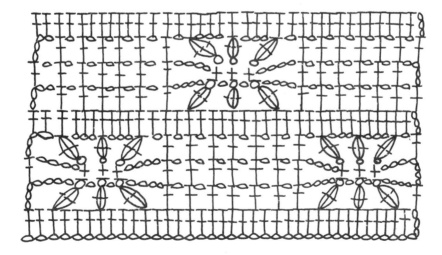

370. Chain multiples of 6 plus 5.

Row 1: 1 dc in 7th ch, * ch 1, 1 dc in 2nd ch, rep from *, ending row with 1 ch and 1 dc, ch 4 and turn.

Row 2: 1 dc in 2nd dc, * ch 1, 1 dc in next dc, rep from *, ending row with 1 dc in the turning ch, ch 3 and turn.

Row 3: 1 dc in the 1st dc, * ch 2, 1 sc in 2nd 1-ch, ch 2, 1 dc in 2nd dc, ch 2, 1 dc in same dc, rep from *, ending row with 2 dc in turning ch, ch 4 and turn.

Row 4: 2-looped cluster in 1st dc, * ch 1, 2-looped cluster in 2-ch between the 2-dc, ch 1, another 2-looped cluster in same ch, ch 1, another 2-looped cluster in the same ch, rep from *, ending row with 2-looped cluster in turning ch, ch 1 and 1 dc in same spot, ch 4 and turn.

Pattern formed by rep rows 1–4.

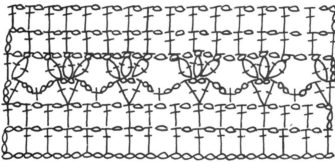

371. Chain multiples of 4 plus 1.

Row 1: 1 sc in the 2nd ch, * ch 5, 1 sc in the 4th ch, rep from *, ending row with 1 sc, ch 2 and turn.

Row 2: Work a 2-looped cluster in the 1st 5-ch, * ch 3, begin a 2-looped cluster in the same 5-ch, begin 2nd 2-looped cluster in the next 5-ch and finish off the 2 clusters together, rep from *, ending row with 2-looped cluster in the last 5-ch and 1 dc in the turning ch, ch 1 and turn.

Row 3: Same as row 1, except that 1 sc is worked in the last ch before the cluster.

Pattern formed by rep rows 1–2.

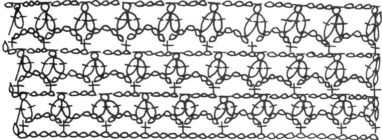

Cluster Stitch—With Double and Single Crochet and Chains 269

372. Chain multiples of 5 plus 4.

Row 1: 2-looped cluster in the 6th ch, * ch 3, 2-looped cluster in the same ch, 2-looped cluster in the 5th ch, rep from *, ending row after last set with 1 dc in the 2nd ch, ch 5 and turn.
Row 2: * 2-looped cluster in 1st cluster, 2-looped cluster in 2nd cluster, ch 3, rep from *, ending row with dc in turning ch after the last set, ch 3 and turn.
Pattern formed by rep rows 1–2.

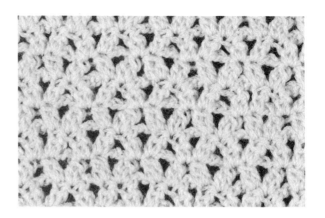

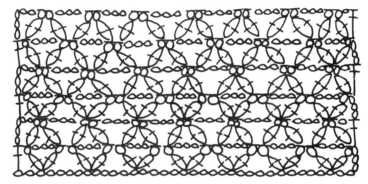

• *26* •
Cluster-Stitch Combinations

373. Chain multiples of 2 plus 4.

Row 1: 2 dc in the 6th ch, * 2 dc in the 2nd ch, rep from *, ending row with last set and 1 extra dc in the 2nd ch, ch 3 and turn.
Row 2: Same as row 1, ch 4 and turn.
Row 3: * work a 3-looped cluster in the middle of the 2 dc worked in the same stitch, ch 1, rep from *, ending row with last cluster, last ch and 1 extra dc in the turning ch, ch 2 and turn.
Row 4: * 1 sc in the 1-ch, ch 2, rep from *, ending row with sc in the last 1-ch and 1 sc in the turning ch, ch 3 and turn.
Pattern formed by rep rows 1–4.

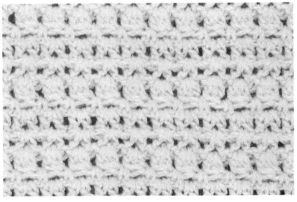

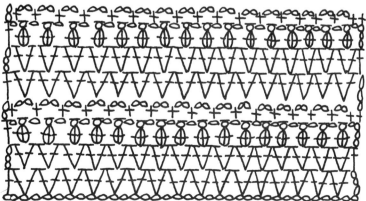

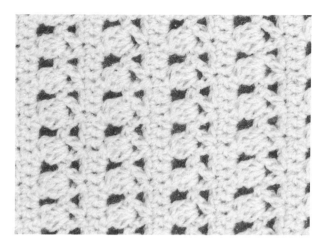

374. Chain multiples of 3 plus 1.

Row 1: Sc in the 2nd ch and in every ch all across the row, ch 3 and turn.
Row 2: 1 dc in the 2nd sc, * ch 1, 1 dc in the same sc, 1 dc in the 3rd sc, rep from *, ending row with an extra dc made together with the last V-set, ch 3 and turn.
Row 3: Work 3-looped cluster in the 1-ch, * ch 2, work 3-looped cluster in the next 1-ch, rep from *, ending row with 1 dc in the turning ch after completion of the last set, ch 1 and turn.
Row 4: 1 sc in the dc, in the 3-looped cluster and in every ch all across the row, ch 1 and turn.
Pattern formed by rep rows 1–4.

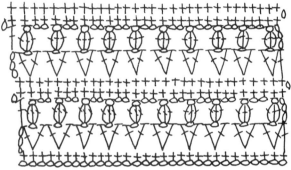

375. Chain multiples of 3 plus 4.

Row 1: 1 dc in the 5th ch, * ch 1, 1 dc in the same ch, 1 dc in the 3rd ch, rep from *, ending row with last dc, 1 ch and dc in the same ch, finished together with 1 extra dc in the last ch, ch 3 and turn.
Row 2: * work a 3-looped cluster in the next 1-ch, ch 2, rep from *, ending row with a 3-looped cluster in the last set and 1 extra dc in the turning ch, ch 3 and turn.
Row 3: 1 dc in each cluster and each ch all the way across the row with 1 extra dc in the turning ch, ch 3 and turn.
Row 4: 1 dc in the 2nd dc, ch 1, 1 dc in the same dc, * 1 dc in the 3rd dc, ch 1, 1 dc in the dc just used, rep from *, ending row with last dc, 1 ch and 2 dc finished together, part in the dc just used and part in the turning ch, ch 3 and turn.
Pattern formed by rep rows 1–4.

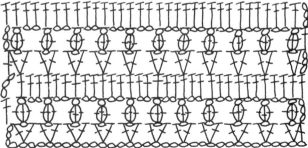

376. Chain multiples of 6 plus 5.

Row 1: 1 dc in the 5th ch, * ch 1, 1 sc in the 3rd ch, ch 1, 1 dc in the 3rd ch, ch 1, 1 dc in the same ch, ch 1, 1 dc in the same ch, rep from *, ending row with 1 dc, 1 ch and 1 dc, ch 1 and turn.
Row 2: 1 sc in the 1st dc, * ch 3, work a 2-looped cluster in the sc, ch 3, 1 sc in the middle dc, rep from *, ending row with 1 sc in the turning ch, ch 4 and turn.
Row 3: Same as row 1, except that the sc is worked in the top of the cluster and the 3 dc with chs are worked in the sc.
Pattern formed by rep rows 1–2.

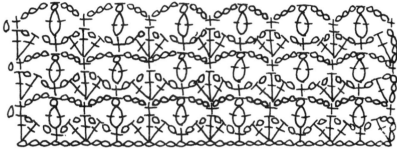

377. Chain multiples of 6 plus 3.

Row 1: 1 dc in the 5th ch, ch 2, * 1 dc in the next ch, ch 2, begin 1 dc in the next ch, and begin the 2nd dc in the 3rd ch, finish together, ch 2, rep from *, ending row with 2 dc finished together in the 3rd to the last ch and the last ch, ch 5 and turn.
Row 2: * work a 2-looped cluster in the single standing dc, ch 2, work 1 dc in the top of the 2 dc finished together, ch 2, rep from *, ending row with 2 chs and 1 dc in the turning ch, ch 2 and turn.
Row 3: Same as row 1, except that the stitches are worked on top of each other.
Pattern formed by rep rows 1–2.

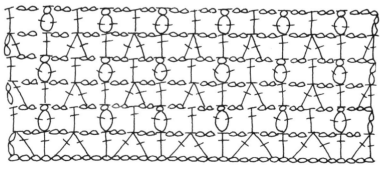

Cluster Stitch Combinations 273

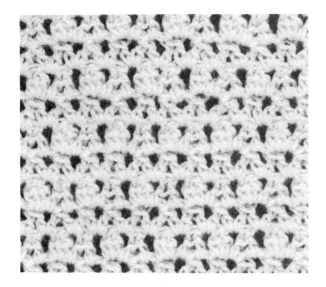

378. Chain multiples of 6 plus 5.

Row 1: Begin 1 dc in the 6th ch, begin 2nd dc in the 2nd ch, finish the 2 dc together, * ch 2, work a 3-looped cluster in the 2nd ch, ch 2, begin dc in the 2nd ch, begin the 2nd dc in the 2nd ch, finish together, rep from *, ending row with final cluster, 1 ch and 1 dc in the last ch, ch 4 and turn.
Row 2: * begin 1st dc in the 1st ch, begin 2nd dc in the next ch, finish off together, ch 2, begin next dc in the next ch, begin dc in the next ch (the 1st after the V-stitch), finish off together, ch 2, rep from *, ending row with the last set, 1 ch and 1 dc in the turning ch, ch 4 and turn.
Row 3: * work a 3-looped cluster in the top of the 1st V-stitch, ch 2, 2 dc around the V-stitch (1 dc on each side), finish off the 2 dc together, ch 2, rep from *, ending row with the last inverted V-stitch, 1 ch and 1 dc in the turning ch, ch 4 and turn.
Row 4: Same as row 2.
Pattern formed by rep rows 1–4.

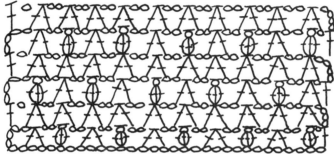

379. Chain multiples of 5 plus 5.

Row 1: Work a 3-looped cluster in the 6th ch, * ch 1, 1 dc in the 3rd ch, 1 dc backwards in the ch before, ch 1, a 3-looped cluster in the 2nd ch, rep from *, ending row with 1 cluster, 1 ch and 1 dc in the 2nd ch, ch 3 and turn.
Row 2: * 1 dc in the ch after the cluster, 1 dc in the ch before the cluster, ch 1, work a 3-looped cluster in the middle of the 2 sides of the X, ch 1, rep from *, ending row with the X worked around the last cluster and 1 dc in the turning ch, ch 4 and turn.
Pattern formed by rep rows 1–2.

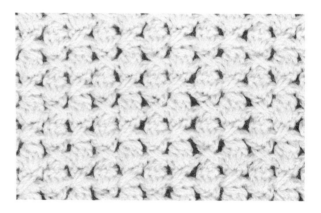

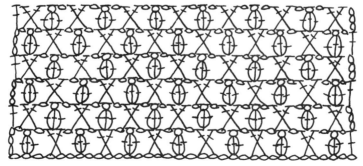

380. Chain multiples of 3 plus 4.

Row 1: 1 dc in the 7th ch, * ch 1, 1 dc backwards, 2 chs, 1 dc in the 3rd ch, rep from *, ending row with 1 dc after last X-stitch, ch 4 and turn.

Row 2: * work a 4-looped cluster in the 1st 1-ch between the 2 sides of the X, ch 3, rep from *, ending row after last set with 2 chs and 1 dc in the turning ch, ch 3 and turn.

Row 3: * 1 dc after cluster, ch 1, 1 dc backwards before the cluster, rep from *, ending row after the last set with 1 dc in the turning ch, ch 4 and turn.

Row 4: * 1 dc in the 1-ch, ch 2, rep from *, ending row with 1 ch and 1 dc in the turning ch, ch 3 and turn.

Row 5: Same as row 1, except that the X is worked around the dc. Pattern formed by rep rows 1–4.

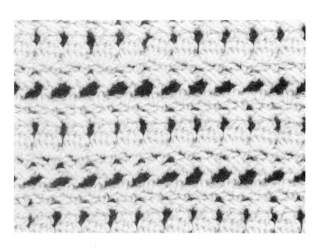

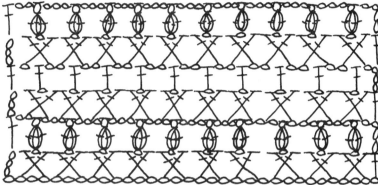

381. Chain multiples of 12 plus 4.

Row 1: 1 dc in the 7th ch, * ch 1, 1 dc backwards 2 chs, 1 dc in the 3rd ch, ch 1, 1 dc backwards 2 chs, ch 3, work a 3-looped cluster in the next ch, work 3-looped cluster in the 5th ch, ch 3, 1 dc in the 3rd ch, rep from *, ending row with 1 dc in the ch after the last X-stitch, ch 3 and turn.

Row 2: Same as row 1, except that the X-stitches are worked in the X-stitches, clusters are worked in the chs just before and after the clusters from the row below.

Pattern formed by rep row 1.

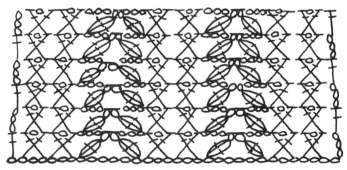

Cluster Stitch Combinations 275

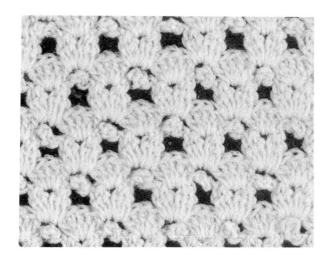

382. Chain multiples of 5 plus 3.

Row 1: Work a 3-looped cluster in the 4th ch, * ch 1, 1 picot, ch 1, work a 3-looped cluster in the 5th ch, ch 1, work a 3-looped cluster in the same ch, rep from *, ending row with a 3-looped cluster in the last ch and 1 dc, ch 3 and turn.
Row 2: 2 dc in the dc, * work 5 dc in the 1-ch between the 2 clusters, rep from *, ending row after the last 5 dc with 3 dc in the turning ch, ch 3 and turn.
Row 3: * work a 3-looped cluster between the 2 sets, ch 1, work 2nd 3-looped cluster in the same stitch, ch 1, 1 picot, ch 1, rep from *, ending row with the last set and then 1 extra dc in the turning ch, ch 2 and turn.
Row 4: * work 5 dc in the 1-ch between the 2 clusters, rep from *, ending row with last set and 1 dc in the turning ch, ch 3 and turn.
Pattern formed by rep rows 1–4.

383. Chain multiples of 6 plus 4.

Row 1: 3 dc in 4th ch, * 3 dc in 6th ch, ch 2, 3 dc in ch just used, rep from *, ending row with 4 dc in last ch, ch 3 and turn.
Row 2: 1 dc in 2nd dc, * ch 5, 3-looped cluster in 2-ch, rep from *, ending row with 2-looped cluster in turning ch, ch 3 and turn.
Row 3: * 3 dc in 3rd ch, ch 2, 3 dc in same ch, rep from *, making set in middle of each 5-ch, ending row with 1 dc in turning ch, ch 5 and turn.
Row 4: 3-looped cluster in 2-ch, * ch 5, 3-looped cluster in 2-ch, rep from *, ending row with 2 chs and 1 dc in turning ch, ch 3 and turn.
Pattern formed by rep rows 1–4.

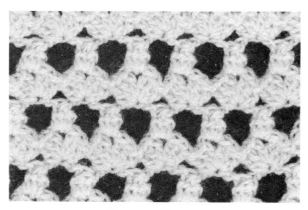

384. Chain multiples of 8 plus 1.

Row 1: 1 sc in the 2nd ch and the ch after that, * ch 4, work 4 dc together in the next ch and the ch after that, then the 2nd ch and the 1 after that, ch 4, 1 sc in the next ch, ch 1, 1 sc in the 2nd ch, rep from *, ending row with 1 sc in each of the last 2 chs, ch 3 and turn.

Row 2: 1 dc in the 1st sc, * ch 3, 1 sc in the last of the 4-ch, ch 1, 1 sc in the 1st of the next 4-ch, ch 3, work a 3-looped cluster in the 1-ch, rep from *, ending row with a 2-looped cluster in the last sc, ch 1 and turn.

Pattern formed by rep rows 1–2.

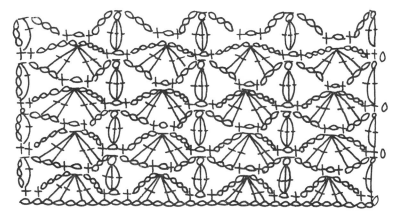

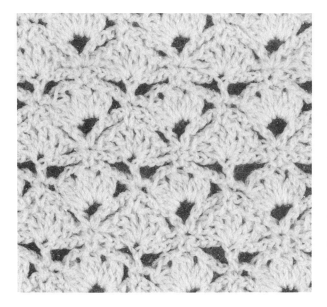

385. Chain multiples of 10 plus 5.

Row 1: 1 dc in the 5th ch, ch 1, 1 dc in the same ch, * ch 1, 1 sc in the 5th ch, ch 1, 1 dc in the 5th ch, ch 1, 5 times, 1 dc in same ch, rep from *, ending row with 1 dc, 1 ch, 1 dc, 1 ch and 1 dc worked in the 5th and last ch, ch 1 and turn.

Row 2: 1 sc in the 1st dc, * ch 3, 1 dc in the sc, ch 3, 1 dc in the same sc, ch 3, 1 sc in the 4th 1-ch (the middle one), rep from *, ending row with 3 chs and 1 sc in the turning ch, ch 1 and turn.

Row 3: 1 sc in the sc, * ch 2, work a 3-looped cluster in the 2nd 3-ch, ch 2, work another 3-looped cluster in the same 3-ch, ch 2, work a 3rd 3-looped cluster in the same 3-ch, ch 2, 1 sc in the sc, rep from *, ending row with 1 sc in the last sc, ch 7 and turn.

Row 4: * 1 sc in the top of the middle cluster, ch 4, 1 dc in the sc, ch 4, rep from *, ending row with 4 chs and 1 dc in the last sc, ch 4 and turn.

Row 5: Same as row 1, except that the sc are worked in the sc and the 5 dc are worked in the dc.

Pattern formed by rep rows 1–4.

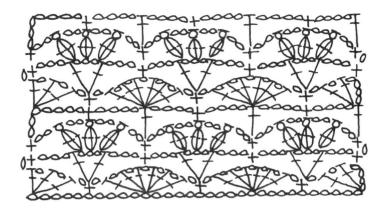

386. Chain multiples of 12 plus 5.

Row 1: 1 sc in the 8th ch, * ch 3, 1 dc in the 4th ch, ch 3, 1 dc in the same ch, ch 3, 1 sc in the 4th ch, ch 5, 1 sc in the 4th ch, rep from *, ending row with sc, ch 2 and 1 dc in the 2nd ch, ch 3 and turn.

Row 2: 4 dc around the 2-ch, * ch 2, work a 2-looped cluster around the 3-ch between the 2 dc, ch 2, work a 2-looped cluster in the same 3-ch, ch 2, work a 2-looped cluster in the same 3-ch, ch 2, work 9 dc around the 5-ch, rep from *, ending row with 5 dc in the turning ch, ch 4 and turn.

Row 3: 1 dc in the 3rd dc and the 2 after that, * 1 dc in the 2nd 2-ch, ch 5, 1 dc in the next 2-ch, 1 dc in each of the 1st 3 dc, ch 3, 1 dc in the 4th dc and the 2 after that, rep from *, ending row with 1 dc in each of the next 3 dc, 1 ch and 1 dc in the turning ch, ch 3 and turn.

Row 4: 1 dc in the 1-ch and in the next 3 dc, * 1 dc in the middle of the 5-ch, ch 5, 1 dc in the same ch, 1 dc in the 2nd dc, the 2 dc after that, 1 dc in each of the 3-chs and 1 dc in each of the last 3 dc, rep from *, ending row with 5 dc, the last 2 in the turning ch, ch 4 and turn.

Row 5: 1 dc in the 1st dc, * ch 3, 1 sc in the 1st of the 5-ch, ch 5, 1 sc in the last of the 5-ch, ch 3, 1 dc in the 5th dc, ch 3, 1 dc in the dc just used, rep from *, ending row with 1 dc, 1 ch and 1 dc in the turning ch, ch 5 and turn.

Row 6: Work a 2-looped cluster in the 1-ch, * ch 2, 9 dc around the 5-ch, ch 2, work a 2-looped cluster in the 3-ch between the 2 dc, ch 2, 2-looped cluster in the same 3-ch, ch 2, 2-looped cluster in the same 3-ch, rep from *, ending row with 2-looped cluster, 1 ch and 1 dc in the turning ch, ch 5 and turn.

Row 7: 1 dc in the 2-ch, * 1 dc in each of the next 3 dc, ch 3, 1 dc in the 4th dc and the 2 after that, 1 dc in the 2nd 2-ch, ch 5, 1 dc in the next 2-ch, rep from *, ending row with 1 dc, 2 chs and 1 dc in the turning ch, ch 5 and turn.

Row 8: 1 dc in the 2-ch, * 1 dc in the 2nd dc, the 2 dc after that, 1 dc in each of the 3-chs, 1 dc in the next dc and the 2 after that, 1 dc in the middle of the 5-ch, ch 5, 1 dc in the same ch, rep from *, ending row with 1 dc, 2 chs and 1 dc in the ch, ch 5 and turn. Pattern formed by rep rows 1–8.

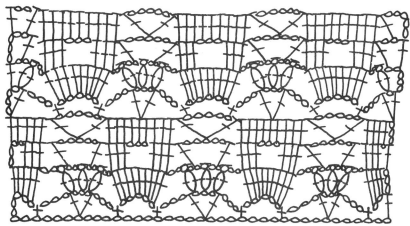

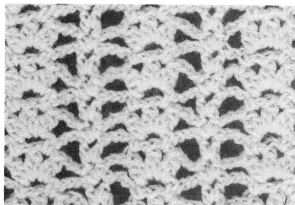

387. Chain multiples of 13 plus 1.

Row 1: 1 sc in the 2nd ch, * ch 3, 1 dc in the 4th ch, ch 1, 1 dc in the same ch, ch 3, 1 sc in the 4th ch, ch 4, 1 sc in the 5th ch, rep from *, ending row with regular set and sc on the end, ch 6 and turn.
Row 2: * 1 sc in the 1st dc, ch 3, 1 sc in the next dc, ch 3, a 2-looped cluster stitch around the 4-ch, ch 2, a 2-looped cluster stitch around the same 4-ch, a 2-looped cluster stitch around the 4-ch, ch 2, a 2-looped cluster stitch around the same 4-ch, rep from *, ending row with 3 chs and 1 dc in the turning ch, ch 1 and turn.
Row 3: Same as row 1, except 2 dc worked in the 3-ch and 1 sc worked between each of the clusters.
Pattern formed by rep rows 1–2.

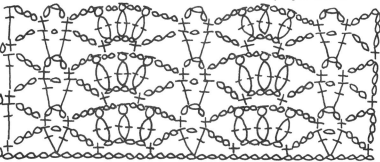

388. Chain multiples of 12 plus 4.

Row 1: 1 sc in the 6th ch, * ch 3, 1 sc in the 4th ch, rep from *, ending row with 1 ch and 1 hdc, ch 3 and turn.
Row 2: 3 dc in 1-ch, * 1 sc in the 1st 3-ch, ch 3, 1 sc in the 3-ch, 7 dc in the next 3-ch, rep from *, ending row with 1 sc, ch 5 and turn.
Row 3: * 1 sc in 3rd dc, ch 3, 1 sc in the 2nd dc, ch 3, a 2-looped cluster in the 3-ch, ch 3, a 2-looped cluster in the same 3-ch, ch 3, rep from *, ending row with 1 ch and 1 hdc in the turning ch, ch 3 and turn.
Row 4: 3 dc in the 1st 1-ch, * 1 sc in the top of the cluster, ch 3, 1 sc in the top of the next cluster, 7 dc around the 2nd 3-ch, rep from *, ending row with sc in the turning ch, ch 3 and turn.
Pattern formed by rep rows 1–4.

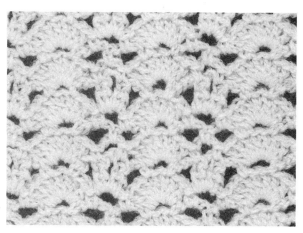

Cluster Stitch Combinations   279

389. Chain multiples of 8 plus 3.

Row 1: 1 dc in the 3rd ch, * ch 2, 1 sc in the 2nd ch, ch 3, 1 sc in the 4th ch, ch 2, a 3-looped cluster in the 2nd ch, rep from *, ending row with 2-looped cluster in the last ch, ch 1 and turn.
Row 2: 1 sc in the top of the cluster, * ch 1, 2 dc in the 3-ch, ch 2, 2 dc in the 3-ch, ch 1, 1 sc in the top of the cluster, rep from *, ending row with 1 ch and 1 sc, ch 1 and turn.
Row 3: 1 sc in the 1st sc, * ch 2, 1 sc in the 1st dc, ch 2, work a 3-looped cluster in the 2-ch, ch 2, 1 sc in the 2nd dc, ch 3, 1 sc in next dc, rep from *, ending row with 2 chs and 1 sc in the sc, ch 3 and turn.
Row 4: 2 dc in the 1st 2-ch, * ch 1, 1 sc in the top of the cluster, ch 1, 2 dc around the 3-ch, ch 2, 2 dc around the 3-ch, rep from *, ending row with 3 dc, 2 in the last 2-ch and 1 in the last sc, ch 2 and turn.
Pattern formed by rep rows 1–4.

390. Chain multiples of 11 plus 6.

Row 1: 1 sc in the 8th ch, * 2-looped cluster in the 4th ch, ch 1, 2-looped cluster in the same ch, ch 1, 2-looped cluster in the same ch, ch 1, 2-looped cluster in the same ch, ch 1, 2-looped cluster in the same ch, 1 sc in the 4th ch, ch 5, 1 sc in the 3rd ch, rep from *, ending row with sc after the last set, 2 chs and 1 hdc in the 2nd ch, ch 5 and turn.
Row 2: 1 sc around the 2-ch, * ch 1, 1 sc in the 1-ch, ch 3, 1 sc in the next 1-ch, ch 3, 1 sc in the next ch, ch 3, 1 sc in the 1-ch, ch 1, 1 sc in the 5-ch, ch 5, 1 sc in the same 5-ch, rep from *, ending row with 2 chs and 1 dc in the turning ch, ch 5 and turn.
Row 3: Same as row 1, except that the clusters are formed in the middle of the middle 3-ch and the 2 sc are worked in the 5-ch.
Pattern formed by rep rows 1–2.

280 **Complete Book of Crochet**

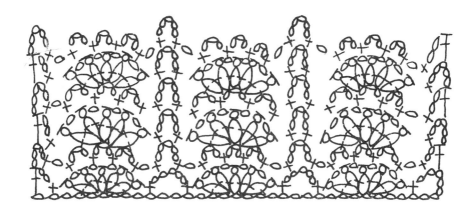

391. Chain multiples of 9 plus 4.

Row 1: 1 dc in the 5th ch, * ch 3, 1 sc in the 3rd ch, ch 3, 1 sc in the 2nd ch, ch 3, 1 dc in the 3rd ch and the ch after that, rep from *, ending row with 2 dc, ch 3 and turn.

Row 2: 1 dc in the 2nd dc, * ch 1, work a 2-looped cluster in the middle 3-ch, 1 picot, ch 1, work a 2-looped cluster in the same 3-ch, 1 picot, 1 ch and work a 2-looped cluster in the same ch, picot, ch 1, 1 dc in each of the next 2 dc, rep from *, ending row with 1 dc in the last dc and 1 in the turning ch, ch 3 and turn.

Row 3: Same as row 1, except that the 2 sc are worked in the 1-ch between the clusters.

Pattern forced by rep rows 1–2.

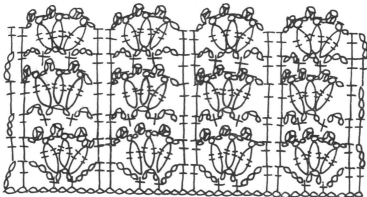

392. Chain multiples of 12 plus 1.

Row 1: 1 sc in the 2nd ch, * ch 2, 1 sc in the 2nd ch, 3 trc in the 4th ch, ch 4, 1 sc in the ch just used, ch 2, 1 sc in the 2nd ch, ch 4, 3 trc in ch just used for the sc, 1 sc in the 4th ch, rep from *, ending row after last set with 1 sc, 2 chs and 1 sc, ch 4 and turn.

Row 2: 1 dc in the 1st 2-ch, * ch 1, 1 sc in the top of the 4-ch, ch 2, 2-looped cluster in the next 2-ch, ch 2, 1 sc in the top of the next 4-ch, ch 1, 1 dc in the 2-ch, ch 1, 1 dc in the same 2-ch, rep from *, ending row with 1 dc in the last 2-ch, ch 1 and 1 dc in the sc, ch 1 and turn.

Row 3: Same as row 1, except 2 sc with the butterfly construction are worked in the chs before and after the cluster stitch and the 2 sc with the 2 chs are worked in the 1-ch before and after the V-stitch.

Pattern formed by rep rows 1–2.

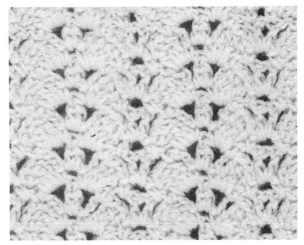

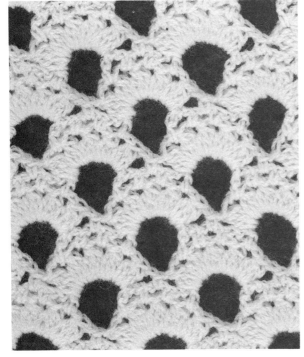

393. Chain multiples of 12 plus 7.

Row 1: 1 sc in the 10th ch and also in the 6 chs following that, * ch 7, work 1 sc in the 6th ch and the 6 chs following that, rep from *, ending row with 4 sc, ch 1 and turn.

Row 2: 1 sc in the 1st sc, * ch 1, work a 3-looped cluster around the 7-ch, ch 2, rep 3 times, ch 2, work a 5th 3-looped cluster in the same chs, ch 1, 1 sc in the 4th sc, rep from *, ending row with a half set (2 clusters, ch 2) and 1 dc in the turning ch, ch 1 and turn.

Row 3: 1 sc in the dc, * 1 sc in the 2-ch, ch 2, 1 dc in the next 2-ch, ch 5, work 1 dc in the next 2-ch, ch 2, 1 sc in the next 2-ch, ch 2, rep from *, ending row with last set, ch 2 and 1 trc in the sc, ch 3 and turn.

Row 4: 1 dc in the 1st trc, * ch 2, work 3-looped cluster in the same 2-ch, ch 2, work 3-looped cluster in the same 2-ch, ch 1, 1 sc in the middle 2-ch from the set below, ch 1, work a 3-looped cluster in the 5-ch, ch 2, work a 3-looped cluster in the same 5-ch, ch 2, work another 3-looped cluster in the same 5-ch, rep from *, ending row with last set, 1 ch and 1 sc in the last sc, ch 8.

Row 5: * 1 dc in the 1st 2-ch, ch 2, 1 sc in the next 2-ch, ch 2, 1 sc in the next 2-ch, ch 2, 1 dc in the next 2-ch, ch 5, rep from *, ending row with 1 ch and 1 sc in the turning ch, ch 1 and turn.
Pattern formed by rep rows 1–5.

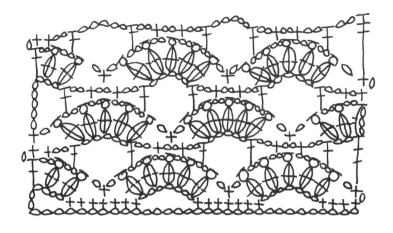

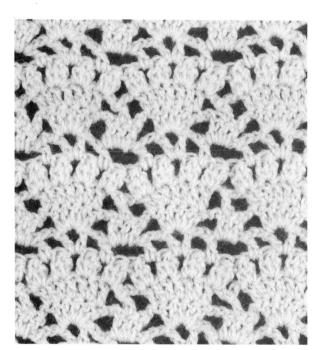

394. Chain multiples of 10 plus 4.

Row 1: 1 dc in the 5th ch, * ch 2, 5 dc in the 4th ch, ch 2, 1 dc in the 4th ch and in each of the next 2 chs, rep from *, ending row with 2 dc, ch 5 and turn.

Row 2: Sk 1st 2 dc, * 1 dc in the 1st dc, 2 dc in the next dc, 1 dc in the next dc, 2 dc in the next dc, 1 dc in the next dc, ch 2, 1 dc in the 2nd dc, ch 2, rep from *, ending row with 1 dc in the turning ch, ch 3 and turn.

Row 3: Sk 1 dc, work a 3-looped cluster in the next dc, * ch 2, work a 3-looped cluster in the 2nd dc, ch 2, work 3-looped cluster in the 2nd dc, ch 2, work a 3-looped cluster in the 2nd dc, finished together with the 3-looped cluster worked in 2nd dc, rep from *, ending row with 1 dc in the turning ch, ch 5 and turn.

Row 4: 1 dc in the 2-ch after the 1st cluster, * ch 2, 1 dc in the 2-ch after the 2nd cluster, ch 2, 1 dc in the ch just used, ch 2, 1 dc after the 3rd cluster, ch 3, rep from *, ending row after last set with 2 chs and 1 dc in the turning ch, ch 3 and turn.

Row 5: Same as row 1, except that the 5 dc are worked in the 2-ch between the sides of the V-stitch and the 3 dc are worked in the 3 chs between the sets.

Pattern formed by rep rows 1–4.

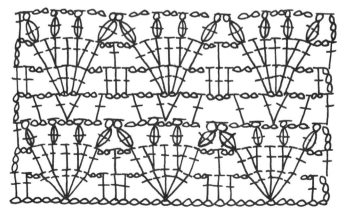

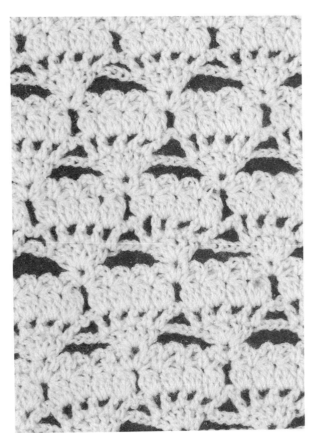

Row 395. Chain multiples of 9 plus 5.

Row 1: 5 dc in the 9th ch, * ch 4, 5 dc in the 9th ch, rep from *, ending row with 1 ch and 1 dc in the 4th ch, ch 3 and turn.
Row 2: Sk 1 dc, * 1 dc in the next dc, ch 1 and 1 dc in the next dc, 4 times, ch 1 and rep from *, ending row with last set and 1 dc in the turning ch, ch 3 and turn.
Row 3: * work a 3-looped cluster in the 1-ch, ch 1, work a 3-looped cluster in the next 1-ch, ch 1, 3-looped cluster in the next 1-ch, ch 1, work 3-looped cluster in the next 1-ch, ch 2, rep from *, ending row with 1 dc in the turning ch, ch 1 and turn.
Row 4: 1 sc in the dc, * ch 3, 1 sc in the 1-ch, ch 3, sc in the 1-ch, ch 3, sc in the 1-ch, ch 3, sc in the 2-ch, ch 4, 1 sc in the same 2-ch, rep from *, ending row with sc in the turning ch, ch 4 and turn.
Row 5: 2 dc in the 1st 3-ch, * ch 4, 5 dc around the 4-ch, rep from *, ending row with 2 dc in the last 3-ch and 1 trc in the last sc, ch 4 and turn.
Row 6: Sk trc, dc in the dc, ch 1, dc in the dc, * ch 1, 1 dc in the next dc, ch 1 and dc in the dc 4 times, rep from *, ending row with dc in the turning ch, ch 4 and turn.
Row 7: * work 3-looped cluster in the 1-ch, ch 1, work 3-looped cluster in the 2nd 1-ch, ch 2, work a 3-looped cluster in the next 1-ch, ch 1, 3-looped cluster in the next 1-ch, ch 1 and rep from *, ending row with 1 cluster and 1 dc in the turning ch, ch 1 and turn.
Row 8: 1 sc in the dc, * ch 3, sc in the next 1-ch, ch 3, sc in the 2-ch, ch 4. sc in the 2-ch, ch 3, sc in the 1-ch, ch 3, sc in the 1-ch, rep from *, ending row with sc in the turning ch.
Pattern formed by rep rows 1–8.

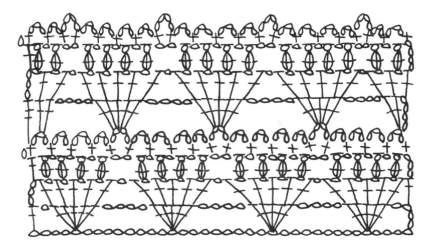

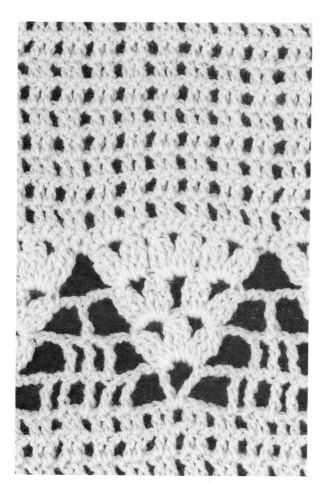

396. Chain multiples of 18 plus 4.

Row 1: 1 dc in the 5th ch, * ch 1, 1 dc in the 2nd ch and the ch after that, rep from *, ending row with 2 dc, ch 3 and turn.

Rows 2–3: Rep row 1, ch 5 and turn.

Row 4: * 1 trc in 1st 1-ch, ch 1, trc in the 2nd dc, ch 1, trc in the next dc, ch 3, 1 trc in the same 1-ch, ch 3, 1 trc in the 2nd 1-ch, ch 3, 1 trc in the same 1-ch, ch 3, 1 trc in the 4th dc, ch 1, 1 trc in the next dc, ch 1, rep from *, ending row with 1 extra trc in the turning ch.

Row 5: 1 trc in the 2nd trc, ch 1, 1 trc in the next trc, * ch 3, work a 3-looped triple cluster in the 3-ch between the 2 sides of the V-stitch, ch 3, work another 3-looped triple cluster in the same 3-ch, ch 3, work another 3-looped triple cluster in the same 3-ch, ch 3, 1 trc in the 2nd trc, ch 1, 1 trc in the next trc, ch 1, 1 trc in the next trc, rep from *, ending row with 1 trc in the turning ch, ch 5 and turn.

Row 6: 1 trc in the 2nd trc, * ch 3, work a 3-looped triple cluster in the 3-ch between the 1st 2 clusters, ch 3, work a 3-looped triple cluster in the same 3-ch, ch 3, work a 3-looped triple cluster in the next 3-ch, ch 3, work a 3-looped triple cluster in the same 3-ch, ch 3, 1 trc in the next trc, rep from *, ending row with 1 trc in the 2nd trc, ch 1, and in the turning ch, ch 6 and turn.

Row 7: * Work a 3-looped triple cluster in the 2nd 3-ch, ch 2, work 2nd 3-looped triple cluster in the same 3-ch, ch 2, work a 3-looped triple cluster in the next 3-ch, ch 2, work a 3-looped triple cluster in the same 3-ch, ch 2, work a 3-looped triple cluster in the next 3-ch, ch 2, work a 3-looped triple cluster in the same 3-ch, ch 2, rep from *, ending row with 1 trc in the turning ch, ch 1 and turn.

Row 8: * 1 sc in the trc, 1 in each of the 2-chs, 1 in the cluster, 3 in the 2-ch, 1 in the cluster, 1 in each 2-ch, 1 in the cluster, 1 in the 2-ch, 1 in the cluster, 1 in each of the chs, 1 in the cluster, 3 in the 2-ch, 1 in the cluster, 1 in the ch, rep from *, ending row with 1 sc in each of the last 3-chs, ch 3 and turn.

Pattern formed by rep rows 1–8.

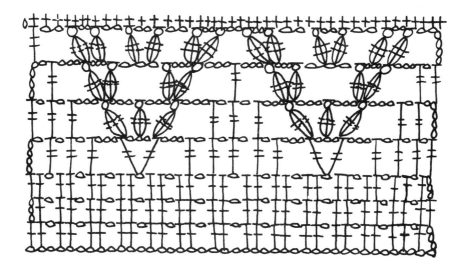

397. Chain multiples of 18 plus 6.

Row 1: 1 dc in the 9th ch, * ch 2, 1 dc in the 3rd ch, 1 dc in the 3rd ch, ch 3, 1 dc in the same ch, 1 dc in the 3rd ch, ch 2, 1 dc in the 3rd ch, ch 2, work a 3-looped cluster in the 3rd ch, ch 2, 1 dc in the 3rd ch, rep from *, ending row with 2 chs and 1 dc in the 3rd ch, ch 5 and turn.

Row 2: 1 dc in the 2nd dc, * ch 2, 6 dc around the 3-ch, ch 2, 1 dc in the dc, ch 2, 1 dc in the cluster, ch 2, 1 dc in the dc, rep from *, ending row with 2 chs and 1 dc in the turning ch, ch 5 and turn.

Row 3: 1 dc in the dc, * 1 dc in the dc and ch 1, 5 times, 1 dc in the last dc of the set, 1 dc in the next dc, ch 2, 1 dc in the dc, ch 2, 1 dc in the dc, rep from *, ending row with 2 chs and 1 dc in the turning ch, ch 5 and turn.

Row 4: Work a 3-looped cluster in the 1st dc, ch 1, until 7 clusters are made, ch 2, 1 dc in the 2 dc, ch 2, rep from *, ending row with 2 chs and 1 dc in the turning ch, ch 5 and turn.

Row 5: * work a 3-looped cluster in the next 1-ch, ch·1, until there are 6 clusters, ch 2, 1 dc in the dc, ch 2, rep from *, ending row with dc in the turning ch, ch 5 and turn.

Row 6: * 1 dc in the cluster, ch 1, work a 3-looped cluster in the 1-ch, ch 1, until 5 clusters are formed, ch 1, 1 dc in the last cluster, ch 2, 1 dc in the dc, ch 2, rep from *, ending row with 2 chs and 1 dc in the turning ch, ch 5 and turn.

Row 7: * 1 dc in the dc, ch 2, work a 3-looped cluster in the 1-ch, ch 1, until 4 clusters are formed, ch 2, 1 dc in the dc, ch 2, 1 dc in the dc, ch 2, rep from *, ending row with 2 chs and 1 dc in the turning ch, ch 5 and turn.

Row 8: Sk 1 dc, * 1 dc in the dc, ch 2, work a 3-looped cluster in each 1-ch, ch 1, until 3 clusters are formed, ch 2, 1 dc in the dc, ch 2, 1 dc in the dc, ch 2, rep from *, ending row with 2 chs and 1 dc in the turning ch, ch 5 and turn.

Row 9: * 1 dc in the dc, ch 2, 1 dc in the 1st cluster, ch 1, work a 3-looped cluster in the 1st 1-ch, ch 1, work a 3-looped cluster in the 1-ch, ch 1, 1 dc in the last cluster, ch 2, 1 dc in the dc, ch 2, 1 dc in the dc, ch 2, dc in the next dc, rep from *, ending row with 1 dc in the turning ch, ch 4 and turn.

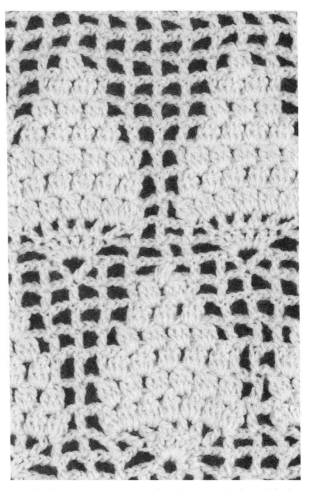

Row 10: Same as row 1, except that the pattern is formed in the middle of the space formed by the 1st set (consult diagram). Pattern formed by rep rows 1–9 and then alternating the spacing in rows 10–18.

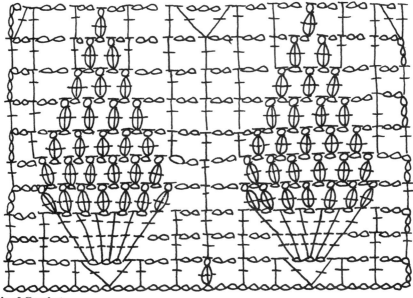

398. Chain multiples of 3 plus 1.

Row 1: 1 sc in the 2nd ch and in each ch all across the row, ch 2 and turn.

Row 2: 1 sc in the 1st sc, * ch 3, 1 sc in the 3rd sc, rep from *, ending row with 1 sc in the last sc, ch 3 and turn.

Row 3: * work a 3-looped cluster around the 3-ch, ch 2, rep from *, ending row with last set, 1 ch and 1 dc in the sc, ch 1 and turn.

Row 4: 1 sc in the dc, 1 sc in each ch and in each cluster, ending row with 1 sc in the turning ch, ch 3 and turn.

Row 5: * 1 relief dc around the base of the cluster, 2 rows below, from the front, 1 dc in each of the next 2 sc, rep from *, ending row with 1 dc in each of the last 2 sc, ch 1 and turn.

Row 6: 1 sc in each of the dc, including 1 in the turning ch.

Pattern formed by rep rows 1–6.

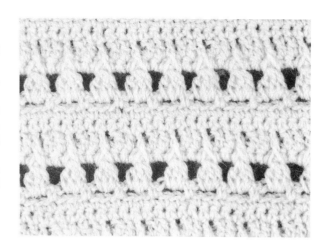

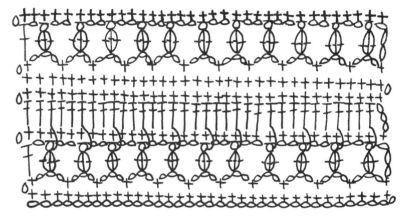

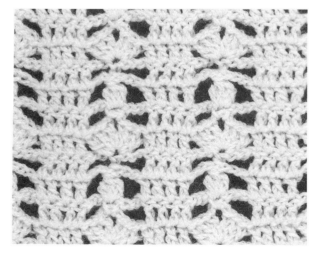

399. Chain multiples of 11 plus 4.

Row 1: 1 dc in 5th ch, ch 3, * 3-looped cluster stitch in 4th ch, ch 3, 1 dc in 4th ch, 1 dc in next 3 chs, ch 3, rep from *, ending with 2 dc in last 2 chs, ch 3 and turn.

Row 2: 1 dc in 2nd dc, ch 3, * 1 relief dc around the post of the cluster below, from the back, ch 3, 1 dc in each of the next 4 dc, ch 3, rep from *, ending row with 2 dc, ch 3 and turn.

Row 3: 1 dc in 2nd dc, * 3 dc in relief dc, ch 3, 3 dc in the same relief dc as just used, 1 dc in each of the next 4 dc, rep from *, ending row with 2 dc following the last set, ch 3 and turn.

Row 4: 1 dc in 2nd dc, * ch 3, 1 sc in the top of the 3-ch, ch 3, 1 dc in each of the next 4 dc, rep from *, ending row with 2 dc.

Row 5: Rep row 1, except that the cluster stitch should be made in the sc.

Pattern formed by rep rows 1–4.

Cluster Stitch Combinations 287

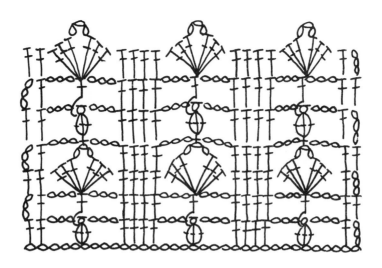

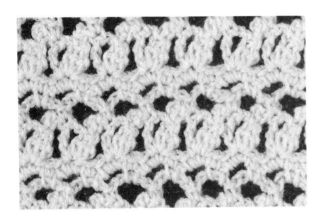

400. Chain multiples of 4 plus 1.

Row 1: 1 sc in the 2nd ch and in every ch all across the row, ch 6 and turn.
Row 2: 1 picot, work a 3-looped double cluster in the 1st sc, * 1 trc in the 4th sc, ch 2, 1 picot, work a 3-looped double cluster in the trc just formed, rep from *, ending row with last set, ch 1 and turn.
Row 3: 1 sc in the 1st trc, * ch 5, 1 sc in the trc, rep from *, ending row with last set, ch 4 and turn.
Row 4: * 1 sc around the 5-ch, ch 3, rep from *, ending row with sc around the 5-ch, ch 1 and 1 dc in the last sc, ch 1 and turn.
Pattern formed by rep rows 1–4.

401. Chain multiples of 16 plus 5.

Row 1: 1 trc in the 7th ch, * ch 3, begin 1 trc in the ch just used, begin next trc in the 4th ch, finish off together, rep from *, ending row with last trc finished together with a trc in the 2nd ch, ch 5 and turn.

Row 2: Begin 1 trc in the 1st trc, begin 2nd part of the trc in the next trc, finish the 2 together, * ch 3, begin 1 trc in the trc just used, begin 2nd part in the next trc, finish the 2 trc together, rep from *, ending row with 1 trc in the turning ch, 1 ch and 1 trc in the same stitch, ch 4 and turn.

Row 3: 1 trc in the top of the 2 trc finished together, * ch 3, begin 1 trc in the trc just formed, begin the 2nd part of the trc in the next trc, finish together, rep 2 trc finished together twice, 3 trc in the same stitch, begin trc in the same stitch, 2nd half of the trc to be worked in the next trc, rep from *, ending row with 2 trc finished together in the turning ch, ch 5 and turn.

Row 4: * work a 3-looped triple cluster in the 1st of the 5 trc, ch 1, rep 4 times, 1 trc in the top of the 2 trc, ch 3, begin 1 trc in the last trc and begin the 2nd half in the next trc, ch 3, 1 trc backwards in the trc just used, rep from *, ending row with a 3-looped triple cluster, 1 ch and 1 trc in the turning ch, ch 4 and turn.

Pattern formed by rep rows 1–4, alternating order in the next 4 rows (consult diagram).

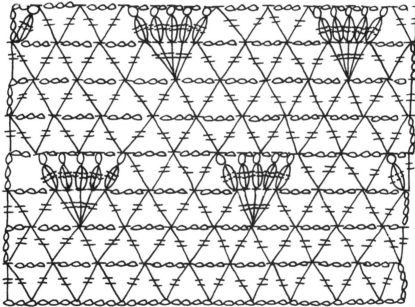

• 27 •
Popcorn Stitch

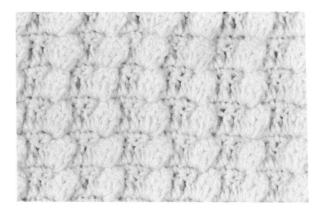

402. Chain multiples of 4 plus 2.

Row 1: 1 dc in the 5th ch from hook and in the next 2 chs, *work a 5-looped popcorn stitch in the next ch, 1 dc in each of the next 3 chs, rep from *, ending row with 3 dc, ch 1 and turn.
Row 2: Sc in each dc and each popcorn stitch all the way across the row, ch 3 and turn.
Pattern formed by rep rows. 1–2.

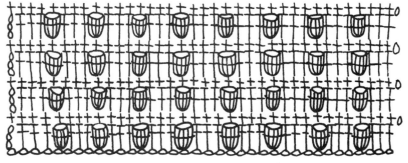

403. Chain multiples of 6 plus 1.

Row 1: 1 sc in the 1st ch and in every ch all the way across the row, ch 1 and turn.

Row 2: 1 sc in the 1st sc, *ch 3, work a 4-looped popcorn stitch in the 3rd sc, ch 3, 1 sc in the 3rd sc, rep from *, ending row after last set with 1 sc, ch 5 and turn.

Row 3: *1 sc in the top of the popcorn stitch, ch 2, 1 dc in the next sc, ch 2, rep from *, ending row with 1 dc in the last sc, ch 1 and turn.

Row 4: 1 sc in each ch and stitch all across the row, ch 1 and turn.

Row 5: Same as row 1.

Pattern formed by rep rows 1–4.

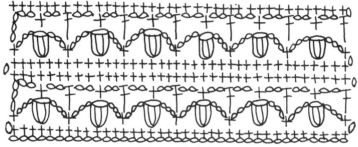

404. Chain multiples of 8 plus 4.

Row 1: 1 dc in the 5th ch and in the following 5 chs, *ch 1, 1 dc in the 2nd ch and the 6 chs following, rep from *, ending row with 7 dc, ch 3 and turn.

Row 2: 1 dc in the 2nd dc, 1 dc in the next dc, *work a 4-looped popcorn stitch in the next dc, 1 dc in each of the next 3 dc, ch 1, 1 dc in the next dc and the 2 dc after that, rep from *, ending row with last set, ch 3 and turn.

Row 3: 1 dc in the 2nd dc, the next dc, the popcorn and in the next 3 dc, *ch 1, 1 dc in the next 3 dc, the popcorn and the next 3 dc, rep from *, ending row with the last set, the last of the 7 dc made in the turning ch, ch 4 and turn.

Row 4: 1 dc in the 3rd dc, ch 1, 1 dc in the 2nd dc, ch 1, 1 dc in the 2nd dc, *ch 1, 1 dc in the 1st, in the 2nd dc, ch 1, 3 times, rep from *, ending row with 1 dc in the turning ch, ch 4 and turn.

Pattern formed by rep rows 1–4.

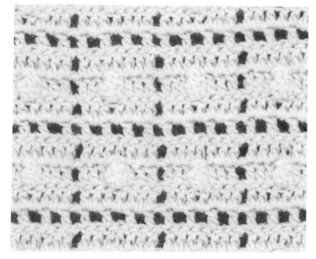

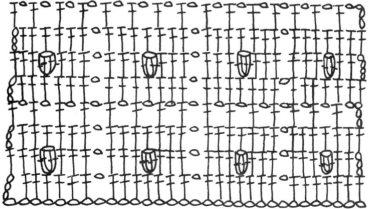

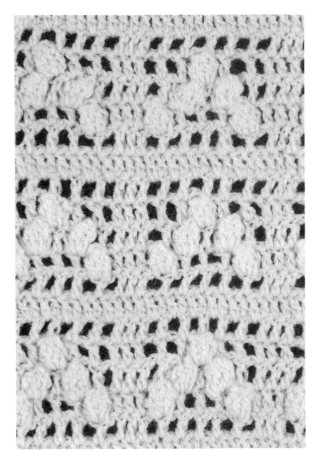

405. Chain multiples of 24 plus 4.

Row 1: 1 dc in the 5th ch and each ch all across the row.
Row 2: 1 dc in the 2nd dc and the dc after that, *ch 1 and dc in the 2nd dc, 6 times, 1 dc in each of the next 2 dc, rep from *, ending row with 2 dc in the dc and 1 in the turning ch, ch 3 and turn.
Row 3: 1 dc in the 2nd dc and the dc after that, *ch 1, work a 5-looped popcorn stitch in the next dc, ch 1, dc in the next dc and ch 1, 3 times, work a 5-looped popcorn stitch in the next dc, ch 1, dc in the next dc and the 2 dc after that, rep from *, ending row with 2 dc and 1 in the turning ch, ch 3 and turn.
Row 4: 1 dc in the 2nd dc and the dc after that, *ch 1, dc in the top of the 5-looped popcorn stitch, ch 1, 5-looped popcorn stitch in the next dc, ch 1, dc in the dc, ch 1, 5-looped popcorn stitch in the next dc, ch 1, dc in the top of the popcorn stitch, ch 1 and 1 dc in each of the next 3 dc, rep from *, ending row with 1 dc in each of the last 2 dc and 1 in the turning ch, ch 3 and turn.
Row 5: 1 dc in the 2nd dc and the 1 after that, *ch 1, dc in the next dc, ch 1, dc in the popcorn stitch, ch 1, 5-looped popcorn stitch in the next dc, ch 1, dc in the dc, ch 1, dc in the dc, ch 1, 1 dc in each of the next 3 dc, rep from *, ending row with 2 dc and 1 in the turning ch, ch 3 and turn.
Row 6: 1 dc in the 2nd and the next dc, *ch 1, dc in the dc, ch 1, dc in the dc, ch 1, dc in the popcorn stitch, ch 1, dc in the dc, ch 1, dc in the dc, ch 1, dc in the dc and in the next 2 dc, rep from *, ending row with 2 dc in the dc and 1 in the turning ch, ch 3 and turn.
Row 7: Same as row 1, except that 1 dc is formed in each ch and in each dc.
Pattern formed by rep rows 1–6.

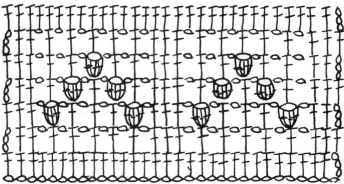

406. Chain multiples of 6 plus 4.

Row 1: 1 dc in the 5th ch and all the way across the row, ch 1 and turn.
Row 2: 1 sc in the 1st 3 dc, *ch 4, 1 sc in the 2nd dc, 1 sc in each of the next 4 dc, rep from *, ending row with 3 sc, ch 3 and turn.
Row 3: 1 dc in the 1st sc, *ch 2, 1 sc in the 4-ch, ch 2, 1 dc in the 4th sc, ch 1, 1 dc backwards in the 2nd sc, rep from *, ending row with 2 dc in the sc, ch 3 and turn.
Row 4: 2 dc in the 1st dc, *work a 5-looped popcorn stitch in the sc, 2 dc in the 1-ch, ch 1, 2 dc in the same 1-ch, rep from *, ending row with 3 dc in the turning ch, ch 3 and turn.
Pattern formed by rep rows 1–4.

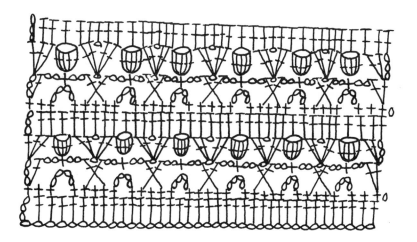

407. Chain multiples of 16 plus 4.

Row 1: 1 dc in the 5th ch and in the 3 chs following, *ch 5, 1 sc in the 5th ch, ch 3, 1 sc in the 2nd ch, ch 5, 1 dc in the 5th ch and in the 4 chs following, rep from *, ending row with 5 dc, ch 3 and turn.

Row 2: Work 1 relief dc from the front around the base of the next 4 dc, *ch 5, 1 dc in the middle of the 5-ch, ch 1, work a 5-looped popcorn stitch in the 3-ch, ch 1, work 1 dc in the middle of the next 5-ch, ch 5, work 1 relief dc from the front around the next 5 dc, rep from *, ending row with 1 extra dc in the turning ch, ch 3 and turn.

Row 3: Same as row 1, except that the relief dc are formed from the back and the sc are formed in the 1-ch.

Pattern formed by rep rows 1–2.

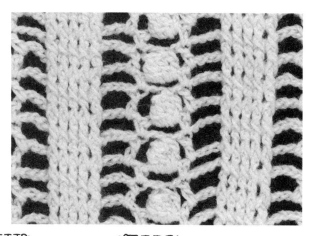

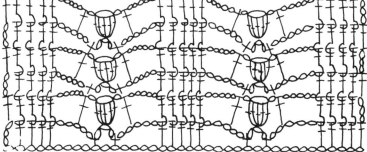

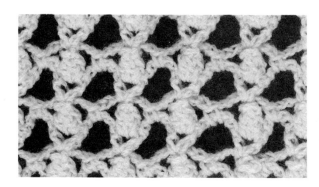

408. Chain multiples of 6 plus 7.

Row 1: 1 sc in the 10th ch, *ch 3, 4-looped popcorn stitch in the 3rd ch, ch 3, 1 sc in the 3rd ch, rep from *, ending row after last set and sc with 3 chs and 1 dc in the turning ch, ch 3 and turn.

Row 2: 1 dc in the 1st dc, *ch 5, 1 dc in the top of the popcorn stitch, ch 1, 1 dc in the same stitch, rep from *, ending row with 2 dc in the turning ch, ch 6.

Row 3: Same as row 1, except that sc are worked in the middle of the 5-ch, popcorn stitch made in the middle of the V-stitch.

Pattern formed by rep rows 1–2.

Popcorn Stitch 293

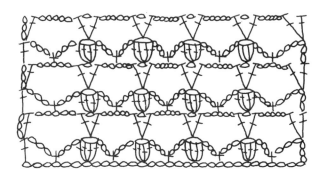

409. Chain multiples of 6 plus 1.

Row 1: 1 sc in the 2nd ch, *ch 3, work a 4-looped popcorn stitch in the 3rd ch, ch 3, sc in the 3rd ch, rep from *, ending row with last sc, ch 1 and turn.

Row 2: 1 sc in the 1st sc, *work 1 sc around each of the 3-chs, work 1 sc around each of the next 3-chs, rep from *, ending row with 1 extra sc in the last sc, ch 2 and turn.

Row 3: Work 1 dc in the 1st sc, *ch 3, 1 sc over the popcorn stitch, ch 3, work a 4-looped popcorn stitch between the 2 sc over the sc of the row below, rep from *, ending row with a 2-looped popcorn stitch in the last sc, ch 1 and turn.

Row 4: 1 sc in the popcorn stitch, *work 1 sc in each of the 3-chs, rep from *, ending row with 1 extra sc in the last dc, ch 1 and turn.
Pattern formed by rep rows 1–4.

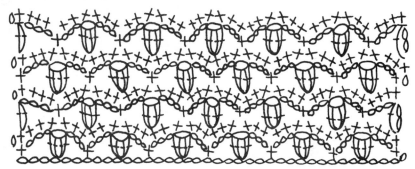

410. Chain multiples of 14 plus 4.

Row 1: 1 dc in the 7th ch, *ch 1, 1 dc in the same ch, ch 1, 1 dc in the same ch, work 5-looped popcorn stitch in the 3rd ch, work another 5-looped popcorn stitch in the 2nd ch, 1 dc in the 3rd ch, ch 1, 1 dc in the same ch, ch 1, 1 dc in the same ch, 1 dc in the 3rd ch, 1 dc in the 3rd ch, rep from *, ending row with 1 dc, ch 4 and turn.

Row 2: 1 dc in the 1st dc, *1 dc in the middle of the 3 dc, ch 1, 1 dc in the top of the popcorn stitch, ch 1, 1 dc in the top of the popcorn stitch, ch 1, 1 dc in the 2nd dc (the middle of the 3 dc), 1 dc in the 2nd dc, ch 1, 1 dc in the same dc, ch 1, 1 dc in the same dc, rep from *, ending row with 1 dc, 1 ch and 1 dc in the turning ch, ch 3 and turn.
Pattern formed by rep rows 1–2.

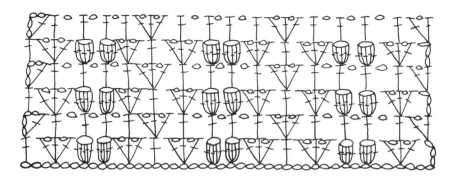

411. Chain multiples of 16 plus 5.

Row 1: 1 dc in the 5th ch, *ch 3, work a 4-looped popcorn stitch in the 4th ch, ch 1, 4-looped popcorn in the 2nd ch, ch 1, 4-looped popcorn in the 2nd ch, ch 1, 4-looped popcorn in the 2nd ch, ch 1, 4-looped popcorn in the 2nd ch, ch 3, 1 dc in the 4th ch, rep from *, ending row with 1 dc in each of the last 2 chs, ch 3 and turn.

Row 2: 1 dc in the 2nd dc and 1 in the 1st ch, *ch 3, work 4-looped popcorn in the 1-ch, ch 1, 4-looped popcorn in the next 1-ch, ch 1, 4-looped popcorn in the next 1-ch, ch 1, work 4-looped popcorn in the next 1-ch, ch 3, 1 dc in the last of the 3-ch, dc in the dc, dc in the 1st of the next 3-ch, rep from *, ending row with 1 dc in the last ch, 1 in the dc and 1 in the turning ch, ch 3 and turn.

Row 3: 1 dc in the 2nd dc and the dc after that, 1 dc in the 1st ch of the 3-ch, *ch 3, work 4-looped popcorn stitch in the 1-ch, ch 1, 4-looped popcorn in the next 1-ch, ch 1, work 4-looped popcorn stitch in the next 1-ch, ch 3, 1 dc in the last of the 3-ch, 1 dc in each of the 3 dc, 1 dc in the 1st of the 3-ch, rep from *, ending row with 1 extra dc in the turning ch, ch 1 and turn.

Row 4: 1 dc in the 2nd dc and the 2 dc after that, 1 in the 1st of the 3-ch, *ch 3, work 4-looped popcorn in the 1-ch, ch 1, work 4-looped popcorn in the next 1-ch, ch 3, 1 dc in the last of the 3-ch, 1 dc in each of the 5 dc and 1 dc in the 1st of the 3-ch, rep from *, ending row with 1 dc in the turning ch, ch 3 and turn.

Row 5: 1 dc in the 2nd dc and 1 in each of the 3 dc following, 1 dc in the 1st of the 3-ch, *ch 3, work a 4-looped popcorn in the 1-ch, ch 3, 1 dc in the last of the 3-ch, 1 dc in each of the 7 dc, 1 dc in the 1st of the 3-ch, rep from *, ending row with 1 extra dc in the turning ch, ch 3 and turn.

Row 6: Work 4-looped popcorn in the 2nd dc, ch 1, work 4-looped popcorn in the 2nd dc, ch 1, work 4-looped popcorn in the 2nd dc, *ch 3, 1 dc in the top of the popcorn stitch, ch 3, work 4-looped popcorn stitch in the next dc, ch 1, work 4-looped popcorn in the 2nd dc, ch 1, 4-looped popcorn in the 2nd dc, ch 1, 4-looped popcorn in the 2nd dc, ch 1, work 4-looped popcorn stitch in the 2nd dc, rep from *, ending row with 1 dc in the turning ch, ch 3 and turn.

Row 7: Work 4-looped popcorn stitch in the 1-ch, ch 1, work 4-looped popcorn stitch in the next 1-ch, *ch 3, 1 dc in the last of the 3-ch, dc in the dc, dc in the 1st of the 3-ch, ch 3, work 4-looped popcorn stitch in the 1-ch, ch 1, work a 4-looped popcorn stitch in the next 1-ch, ch 1, work 4-looped popcorn stitch in the

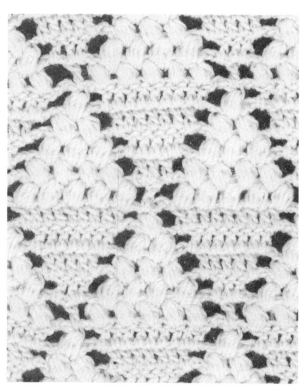

next 1-ch, ch 1, work 4-looped popcorn in the next 1-ch, rep from *, ending row with 1 dc in the turning ch, ch 3 and turn.

Row 8: 4-looped popcorn in the 1-ch, ch 1, 4-looped popcorn in the next 1-ch, *ch 3, 1 dc in the last of the 3-ch, 1 dc in each of the 3 dc, 1 dc in the 1st of the 3-ch, ch 3, work 4-looped popcorn in the 1-ch, ch 1, 4-looped popcorn in the 1-ch, ch 1, work 4-looped popcorn in the next 1-ch, rep from *, ending row with 1 dc in the turning ch, ch 3 and turn.

Row 9: 4-looped popcorn in the 1-ch, *ch 3, 1 dc in the last of the 3-ch, 1 dc in each of the next 5 dc, 1 dc in the 1st of the 3-ch, ch 3, 4-looped popcorn in the 1-ch, ch 1, 4-looped popcorn in the next 1-ch, rep from *, ending row with 1 dc in the turning ch, ch 3 and turn.

Row 10: 4-looped popcorn in the 1-ch, *ch 3, 1 dc in the last of the 3-ch, 1 dc in each of the 7 dc and 1 in the 1st of the next 3-ch, ch 3, work 4-looped popcorn in the 1-ch, rep from *, ending row with 1 dc in the turning ch.

Pattern formed by rep rows 1–10.

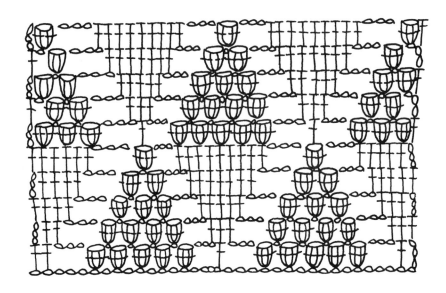

412. Chain multiples of 12 plus 1.

Row 1: 1 sc in the 2nd ch, ch 5, 1 sc in the same ch, *ch 5, work a 5-looped popcorn in the 6th ch, ch 5, 1 sc in the 6th ch, ch 5, 1 sc in the same ch, ch 5, 1 sc in the same ch, rep from *, ending row with 1 sc in the last ch, ch 5 and 1 sc in the last ch, ch 8 and turn.
Row 2: *1 sc in the top of the popcorn, ch 5, 1 sc in the same ch, ch 5, 1 sc in the same stitch, ch 5, work a 5-looped popcorn in the 3 sc, ch 5, rep from *, ending row with 5 chs and 1 dc in the last sc, ch 1 and turn.
Pattern formed by rep rows 1–2.

· *28* ·
Dropped Stitch

413. Chain multiples of 14 plus 1.

Row 1: 1 sc in the 2nd ch and in the 3 chs following, *ch 8, 1 sc in the 8th ch and in the 6 chs following, rep from *, ending row with 4 sc, ch 1 and turn.
Rows 2–3: Same as row 1, ch 1 and turn.
Row 4: 1 sc in each of the 1st 4 sc, *ch 3, work 1 sl st around the 3 chs below, gathering all 3 together, ch 3, 1 sc in each of the next 7 sc, rep from *, ending row with 4 sc, ch 1 and turn.
Pattern formed by rep rows 1–4.

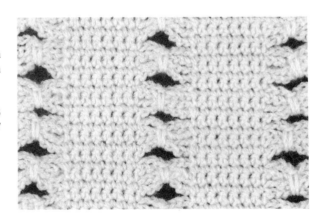

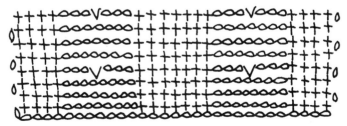

414. Chain multiples of 14 plus 1.

Row 1: 1 sc in the 2nd ch, ch 2, 1 sc in the 3rd ch, *sc in each of the next 4 chs, ch 5, 1 sc in the 6th ch, rep from *, ending row with 2 chs and 1 sc in the 3rd ch, ch 1 and turn.
Row 2: Same as row 1, ch 1 and turn.
Row 3: 1 sc in the 1st sc, 1 sc in each of the next 2 chs, *ch 5, 1 sc in each of the next 2 chs, work 1 sl st around the 2 rows of chs below, 1 sc in the last 2 chs, rep from *, ending row with 2 sc in the 2 chs and 1 sc in the last sc, ch 1 and turn.
Row 4: 1 sc in each of 1st 3 sc, *ch 5, 1 sc in the next 2 sc, the sl st and the next 2 sc, rep from *, ending row with sc in the 3rd sc, ch 1 and turn.
Pattern formed by rep rows 1–4.

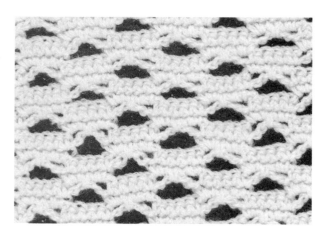

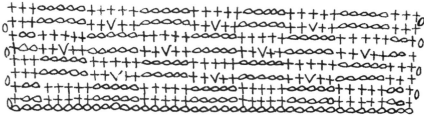

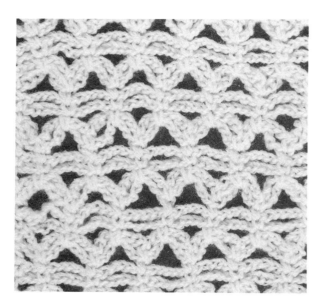

415. Chain multiples of 6 plus 1.

Row 1: 1 sc in the 2nd ch, *ch 5, 1 sc in the 6th ch, rep from *, ending row with last sc, ch 1 and turn.
Row 2: Same as row 1, ch 1 and turn.
Row 3: 1 sc in the 1st sc, *ch 7, 1 sc in the next sc, rep from *, ending row with sc after the last set, ch 1 and turn.
Row 4: Same as row 3, ch 5 and turn.
Row 5: *work 1 sc around the middle of the chs in the 2 rows below, ch 5, rep from *, ending row with last sc around the 2 rows, ch 2, 1 dc in the sc, ch 1 and turn.
Row 6: Sc in 1st dc, ch 2, * sc in sc, ch 5, rep from *, ending row with sc in turning ch.
Row 7: *1 sc in the sc, ch 7, rep from *, ending row after last set with a sc, ch 3 and 1 dc in the sc, ch 1 and turn.
Row 8: 1 sc in the dc, ch 3, *1 sc in the sc, ch 7, rep from *, ending row with 1 sc in the turning ch, ch 1 and turn.
Pattern formed by rep rows 1–8.

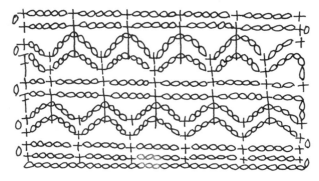

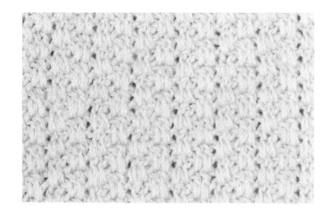

416. Chain multiples of 4 plus 4.

Row 1: 1 dc in the 5th ch, 1 dc in the next ch, *ch 2, 1 dc in the 3rd and the next dc, rep from *, ending row with 3 dc, ch 5 and turn.
Row 2: *work 2 dc around the 2-ch and down to the ch of the row below, ch 2, rep from *, ending row with last 2 chs and 1 dc in the turning ch, ch 3 and turn.
Row 3: Same as row 1, except that the dc are always worked in the row below.
Pattern formed by rep rows 1–2.

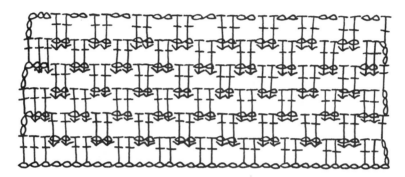

417. Chain multiples of 6 plus 4.

Row 1: 1 dc in the 5th ch, *ch 1, 1 dc in the 2nd ch and in the 4 chs following, rep from *, ending row with 2 dc, ch 3 and turn.
Row 2: 1 dc in the 2nd dc, *1 dc worked in the row underneath, 1 dc in each of the next 2 dc, ch 1, 1 dc in each of the next 2 dc, rep from *, ending row with 1 dc in the turning ch, ch 3 and turn.
Row 3: Same as row 1, except that the middle dc of the 5 is worked in the row underneath.
Pattern formed by rep rows 1–2.

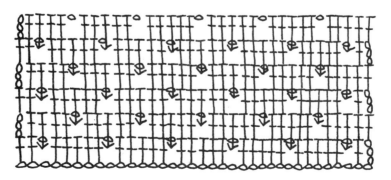

418. Chain multiples of 14 plus 4.

Row 1: 1 dc in the 5th ch and the 6 chs following, *ch 7, 1 dc in the 8th ch and the 6 chs following, rep from *, ending row after the 7 chs with 1 dc in the 8th and last ch, ch 10 and turn.
Row 2: *dc in each dc, ch 7, rep from *, ending row with 1 extra dc in the turning ch, ch 10 and turn.
Row 3: *1 dc in each of the 1st 3-chs, form 1 dc around the next ch, catching also the middle of the 2 chs below, 1 dc in each of the next 3-chs, ch 7, rep from *, ending row with 8 dc, ch 3 and turn.
Row 4: *1 dc in each dc, ch 7, rep from *, ending row with 7 chs and 1 dc in the turning ch, ch 3 and turn.
Row 5: Same as row 1, except that the middle of the 7 dc are worked as a dropped dc.
Pattern formed by rep rows 1–5.

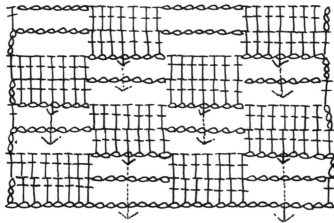

419. Chain multiples of 2 plus 1.

Row 1: 1 sc in the 2nd ch and all across the row, ch 3 and turn.
Row 2: 1 sc in the 2nd sc, *1 dc in the next sc, 1 sc in the next stitch, rep from *, ending row with 1 dc in the sc, ch 1 and turn.
Row 3: 1 sc in the 2nd stitch and in each stitch all the way across the row, ch 2 and turn.
Row 4: 1 sc in the 2nd sc, *work 1 relief dc, from the front, around the base of the dc of the row 2 rows below, 1 sc in the next sc, rep from *, ending row with 1 dc in the sc, ch 2 and turn.
Pattern formed by rep rows 3–4.

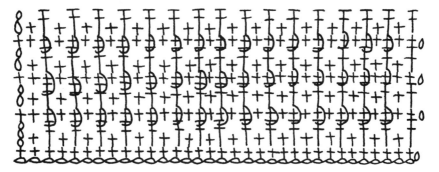

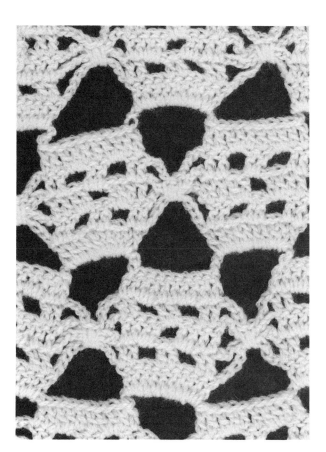

420. Chain multiples of 30 plus 6.

Row 1: 1 dc in the 5th ch and all across the row, ch 3 and turn.
Row 2: 1 dc in the 2nd dc, *ch 10, 1 dc in the 11th dc and 9 dc following that, rep from *, ending row with 1 dc in the last dc and 1 in the turning ch, ch 3 and turn.
Row 3: 1 dc in the 2nd dc, *ch 10, 1 dc in the 1st and the next dc, ch 2, 1 dc in the 3rd dc and the dc after that, ch 2, 1 dc in the 3rd dc and the dc after that, rep from *, ending row with 1 dc in the last dc and in the turning ch, ch 3 and turn.
Row 4: 1 dc in the 2nd dc, *ch 10, 1 dc in the next dc and the dc after that, 1 dc in each of the 2-chs, ch 2, 1 dc in each of the 2-chs, 1 dc in each of the 2 dc, rep from *, ending row with 1 dc in the dc and 1 in the turning ch, ch 3 and turn.
Row 5: 1 dc in the 2nd dc, *ch 4, work 1 sc around the 3 chs below, work another sc around the 3-chs below, ch 4, 1 dc in the next dc and the dc after that, ch 2, 1 dc in each of the 2-chs, ch 2, 1 dc in the 3rd dc and the dc after that, rep from *, ending row with 1 dc in the last dc and 1 in the turning ch, ch 3 and turn.
Row 6: 1 dc in the 2nd dc, *ch 10, 1 dc in each of the 2 dc, the 2-chs, the 2 dc, the 2-chs and the 2 dc, rep from *, ending row with 1 dc in the last dc and 1 in the turning ch, ch 3 and turn.
Row 7: 1 dc in the 2nd dc, *10 dc around the 10-ch, ch 10, rep from *, ending row with 1 dc in the last dc and 1 in the turning ch, ch 3 and turn.
Rows 7–10: Alternate the pattern, but blocks are formed the same as rows 1-6.
Pattern formed by rep rows 1–10.

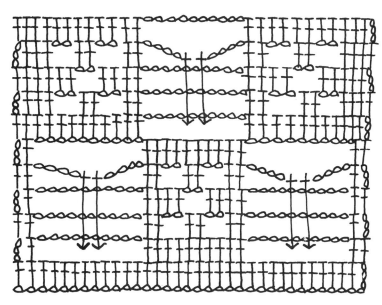

421. Chain multiples of 2 plus 4.

Row 1: 1 dc in the 5th ch and in each ch all across the row, ch 1 and turn.
Row 2: 1 sc in the 1st dc and in each dc all across the row, ch 3 and turn.
Row 3: *work 1 relief dc, from the front, around the base of the dc in the 1st row, 1 dc in the next sc, rep from *, ending row with 1 dc in the sc, ch 3 and turn.
Row 4: 1 sc in the top of each stitch all across the row, ch 3 and turn.
Pattern formed by rep rows 3–4.

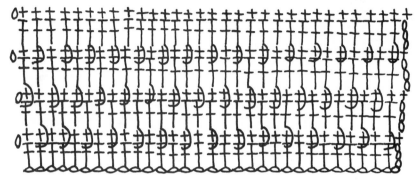

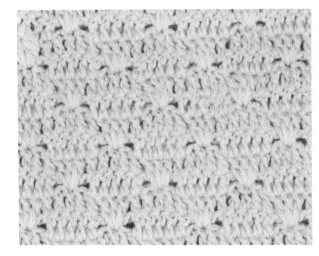

422. Chain multiples of 8 plus 4.

Row 1: 1 dc in the 5th ch and the ch after that, *ch 3, work 1 dc in the 4th ch and in the 4 chs following, rep from *, ending row with 3 dc, ch 3 and turn.
Row 2: 1 dc in the 2nd dc and the dc after that, *work 3 dc through the next 3-ch and around the chs in the row below, 1 dc in each of the next 5 dc, rep from *, ending row with 3 dc, ch 3 and turn.
Row 3: 1 dc in the 2nd dc and in each of the next 5 dc, *ch 3, 1 dc in the 4th dc and the 4 dc after that, rep from *, ending row with 1 dc in each dc and 1 in the turning ch, ch 3 and turn.
Row 4: 1 dc in the 2nd dc and in the next 5 dc, *work 3 dc through 2 rows below, work 1 dc in each of the next 5 dc, rep from *, ending row with 7 dc, ch 3 and turn.
Pattern formed by rep rows 1–4.

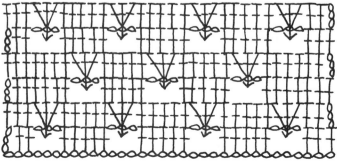

423. Chain multiples of 7 plus 4.

Row 1: 3 dc in the 5th ch, ch 2, *3 dc in the 7th ch, ch 1, 3 dc in the ch just used, ch 2, rep from *, ending row with 2 chs, 3 dc in the 7th ch and 1 dc in the next ch, ch 3 and turn.
Row 2: Same as row 1.
Row 3: 3 dc in the 2nd dc, *ch 1, sl st around the 2 rows below, ch 1, 3 dc in the next 1-ch, ch 1, 3 dc in the same 1-ch, rep from *, ending row with 1 dc in the turning ch, ch 3 and turn.
Pattern formed by rep rows 1–3.

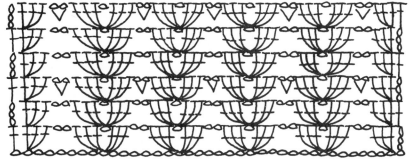

424. Chain multiples of 5 plus 4.

Row 1; Work 2 dc in the 7th ch, *ch 1, 2 dc in the ch just used, 2 dc in the 5th ch, rep from *, ending row with last set and 1 dc in the 3rd ch, ch 3 and turn.
Row 2: Same as row 1, ch 1 and turn.
Row 3: 1 sc in the dc, *ch 1, 1 sc in the 1-ch, ch 1, work 1 dc in the space between the sets of dc, 2 rows below, ch 1, rep the same dropped dc just used in the same space, rep from *, ending row with last set and a sc in the turning ch, ch 3 and turn.
Row 4: 1 dc in the 1st sc, *work 2 dc in the 1-ch between the 2 sides of the dropped dc, ch 1, 2 dc in the same 1-ch, rep from *, ending row with 2 dc in the sc, ch 3 and turn.
Row 5: Same as row 4, ch 1 and turn.
Row 6: 1 sc in the 1st dc, *work 1 dc in the space between the sets of dc, 2 rows below, ch 1, rep same dropped crochet just used in the same space, ch 1, 1 sc in the 1-ch between the 2 dc, ch 1 and rep from *, ending row with 1 sc in the turning ch, ch 3 and turn.
Pattern formed by rep rows 1–6.

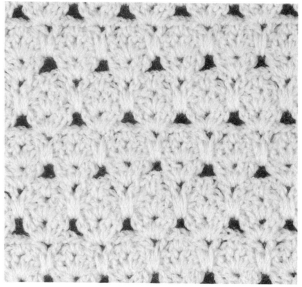

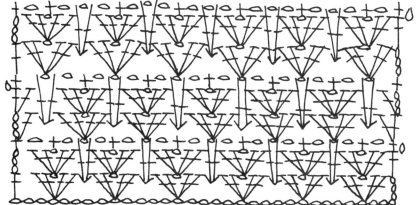

425. Chain multiples of 5 plus 4.

Row 1: 1 dc in the 7th ch, *ch 2, 1 dc in the ch just used, ch 1, 1 dc in the 5th ch, rep from *, ending row with last set and 1 extra dc in the 3rd ch, ch 1 and turn.
Row 2: 1 sc in the 1st dc, *ch 5, 1 sc in the 1-ch, rep from *, ending row with last sc of the set in the turning ch, ch 1 and turn.
Row 3: Work 1 relief sc around the base of the turning ch, 2 rows below, *work 6 sc around the 5-ch, 1 sc around both the sc from the row below and the 1-ch from the row below that, rep from *, ending row with 1 sc around the sc of the row below and the dc from the row below that, ch 7 and turn.
Row 4: *work 1 dc in the 1st relief sc (the one worked in the rows below), ch 4, rep from *, ending row with regular set, ch 4 and turn.
Row 5: 1 dc in the dc, *ch 1, 1 dc in the next dc, ch 2, 1 dc in the ch just used, rep from *, ending row with 1 dc in the turning ch, 1 ch and 1 dc in the turning ch, ch 4 and turn.
Row 6: *1 sc in the 1-ch, ch 5, rep from *, ending row with 2 chs and 1 hdc in the turning ch, ch 1 and turn.
Row 7: 1 sc in the hdc, 3 sc in 2-ch, *work 1 relief sc around the sc of the row below and the 1-ch of the row below that, work 6 sc around the 5-ch, rep from *, ending row with 4 sc around the turning ch, ch 4 and turn.
Row 8: *1 dc in the extended sc, ch 4, rep from *, ending row with 2 chs and 1 hdc in the last sc.
Pattern formed by rep rows 1–8.

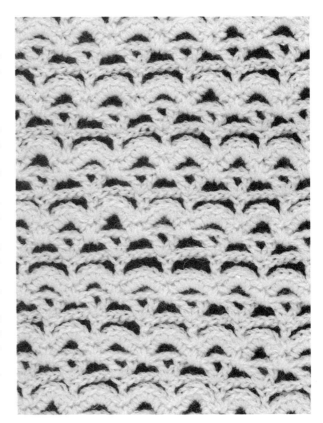

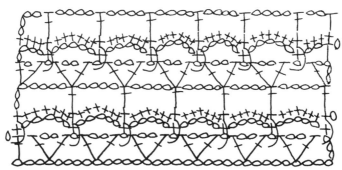

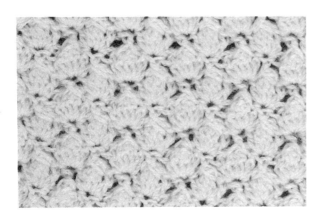

426. Chain multiples of 6 plus 4.

Row 1: 5 dc in the 7th ch, *1 dc in the 3rd ch, 5 dc in the 3rd ch, rep from *, ending row after last set with 1 dc, ch 3 and turn.
Row 2: 2 dc in the 1st dc, *work 1 relief dc around the base of the middle 3 dc from the back, 5 dc in the next dc, rep from *, ending row with 3 dc in the turning ch, ch 3 and turn.
Row 3: *5 dc in the relief dc, work 1 relief dc around the middle 3 dc from the front, rep from *, ending row with 1 dc after the last set in the turning ch, ch 3 and turn.
Pattern formed by rep rows 2–3.

427. Chain multiples of 4 plus 4.

Row 1: 1 dc in the 5th ch and in each ch all across the row, ch 1 and turn.

Row 2: 1 sc in the 1st dc and all across the row, ch 4 and turn.

Row 3: Work 2 relief dc around the base of the 2nd dc and the 2nd dc, from the front with the 2 stitches finished up together, * ch 1, 1 dc in the 2nd sc, ch 1, work 2 relief dc around the base of the 2nd and 4th dc from the front with the 2 dc finished up together, rep from *, ending row with 1 dc in the last sc, ch 1 and turn.

Row 4: 1 sc in each crochet and each ch all across the row, ch 3 and turn.

Pattern formed by rep rows 1–4.

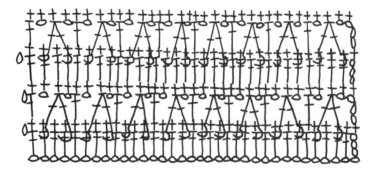

· 29 ·
Relief Stitch

428. Chain multiples of 4 plus 3.

Row 1: 1 dc in the 5th ch and in each ch all across the row, ch 3 and turn.
Row 2: 1 dc in the 2nd and next dc, * from the front, work 1 relief dc around the base of the next dc, 1 dc in each of the next 3 dc, rep from *, ending row with 1 extra dc in the turning ch, ch 3 and turn.
Row 3: 1 dc in the 2nd dc and in each dc all across the row, ch 3 and turn.
Row 4: From the front, work 1 relief dc around the base of the 2nd dc, * dc in each of the next 3 dc, work, from the front, 1 relief dc around the base of the next dc, rep from *, ending row with a dc in the turning ch, ch 3 and turn. (Make sure that the relief dc are staggered so that every 4th row is above each relief stitch and the other is in the middle.)
Pattern formed by rep rows 1–4.

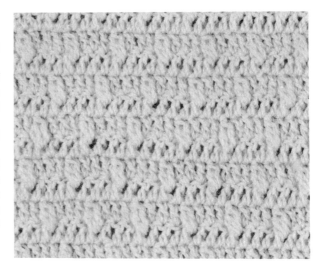

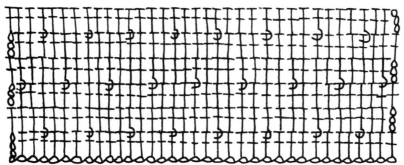

429. Chain multiples of 8 plus 3.

Row 1: 1 dc in 5th dc and in each dc all across the row, ch 3 and turn.
Row 2: 1 dc in the 2nd and the next dc, * ch 1, 1 dc in each of the next 3 dc, work, from the front, 1 relief dc around the base of the next dc, work 1 dc in each of the next 3 dc, rep from *, ending row with dc, ch 3 and turn.
Row 3: Same as row 2, except the relief dc are worked from the back.
Pattern formed by rep rows 2–3.

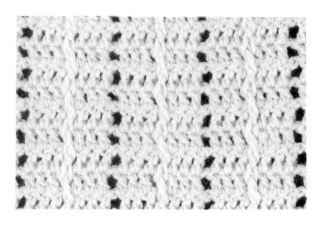

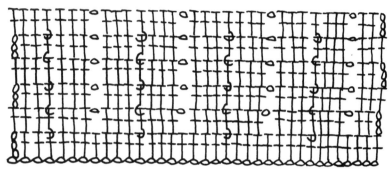

430. Chain multiples of 4 plus 2.

Row 1: 1 sc in the 2nd ch and all across the row, ch 3 and turn.
Row 2: 1 dc in the 2nd sc, * ch 1, 1 dc in the same sc, 1 dc in the 2nd sc, 1 dc in the 2nd sc, rep from *, ending row with 1 dc in the last sc, ch 3 and turn.
Row 3: * 1 dc in the 1-ch, ch 1, 1 dc in the same 1-ch, work, from the front, 1 relief dc around the base of the single standing dc, rep from *, ending row with 1 dc in the turning ch, ch 3 and turn.
Row 4: Same as row 3, except that the relief dc is worked from the back.
Pattern formed by rep rows 3–4.

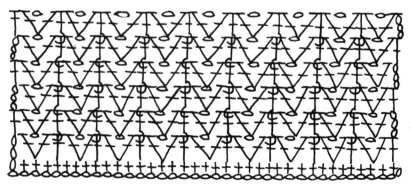

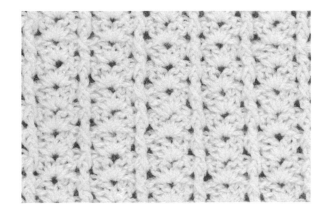

431. Chain multiples of 6 plus 4.

Row 1: 2 dc in the 7th ch, ch 1, 2 dc in the same ch, * 1 dc in the 3rd ch, 2 dc in the 3rd ch, ch 1, 2 dc in the same ch, rep from *, ending row with last set and the last dc, ch 3 and turn.
Row 2: * 2 dc in the 1-ch, ch 1, 2 dc in the same 1-ch, work, from the back, 1 relief dc around the base of the 3rd dc, rep from *, ending row with 1 dc in the turning ch, ch 3 and turn.
Row 3: Same as row 2, except that the relief dc are worked from the front.
Pattern formed by rep rows 2–3.

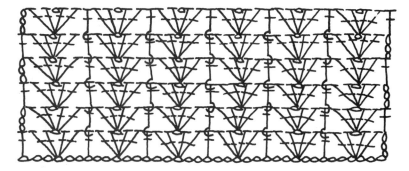

432. Chain multiples of 11 plus 4.

Row 1: 1 dc in the 5th ch, * 3 dc in the 3rd ch, 1 dc in the next ch and 3 dc in the next ch, 1 dc in the 3rd ch and in the next 3 chs, rep from *, ending row with 2 dc, 1 each in the last 2 chs, ch 3 and turn.
Row 2: 1 dc in the 2nd dc, * ch 2, 1 relief dc worked, from the back, around the base of the 3rd dc, 1 dc in the next dc, 1 relief dc worked, from the back, around the base of the next dc, ch 2, 1 dc in each of the next 4 dc, rep from *, ending row with 2 dc, 1 in the last dc and 1 in the turning ch, ch 3 and turn.
Pattern formed by rep rows 1–2.

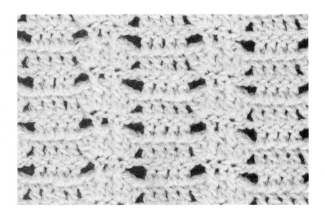

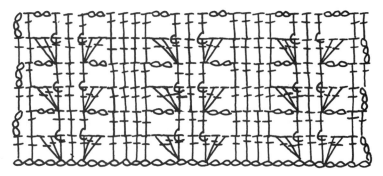

433. Chain multiples of 11 plus 5.

Row 1: 1 dc in the 7th ch, * 3 dc in the 3rd ch, 3 dc in the next ch, 1 dc in the 3rd ch, ch 1, 1 dc in the 2nd ch, ch 1, 1 dc in the 2nd ch, rep from *, ending row with 3 dc in the 2nd to the last ch and 1 in the last ch, ch 3 and turn.
Row 2: 3 dc in the 2nd dc, 1 relief dc worked, from the front, around the base of the 2nd dc, ch 1, * 1 dc in the 2nd dc, ch 1, 1 relief dc worked, from the front, around the base of the 2nd dc, 3 dc in the 2nd dc, 3 dc in the next dc, 1 relief dc worked, from the front, around the base of the 2nd dc, ch 1, rep from *, ending row with 1 ch and 1 dc in the turning ch, ch 4 and turn.
Row 3: Same as row 2, except that the relief dc are worked from the back and not the front. Pattern formed by rep rows 2–3.

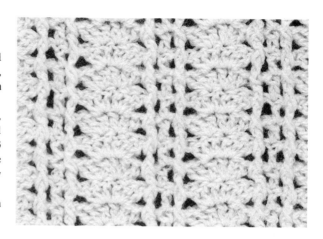

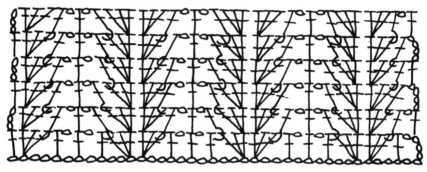

434. Chain multiples of 2 plus 3.

Row 1: 1 dc in 4th ch, * ch 1, begin 1 dc in the same ch, begin 2nd part of the dc in the 2nd ch, finish off the 2 dc together, rep from *, ending row after last set with 1 dc in the next ch, finished together with the stitch before, ch 4 and turn.
Row 2: Sk 1st 2 dc finished together, * from the front, work relief dc around the base of the 2 dc finished together, ch 1, rep from *, ending row with 1 ch and 1 dc in the turning ch, ch 2 and turn. Pattern formed by rep rows 1–2.

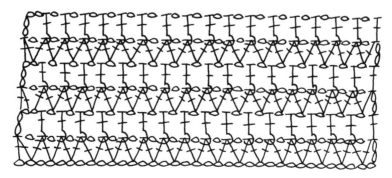

435. Chain multiples of 3 plus 4.

Row 1: 1 dc in the 5th ch and in each ch all across the row, ch 3 and turn.
Row 2: * 1 dc in the 3rd dc, ch 1, 1 dc in the same dc, rep from *, ending row with 1 dc in the turning ch after the last set, ch 3 and turn.
Row 3: * from the back, work 1 relief dc around the base of the 1st part of the V-stitch, 1 dc in the 1-ch, work, from the back, 1 relief dc around the base of the 2nd part of the V-stitch, rep from *, ending row with 1 dc in the turning ch, after the last set, ch 4 and turn.
Row 4: From the front, work 1 relief dc around the base of the 3rd dc, * ch 2, from the front, work 1 relief dc around the base of the 3rd dc, rep from *, ending row with 1 ch and 1 dc in the turning ch, ch 3 and turn.
Row 5: Same as row 1, except that 2 dc are worked in the 2-ch and 1 dc in each dc, ch 3 and turn.
Pattern formed by rep rows 1–4.

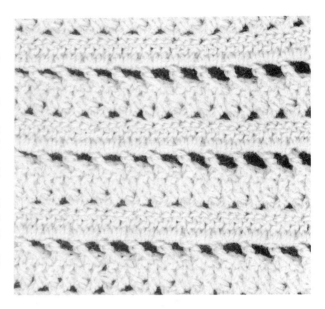

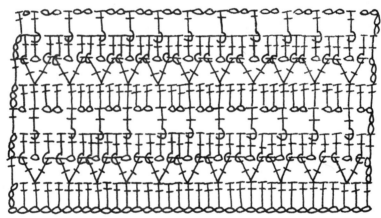

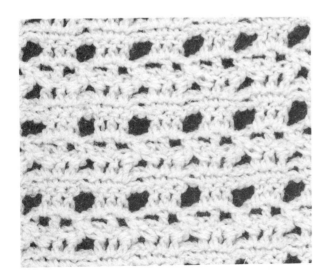

436. Chain multiples of 6 plus 4.

Row 1: 1 dc in the 5th ch, * ch 3, 1 dc in the 4th ch, 1 dc in next ch and 1 dc in following ch, rep from *, ending row with 2 dc in the last 2 chs, ch 5 and turn.
Row 2: * From the front, begin 1 relief dc around the base of the 2nd dc, begin 2nd relief dc, from the front, around the base of the next dc, finish the 2 stitches together, ch 2, 1 dc in next dc, ch 2, rep from *, ending row with 2 chs and 1 dc, ch 3 and turn.
Row 3: 1 dc in the 1st ch, * ch 3, 1 dc in the last ch of the next 2-ch, 1 dc in dc, 1 dc in the 1st ch, rep from *, ending row with 2 dc in the turning ch, ch 1 and turn.
Row 4: * 1 sc in 1st dc and in next dc, ch 3, 1 sc in each of the next 3 dc, ch 3, rep from *, ending row with 1 sc in last dc and 1 in the turning ch, ch 3 and turn.
Pattern formed by rep rows 1–4.

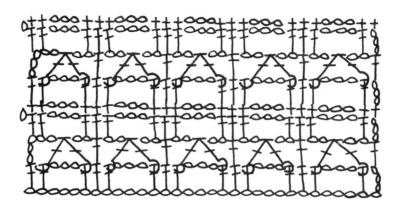

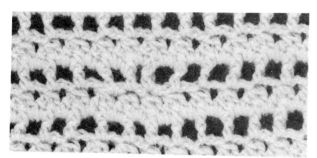

437. Chain multiples of 3 plus 6.

Row 1: 1 dc in the 9th ch, * ch 2, 1 dc in the 3rd ch, rep from *, ending row with last dc, ch 3 and turn.

Row 2: 1 dc around the 1st 2-ch, * ch 2, begin 1 dc around the same 2-ch, begin, from the front, 1 relief dc around the base of the dc, begin 3rd dc in the ch following and finish up the 3 dc together, rep from *, ending row with 2 dc in the turning ch, ch 5 and turn.

Pattern formed by rep rows 1–2.

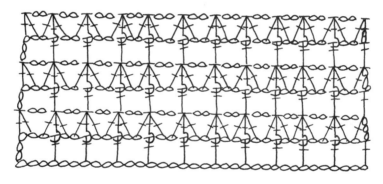

438. Chain multiples of 6 plus 3.

Row 1: 1 dc in 4th ch, * ch 2, 1 dc in the 2nd ch, ch 2, work 3 dc together in the 2nd ch and the 2 after that, rep from *, ending row with 2 chs and 2 dc finished together in the last 2 chs, ch 1 and turn.

Row 2: 1 sc in the top of the 2 dc finished together, * ch 2, 1 sc in the next dc, ch 2, 1 sc in the top of the 3 dc finished together, rep from *, ending row with 1 sc in the turning ch, ch 2 and turn.

Row 3: 1 dc in the 2-ch, * ch 2, from the front, work 1 relief dc around the base of the sc, ch 2, work together 1 dc in the last of the next 2-ch, from the front, work 1 relief dc around the base of the sc, 1 dc in the 1st of the next 2-ch, rep from *, ending row with 2 dc finished together in the last 2-ch and sc, ch 1 and turn.

Row 4: 1 sc in the top of the 2 dc finished together, * ch 2, 1 sc in the relief dc, ch 2, 1 sc in the top of the 3 dc finished together, rep from *, ending row with 1 sc in the turning ch, ch 2 and turn.

Pattern formed by rep rows 1–4.

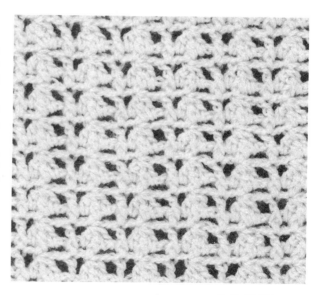

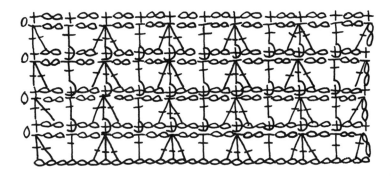

439. Chain multiples of 12 plus 4.

Row 1: 1 dc in the 5th ch and all the way across the row, ch 3 and turn.

Row 2: 1 dc in the 2nd dc, 1 dc in the 2nd dc, ch 1, 1 dc in the dc just used, * worked, from the front, 1 relief dc around the base of the 2nd dc, work relief dc around the base of the next dc and the 1 after that, 1 dc in the 2nd dc, ch 1, 1 dc in the same dc, dc in the 3rd dc, ch 1, 1 dc in the same dc, dc in the 3rd dc, ch 1, dc in the same dc, rep from *, ending row with 1 dc in the turning ch, ch 3 and turn.

Row 3: Same as row 2, except that the relief dc are worked from the back.

Row 4: Same as row 2 (worked from the front).

Row 5: Same as row 2 (worked from the back).

Row 6: Same as row 2 (worked from the front).

Row 7: Continue pattern of relief dc over the columns of relief dc (from the back), work dc above all the other stitches.

Pattern formed by rep rows 2–7.

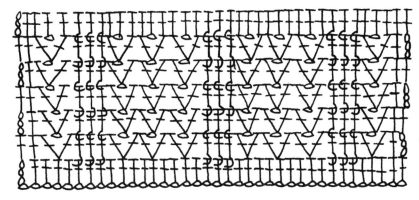

440. Chain multiples of 8 plus 4.

Row 1: 2 dc in the 4th ch, * 1 dc in the 4th ch, ch 1, 1 dc in the same ch, 2 dc in the 4th ch, ch 1, 2 dc in the same ch, rep from *, ending row with 3 dc in the last ch, ch 3 and turn.

Row 2: 2 dc in the 1st dc, * work, from the front, 1 relief dc around the base of the 3rd dc, ch 1, work, from the front, 1 relief dc around the base of the next dc, 2 dc in the 1-ch, ch 1, 2 dc in the same 1-ch, rep from *, ending row with 3 dc in the turning ch, ch 3 and turn.

Row 3: Same as row 2, except that the relief stitch is worked from the back instead of the front, ch 3 and turn.

Row 4: 1 dc in the 1st dc, *2 dc in the 1-ch, ch 1, 2 dc in the same 1-ch, 1 dc in the next 1-ch, ch 1, 1 dc in the same 1-ch, rep from *, ending row with 2 dc in the turning ch, ch 3 and turn.

Row 5: Work from the front, 1 relief dc around the base of the 2nd dc, * 2 dc in the 1-ch, ch 1, 2 dc in the same 1-ch, work, from the front, 1 relief dc around the base of the 3rd dc, ch 1, work from the front, 1 relief dc around the base of the next dc, rep from *, ending row with 1 relief dc in the last dc and 1 dc in the turning ch, ch 3 and turn.

Row 6: Same as row 5, except that the relief dc are worked from the back, ch 3 and turn.

Pattern formed by rep rows 1–6.

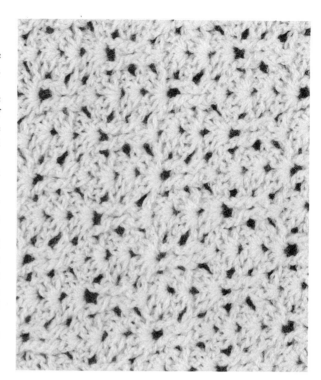

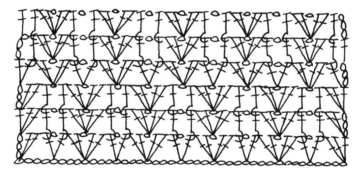

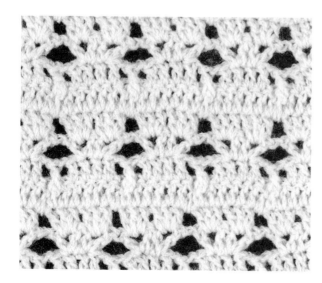

441. Chain multiples of 7 plus 4.

Row 1: 1 dc in the 5th ch and in each ch all across the row, ch 3 and turn.

Row 2: 1 dc in the 2nd dc, * ch 1, 1 relief dc, worked from the front, around the base of the 2nd dc, ch 1, 1 dc in the 2nd dc and in the 3 chs after, rep from *, ending row with 2 dc, ch 4 and turn.

Row 3: 1 dc in the 1st dc, * ch 1, 1 dc in the 2nd dc of the 4-group, ch 1, 1 dc in the same ch, 1 dc in the next ch, ch 1, 1 dc in the ch just used, rep from *, ending row with 1 dc, 1 ch and 1 dc in the turning ch.

Row 4: 2 dc in the 1-ch, * ch 1, 3 dc in the 2nd 1-ch, 3 dc in the next 1-ch, rep from *, ending row with 3 dc in the turning ch, ch 3 and turn.

Row 5: Same as row 1, except that a dc is worked in each dc and each ch.

Pattern formed by rep rows 1–4.

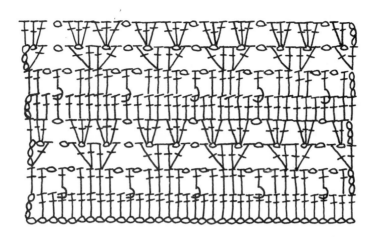

442. Chain multiples of 4 plus 4.

Row 1: 1 dc in the 6th ch, * ch 2, 1 dc in the same ch, 1 dc in 4th ch, rep from *, ending row in 3rd ch with a dc, ch 4 and turn.
Row 2: * From the front, work 1 relief dc around the base of the dc below, relief stitch worked, around the 2nd dc, ch 2, rep from *, ending row with 1 ch and 1 dc in turning ch, ch 3 and turn.
Row 3: * 1 dc between the 2 relief dc of the row below, ch 2, 1 dc in same space, rep from *, ending row with 1 dc in the turning ch, ch 4 and turn.
Pattern formed by rep rows 1–3.

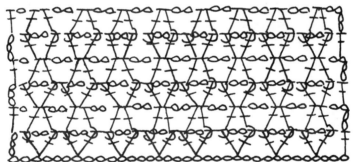

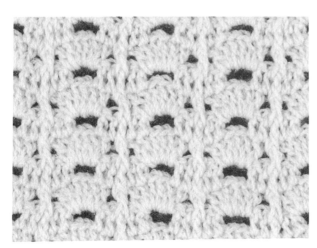

443. Chain multiples of 7 plus 5.

Row 1: 1 dc in the 5th ch and the next ch, * ch 2, 1 dc in the 3rd ch and the next 4 chs, rep from *, ending row with 2 chs and 3 dc, ch 3 and turn.
Row 2: * 6 dc around the 2-ch, work, from the front, 1 relief dc around the base of the 3rd dc, rep from *, ending row with 1 dc in the turning ch after the last set, ch 3 and turn.
Row 3: 1 dc in the 2nd dc and the dc after that, * ch 2, 1 dc in the 3rd dc and the dc after that, work, from the back, 1 relief dc around the base of the next dc, 1 dc in each of the next 2 dc, rep from *, ending row with 1 extra dc in the turning ch, ch 3 and turn.
Row 4: Same as row 2.
Pattern formed by rep rows 1–4.

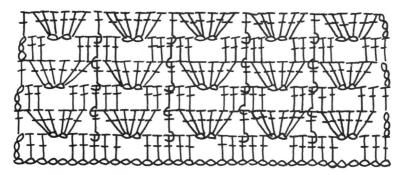

444. Chain multiples of 7 plus 6.

Row 1: 1 dc in the 9th ch and in each of the next 2 chs, * ch 4, 1 dc in the 5th ch and in each of the next 2 chs, rep from *, ending row with 2 dc, ch 1 and turn.

Row 2: From the front, work 1 relief dc around the base of the 1st dc, * work 7 dc around the 4-ch, work, from the front, 1 relief dc around the base of the 2nd dc, rep from *, ending row with 4 dc around the turning ch, ch 3 and turn.

Row 3: 1 dc in the 3rd dc, * ch 4, 1 dc in the 2nd dc, 1 dc in the 2nd dc, 1 dc in the 2nd dc, rep from *, ending row with 2 chs and 1 dc in the relief dc, ch 3 and turn.

Row 4: Work 4 dc in the 2-ch, * from the front, work 1 relief dc around the base of the 2nd dc, 7 dc around the base of the 4-ch, rep from *, ending row with 1 sc in the turning ch, ch 5 and turn.

Row 5: Same as row 1, except dc made in every 2nd dc.

Pattern formed by rep rows 1–4.

445. Chain multiples of 13 plus 1.

Row 1: 1 sc in the 2nd ch, ch 1, 1 sc in the 2nd ch, * ch 1, 1 dc in the 4th ch, ch 1, 1 dc in the same ch, ch 1, 1 dc in the same ch, ch 1, 1 sc in the 4th ch, ch 5, 1 sc in the 5th ch, rep from *, ending row with 1 dc, 1 ch and 1 dc in the last ch, ch 4 and turn.

Row 2: From the front, work 1 relief dc around the 2nd dc, * work 8 dc around the 5-ch, work, from the front, 1 relief dc around the next dc, ch 3, work, from the front, 1 relief dc around the 2nd dc, rep from *, ending row with 3 dc in the last 1-ch and 1 in the sc, ch 1 and turn.

Row 3: Same as row 1, except that the sc are worked in the 2nd and 5th dc and the 3 dc are worked in the 3-ch.

Pattern formed by rep rows 1–2.

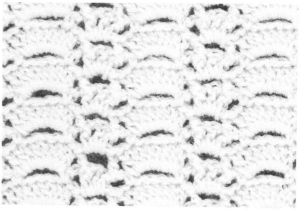

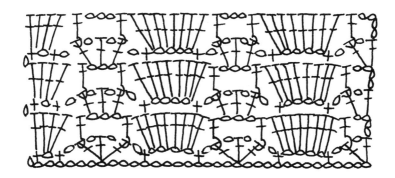

446. Chain multiples of 18 plus 4.

Row 1: 1 dc in the 5th ch and in the following 5 chs, * 1 dc in the 2nd ch, ch 1, 1 dc in the same ch, 1 dc in the 2nd ch and in the 14 chs following, rep from *, ending row with 6 dc, ch 3 and turn.

Row 2: 1 dc in the 2nd dc and the 3 following, * work, from the front, 1 relief dc around the base of the 2nd dc, 1 dc in the 1-ch, ch 1, 1 dc in the 1-ch, work, from the front, 1 relief dc around the base of the next dc, 1 dc in the 2nd dc and the next 12 dc, rep from *, ending row with 6 dc, the last in the turning ch, ch 3 and turn.

Row 3: 1 dc in the 2nd dc and in the following 3 dc, * work 1 relief dc around the base of the 2nd dc, from the back, 2 dc in the 1-ch, ch 1, 2 dc in the same 1-ch, work, from the back, 1 relief dc around the base of the 2nd dc, 1 dc in the 2nd dc and in the next 10 dc, rep from *, ending row with 4 dc, the last in the turning ch, ch 3 and turn.

Row 4: 1 dc in the 2nd dc and the 1 after, * from the front, work 1 relief dc around the base of the 2nd dc, work 3 dc in the 1-ch, ch 1, work 3 dc in the same 1-ch, work, from the front, 1 relief dc around the base of the 3rd dc, 1 dc in the 2nd dc and in the 8 dc following, rep from *, ending row with 4 dc, the last in the turning ch, ch 3 and turn.

Row 5: 1 dc in the 2nd dc and the 1 after, * work from the back, 1 relief dc around the base of the 2nd dc, work 4 dc in the 1-ch, ch 1, work 4 dc in the same 1-ch, work, from the back, 1 relief dc around the base of the 4th dc, 1 dc in the 2nd dc and the 6 dc after that, rep from *, ending row with 2 dc, the last in the turning ch, ch 3 and turn.

Row 6: Same as row 1, except that dc are worked in all except the dc before and after the 1-ch, 2 dc are worked in the 1-ch with 1 ch between.

Pattern formed by rep rows 1–6.

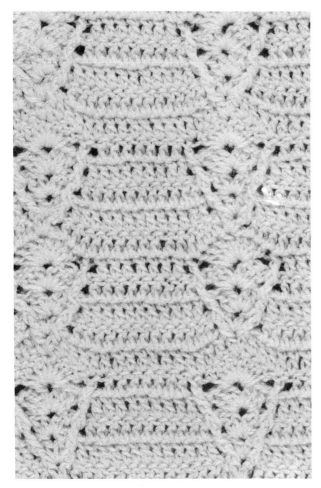

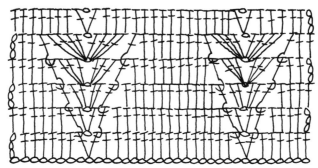

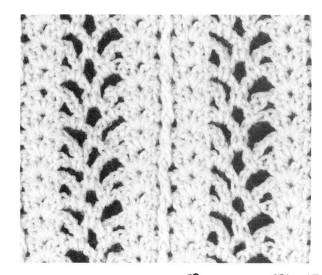

447. Chain multiples of 14 plus 4.

Row 1: 2 dc in the 7th ch, * ch 1, 2 dc in the same ch, ch 3, 1 sc in the 4th ch, ch 3, 2 dc in the 4th ch, ch 1, 2 dc in the ch just used, 1 dc in the 3rd ch, 2 dc in the 3rd ch, rep from *, ending row with 1 final set and 1 dc in the 3rd ch, ch 3 and turn.

Row 2: * 2 dc around the 1-ch, ch 1, 2 dc around the same ch, ch 3, 1 sc around the 3-ch, ch 3, 1 sc around the 3-ch, ch 3, 2 dc around the 1-ch, ch 1, 2 dc around the 1-ch just used, from the front, work 1 relief dc around the base of the single standing dc, rep from *, ending row with 1 dc in the turning ch, ch 3 and turn.

Row 3: * 2 dc in the 1-ch, ch 1, 2 dc in the same 1-ch, ch 3, 1 sc around the 3-ch, ch 3, 2 dc in the next 1-ch, ch 1, 2 dc in the same 1-ch, work, from the back, 1 relief dc around the base of the relief dc, rep from *, ending row with 1 dc in the turning ch, ch 3 and turn.

Pattern formed by rep rows 2–3.

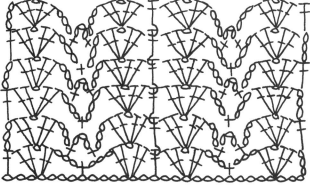

448. Chain multiples of 11 plus 5.

Row 1: 1 dc in the 7th ch, 1 dc in each of the next 6 chs, * ch 1, 1 dc in 2nd ch and the next ch, ch 1, 1 dc in the 2nd ch and each of the next 6 chs, rep from *, ending row with 1 ch and 1 dc in the last ch, ch 3 and turn.

Row 2: 3 dc in the 1st dc, * ch 1, work, from the front, 1 relief dc around the base of the 4th dc, ch 1, 4 dc in the 4th dc, 4 dc in the next dc, rep from *, ending row with 4 dc in the turning ch, ch 3 and turn.

Row 3: 2 dc in the 1st dc, * ch 1, 1 dc in the 1-ch, work from the back, 1 relief dc around the base of the next relief dc, 1 dc in the next 1-ch, ch 1, 3 dc in the 4th dc, 3 dc in the next dc, rep from *, ending row with 3 dc in the turning ch, ch 3 and turn.

Row 4: 1 dc in the 1st dc, * ch 1, 1 dc in the 1-ch, 1 dc in the dc, work, from the front, 1 relief dc around the base of the next relief dc, 1 dc in the dc, 1 dc in the 1-ch, ch 1, 2 dc in the 3rd dc, 2 dc in the next dc, rep from *, ending row with 2 dc in the turning ch, ch 4 and turn.

Row 5: * 1 dc in the 1-ch, 1 dc in each of the next 2 dc, work, from the back, 1 relief dc around the base of the next relief dc, 1 dc in each of the 2 dc, 1 dc in the 1-ch, ch 1, 1 dc in the 2nd dc, 1 dc in the next dc, ch 1, rep from *, ending row with 1 dc in the turning ch, ch 3 and turn.

Pattern formed by rep rows 1–4.

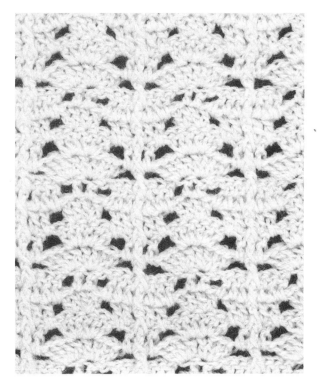

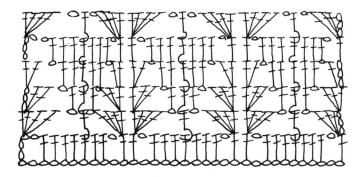

449. Chain multiples of 26 plus 4.

Row 1: 1 dc in the 5th ch, * 1 dc in the 4th ch, 1 dc in the next ch, ch 3, 1 dc in the next ch, 1 dc in the ch following, ch 1, 7 dc in the 5th ch, ch 1, 1 dc in the 5th ch, 1 dc in the next ch, ch 3, 1 dc in the next ch, 1 dc in the next ch, 1 dc in the 4th ch and in the following 2 chs, rep from *, ending row with 2 dc, ch 3 and turn.

Row 2: 1 dc in the 2nd dc, * work, from the front, 1 relief dc around the base of the next dc, work another relief dc from the front around the base of the next dc, ch 3, 1 dc in each of the 3 dc, ch 3, work, from the front, 1 relief dc around the base of the next dc, work another relief dc, from the front, around the base of the next dc, 1 dc in the next dc and in the dc after that, ch 1, 1 dc, ch 1, 1 dc, ch 1, 1 dc, ch 1, 1 dc, ch 1, dc in 4th dc and dc in next dc, rep from *, ending row with 1 dc in the turning ch, ch 3 and turn.

Pattern formed by rep rows 1–2.

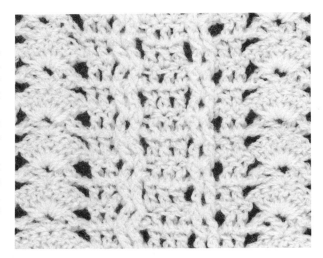

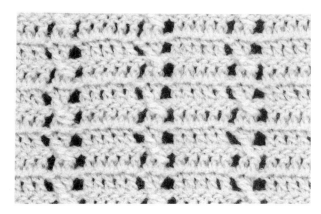

450. Chain multiples of 9 plus 4.

Row 1: 1 dc in the 5th ch and also in the next ch, * ch 1, 1 dc in the 2nd ch and the next ch, ch 1, 1 dc in the 2nd ch and in the 4 chs following, rep from *, ending row with 3 dc, ch 3 and turn.

Row 2: 1 dc in the 2nd dc and also in the next dc, * ch 1, 1 dc in the 2nd dc, work, from the front, 1 double relief stitch backwards around the 1st dc, ch 1, 1 dc in each of the next 5 dc, rep from *, ending row with 3 dc.

Row 3: Same as row 1, except that the 2 dc are worked in the top of the X-stitch.

Pattern formed by rep rows 1–2.

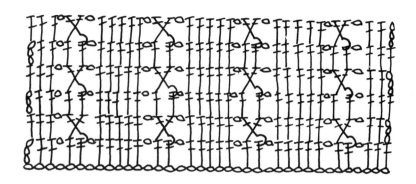

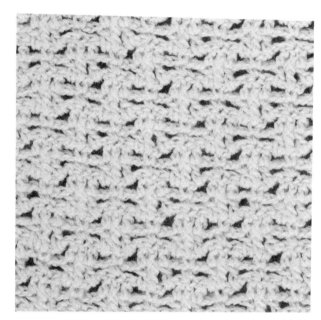

451. Chain multiples of 8 plus 1.

Row 1: 1 sc in the 2nd ch, * ch 2, 1 dc in the 3rd ch and in the 2 chs following, ch 2, 1 sc in the 3rd ch, rep from *, ending row with 1 sc, ch 3 and turn.

Row 2: 1 dc in the 2-ch, * ch 2, 1 sc in the 2nd dc, ch 2, 1 dc in the 2-ch, 1 dc in the sc and 1 dc in the next 2-ch, rep from *, ending row with 1 dc in the 2-ch and 1 in the sc, ch 3 and turn.

Row 3: 1 dc in the 2nd dc, * ch 2, 1 sc in the sc, ch 2, 1 dc in the dc, work, from the back, 1 relief dc around the base of the next dc, 1 dc in the dc, rep from *, ending row with 1 dc in the dc and 1 in the turning ch, ch 1 and turn.

Row 4: 1 sc in the 1st dc, * ch 2, 1 dc in the 2-ch, 1 dc in the sc, 1 dc in the 2-ch, ch 2, 1 sc in the 2nd dc, rep from *, ending row with 1 sc in the turning ch, ch 1 and turn.

Row 5: 1 sc in the sc, * ch 2, 1 dc in the dc, work, from the back, 1 relief dc around the base of the next dc, 1 dc in the next dc, ch 2, 1 sc in the sc, rep from *, ending row with 1 sc in the sc, ch 3 and turn.

Pattern formed by rep rows 2–5.

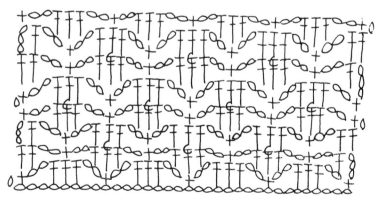

452. Chain multiples of 7 plus 4.

Row 1: 1 dc in the 5th ch, * ch 1, 1 dc in 2nd ch, ch 1, 1 dc in 2nd ch and in the next 3 chs, rep from *, ending row with 2 dc in the last 2 chs, ch 1 and turn.
Row 2: 1 sc in the 1st dc, * 1 dc, ch 1, 2 dc, ch 1 and 1 dc all worked in the single standing dc, 1 sc in the 2nd dc, 1 sc in the next dc, rep from *, ending row with 1 sc in the turning ch, ch 3 and turn.
Row 3: 1 dc in 1st dc, * ch 1, 1 relief dc worked from the back around the 2nd dc, raised dc, ch 1, 1 dc in next dc, 1 dc in each of the next 2 sc, 1 dc in the next dc, rep from *, ending row with 2 dc, ch 1 and turn.
Pattern formed by rep rows 1–3.

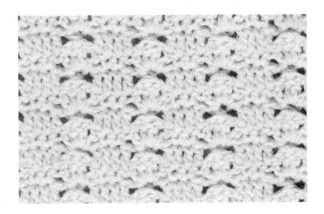

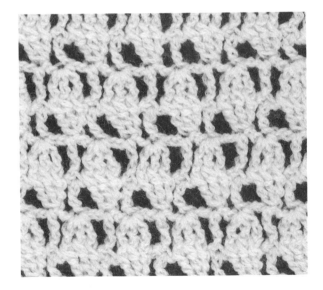

453. Chain multiples of 6 plus 6.

Row 1: Work 3 trc in the 9th ch, * ch 1, 1 trc in the 3rd ch, ch 1, 3 trc in the 3rd ch, rep from *, ending row with 1 ch and 1 trc in the 3rd ch, ch 6 and turn.
Row 2: * work 3 triple relief crochet together, from the front, begin 1 trc around the base of the 1st trc, the 2nd trc around the base of the 2nd trc, the 3rd trc around the base of the 3rd trc and finish off all 3 together, ch 2, 1 trc in the next trc, ch 2, rep from *, ending row with 2 chs and 1 trc in the turning ch, ch 4 and turn.
Row 3: 1 trc in the 1st trc, * ch 1, 1 trc in the top of the 3 trc worked together, ch 1, work 3 trc in the trc, rep from *, ending row with last trc, 1 ch and 2 trc in the turning ch, ch 3 and turn.
Row 4: From the front, work 1 triple relief crochet around the base of the 2nd trc, * ch 2, 1 trc in the next trc, ch 2, work, from the front, 3 relief trc together around the base of the next 3 trc, rep from *, ending row with 2 chs and 2 trc finished together.
Pattern formed by rep rows 1–4.

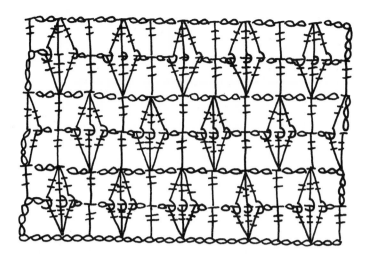

454. Chain multiples of 6 plus 5.

Row 1: 1 dc in the 9th ch, * ch 1, 1 dc backwards 2 chs, ch 1, 1 dc in the 2nd ch, ch 1, 1 dc in the 4th ch, rep from *, ending row with last set, 1 ch and 1 dc in the 2nd ch, ch 4 and turn.

Row 2: Sk 1 dc, * 1 dc in the 2nd dc, ch 1, 1 dc backwards in the last dc, ch 1, from the front, 1 relief dc around the base of the dc, ch 1, rep from *, ending row with 1 dc in the turning ch, ch 4 and turn.

Pattern formed by rep rows 1–2.

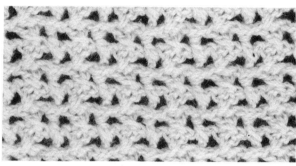

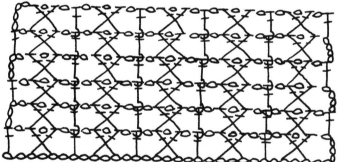

455. Chain multiples of 12 plus 4.

Row 1: 1 dc in the 5th ch and the 4 chs after, * 1 dc in the 2nd ch, 1 dc backwards 1 ch, 1 dc in the 2nd ch and 1 dc backwards 1 ch, 1 dc in the 2nd ch and 1 dc backwards 1 ch, 1 dc in the next ch and the 5 chs after that, rep from *, ending row with 6 dc, ch 3 and turn.

Row 2: 1 dc in the 2nd dc and the 4 dc after that, * work, from the front, 1 relief dc around the base of the 2nd dc, 1 dc backwards around the base of the last dc, also from the front, rep the same process around the next 2 sets of X-stitches, 1 dc in the next dc and the 5 dc after, rep from *, ending row with 5 dc, and 1 dc in the turning ch, ch 3 and turn.

Pattern formed by rep rows 1–2.

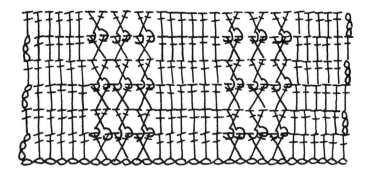

456. Chain multiples of 16 plus 4.

Row 1: 1 dc in the 5th ch and the 2 chs after, * ch 2, 2 dc in the 5th ch, ch 1, 2 dc in the same ch, ch 2, 1 dc in the 5th ch and in each of the 6-chs after, rep from *, ending row with 1 dc in each of the last 4-chs, ch 3 and turn.

Row 2: 1 dc in the 2nd dc, finish together 1 dc in the next dc and 1 relief dc, from the front, around the base of the next dc, * ch 2, 3 dc in the 1-ch, ch 1, 3 dc in the same 1-ch, ch 2, finish together, from the front, 1 relief dc around the base of the 3rd dc and 1 dc in the 2nd dc, 1 dc in each of the next 3 dc, finish together 1 dc in the next dc and 1 relief dc, from the front, around the base of the next dc, rep from *, ending row with 1 dc in the turning ch, ch 3 and turn.

Row 3: Finish together 1 dc in the 2nd dc and 1 relief dc, from the front, around the base of the relief dc, * ch 2, 2 dc in the 2nd dc, ch 1, 2 dc in the same stitch, ch 1, 2 dc in the 3rd dc, ch 1, 2 dc in the same stitch, ch 2, finish together 1 relief dc, from the front, around the base of the relief dc and 1 dc in the next dc, 1 dc in the dc, finish 1 dc in the next dc together with 1 relief dc around the base of the next relief dc, from the front, rep from *, ending row with 1 dc in the turning ch, ch 5 and turn.

Row 4: * 2 dc in the 1-ch, ch 1, 2 dc in the same 1-ch, ch 1, 2 dc in the 2nd 1-ch, ch 1, 2 dc in the same 1-ch, ch 2, work 1 relief dc from the front around the middle dc of the row below, ch 2, rep from *, ending row with 1 dc in the turning ch, ch 3 and turn.

Row 5: 2 dc in the dc, * ch 2, 1 dc in the 1-ch, 1 dc in each of the 2 dc, 1 dc in the 1-ch, 1 dc in each of the 2 dc, 1 dc in the 1-ch, ch 2, 2 dc in the relief dc, ch 1, 2 dc in the same relief dc, rep from *, ending row with 3 dc in the turning ch, ch 3 and turn.

Row 6: 3 dc in the 1st dc, * ch 2, finish together, from the front, 1 relief dc around the relief dc and 1 dc in the next dc, 1 dc in each of the next 3 dc, finish together 1 dc in the next dc and 1 relief dc, from the front, around the base of the relief dc, ch 2, 3 dc in the 1-ch, ch 1, 3 dc in the same 1-ch, rep from *, ending row with 1 dc in the turning ch, ch 3 and turn.

Row 7: 2 dc in the 3rd dc, ch 1, 2 dc in the same 1-ch, * ch 2, finish together 1 relief dc, from the front, around the base of the relief dc and 1 dc in the next dc, 1 dc in the next dc, finish together 1 dc in the next dc and 1 relief dc, from the front, around the base of the relief dc, ch 2, 2 dc in the 2nd dc, ch 1, 2 dc in the same dc, ch 1, 2 dc in the 3rd dc, ch 1, 2 dc in the same dc, rep from *, ending row with 1 dc in the turning ch, ch 3 and turn.

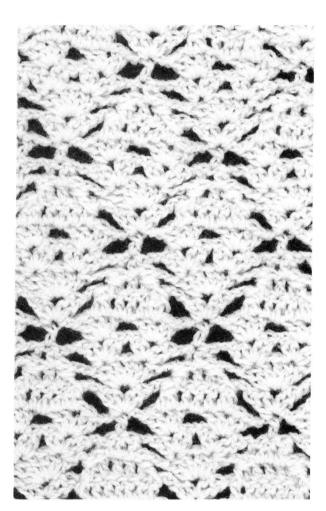

Row 8: 2 dc in the 1-ch, ch 1, 2 dc in the same 1-ch, * ch 2, work 1 relief dc, from the front, around the middle dc, ch 2, 2 dc in the 1-ch, ch 1, 2 dc in the same 1-ch, ch 1, 2 dc in the 2nd 1-ch, ch 1, 2 dc in the same 1-ch, rep from *, ending row with 1 dc in the turning ch.

Pattern formed by rep rows 1–8.

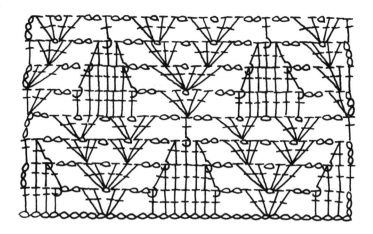

457. Chain multiples of 12 plus 4.

Row 1: 1 dc in the 5th ch and the ch after, * ch 1, 1 dc in the 2nd ch, ch 1, 1 dc in the 2nd ch, ch 1, 1 dc in the 2nd ch and 1 dc in each of the next 6 chs, rep from *, ending row with 1 dc in each of the last 3 chs, ch 3 and turn.

Row 2: 1 dc in the 2nd dc, * from the front, work 1 relief dc around the base of the next dc, ch 2, finish 2 dc together in the next 2 dc, ch 3, work, from the front, 1 relief dc around the base of the next relief dc, 1 dc in each of the next 5 dc, rep from *, ending row with 1 extra dc in the turning ch, ch 3 and turn.

Row 3: 1 dc in the 2nd dc, * work, from the front, 1 relief dc around the base of the next relief dc, ch 1, 1 dc in the top of the 2 dc finished together, ch 1, 1 dc in the spot just used, ch 1, 1 relief dc from the front, around the base of the next relief dc, 1 dc in each of the next 5 dc, rep from *, ending row with 1 extra dc in the turning ch, ch 3 and turn.

Pattern formed by rep rows 1–3.

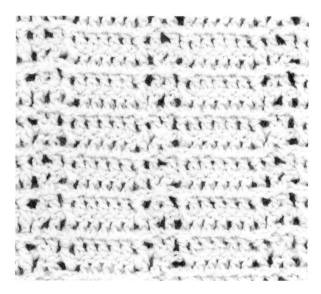

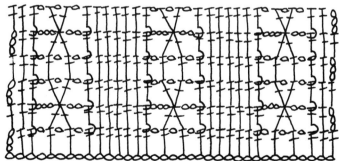

458. Chain multiples of 17 plus 4.

Row 1: 1 dc in the 5th ch, 1 dc in each of the next 2 chs, * ch 3, 1 sc in the 2nd ch, ch 3, 1 dc in the 2nd ch and the 2 chs following, ch 3, 1 sc in the 2nd ch, ch 3, 1 dc in the 2nd ch and the 7 chs following, rep from *, ending row with 1 dc in each of the last 4 chs, ch 3 and turn.

Row 2: 1 dc in the 2nd dc, work, from the front, 1 relief dc around the base of the next dc, 1 dc in the next dc, * ch 1, finish 2 dc together, 1 in each of the 3-chs, ch 1, 1 dc in each of the 3 dc, ch 1, finish 2 dc together in each of the 3-chs, ch 1, 1 dc in the next dc, work, from the front, 1 relief dc around the base of the next dc, 1 dc in each of the next 4 dc, work, from the front, 1 relief dc around the base of the next dc, dc in the next dc, rep from *, ending row with 1 dc in the turning ch, ch 3 and turn.

Row 3: Same as row 1, except that the sc are worked in the top of the 2 dc finished together and the relief dc are worked from the back instead of the front.

Row 4: Same as row 2, except that the relief dc are worked from the front.

Pattern formed by rep rows 1–4.

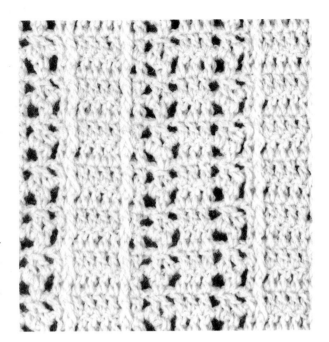

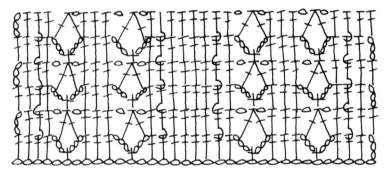

459. Chain multiples of 12 plus 4.

Row 1: 1 dc in the 5th ch and the ch after, * ch 3, 1 sc in the 3rd ch, 1 hdc in the next ch, 3 dc in the same ch, 1 hdc in the same ch, 1 sc in the next ch, ch 3, 1 dc in the 3rd ch and in the 4 chs following, rep from *, ending row with 3 dc, ch 3 and turn.

Row 2: From the back, work 1 relief dc around the base of each of the next 2 dc, * ch 3, 1 sc in the 2nd dc, ch 3, work, from the back, 1 relief dc around the base of the next dc, rep the same stitch in the next 4 dc, rep from *, ending row with 2 relief dc around the base of the dc worked from the back and 1 dc in the turning ch, ch 3 and turn.

Pattern formed by rep rows 1–2.

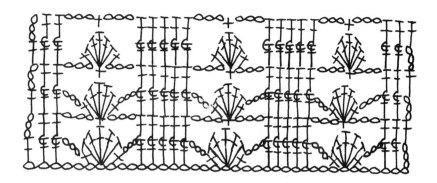

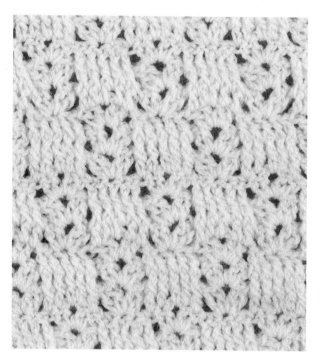

460. Chain multiples of 10 plus 4.

Row 1: 1 dc in the 5th ch and the next ch, * work 2 dc in the 3rd ch, ch 2, work 2 dc in the same ch, 1 dc in the 3rd ch and the 4 chs after that, rep from *, ending row with 3 dc, ch 3 and turn.

Row 2: From the front, work 1 relief dc around the base of the 2nd dc, work another relief dc in the next dc, * 2 dc in the 2-ch, ch 2, 2 dc in the same 2-ch, work, from the front, 1 relief dc around the base of the 3rd dc, same stitch in the next 4 dc, rep from *, ending row with 2 relief dc, from the front, around the base of the last 2 dc and 1 dc in the turning ch, ch 3 and turn.

Row 3: From the back, work 1 relief dc around the base of the relief dc, rep in the next stitch, * 2 dc in the 2-ch, ch 2, 2 dc in the same 2-ch, work, from the back, 1 relief dc around the base of the relief dc, rep in the next 4 stitches, rep from *, ending row with the last 2 relief dc, from the back, around the last 2 relief dc, 1 dc in the turning ch, ch 3 and turn.

Row 4: Patterns are worked alternatively, work 5 dc over the shell pattern (1 dc in each of the dc and 1 in the 2-ch), 5 dc comes over the shell pattern (all dc worked in the middle of the 5 dc), row ends with 3 dc, ch 3 and turn.

Pattern formed by rep rows 1–3 and rep the next 3 rows in alternative positions.

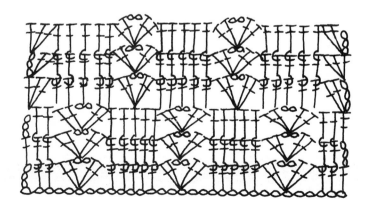

461. Chain multiples of 20 plus 4.

Row 1: 1 dc in the 5th ch, ch 1, 1 dc in the 2nd ch, 5 times, 1 dc in each of the next 10 chs, ch 1, 1 dc in the 2nd ch, 4 times, 1 dc in the next ch, ch 3 and turn.

Row 2: 1 dc in the 2nd dc, dc in the next ch and dc, ch and dc, ch and dc, ch and work, from the front, 1 relief dc around the base of the next dc, work from the back of the next 9 dc relief dc around the base, work, from the front, 1 relief dc around the next dc, 1 dc in each of the next chs and dc (totalling 9), work, from the front, 1 relief dc around the last dc, 1 dc in the turning ch, ch 3 and turn.

Row 3: From the front, work 1 relief dc around the base of the 2nd dc, work, from the back, relief dc around the bases of the next 9 dc, work, from the front, 1 relief dc around the next relief dc, ch 1 and 1 dc in every other dc until 4 sets are made, ch 1, work, from the front, 1 relief dc around the base of the relief dc formed, work 8 relief dc in the dc (from the back), work 1 dc in the turning ch, ch 3 and turn.

Row 4: 1 dc in the 2nd dc, ch 1, dc in 2nd dc, 3 times, ch 1, work 1 relief dc around the base of the relief dc formed from the front, 1 dc in the next chs and dc until 9 are formed, work, from the front, 1 relief dc around the next double relief stitch, ch 1, 1 dc in the 2nd relief dc until 4 are formed, ch 1, from the front, form 1 relief dc around the next relief dc, dc in turning ch, ch 3 and turn.
Pattern formed by rep rows 1–4.

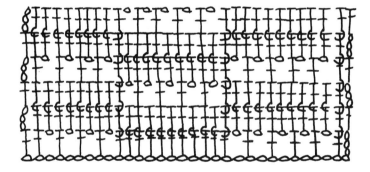

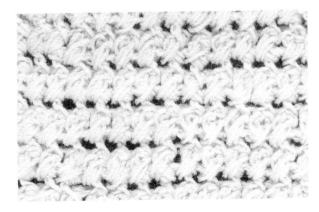

462. Chain multiples of 3 plus 4.

Row 1: Work 2-looped puff stitch in the 7th ch, * ch 1, work 2-looped puff stitch backwards in the 2nd ch, work 2-looped puff stitch in the 3rd ch, rep from *, ending row after the last set of crossed puff stitches with 1 dc, ch 4 and turn.

Row 2: * from front to back, work 1 relief dc around the base of the 2 sets of puff stitches, ch 2, rep from *, ending row after last relief dc with 1 ch and 1 dc in the turning ch, ch 3 and turn.

Row 3: Same as row 1, except 2 sides of the puff stitch sets are worked on either side of the relief dc.
Pattern formed by rep rows 1–2.

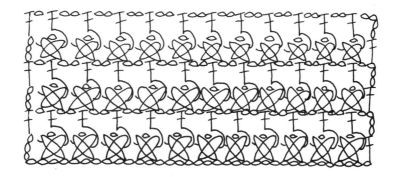

463. Chain multiples of 16 plus 1.

Row 1: 1 sc in the 2nd ch, ch 3, sc in the 3rd ch, * ch 3, 1 dc in the 4th ch, dc in the next ch, ch 3, 1 sc in the 4th ch, ch 7, sc in the 7th ch, rep from *, ending row with 1 dc in the last ch, ch 6 and turn.

Row 2: * 10 dc around the 7-ch, ch 3, work 1 relief dc, from the front, around each of the next 2 dc, ch 3 and rep from *, ending row with 4 dc in the 3-ch and 1 dc in the sc, ch 1 and turn.

Row 3: Sc in the 1st dc, * ch 3, work 1 relief dc, from the front, around the base of the next dc, ch 3, work 1 relief dc around the base of the 2nd dc, ch 3, from the front, work 2 relief dc together around the base of the relief dc and work 2 relief dc, from the front, around the base of the next relief dc, ch 3, work, from the front, 1 relief dc around the next dc, ch 3, relief dc around the base of the 2nd dc and ch 3, 4 times, rep from *, ending row with 2 dc in the turning ch, ch 3 and turn.

Row 4: 2 dc in the 2nd dc, * ch 3, sk 3 chs, sc in the next 3-ch, 4 times, ch 3, from the front, work 2 relief dc together around the base of the next relief dc, work, from the front, relief dc around each of the next 2 relief dc, work 2 relief dc together, from the front, around the base of the next relief dc, rep from *, ending row with 1 dc in the last sc, ch 1 and turn.

Row 5: Sc in the dc, ch 3, sc in the next 3-ch, * ch 3, work 2 relief dc together, from the front, around the base of the next relief dc, work, from the front, relief dc around the bases of the next 4 relief dc, work 2 relief dc from the front, around the base of the next relief dc, ch 3, sc in the 2nd 3-ch, ch 3, sc in the next 3-ch, ch 3, sc in the next 3-ch, ch 3, rep from *, ending row with 1 dc in the turning ch, ch 3 and turn.

Row 6: From the front, work 1 relief dc around the base of the relief dc, work the same stitch around the next relief dc, work 2 relief dc together, from the front, around the base of the next relief dc, * ch 3, sc in the 2nd 3-ch, ch 3, sc in the next 3-ch, ch 3, from the front, work 2 relief dc around the base of the next relief dc, work, from the front 1 relief dc around the bases of the next 6 relief dc, work 2 relief dc together around the base of the next relief dc, rep from *, ending row with 1 dc in the sc, ch 1 and turn.

Row 7: 1 sc in the dc, * ch 3, work 2 relief dc, from the front, around the base of the relief dc, work, from the front, relief dc around the bases of the next 8 relief dc, work 2 relief dc together, from the front, around the base of the next relief dc, ch 3, 1 sc in the 2nd 3-ch, rep from *, ending row with 1 dc in the turning ch, ch 3 and turn.

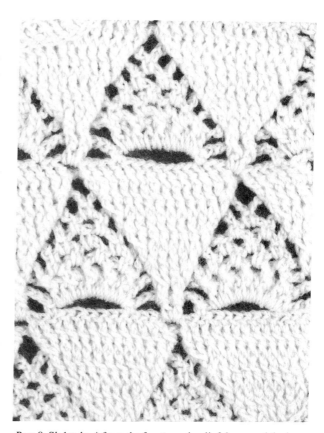

Row 8: Sk 1st dc, * from the front, work relief dc around the base of the next relief dc, rep same stitch around next 2 relief dc, work 2 relief dc together around the base of the next relief dc, ch 2, work, from the front, 2 relief dc together around the base of the next relief dc, work, from the front, relief dc around the bases of each of the next relief dc, rep from *, ending row with 1 trc in the sc, ch 3 and turn.

Row 9: Sk 1st trc, * from the front, work 1 relief dc around the bases of each of the next 14 relief dc, ch 2 and rep from *, ending row with 1 dc in the turning ch, ch 1 and turn.

Row 10: 1 sc in the dc, ch 3, 1 sc in the 3rd relief dc, * ch 3, 1 dc in each of the 2-chs, ch 3, sc in the 4th relief dc, ch 7, 1 sc in the 8th relief dc, rep from *, ending row with 1 dc in the turning ch.

Rows 10–18 should be continued the same way as the 1st 9, alternating the position.

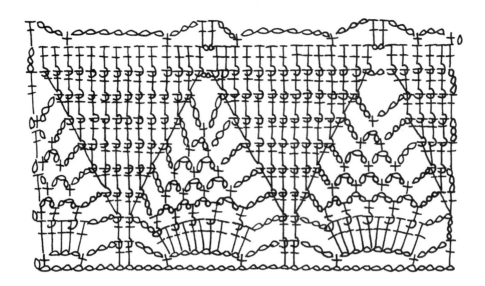

464. Chain multiples of 12 plus 4.

Row 1: 1 dc in the 5th ch and in the 2 chs following, * ch 2, 3-looped cluster in the next ch, work a 3-looped cluster in the 4th ch, ch 2, 1 dc in the next ch and in the next 6 chs, rep from *, ending row with 4 dc, ch 3 and turn.

Row 2: 1 dc in the 2nd dc and in the next dc, work, from the front, 1 relief dc around the base of the next dc, ch 2, work a 3-looped cluster in the 2-ch, work a 3-looped cluster in the next 2-ch, ch 2, work, from the front, 1 relief dc around the base of the next dc, work 1 dc in each of the next 5 dc, rep from *, ending row with 1 extra dc in the turning ch, ch 3 and turn.

Row 3: Same as row 1, except that the relief dc is worked from the back.

Pattern formed by rep rows 1–2.

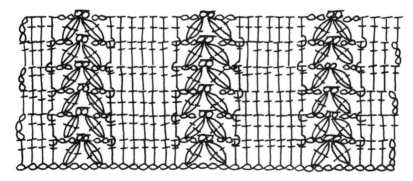

· 30 ·
Strip Horizontal Patterns

465. Chain multiples of 3 plus 4.

Row 1: 1 dc in the 5th ch and all the way across the row, ch 1 and turn.
Row 2: 1 sc in the 1st dc, * ch 4, 1 sc in the 3rd dc, rep from *, ending row with the last set, ch 5 and turn.
Row 3: * 1 sc around the middle of the 4-ch, ch 4, rep from *, ending row with 2 chs and 1 dc in the last sc, ch 1 and turn.
Row 4: 1 sc in the dc, * ch 4, 1 sc around the middle of the 4-ch, rep from *, ending row with the last set and the sc in the turning ch, ch 3 and turn.
Row 5: * work 3 dc around the 4-ch, rep from *, ending row with the last set, ch 3 and turn.
Row 6: 1 dc in the 2nd dc, * ch 1, 1 dc in the 2nd dc and the one after, ch 1, rep from *, ending row after last set with 1 ch and 1 dc in the turning ch, ch 3 and turn.
Row 7: Same as row 1, except that 1 dc should be made in each dc and in each ch.
Pattern formed by rep rows 1–4.

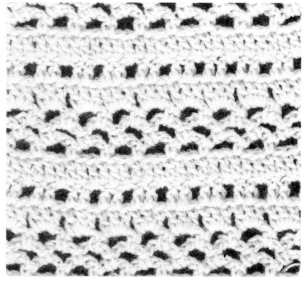

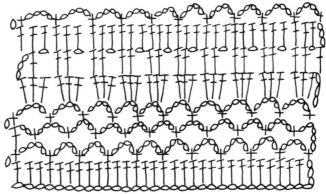

466. Chain multiples of 4 plus 1.

Row 1: 1 sc in the 2nd ch, * ch 5, 1 sc in the 4th ch, rep from *, ending row with 1 sc, ch 4 and turn.
Row 2: * 3 dc around th 5-ch, ch 1, rep from *, ending row after last set with 1 trc in the sc, ch 3 and turn.
Row 3: * 1 dc in each of the 3 dc, ch 1, rep from *, ending row with 1 extra dc in the turning ch, ch 6 and turn.
Row 4: Sk 1st dc, * finish 3 dc together in the next 3 dc, ch 5, rep from *, ending row with last set, 2 chs and 1 trc in the turning ch, ch 1 and turn.
Row 5: Same as row 1, made of 5 chs and the sc made around the middle of the 5-ch.
Pattern formed by rep rows 1–4.

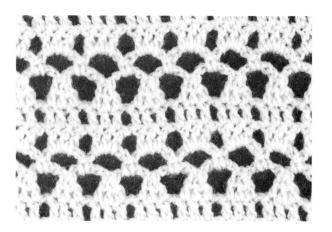

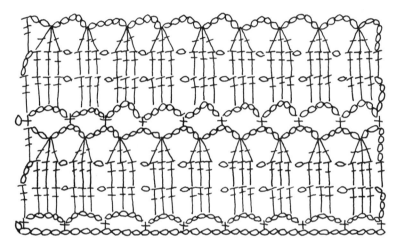

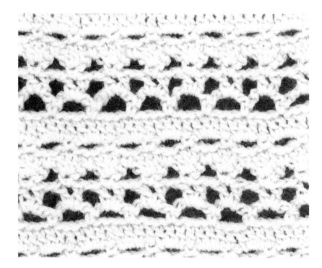

467. Chain multiples of 4 plus 4.

Row 1: 1 dc in 5th ch and dc all across row, ch 1 at the end of the row and turn.
Row 2: 1 sc in 1st dc, * ch 5, 1 sc in 4th dc, rep from *, ending row with 1 sc in the turning ch, ch 4 and turn.
Row 3: * 1 dc, 1 ch and 1 dc in the middle of the 1st 5-ch, ch 1, rep from *, ending row after last set with 1 trc in sc, ch 5 and turn.
Row 4: * 1 sc in the 1-ch, ch 5, 1 sc in next 1-ch, rep from *, ending row after last set with 2 chs and 1 dc, ch 1 and turn.
Row 5: 1 sc in 1st dc, * 3 dc in 1st sc, 1 sc around 5-ch, rep from *, ending row with last set and 1 sc in the turning ch, ch 3 and turn.
Row 6: * 1 sc in 2nd dc of the set, ch 3, rep from *, ending row after last set with 1 ch and 1 hdc, ch 3 and turn.
Row 7: 1 dc in 1st ch, 1 dc in 1st sc, 3 dc in next 3-ch, rep process across entire row.
Pattern formed by rep rows 1–6.

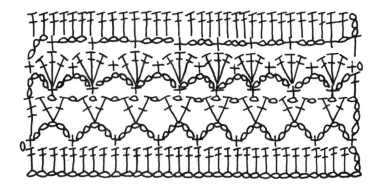

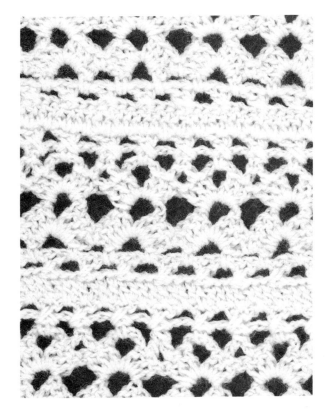

468. Chain multiples of 8 plus 4.

Row 1: 1 dc in the 5th ch and in each ch all across the row, ch 3 and turn.

Row 2: 1 dc in the 2nd dc, * ch 1, 1 dc in the 4th dc, ch 1, 1 dc backwards in the 2nd dc, rep from *, ending row with last set, 1 ch and 1 dc in the last dc and 1 in the turning ch, ch 5 and turn.

Row 3: * 1 sc around the 1-ch, ch 5, rep from *, ending row with last sc, 2 chs and 1 dc in the turning ch, ch 1 and turn.

Row 4: 1 sc in the dc, * 3 dc around the next 5-ch, ch 5, 3 dc around the same 5-ch, 1 sc in the next 5-ch, rep from *, ending row with 1 sc in the turning ch, ch 3 and turn.

Row 5: * work 3 dc around the 5-ch, ch 5, 3 dc around the same 5-ch, rep from *, ending row with 1 dc in the sc after the last set, ch 3 and turn.

Row 6: 1 dc in the 3rd dc, ch 3, * 1 sc around the 5-ch, ch 3, begin 1 dc in the 2nd dc, begin 1 dc in the 3rd dc and finish the 2 dc together, rep from *, ending row with 3 chs and 2 dc finished together and worked in the 2nd to the last dc and in the turning ch, ch 3 and turn.

Row 7: 1 dc in the 3-ch, * ch 1, work 1 dc in the 3-ch after the sc, ch 1, work 1 dc in the ch before the sc just used, ch 1, 1 dc after the 2 dc finished together, ch 1, 1 dc in the ch before the 2 dc finished together, rep from *, ending row with 1 dc in the last 3-ch and 1 dc in the last dc, ch 3 and turn.

Pattern formed by rep rows 1–7.

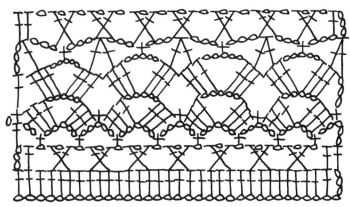

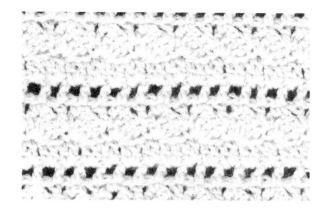

469. Chain multiples of 4 plus 1.

Row 1: 1 sc in 2nd ch, * ch 3, 3 dc in sc just used, 1 sc in 4th ch, rep from *, ending row with 1 sc, ch 4 and turn.
Row 2: * 1 sc in ch, ch 1, 1 dc in sc, ch 1, rep from *, ending row with 1 dc, ch 4 and turn.
Row 3: * 1 dc in sc, ch 1, 1 dc in dc, ch 1, rep from *, ending row with 1 dc, ch 3 and turn.
Row 4: 1 dc in 1st ch, * 2 dc in next ch, rep from *, ending row with 1 dc, ch 1 and turn.
Row 5: Same as row 1, except that the sc, 3 chs and 3 dc should be formed in the 1st dc and in each 4th dc.
Pattern formed by rep rows 1–4.

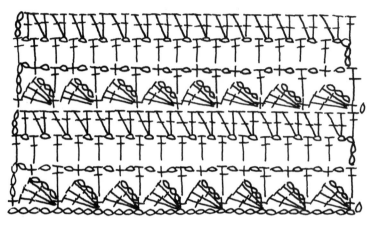

470. Chain multiples of 7 plus 4.

Row 1: 1 dc in the 5th ch and in each ch all across the row, ch 5 and turn.
Row 2: 3 dc in the 5th dc, * ch 5, 3 dc in the same dc, ch 5, 3 dc in the 7th dc, rep from *, ending row with 2 chs and 1 extra dc in the turning ch, ch 1 and turn.
Row 3: 1 sc in the dc, * work 4 dc in the next 5-ch, ch 5, work 4 dc in the same ch, 1 sc in the next 5-ch, rep from *, ending row with 1 sc in the last sc after completion of the last set, ch 3 and turn.
Row 4: 1 sc in the 1st sc, * ch 3, work 4 dc around the 5-ch, ch 5, work 4 more dc in the same 5-ch, ch 3, 1 sc in the sc, ch 3, rep from *, ending row with last set and 1 sc in the sc, ch 8 and turn.
Row 5: * 5 sc in the 5-ch, ch 2, rep from *, ending row with 1 ch after the last 5 sc and 1 quadruple crochet in the ch, ch 1 and turn.
Row 6: 1 sc in each ch and in each sc all across the row, ending row with 2 sc in the turning ch, ch 4 and turn.
Row 7: Work 1 dc in the 3rd sc, * ch 1, work 1 dc in the 2nd sc, rep from *, ending row with dc in the last sc, ch 1 and turn.
Row 8: 1 sc in each ch and in each dc, ch 3 and turn.
Pattern formed by rep rows 1–8.

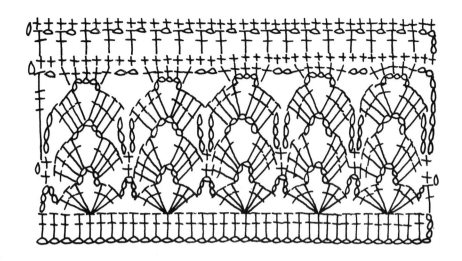

471. Chain multiples of 8 plus 4.

Row 1: 1 dc in the 5th ch and in every ch all across the row, ch 1 and turn.

Row 2: 1 sc in the 1st dc, * ch 3, work a 3-looped puff stitch in 4th dc, ch 3, 3-looped puff stitch in the 4th dc, ch 3, work a 3-looped puff stitch in the same dc, ch 3, 1 sc in the 4th dc, rep from *, ending row with a sc in the turning ch, ch 3 and turn.

Row 3: 1 dc in the 3-ch, * ch 3, work a 3-looped puff stitch in the next 3-ch, ch 1, 1 picot, ch 1, work a 3-looped puff stitch in the same 3-ch, ch 3, begin 1 dc in the next 3-ch, begin the 2nd dc in the next 3-ch and finish together, rep from *, ending row with 2 dc finished together in the last ch and the sc, ch 3 and turn.

Row 4: 2 dc in the top of the 2 dc finished together, * ch 3, 5 dc in the top of the 2 dc finished together, rep from *, ending row with 3 dc in the turning ch, ch 3 and turn.

Row 5: Rep row 1, with 1 dc in every dc, and 1 in each of the chs. Pattern formed by rep rows 1–4.

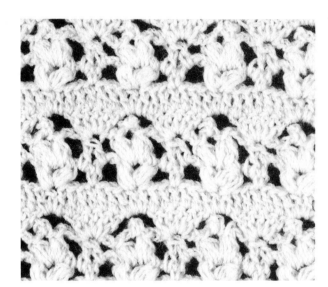

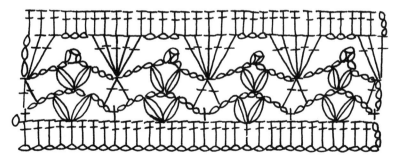

472. Chain multiples of 8 plus 4.

Row 1: 1 dc in the 5th ch and in each ch all across the row, ch 1 and turn.

Row 2: 1 sc in the 1st dc and in the next 3 dc, * ch 7, slip the last stitch into the 1st, 1 sc in the next dc, ch 7 attach the last ch into the 1st, 1 sc in the next dc and in the next 6 dc, rep from *, ending row with 3 sc in dc and 1 sc in the turning ch, ch 3 and turn.

Row 3: * 1 sc in the middle of the 7-ch, ch 2, work a 3-looped puff stitch in the space where the 7-chs join the sc, ch 4, 1 sc around the middle of the 3rd 7-ch, work 1 relief dc around the base of the dc 2 rows below, from the front, rep from *, ending row with last set and 1 dc in the sc, ch 3 and turn.

Row 4: * 1 dc in the sc, ch 2, 1 sc in the top of the 4-ch, ch 2, 1 dc in the sc, 1 dc in the relief dc, rep from *, ending row with 1 dc in the sc and 1 dc in the last dc, ch 1 and turn.

Row 5: 1 sc in each ch and each dc, the last 1 in the turning ch, ch 3 and turn.

Pattern formed by rep rows 1–5.

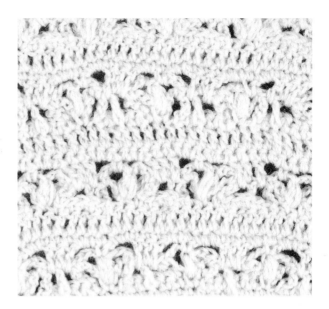

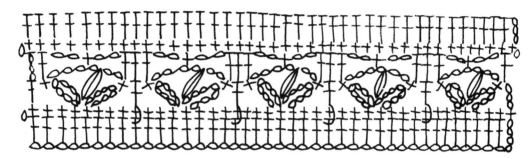

· *31* ·
Vertical Columns

473. Chain multiples of 7 plus 4.

Row 1: 1 dc in the 5th ch and the ch after that, * ch 2, 1 dc in the 3rd ch and the 4 chs following, rep from *, ending row with 3 dc, ch 3 and turn.
Pattern formed by rep row 1.

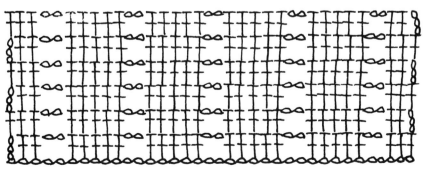

474. Chain multiples of 12 plus 4.

Row 1: 1 dc in the 5th ch, * ch 4, 1 dc in the 4th ch, 1 dc in the next ch, ch 4, 1 dc in the 4th ch, 1 dc in each of the next 3 chs, rep from *, ending row with 2 dc, ch 3 and turn.

Row 2: 1 dc in the 2nd dc, * ch 2, 3 dc around the 4-ch, 3 dc around the next 4-ch, ch 2, 1 dc in each of the next 4 dc, rep from *, ending row with 1 dc in the dc and 1 in the turning ch, ch 3 and turn.

Row 3: 1 dc in the 2nd dc, * ch 4, begin 1 dc in the 2nd dc, begin the 2nd dc in the 3rd dc, finish off together, ch 4, 1 dc in each of the 4 dc of the column, rep from *, ending row with 1 dc in the dc and 1 in the turning ch, ch 3 and turn.

Row 4: Same as row 2.

Pattern formed by rep rows 2–3.

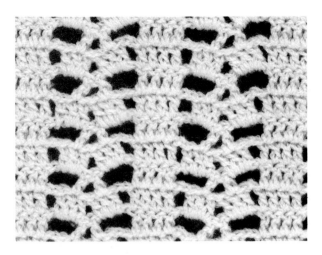

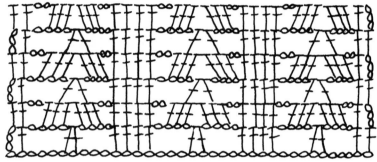

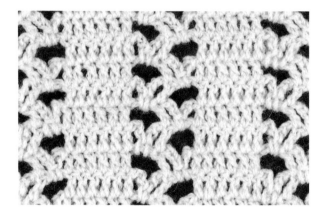

475. Chain multiples of 11 plus 4.

Row 1: 1 dc in the 5th ch and in each of the 4 chs following, * ch 3, 1 sc in the next ch, ch 3, 1 dc in the 2nd ch, ch 2, 1 dc in the 3rd ch and in the 5 chs following, rep from *, ending row with 6 dc, ch 3 and turn.

Row 2: 1 dc in the 2nd dc and in the next 4 dc, * ch 3, 1 sc around the 2-ch, ch 3, 1 dc in the dc, ch 2, 1 dc in each of the 6 dc, rep from *, ending row with the 6 dc, ch 3 and turn.

Pattern formed by rep rows 1–2.

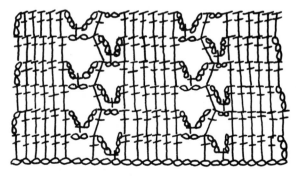

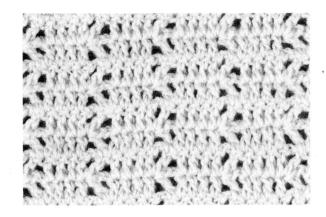

476. Chain multiples of 7 plus 3.

Row 1: 1 dc in 5th ch, * ch 2, 1 dc in same ch as 1st dc, 1 dc in 4th ch, 1 dc in each of the next 3 chs, totalling 4, rep from *, ending row with 2 dc in last 2 chs, ch 3 and turn.

Row 2: 1 dc in 2nd dc, * ch 2, 1 dc in same dc as 1st dc, 1 dc in dc following 2-ch, 1 dc in each of the next 3 dc, totalling 4, rep from *, ending row with 1 dc in the last dc and 1 in the turning ch, ch 3 and turn.

Pattern formed by rep rows 1–2.

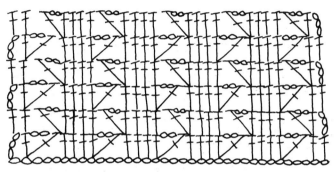

477. Chain multiples of 7 plus 4.

Row 1: 1 dc in 7th ch, * ch 3, 1 dc in same ch, 1 dc in 3rd ch, 1 dc in next ch, 1 dc in 3rd ch, rep from *, ending row with set and 1 dc, ch 5 and turn.

Row 2: * 1 dc around the middle of the 3-ch, ch 2, 1 dc in 1st dc and 1 dc in next dc, ch 2, rep from *, ending row with 2 chs and 1 dc, ch 3 and turn.

Row 3: Same as row 1, except that the dc, 3 chs and dc should be worked in the single standing dc.

Pattern formed by rep rows 1–2.

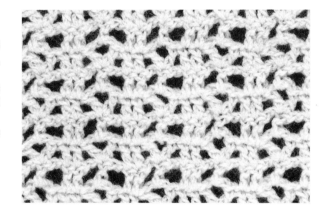

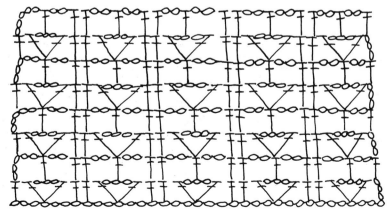

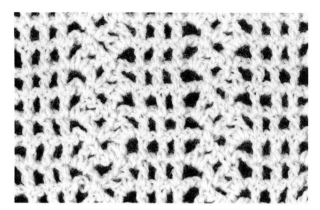

478. Chain multiples of 11 plus 4.

Row 1: 1 dc in the 7th ch, * ch 3, 1 dc in the next ch, ch 1, 1 dc in the same ch, 1 sc in the 4th ch, ch 3, 1 dc in the 2nd ch, ch 1, 1 dc in the 2nd ch, ch 1, 1 dc in the 2nd ch, rep from *, ending row with 1 ch and 1 dc in the turning ch, ch 4 and turn.
Row 2: 1 dc in the 2nd dc, * ch 3, 1 dc in the 3-ch, ch 1, 1 dc in the same 3-ch, 1 sc in the next 3-ch, ch 3, 1 dc in the next dc, ch 1, 1 dc in the next dc, ch 1, 1 dc in the next dc, rep from *, ending row with dc in the turning ch, ch 4 and turn.
Pattern formed by rep rows 1–2.

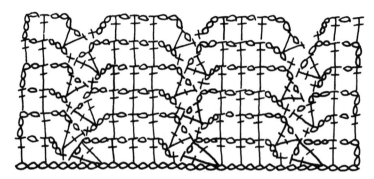

479. Chain multiples of 10 plus 4.

Row 1: 1 dc in the 5th ch and 1 dc in the next ch, * work 2 dc in the 4th ch, ch 2, 2 dc in the ch just used, 1 dc in the 4th ch and in each of the next 2 chs, rep from *, ending row with 3 dc, ch 3, and turn.
Pattern formed by rep row 1.

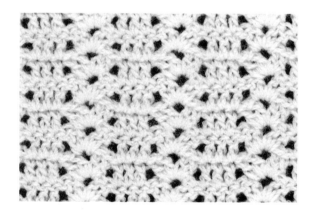

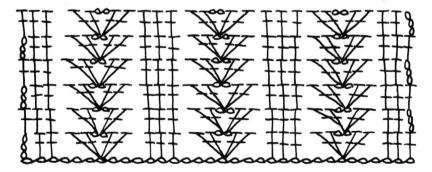

480. Chain multiples of 8 plus 4.

Row 1: 1 dc in the 5th ch, * ch 3, 1 sc in the 3rd ch, ch 3, 1 dc in the 3rd dc and in the next 2 dc, rep from *, ending row with 2 dc, ch 3 and turn.

Row 2: 1 dc in the 2nd dc, * ch 2, begin 1 dc around the middle of the 3-ch, begin 2nd dc around the middle of the next 3-ch, finish off the 2 dc together, ch 2, 1 dc in each of the next 3 dc, rep from *, ending row with 2 dc, ch 3 and turn.

Row 3: Same as row 1, except that the sc are worked in the top of the 2 dc finished together.

Pattern formed by rep rows 1–2.

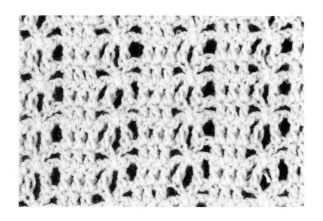

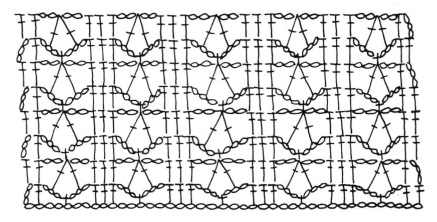

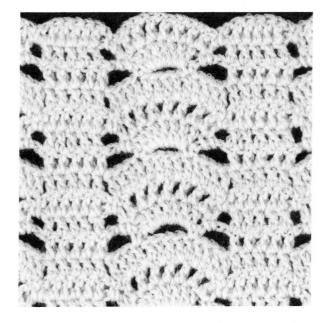

481. Chain multiples of 16 plus 4.

Row 1: 1 dc in the 5th ch and the ch after that, * ch 3, 1 sc in the 4th ch, ch 3, 1 sc in the 4th ch, ch 3, 1 dc in the 4th ch and the 4 chs following, rep from *, ending row with 1 dc in each of the last 3 chs, ch 3 and turn.

Row 2: 1 dc in the 2nd dc and the next dc, * ch 3, 1 sc around the 3-ch, 7 dc around the next 3-ch, 1 sc around the next 3-ch, ch 3, 1 dc in each of the 5 dc, rep from *, ending row with 1 dc in the turning ch, ch 3 and turn.

Row 3: 1 dc in the 2nd dc and the dc after that, * ch 1 and 1 sc in the 3-ch, 1 dc in the next dc, followed by 1 ch, 6 times, dc in the next dc, sc around the 3-ch, ch 1, 1 dc in each of the 5 dc, rep from *, ending row with 1 extra dc in the turning ch, ch 3 and turn.

Row 4: 1 dc in the 2nd dc and the dc after, * 1 dc in each dc and in each ch, totalling 13, 1 dc in each of the next 5 dc, rep from *, ending row with 1 extra dc in the turning ch, ch 3 and turn.

Row 5: Same as row 1, except that the sc are worked in the 5th dc of the set and the 4th.

Pattern formed by rep rows 1–4.

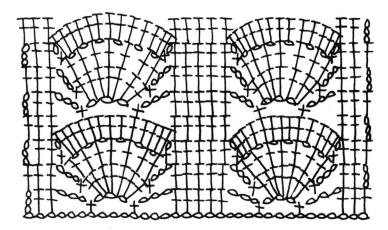

482. Chain multiples of 10 plus 4.

Row 1: 1 dc in 5th ch, * 4 dc in 2nd ch, ch 2, 1 dc in same ch as 1st 4 dc, 1 dc in 4th ch, 1 dc in each of next 4 chs, rep from *, ending row with 2 dc, ch 3 and turn.
Row 2: 1 dc in 2nd dc, * 4 dc in 2-ch, ch 2, 1 dc in same ch as 4 dc, 1 dc in each of the 5 dc, rep from *, end row with 2 dc, ch 3 and turn.
Pattern formed by rep rows 1–2.

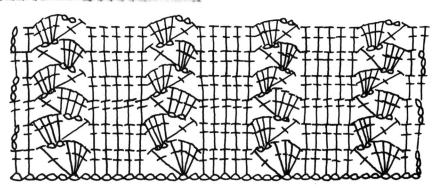

483. Chain multiples of 15 plus 4.

Row 1: 1 dc in 5th ch, 1 dc in next ch and the one after that, * 1 dc in 4th ch, ch 2, 2 dc in same ch, ch 2, 1 dc in same ch, 1 dc in 4th ch and in the 7 chs following, totalling 8 dc, rep from *, ending row with 4 dc in last 4 chs, ch 5 and turn.
Row 2: * 1 dc in the last dc of the set, ch 2, 1 sc around the 1st 2-ch, ch 3, 1 sc around the 2-ch, ch 2, 1 dc in 1st dc, ch 2, 1 dc in 3rd dc and also in the next dc, ch 2 and rep from *, ending row with 2 chs and 1 dc, ch 3 and turn.
Pattern formed by rep rows 1–2.

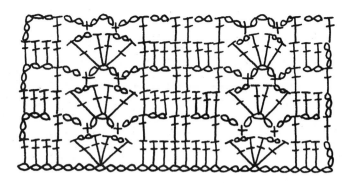

484. Chain multiples of 12 plus 4.

Row 1: 1 dc in 5th ch, * ch 2, 6 dc in the 3rd ch, 1 sc in the 5th ch, ch 2, 1 dc in the 3rd ch and in the next ch, rep from *, ending row with 1 sc in the last ch, ch 3 and turn.
Row 2: 5 dc in the 1st sc, * 1 sc in the 6th dc of the row below, ch 2, 1 dc in next dc and in the next dc, ch 2, 6 dc in the next sc, rep from *, ending row with 2 dc, the last in the turning ch, ch 3 and turn.
Pattern formed by rep rows 1–2.

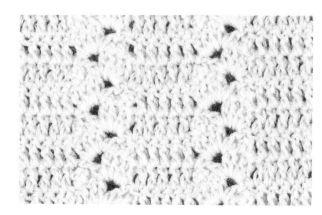

485. Chain multiples of 12 plus 4.

Row 1: 1 dc in the 5th ch, 1 dc in the next ch, * 2 dc in the 4th ch, 1 picot, 2 dc in the same ch, ch 2, 1 dc in the same ch, 1 dc in the 4th ch and in the 4 chs following, rep from *, ending row with 3 dc after the last set, ch 3 and turn.
Row 2: 1 dc in the 2nd dc and in the next dc, * 2 dc in the 2-ch, 1 picot, 2 dc in the same 2-ch, ch 2, 1 dc in the same 2-ch, 1 dc in each of the next 5 dc, rep from *, ending row with 3 dc after the last set, the last in the turning ch, ch 3 and turn.
Pattern formed by rep rows 1–2.

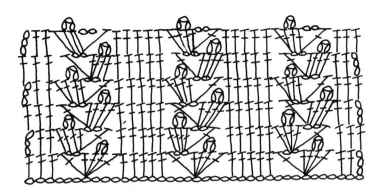

486. Chain multiples of 10 plus 3.

Row 1: 1 dc in the 5th ch and in each of the following 3 chs, * ch 5, 1 sc in the 3rd ch, ch 5, 1 dc in the 3rd ch and in the next 4 chs, rep from *, ending row with 5 dc, ch 3 and turn.
Row 2: 1 dc in the 2nd dc and in the next 3 dc, * ch 3, 1 sc around the 5-ch, ch 3, 1 sc around the next 5-ch, ch 3, 1 dc in each of the next 5 dc, rep from *, ending row with 5 dc, the last in the turning ch, ch 3 and turn.
Row 3: 1 dc in the 2nd dc and in the next 3 dc, * work 7 dc in the 2nd 3-ch, 1 dc in each of the next 5 dc, rep from *, ending row with 5 dc, the last in the turning ch, ch 3 and turn.
Row 4: Same as row 1, except that the sc is formed in the 4th dc of the set.
Pattern formed by rep rows 1–4.

487. Chain multiples of 9 plus 4.

Row 1: 1 dc in the 5th ch, * 1 dc in the 3rd ch, ch 3, finish off 4 dc together, all worked around the last dc, 1 dc in the 3rd ch and the 3 chs following, rep from *, ending row with 2 dc, ch 3 and turn.
Row 2: 1 dc in the 2nd dc, * ch 2, 1 sc in the middle of the 3-ch, ch 2, 1 dc in each of the next 4 dc, rep from *, ending row with 2 dc, ch 3 and turn.
Pattern formed by rep rows 1–2.

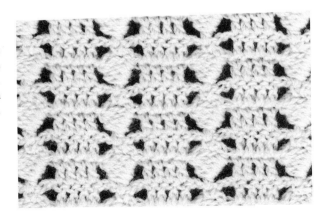

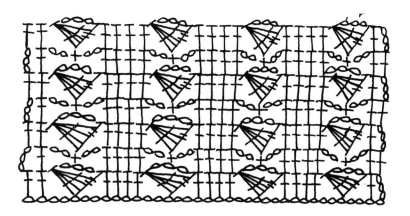

488. Chain multiples of 14 plus 4.

Row 1: 1 dc in the 4th ch and in the 3 chs following, * 1 dc in the 4th ch, ch 1, 4 times, 1 dc in the same ch, 1 dc in the 4th ch and the 2 chs following, 3 dc in the next ch, 1 dc in each of the next 3 chs, rep from *, ending row with 3 dc and 2 dc in the last ch, ch 3 and turn.

Row 2: 1 dc in the 1st dc and in the next 3 dc, * 1 sc in the 1-ch, ch 3, 1 sc in the next 1-ch, ch 3, 1 sc in the next 1-ch, ch 3, 1 sc in the last 1-ch, 1 dc in the 2nd dc and the next 2 dc, 3 dc in the next dc, 1 dc in each of the next 3 dc, rep from *, ending row with 5 dc, the last 2 in the turning ch, ch 3 and turn.

Pattern formed by rep rows 1–2.

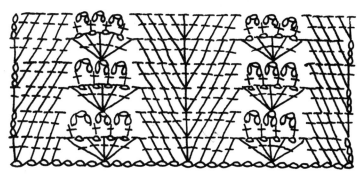

489. Chain multiples of 17 plus 4.

Row 1: 1 dc in the 5th ch and in the 4 chs following, * ch 2, 1 dc in the 6th ch, ch 1, 1 dc in the same ch, ch 1, 1 dc in the same ch, ch 1, 1 dc in the same ch, ch 2, 1 dc in the 6th ch, and the next 5 chs, rep from *, ending row with 6 dc, ch 3 and turn.

Row 2: Sk 1 dc, * 1 dc in each of the 5 dc, ch 2, 1 sc in the 1st 1-ch, ch 3, 1 sc in the same ch, 1 sc in the next 1-ch, ch 3, 1 sc in the same ch, 1 sc in the next 1-ch, ch 3, 1 sc in the same 1-ch, ch 2, rep from *, ending row with 1 dc in each of the last 5 dc and 1 in the turning ch, ch 3 and turn.

Row 3: Same as row 1, except that all 4 dc are worked in the middle of the middle 3-ch.

Pattern formed by rep rows 1–2.

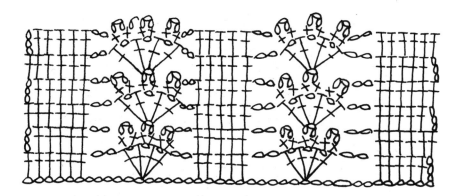

490. Chain multiples of 16 plus 4.

Row 1: 1 dc in 5th ch and 1 dc in each of the next 3 chs, * ch 2, 1 dc in 4th ch, ch 2, 1 dc in ch just used, ch 2, 1 dc in the 4th ch and in next 8 chs, rep from *, ending row with 5 dc, ch 3 and turn.
Row 2: 1 dc in 2nd dc and in next 2 dc, * ch 2, 2 dc, ch 2 and 2 dc all worked in the 2-ch between the 2 dc, ch 2, 1 dc in 2nd dc and in the next 6 dc, rep from *, ending row with 3 dc worked in last 3 dc, 1 dc in the turning ch, ch 3 and turn.
Row 3: 1 dc in 2nd dc and in the next dc, * ch 2, 3 dc, ch 2 and 3 dc all worked in the 2-ch between the 2 sets of dc, ch 2, 1 dc in 2nd dc in the middle set and in the next 4 dc, rep from *, ending row with 3 dc, the last in the turning ch, ch 3 and turn.
Row 4: 1 dc in 2nd dc, * ch 2, 4 dc in 2-ch, ch 2, 4 dc around same 2-ch, ch 2 and 1 dc in 2nd dc of middle set and in the next 2 dc, rep from *, ending row with 2 dc, the last in the turning ch, ch 3 and turn.
Row 5: Same as row 1, except that the 1 dc, 1 ch 1 dc are worked in the 2-ch.
Pattern formed by rep rows 1–4.

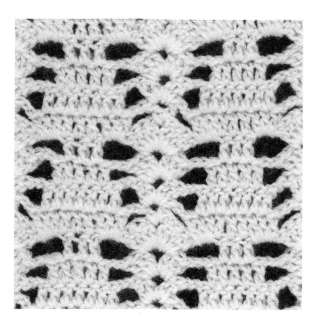

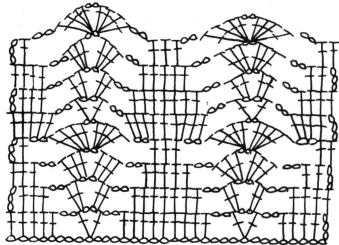

491. Chain multiples of 11 plus 4.

Row 1: 1 dc in 5th ch, 1 dc in next ch, * ch 3, 1 sc in 3rd ch, ch 3, 1 dc in 3rd ch, 1 dc in each of the next 5 chs, rep from *, ending row with 3 dc, ch 3 and turn.

Row 2: 1 dc in 2nd dc and also in the next dc, * ch 2, 1 sc around the 3-ch, ch 3, 1 sc around the 3-ch, ch 2, 1 dc in each of the next 6 dc, rep from *, ending row with 3 dc, the last in the turning ch, ch 3 and turn.

Row 3: 1 dc in 2nd dc, 1 dc in next ch, * 1 picot, 5 dc around the 3-ch, 1 picot 1 dc in each of the next 6 dc, rep from *, ending row with 3 dc the last in the turning ch, ch 3 and turn.

Row 4: Same as row 1, except that sc are worked in middle (3rd) dc.

Pattern formed by rep rows 1–3.

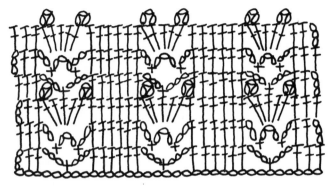

· *32* ·
Multi-stitches

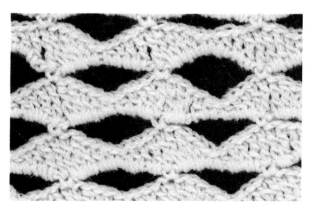

492. Chain multiples of 11 plus 5.

Row 1: 1 trc in the 6th ch, 1 dc in the next ch and the ch after that, 1 hdc in the next ch, * 1 sc in the next ch, 1 hdc in the next ch, 1 dc in each of the next 2 chs, 1 trc in each of the next 4 chs, 1 dc in each of the next 2 chs, 1 hdc in the next ch, rep from *, ending row with 2 trc, ch 1 and turn.
Row 2: 1 sc in the 1st trc, * ch 10, 1 sc in the 4th trc, rep from *, ending row with 1 sc in the turning ch, ch 4 and turn.
Pattern formed by rep rows 1–2.

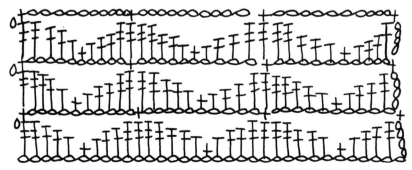

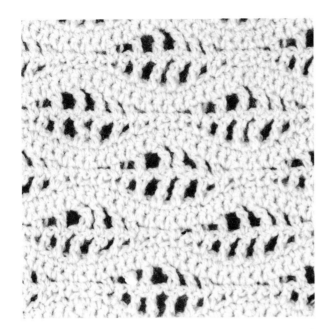

493. Chain multiples of 16 plus 1.

Row 1: 1 sc in the 2nd ch, * 1 sc in the next ch, ch 1, 1 hdc in the 2nd ch, ch 1, 1 dc in the 2nd ch, ch 1, 1 trc in the 2nd ch, ch 1, 1 trc in the 2nd ch, ch 1, 1 dc in the 2nd ch, ch 1, 1 hdc in the 2nd ch, ch 1, 1 sc in the 2nd ch, ch 1, rep from *, ending row with sc in each of last 2 chs after the last set, ch 1 and turn.
Row 2: 1 sc in each ch and in each stitch, ch 1 and turn.
Row 3: Rep row 2, ch 4 and turn.
Row 4: Sk 1 sc, * 1 trc in next sc, ch 1, 1 dc in the 2nd sc, ch 1, 1 hdc in the 2nd sc, ch 1, 1 sc in the 2nd sc, ch 1, 1 sc in the 2nd sc, ch 1, 1 hdc in the 2nd sc, ch 1, 1 dc in the 2nd sc, ch 1, 1 trc in the 2nd sc, rep from *, ending row with 2 trc in the last 2 sc, ch 4 and turn.
Row 5: * 1 trc in the 2nd trc, ch 1, 1 dc in the dc, ch 1, 1 hdc in the hdc, ch 1, 1 sc in the sc, ch 1, 1 sc in the sc, ch 1, 1 hdc in the hdc, ch 1, 1 dc in the dc, ch 1, 1 trc in the trc, ch 1, rep from *, ending row with 1 trc in the last trc and 1 in the turning ch, ch 1 and turn.
Rows 6–7: 1 sc in each stitch, ch 1 and turn.
Pattern formed by rep rows 1–7.

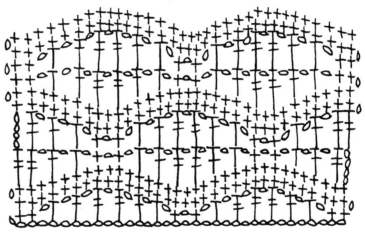

494. Chain multiples of 4 plus 1.

Row 1: 1 sc in 2nd ch, * ch 3, 1 sc in 4th ch, rep from *, ending row with last set, ch 3 and turn.
Row 2: * 2 dc, 1 hdc and 1 sc around the 1st 3-ch, 1 sc in 1st ch, ch 3 and rep from *, ending row after last set, ch 6.
Row 3: Same as row 1, except sc comes in the top of the ch.
Pattern formed by rep rows 1–2.

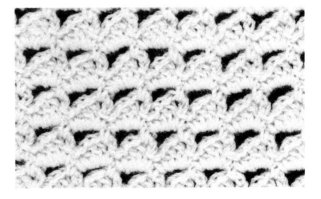

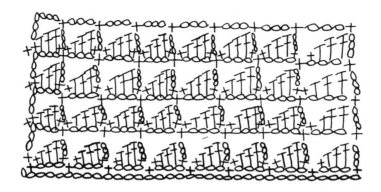

495. Chain multiples of 4 plus 6.

Row 1: 1 sc in the 2nd ch, * ch 6 and turn, work 1 sc in the 3rd ch, 1 hdc in the next ch, 1 dc in the next ch, and 1 trc in the next ch, sl st in the 4th ch, rep from *, ending row after last set with 1 sl st and ch 6 and turn.
Row 2: * 1 sc in the top of the 6-ch, ch 3, rep from *, ending row with last sc, 1 ch and 1 trc in the last sc, ch 1 and turn.
Row 3: 1 sc in the trc, * ch 3, 3 dc in the 1-ch, sc in the next 3-ch, rep from *, ending row with sc in the turning ch, ch 4 and turn.
Row 4: * 1 sc in the top of the 3-ch, ch 3, rep from *, ending row with last sc, 1 ch and 1 dc in the last sc, ch 6 and turn.
Pattern formed by rep rows 1–4.

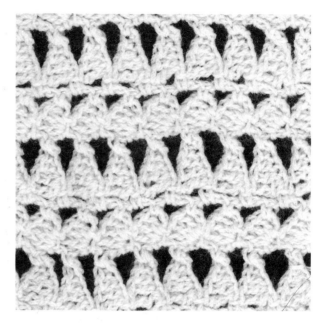

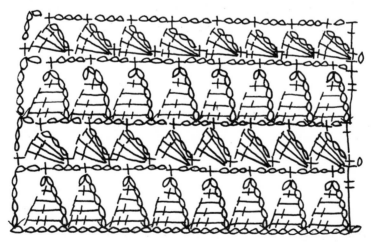

496. Chain multiples of 4 plus 1.

Row 1: 1 sc in the 2nd ch, * ch 6, 1 sc back in the turning ch, 3 dc around the same ch, 1 sc in the 4th ch, rep from *, ending row with last set, ch 6 and turn.

Row 2: 1 sc in the top of the ch, * ch 3, 1 sc in the top of the ch, rep from *, ending row after last set with 1 ch and 1 trc in the turning ch, ch 10 and turn.

Row 3: 1 sc in the sc, * ch 6, 1 sc back around the ch, work 3 dc around the same ch, 1 sc in the sc, rep from *, ending row with last set, 5 chs and 1 trc in the turning ch, ch 1 and turn.

Row 4: 1 sc in the trc, * ch 3, 1 sc in the top of the ch, rep from *, ending row with last set, ch 1 and turn.

Pattern formed by rep rows 1–4.

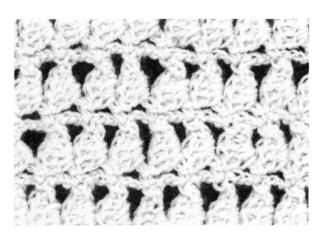

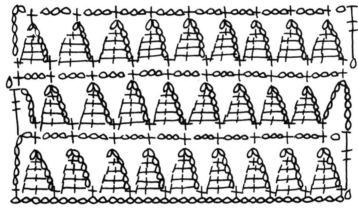

· 33 ·
Miscellaneous

497. Chain multiples of 6 plus 4.

Row 1: 1 trc in the 8th ch, * ch 4, 1 trc in the ch just used, finish 2 trc together in the next ch and the 5th ch, rep from *, ending row with 2 trc formed in the next ch after the last set and the 3rd ch, ch 6 and turn.
Row 2: 1 trc in the top of the 2 trc finished together, * finish 2 trc together in the next trc and the trc after that, ch 4, 1 trc in the next trc set, rep from *, ending row with 2 chs and 1 trc in the turning ch, ch 4 and turn.
Pattern formed by rep rows 1–2.

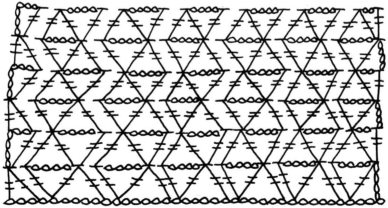

498. Chain multiples of 20 plus 4.

Row 1: 1 dc in the 6th ch, * ch 1, dc in the 2nd ch, 4 times, ch 3, 1 dc in the ch used for the last dc, ch 1, 1 dc in the 2nd ch, 3 times, ch 1, begin 1 dc in the 2nd ch, 2nd half in 4th ch, rep from *, ending row with 1 dc, 1 ch and 1 dc in the same ch, begin next dc in the 4th ch, finish together, ch 3 and turn.
Row 2: 2 dc in the 1st dc, * make a total of 7 dc in the next dc, begin 1 dc in the dc before the inverted V-stitch, begin the 2nd half in the dc just after the inverted V-stitch, make 8 dc in the dc and chs, ch 3, 1 dc in the dc used for the last dc, rep from *, ending row with 2 dc finished together in the last 2 dc, ch 3 and turn.
Pattern formed by rep rows 1–2.

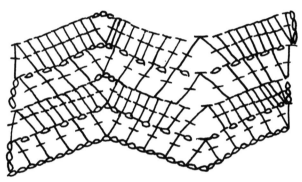

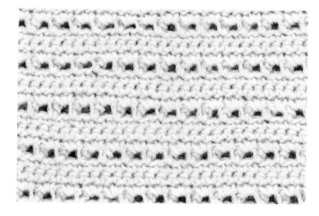

499. Chain multiples of 2 plus 1.

Row 1: 1 sc in the 2nd ch and all the way across the row, ch 1 and turn.
Rows 2–3: Same as row 1, ch 4 and turn.
Row 4: 1 hdc in the 3rd sc, * ch 1, 1 hdc in the 2nd sc, rep from *, ending row with 1 hdc, ch 1 and turn.
Pattern formed by rep rows 1–4.

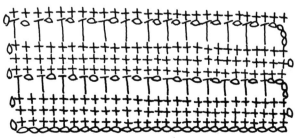

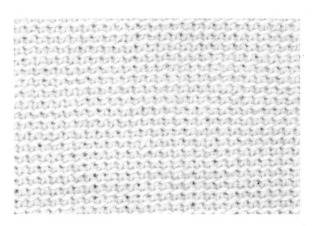

500. Chain any amount of chains plus 1.

Use Tunisian crochet hook.
Row 1: Sk 1 ch, * insert the hook into the next ch, draw up a loop and leave it on the needle, rep from *.
Row 2: Yarn over, draw through 1 loop, * yarn over and draw through 2 loops, rep from *, ch 3.
Row 3: * insert hook right to left under next vertical stitch, draw up a loop.
Pattern formed by rep rows 2–3.

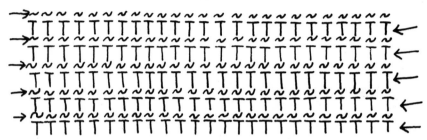